Ill-Equipped:
U.S. Prisons and Offenders with Mental Illness

Human Rights Watch

New York **Washington** **London** **Brussels**

ISBN: 1564322904

Cover photo: Copyright © 1999 Andrew Lichtenstein
Caption: Stiles Unit, Beaumont, Texas, 1999.
Cover design by Rafael Jimenez

Addresses for Human Rights Watch
350 Fifth Avenue, 34th Floor, New York, NY 10118-3299
Tel: (212) 290-4700, Fax: (212) 736-1300, E-mail: hrwnyc@hrw.org

1630 Connecticut Avenue, N.W., Suite 500, Washington, DC 20009
Tel: (202) 612-4321, Fax: (202) 612-4333, E-mail: hrwdc@hrw.org

2nd Floor, 2-12 Pentonville Road London N1 9HF, UK
Tel: (44 20) 7713 1995, Fax: (44 20) 7713 1800, E-mail: hrwuk@hrw.org

15 Rue Van Campenhout, 1000 Brussels, Belgium
Tel: (32 2) 732-2009, Fax: (32 2) 732-0471, E-mail: hrwbe@hrw.org

Web Site Address: http://www.hrw.org

Listserv address: To receive Human Rights Watch news releases by email, subscribe to the HRW news listserv of your choice by visiting http://hrw.org/act/subscribe-mlists/subscribe.htm

Human Rights Watch is dedicated to
protecting the human rights of people around the world.

We stand with victims and activists to prevent
discrimination, to uphold political freedom, to protect people from inhumane conduct in wartime,
and to bring offenders to justice.

We investigate and expose
human rights violations and hold abusers accountable.

We challenge governments and those who hold power to end abusive practices and respect
international human rights law.

We enlist the public and the international
community to support the cause of human rights for all.

HUMAN RIGHTS WATCH

Human Rights Watch conducts regular, systematic investigations of human rights abuses in some seventy countries around the world. Our reputation for timely, reliable disclosures has made us an essential source of information for those concerned with human rights. We address the human rights practices of governments of all political stripes, of all geopolitical alignments, and of all ethnic and religious persuasions. Human Rights Watch defends freedom of thought and expression, due process and equal protection of the law, and a vigorous civil society; we document and denounce murders, disappearances, torture, arbitrary imprisonment, discrimination, and other abuses of internationally recognized human rights. Our goal is to hold governments accountable if they transgress the rights of their people.

Human Rights Watch began in 1978 with the founding of its Europe and Central Asia division (then known as Helsinki Watch). Today, it also includes divisions covering Africa, the Americas, Asia, and the Middle East. In addition, it includes three thematic divisions on arms, children's rights, and women's rights. It maintains offices in New York, Washington, Los Angeles, London, Brussels, Moscow, Tashkent, Tblisi, and Bangkok. Human Rights Watch is an independent, nongovernmental organization, supported by contributions from private individuals and foundations worldwide. It accepts no government funds, directly or indirectly.

The staff includes Kenneth Roth, executive director; Michele Alexander, development director; Carroll Bogert, associate director; Barbara Guglielmo, finance director; Lotte Leicht, Brussels office director; Maria Pignataro Nielsen, human resources director; Iain Levine, program director; Rory Mungoven, advocacy director; Wilder Tayler, legal and policy director; and Joanna Weschler, United Nations representative.

The regional division directors of Human Rights Watch are Peter Takirambudde, Africa; José Miguel Vivanco, Americas; Brad Adams, Asia .The thematic division directors are Steve Goose, Arms, Lois Whitman, Children's Rights; and LaShawn R. Jefferson, Women's Rights. Jamie Fellner is director of the U.S. Program.

Jonathan Fanton is the chair of the board. Robert L. Bernstein is the founding chair. The members of the board are Khaled Abou El Fadl, Lisa Anderson, Lloyd Axworthy, David Brown, William Carmichael, Dorothy Cullman, Edith Everett, Michael Gellert, Vartan Gregorian, James F. Hoge, Jr., Stephen L. Kass, Marina Pinto Kaufman, Wendy Keys, Robert Kissane, Bruce Klatsky, Joanne Leedom-Ackerman, Josh Mailman, Joel Motley, Samuel K. Murumba, Jane Olson, Peter Osnos, Kathleen Peratis, Catherine Powell, Sigrid Rausing, Orville Schell, Sid Sheinberg, Gary G. Sick, Domna Stanton, John J. Studzinski, Shibley Telhami, Maureen White, and Maya Wiley. Emeritus Board: Roland Algrant, Adrian DeWind, Alice H. Henkin, Bruce Rabb, and Malcolm Smith.

ACKNOWLEDGMENTS

Human Rights Watch wishes to thank each of the prisoners, correctional staff, mental health professionals, attorneys, and advocates who shared experiences, information, materials, and insights with us in the course of research for this report. We want to acknowledge especially the invaluable assistance from correctional mental health and law experts who generously contributed time to helping us understand and synthesize the concepts addressed in this report, including Professor Fred Cohen, L.L.B., L.L.M., Dr. Jane Haddad, Lindsey Hayes, Dr. Terry Kupers, Dr. Richard Lamb, David Lovell, Ph.D., Steve Martin, Esq., Dr. Jeffrey Metzner, and Professor Hans Toch, Ph.D. Dr. Terry Kupers also participated in a research mission to Indiana with Human Rights Watch in 1997. Several state corrections authorities, convinced of the importance of this project, were particularly helpful in giving us access to their staff and facilities, including: Secretary of the Washington State Department of Corrections Joseph D. Lehman; Robert Horel at the California Department of Corrections; Beth Anderson, health services administrator, Washington Department of Corrections; Brett Rayford, Connecticut Department of Correction; Lance Couturier, chief psychologist, Pennsylvania Department of Corrections; and Dr. Thomas Powell, director of clinical services, Vermont Department of Corrections. They were all extremely gracious with their time and energy. We also want to specially note extraordinary assistance from attorneys Donna Brorby, David Fathi, Tara Herivel, Sarah Kerr, Patricia Perlmutter, Antonio Poinvert, Betsy Sterling, and Todd Winstrom, all of whom we interviewed numerous times during the research for this report. In addition, our deepest thanks go to the staff at the Council on State Government and the Correctional Association of New York, who were more than generous in sharing information and ideas with us. Finally, we with to express our great gratitude to Fred Cohen, David Fathi, Craig Haney, Terry Kupers, and Jeffrey Metzner for carefully reviewing and commenting on earlier drafts of this report.

Sasha Abramsky, a consultant to Human Rights Watch, and Jamie Fellner, director of the U.S. Program at Human Rights Watch are the authors of this report. It was edited by Joseph Saunders, deputy program director at Human Rights Watch, and James Ross, senior legal advisor. It is based principally on research by Mr. Abramsky, with additional research by Ms. Fellner. Paul Jacobs, a program associate at Human Rights Watch and Sarah Kunstler, a Human Rights Watch intern, also provided research assistance. Paul Jacobs also prepared the report for publication.

Human Rights Watch is grateful to the Open Society Institute for its support of the U.S. Program that made this report possible.

CONTENTS

"It is deplorable and outrageous that this state's prisons appear to have become a repository for a great number of its mentally ill citizens. Persons who, with psychiatric care, could fit well into society, are instead locked away, to become wards of the state's penal system. Then, in a tragically ironic twist, they may be confined in conditions that nurture, rather than abate, their psychoses."
— Judge William Wayne Justice, *Ruiz v. Johnson*, 37 F. Supp.2d 855 (S.D. Texas, 1999).

I.   SUMMARY

Somewhere between two and three hundred thousand men and women in U.S. prisons suffer from mental disorders, including such serious illnesses as schizophrenia, bipolar disorder, and major depression. An estimated seventy thousand are psychotic on any given day. Yet across the nation, prison mental health services are woefully deficient, crippled by understaffing, insufficient facilities, and limited programs. Many seriously ill prisoners receive little or no meaningful treatment. They are neglected, accused of malingering, treated as disciplinary problems.

Without the necessary care, mentally ill prisoners suffer painful symptoms and their conditions can deteriorate. They are afflicted with delusions and hallucinations, debilitating fears, extreme and uncontrollable mood swings. They huddle silently in their cells, mumble incoherently, or yell incessantly. They refuse to obey orders or lash out without apparent provocation. They beat their heads against cell walls, smear themselves with feces, self-mutilate, and commit suicide.

Prisons were never intended as facilities for the mentally ill, yet that is one of their primary roles today. Many of the men and women who cannot get mental health treatment in the community are swept into the criminal justice system after they commit a crime. In the United States, there are three times more mentally ill people in prisons than in mental health hospitals, and prisoners have rates of mental illness that are two to four times greater than the rates of members of the general public. While there has been extensive documentation of the growing presence of the mentally ill in prison, little has been written about their fate behind bars.

Drawing on interviews with correctional officials, mental health experts, prisoners and lawyers, this report seeks to illuminate that fate. We identify the mentally ill in prison — their numbers, the nature of their illnesses, and the reasons for their incarceration. We set out the international human rights and U.S. constitutional framework against which their treatment should be assessed. We review their access to mental health services and the treatment they receive. We examine the various levels of care available to them, their confinement in long-term segregation facilities, the way prisons respond to their self-mutilation and suicide attempts, and the services they receive upon release from prison.

Our research reveals there are competent and committed professionals working in prisons who struggle to provide mental health services to those who need them. They face, however, daunting obstacles — including facilities and rules designed for punishment. The current fiscal crisis in states across the country also threatens the gains they have made.

But our research also indicates the persistence in many prisons of deep-rooted patterns of neglect, mistreatment, and even cavalier disregard for the well-being of vulnerable and sick human beings. A

1

federal district judge, referring in 1999 to conditions in Texas' prisons, made an observation that is still too widely applicable:

> Whether because of a lack of resources, a misconception of the reality of psychological pain, the inherent callousness of the bureaucracy, or officials' blind faith in their own policies, the [corrections department] has knowingly turned its back on this most needy segment of its population.[1]

In the most extreme cases, conditions are truly horrific: mentally ill prisoners locked in segregation with no treatment at all; confined in filthy and beastly hot cells; left for days covered in feces they have smeared over their bodies; taunted, abused, or ignored by prison staff; given so little water during summer heat waves that they drink from their toilet bowls. A prison expert recently described one prison unit as "medieval...cramped, unventilated, unsanitary...it will make some men mad and mad men madder." Suicidal prisoners are left naked and unattended for days on end in barren, cold observation cells. Poorly trained correctional officers have accidentally asphyxiated mentally ill prisoners whom they were trying to restrain.

Offenders who need psychiatric interventions for their mental illness should be held in secure facilities if they have committed serious crimes, but those facilities should be designed and operated to meet treatment needs. Society gains little from incarcerating offenders with mental illness in environments that are, at best, counter-therapeutic and, at worst dangerous to their mental and physical well-being. As another federal judge eloquently noted:

> All humans are composed of more than flesh and bone — even those who, because of unlawful and deviant behavior, must be locked away.... Mental health, just as much as physical health, is a mainstay of life. Indeed, it is beyond any serious dispute that mental health is a need as essential to a meaningful human existence as other basic physical demands our bodies may make for shelter, warmth, or sanitation.[2]

Doing time in prison is hard for everyone. Prisons are tense and overcrowded facilities in which all prisoners struggle to maintain their self-respect and emotional equilibrium despite violence, exploitation, extortion, and lack of privacy; stark limitations on family and community contacts; and a paucity of opportunities for meaningful education, work, or other productive activities. But doing time in prison is particularly difficult for prisoners with mental illness that impairs their thinking, emotional responses, and ability to cope. They have unique needs for special programs, facilities, and extensive and varied health services. Compared to other prisoners, moreover, prisoners with mental illness also are more likely to be exploited and victimized by other inmates.

Mental illness impairs prisoners' ability to cope with the extraordinary stresses of prison and to follow the rules of a regimented life predicated on obedience and punishment for infractions. These prisoners are less likely to be able to follow correctional rules. Their misconduct is punished — regardless of whether it results from their mental illness. Even their acts of self-mutilation and

---

[1] *Ruiz v. Johnson*, 37 F.Supp. 2d 855, 914 (S.D. Texas, 1999), rev'd 178 F.3d 385 (5th Cir. Tex., 1999), adhered to on remand, 243 F.3d 941 (5th Cir. Tex., 2001).
[2] *Madrid v. Gomez*, 889 F. Supp. 1146, 1261 (N.D. California, 1995).

suicide attempts are too often seen as "malingering" and punished as rule violations. As a result, mentally ill prisoners can accumulate extensive disciplinary histories.

Our research suggests that few prisons accommodate their mental health needs. Security staff typically view mentally ill prisoners as difficult and disruptive, and place them in barren high-security solitary confinement units. The lack of human interaction and the limited mental stimulus of twenty-four-hour-a-day life in small, sometimes windowless segregation cells, coupled with the absence of adequate mental health services, dramatically aggravates the suffering of the mentally ill. Some deteriorate so severely that they must be removed to hospitals for acute psychiatric care. But after being stabilized, they are then returned to the same segregation conditions where the cycle of decompensation begins again.[3] The penal network is thus not only serving as a warehouse for the mentally ill, but, by relying on extremely restrictive housing for mentally ill prisoners, it is acting as an *incubator* for worse illness and psychiatric breakdowns.

International human rights law and standards specifically address conditions of confinement, including the treatment of mentally ill prisoners. If, for example, U.S. officials honored in practice the International Covenant on Civil and Political Rights, to which the United States is a party, and the United Nation's Standard Minimum Rules for the Treatment of Prisoners, which sets out detailed guidelines on how prisoners should be treated, practices in American prisons would improve dramatically. These human rights documents affirm the right of prisoners not to be subjected to cruel, inhuman, or degrading conditions of confinement and the right to mental health treatment consistent with community standards of care. That is, human rights standards do not permit corrections agencies to ignore or undertreat mental illness just because a person is incarcerated. The Eighth Amendment to the U.S. Constitution, which prohibits cruel and unusual punishment, also provides prisoners a right to humane conditions of confinement, including mental health services for serious illnesses.

Prisoners are not, however, a powerful public constituency, and legislative and executive branch officials typically ignore their rights absent litigation or the threat of litigation. U.S. reservations to international human rights treaties mean that prisoners cannot bring suit based on violations of their rights under those treaties. Lawsuits under the U.S. Constitution can only accomplish so much. Federal courts have interpreted the U.S. Constitution as violated only when officials are "deliberately indifferent" to prisoners' known and serious mental health needs. Neglect or malpractice are not constitutional violations. In most states, prisoners cannot sue public officials under state law for medical malpractice. Finally, the misguided Prison Litigation Reform Act, enacted in 1996, has seriously hampered the ability of prisoners to achieve effective and timely help from the courts.

Mental health treatment can help some people recover from their illness, and for many others it can alleviate its painful symptoms. It can enhance independent functioning and encourage the development of more effective internal controls. In the context of prisons, mental health services play an even broader role. By helping individual prisoners regain health and improve coping skills, they promote safety and order within the prison community as well as offer the prospect of enhancing community safety when the offenders are ultimately released.

---

[3] Decompensation refers to the aggravation of symptoms of mental illness leading to a marked deterioration from previously adequate levels of functioning and coping in daily life.

The components of quality, comprehensive mental health care in prison are well known. They include systematic screening and evaluation for mental illness; mechanisms to provide prisoners with prompt access to mental health personnel and services; mental health treatment that includes a range of appropriate therapeutic interventions including, but not limited to, appropriate medication; a spectrum of levels of care including acute inpatient care and hospitalization, long-term intermediate care programs, and outpatient care; a sufficient number of qualified mental health professionals to develop individualized treatment plans and to implement such plans for all prisoners suffering from serious mental disorders; maintenance of adequate and confidential clinical records and the use of such records to ensure continuity of care as prisoners are transferred from jail to prison and between prisons; suicide prevention protocols for identifying and treating suicidal prisoners; and discharge planning that will provide mentally-ill prisoners with access to needed mental health and other support services upon their release from prison. Peer review and quality assurance programs help ensure that proper policies on paper are translated into practice inside the prisons.

We found no state prison system that has instituted all of the components of quality care for all prisoners with serious mental disorders. Many prison systems have good policies on paper, but implementation can lag far behind. In recent years, some prison systems have begun to implement system-wide reforms — often prompted by litigation — and innovative programs to attend to the mentally ill. But even these reforms are inadequate.

Across the country, seriously ill prisoners continue to confront a paucity of qualified staff who can evaluate their illness, develop and implement treatment plans, and monitor their conditions; they confront treatment that consists of little more than medication or no treatment at all; they remain at unnecessarily high risk for suicide and self-mutilation; they live in the chaos of the general prison population[4] or under the strictures of solitary confinement — with brief breaks in a hospital — because of the lack of specialized facilities that would provide the long-term supportive, therapeutically-oriented environment they need.

Providing mental health services to incarcerated offenders is frustrated by lack of resources. It is also frustrated by the realities of prison life. Correctional mental health professionals work in facilities run by security staff according to rules never designed for or intended to accommodate the mentally ill. For example, mentally ill prisoners are consigned to segregated units even though the harsh, isolated confinement in such units can provoke psychiatric breakdown. Moreover, the rules designed by security staff for prisoners in solitary confinement prevent mental health professionals from providing little more than medication to the mentally ill confined in these units; they cannot provide much needed private counseling, group therapy, and structured activities. Correctional staff who have the most contact with prisoners and who are often called upon to make decisions regarding their needs — particularly in the evenings when mental health staff are not present — often lack the training to recognize symptoms of mental illness and to handle appropriately prisoners who are psychotic or acting in bizarre or even violent ways. It is easy for untrained correctional staff to assume an offender is deliberately breaking the rules or is faking symptoms of illness for secondary gain, such as to obtain a release from solitary confinement into a less harsh hospital setting.

---

[4] Prisoner's are part of the "general population" of a prison unless they have been placed in segregated or special housing units for such purposes as discipline, protective custody, security, or medical care.

Many experts with whom we spoke also noted that, unfortunately, the judgment of some mental health professionals working in prisons becomes compromised over time. They become quick to find malingering instead of illness; to see mentally ill prisoners as troublemakers instead of persons who may be difficult but are nonetheless deserving of serious medical attention. The tendency to limit treatment to the most acutely and patently ill is also encouraged by the lack of resources; since everyone cannot receive appropriate treatment, mental health staff limit their attention to only a few.

* * *

The growing number of mentally ill persons who are incarcerated in the United States is an unintended consequence of two distinct public policies adopted over the last thirty years.

First, elected officials have failed to provide adequate funding, support, and direction for the community mental health systems that were supposed to replace the mental health hospitals shut down as part of the "deinstitutionalization" effort that began in the 1960s.

A federal advisory commission appointed by President George W. Bush, the President's New Freedom Commission on Mental Health, recently reported that the U.S. mental health system was "in shambles." People with serious mental illnesses — particularly those who are also poor, homeless, and suffering as well from untreated alcoholism or drug addiction — often cannot obtain the mental health treatment they need. Left untreated and unstable, they enter the criminal justice system when they break the law. Most of their crimes are minor public order or nuisance crimes, but some are felonies which lead to prison sentences.

Second, elected officials have embraced a punitive anti-crime effort, including a national "war on drugs" that dramatically expanded the number of persons brought into the criminal justice system, the number of prison sentences given even for nonviolent crimes (particularly drug and property offenses), and the length of those sentences. Prison and jail populations have soared, more than quadrupling in the last thirty years. A considerable proportion of that soaring prison population consists of the mentally ill.

There is growing recognition in the United States that the country can ill-afford its burgeoning prison population, and that for many crimes, public goals of safety and crime reduction would be equally — if not better — served by alternatives to incarceration, including drug and mental health treatment programs. Momentum is building, albeit slowly, to divert low-level nonviolent offenders from prison — an effort that would benefit many of the mentally ill. But until the country makes radical changes in its approach to community mental health — as well as poverty and homelessness — there is every likelihood that men and women with mental illness will continue to be over-represented among prison populations.

Corrections officials recognize the challenge posed to their work by the large and growing number of prisoners with mental illness. They recognize they are being asked to serve a function for which they are ill equipped. Most of what we say in this report will not be new to them. We hope our report, and the extensive documentation of human suffering that it contains, will support their efforts to ensure appropriate conditions of confinement and mental health services for the mentally ill men and women consigned to them. We hope it helps marshal political sentiments and public opinion to understand the need for enhanced mental health resources — for those in as well as outside of prison. We also hope it encourages dramatic changes in the use of prisons in the United States — reserving them for dangerous violent offenders who must be securely confined and not for low-level nonviolent offenders. The problems we document in this report can be solved — but to do so requires drastically more public commitment, compassion, and common sense than have been shown to date.

The Scope of this Report

We are keenly aware of the many related problems that we have excluded from this report. Our inquiry is limited to adults, although a high percentage of youth in the juvenile justice system are also mentally ill. We concentrate on mental illness, while recognizing that prisoners who are developmentally disabled or suffer from organic brain damage also face unique and important problems. And our inquiry is limited to prisons, although we acknowledge — as all who are familiar with jails must — that jails are equally, if not more, overwhelmed by mentally ill prisoners for whom they are ill-equipped to care.

There are approximately fourteen hundred adult prisons in the United States, operated by or responsible to fifty state correctional agencies and the federal bureau of prisons. We have not attempted to produce a comprehensive assessment of the treatment of mentally ill prisoners in any one of these prisons or prison systems. Rather, we have sought to identify conditions and problems that are shared by many and to present illustrative examples. The time period covered in this report is from the mid-1990s to the present. Examples of specific problems in individual prisons presented in this report may have been subsequently addressed by correctional authorities, and, where we are aware of such remedial measures, we have described them.

A Note on Methodology

This report is based on research, interviews, and visits to numerous correctional facilities conducted primarily between 2001 and 2003, although we visited some prisons in earlier years. Human Rights Watch interviewed and/or corresponded with at least three hundred prisoners, mental health experts, prison officials, and lawyers from many parts of the country. We have visited prisons and conducted in-person, on-site interviews with prisoners and staff in California, Colorado, Connecticut, Illinois, Indiana, Minnesota, New York, Ohio, Oklahoma, Pennsylvania, Texas, Vermont, and Washington. We also interviewed by telephone many correctional staff, including mental health professionals, in a number of states whose facilities we did not visit. In the course of our research, we have consulted experts in numerous fields, including psychiatry, psychology, bio-statistics, law, correctional security classifications, prison architecture, suicide protocols, prison mental health care, public health care, community mental health, counseling, and substance abuse treatment. We have also drawn on many other resources, including opinions generated in court rulings; information gathered by court monitors as well as experts hired for court challenges to prison mental health services; academic and professional writing on correctional mental health issues; and unpublished studies.

Prisoners were contacted through advertisements placed in *Prison Legal News* asking seriously mentally-ill prisoners to write to Human Rights Watch, through attorneys who had been involved in litigating cases on mental illness in prisons, through family members who believed their incarcerated relatives needed mental health help that they were not receiving, and through organizations such as state protection and advocacy groups.[5] The staff at many of the institutions Human Rights Watch visited while researching this report also agreed to provide us access, with prisoner consent, to

---

[5] In recent years, an increasing number of protection and advocacy groups, including NAMI (formerly known as the National Alliance for the Mentally Ill) have begun focusing on the issue of the mentally ill in prison.

individuals randomly selected from the mental health caseload and prisoners whose behavior and correctional histories met Human Rights Watch research criteria. Throughout this report, we provide extracts from letters prisoners with mental illness sent us. We have not sought to verify the specific allegations made in them and recognize that some may be embellished or altered in the telling. Nevertheless, the letters are eloquent testimony to the prisoners' sense of their experience. Where prisoners' letters are quoted, we have left in place spelling and grammatical errors.

It is impossible to do justice to the wealth of information accumulated during research for this report without creating a publication that was thousands of pages in length. Yet, because prisons operate in secret, for the most part, it is important for the public to have access to as much material as is possible. We have placed some of the expert reports produced during litigation on our website, as they are not readily available to the public, and reveal, in often harrowing detail, problems with specific prisons regarding the treatment of mentally ill offenders. They can be found at http://www.hrw.org.

R.U., Nevada, June 4, 2002

At one point and time in my life here in prison I wanted to just take my own life away. Why? Everything in prison that's wrong is right, and everything that's right is wrong. I've been jump, beat, kick and punch in full restraint four times.... Two times I've been put into nude four point as punishment and personal harassment.... During the time I wanted to just end my life thre was no counseling, no programs to attend. I was told if I didn't take my psych meds I was "sol." Three times I attempt suicidal by way to hang myself. I had no help whatsoever days and week and months I had to deal with myself. Depression, not eating, weight loss, everyday, overwhelmed by the burdens of life. I shift between feeling powerless and unworthy to feeling angry and victimized. I would think about death or killing myself daily. For eight months or a year I was not myself. From Oct 2000 to like Sept or Nov of 2001.... I was just kept into a lock cell ready to end my life at any given time. Each [time] I would try to hang myself it never work out. I cut my arms. I really was going thru my emotions and depression.... I would rather live inside a zoo. The way I've been treated here at this prison I couldn't do a dog this way.

II.   RECOMMENDATIONS

No prison system in the United States intentionally harms mentally ill prisoners through a policy of providing substandard care. Nevertheless, poor mental health treatment for mentally ill prisoners is a national reality. The government is responsible for protecting basic human rights, particularly those of the most vulnerable, and making wise use of limited criminal justice resources. Public officials must make the necessary improvements. Public support, particularly in times of tight budgets, is crucial to ensuring officials fulfill their responsibilities.

Prescriptions for quality mental health care in prisons are plentiful. They are found in the standards and guidelines of the American Correctional Association, the National Commission on Correctional Health Care (NCCHC), the Criminal Justice/Mental Health Consensus Project coordinated by the Council of State Governments, in court rulings, expert reports, and in a voluminous professional literature. Little would be served by repeating here all those recommendations. Our research suggests that what is lacking in prison mental health services is not knowledge about what is needed, but the resources and commitment to do it.

We therefore present here three sets of recommendations: one directed at the U.S. Congress specifically; one directed at public officials, community leaders and members of the general public; and one directed at prison officials and their staff.

Recommendations to the U.S. Congress

Human Rights Watch recommends that the U.S. Congress promptly:

1) Enact the Mentally Ill Offender Treatment and Crime Reduction Act

Currently pending before the U.S. Senate and House of Representatives is the Mentally Ill Offender Treatment and Crime Reduction Act introduced by Congressman Ted Strickland and Senator Mike DeWine. If enacted, the bill could catalyze significant reforms across the country in the way the criminal justice system responds to people with mental illness. The bill authorizes grants to help communities establish diversion programs (pre-booking, jail diversion, mental health courts) for mentally ill offenders, treatment programs for mentally ill offenders who are incarcerated, and transitional and discharge programs for mentally ill offenders who have completed their sentences. The grants program would be administered by the Department of Justice in consultation with the Department of Health and Human Services and could be used to help pay for mental health treatment services in addition to program planning and administration, education and training, and temporary housing.

2) Improve access to public benefits covering all needed mental health services.

Congress should tackle serious deficiencies in federal programs that fund mental health services, including problems of limited coverage and access that keep many mentally ill persons from being able to obtain the treatment they need. For offenders released from prisons, current law leads to long delays in the restoration of eligibility for benefits. Relatively simply changes in the rules governing Medicaid, Supplemental Security Income (SSI) and Social Security Disability Insurance (SSDI) would enable ex-offenders with mental illness to avoid those delays and to obtain quickly the

9

ability to pay for needed medication and mental health services in the community and to ensure continuity of care. Rapid restoration of benefits to released offenders with mental illness not only helps them manage their illness; it also supports public safety by reducing the risk of new involvement with the criminal justice system.

3) Amend or repeal the Prison Litigation Reform Act (PLRA)

Human Rights Watch also urges Congress to amend or repeal the Prison Litigation Reform Act (PLRA) which severely hinders prisoners in their efforts to remedy unconstitutional conditions in state correctional facilities. We urge Congress to: 1) modify the excessively stringent exhaustion requirement in the PLRA that requires prisoners to comply with all internal prison grievance procedures and appeals before being allowed to bring a federal lawsuit which frustrates the prosecution of many meritorious prisoner lawsuits; 2) repeal the requirement that judicially enforceable consent decrees contain findings of federal law violations; 3) repeal the requirement that all judicial orders automatically terminate two years after they are issued; and 4) restore special masters' and attorneys' fees to reasonable levels.

Recommendations to Public Officials, Community Leaders and the General Public

Public officials — elected and appointed — must act decisively to improve mental health services in U.S. prisons. An ongoing concern should be reducing the population of prisoners who have severe mental illnesses. Second, public officials must develop standards, provide oversight mechanisms, and mobilize resources to ensure effective, quality mental health care in prisons.

1) Reduce the incarceration of persons with mental illness.

Steps should be taken at the federal, state, and local levels to reduce the unnecessary and counterproductive incarceration of low-level nonviolent offenders with mental illness. Mandatory minimum sentencing laws should be revised to ensure prison is reserved for the most serious offenders (whether or not mentally ill) and prison sentences are not disproportionately harsh. Mental health courts, prosecutorial pretrial diversion, and other efforts should be supported which will divert mentally ill offenders from jails and into community based mental health treatment programs. Reducing the numbers of mentally ill offenders sent to prison will also free up prison resources to ensure appropriate mental health treatment for those men and women with mental illness who must, in fact, be incarcerated for reasons of public safety.

2) Set high standards for prison mental health services.

Public officials must not accept low quality mental health services for mentally ill prisoners. They should set standards higher than the constitutional minimum required under the Eighth Amendment, which permits malpractice even on a massive scale. International human rights standards require officials to ensure the highest attainable standard of mental health, including accessible, acceptable, and appropriate and good quality mental health services, provided by trained professionals. Officials should not tolerate the misery and pain of prisoners whose mental illness is left untreated or undertreated. Quality mental health services in prison will not only help prisoners, but will improve safety within prisons, benefiting others prisoners and staff. Good correctional mental health services will also increase the likelihood that prisoners will be able to return successfully to their communities following release.

3) Improve conditions of confinement.

Public officials must ensure that all prisoners are confined in conditions consistent with their human dignity. No prisoner should be confined in overcrowded, dangerous, filthy, vermin- or bug-ridden, or unbearably hot cells. Such conditions violate the rights of all prisoners, but they have an especially detrimental effect on prisoners with mental illness.

4) Establish effective performance reviews using independent experts.

Public officials cannot exercise their obligation to ensure appropriate mental health services for prisoners if they do not have objective information provided by independent and qualified experts. Correctional officials often do not have an adequate understanding of the limitations on mental health services provided in their prisons, and other elected officials often have even less understanding. Expert reports presented during litigation are often the only way light is shed on prison conditions. Public officials should not wait, however, until an inmate or family member brings a lawsuit. Existing prison accreditation mechanisms—by the American Correctional Association and the National Commission on Correctional Health Care (NCCHC)—focus primarily on the existence of appropriate policies; they do not assess their implementation or the quality of services actually provided. Experience reveals that implementation often lags far behind even the best of policies.

Each prison system should have performance evaluations of its mental health services by independent qualified professionals. The results of those evaluations should be public (with the names of prisoners kept confidential). To be able to undertake the evaluations, the experts should have unfettered access to medical records, staff, and prisoners. The experts should be charged with monitoring the ways in which prisons diagnose and treat prisoners; the availability of qualified staff in numbers adequate for prisoner mental health needs; the availability of appropriate facilities to provide different levels of care; the range of therapeutic interventions provided to prisoners and the extent to which prisoners have access to services, programs, and facilities; and policies and practices concerning the use of disciplinary measures such as administrative segregation and physical restraints to respond to inmates with serious mental illnesses.

5) Establish comprehensive internal quality review mechanisms for each prison system and prison.

Quality controls for mental health services are often rudimentary, ineffective, or nonexistent. Mental health staff often lack an effective opportunity to engage in candid self-criticism, gather data, identify and discuss shared problems, and work with senior corrections officials to develop solutions to problems in the delivery of mental health services. Establishment of internal quality review procedures and the commitment of prison officials and mental health staff to effectively implement those procedures will provide a vital and ongoing complement to external quality assurance audits.

6) Solicit and heed prisoners' concerns.

As consumers of mental health services, prisoners are singularly without power to protest poor treatment. They cannot switch to another provider, and their legitimate complaints and concerns are rarely acknowledged, much less responded to by corrections officials. Prisons should establish at an institutional as well as departmental level procedures by which prisoner perspectives about mental health services (indeed all medical services) are solicited and heeded. Prisoner views should be incorporated into the outside as well as internal quality review mechanisms recommended above. Special prisoner mental health grievance systems should be established predicated on recognition that prisoners are mental health service consumers and their concerns warrant prompt, careful responses. Current grievance mechanisms are difficult to comply with, rarely result in any meaningful response, and can prompt retaliation from staff. Mentally ill prisoners can have a particularly difficult time following the rules regarding grievances and meeting grievance procedure deadlines. If prison systems attended to prisoner concerns — at the very least communicating to them that they are being listened to — this could well have a beneficial impact on the prisoners' adherence to treatment plans, medication compliance, and other measures critical to their health. If other prisoner-responsive quality control mechanisms are not available, we also recommend the creation of an impartial external entity (within individual prisons or system-wide) staffed with persons with mental health expertise to evaluate prisoner complaints regarding mental health care and treatment.

7) Support funding for appropriate prison mental health services.

We recognize that even corrections departments are not immune from the budget slashing occasioned by current fiscal crises. But even in the best of times, it is difficult to secure adequate funding for services and programs for prisoners. Improvements in mental health services in prison are, unfortunately, heavily dependent on financial resources. Qualified, competent staff cannot be hired and retained in sufficient numbers absent funding. Governors must support adequate funding levels for mental health services and permit corrections officials and mental health staff to argue forcefully, extensively, and publicly on behalf of such funding. They must present candid analyses to the public of existing problems with correctional mental health treatment, the consequences of those problems and the need for resources to address them. They should encourage legislators to reduce prison populations, by lowering unnecessarily harsh mandatory sentencing laws and by supporting alternatives to incarceration for low-level nonviolent offenders, rather than by cutting indispensable services for those prisoners who must be incarcerated.

Recommendations to Prison Officials and Staff

Correctional agencies need to act decisively to improve the delivery of mental health services in prisons and prison systems. We recommend they:

1) Provide sufficient numbers of qualified prison mental health staff.

- Quality mental health services cannot be provided without sufficient numbers of qualified staff with different areas of expertise (from occupational therapists to psychiatrists). Determination of optimal staffing levels should be based on assessment of accurate data regarding prisoner demographics, mental health histories, and service utilization. Each prison system should have department-wide internal credential requirements for mental health staff, and effective mechanisms for monitoring mental health staff competency, performance, and compliance with official protocols and procedures. Mental health staff should be provided and encouraged to engage in ongoing professional education to keep up to date in their fields.

• Recruiting qualified, competent mental health staff is often frustrated by salaries that are below community levels. Low pay also contributes to high rates of staff turnover, which diminishes the quality of care provided. Prison systems and agencies contracted to provide prison medical and mental health services should create employment incentives and introduce competitive pay rates comparable to those offered in community mental health settings, to reduce staff turnover. For prisons in out-of-the-way, undesirable locations, additional incentives ought to be provided to hire and retain quality staff.

2) Provide mental health training for correctional staff.

• It is counterproductive and dangerous for correctional staff who have little or no training in mental illness to work in housing units, on the yards, and elsewhere in prison with prisoners who have serious mental illnesses. Effective training should be provided to all new officers in such areas as: signs of mental illness; different treatments for mental illnesses; side-effects of medications used for the treatment of mental illnesses; effective interaction with mentally ill prisoners; defusing potentially escalating situations; recognition of the signs of possible suicide attempts; and training on the safe use of physical and mechanical restraints for mentally ill offenders. Additional information pertinent to working with mentally ill prisoners should be provided during in-service training.

• Staff should be trained to view suicide attempts and extreme acts of self-mutilation as probable signs of mental illness rather than as indications that prisoners are "malingering" or acting-out simply to gain attention or to be temporarily removed from their cell. Staff should be given guidance, working with mental health staff, to better distinguish between prisoners who deliberately and consciously break rules and undermine prison security, and prisoners whose conduct reflects a serious mental illness.

• Senior officials should carefully monitor the conduct of custodial staff, take seriously prisoner allegations of misconduct, and investigate individual cases as well as patterns of staff misconduct. Staff should be held individually accountable for mistreating prisoners. But prison officials should not rely solely on disciplinary mechanisms for individual staff. They should use their institutional authority to communicate forcefully that mistreatment will not be condoned, to reassign or more closely monitor problematic staff, and to provide better training.

3) Ensure sufficient specialized facilities for seriously mentally ill prisoners.

• Corrections departments should ensure they have a sufficient number of hospital beds and acute care facilities to meet the needs of the prison population. Prisoners with serious mental health needs should not be removed from such facilities simply to free up space for others; nor should prisoners have to wait to be able get the services they need because of insufficient beds. Prisoners with mental illness who have been in acute care facilities should be placed in "step-down" or transitional programs before they are returned to the general prisoner population. Corrections departments should also establish additional intermediate care facilities to provide mentally ill prisoners who have sub-acute care needs with more intensive and long-term mental health services in a more supportive and structured setting than is available to the general population. While not all of those who are seriously mentally ill need to be, or should be, housed in separate facilities, states need to have sufficient specialized facility space available to accommodate those whom the mental health teams determine would benefit from such housing.

- States should focus more resources on providing specialist mental health facilities for seriously mentally ill female prisoners. Since the absolute number of women prisoners is much smaller than that of male prisoners, states frequently lack comprehensive mental health facilities for their female prisoners.

4) Ensure mental health input and impact in disciplinary proceedings.

Prisoners with mental illness can have unique difficulties complying with prison rules and may engage in bizarre or disruptive behavior because of their illness. Punitive responses to such conduct do little to reduce or deter it. When prisoners who are on the mental health caseload violate rules, disciplinary procedures should require mental health input to the disciplinary officers regarding whether the prisoner's behavior was connected to or caused by mental illness, and regarding what sanctions might be appropriate. In specialized units housing only mentally ill prisoners, corrections officials should work with mental health staff to determine whether the normal prison disciplinary system should be suspended, and mental health staff should determine appropriate responses to prisoner misconduct consistent with his or her mental diagnosis and treatment plan.

5) Exclude the seriously mentally ill from segregated confinement or supermax prisons.

Human Rights Watch opposes the prolonged and unnecessary incarceration of any prisoner in isolated segregation or supermaximum security units. Prisoners with serious mental illnesses, even if they are currently stabilized or asymptomatic, should never be confined for prolonged periods in the harsh isolation conditions typical of segregation or supermax prisons. There is an unacceptably high risk that the isolation, reduced mental stimulus, lack of structured activities, and the absence of social interaction will provoke a deterioration of their symptoms and increased suffering. We recognize there are some prisoners with mental illness who require extreme security precautions even when under mental health treatment. For these individuals, prisons should provide specialized secure units that ensure human interaction and purposeful activities in addition to mental health services.

Corrections officials should also make sure that all prisoners in segregated housing have their mental health monitored carefully and continually; that they be able to communicate confidentially with mental health staff; and that they have access to whatever services and therapeutic interventions mental health staff determine are necessary. To the extent that accommodating mental health needs requires changes in regular rules and protocols governing prisoners in isolation, the changes should be undertaken consistent with reasonable security requirements.

6) Develop and expand continuity-of-care protocols between prisons and the community.

Ill-Equipped

Prisons and community mental health systems need to develop comprehensive continuity-of-care protocols and programs to break the cycle of release-recidivism-reincarceration. Prisoners that have serious mental illnesses should be released from prison with arrangements in place to provide them with access to medication and mental health services. Moving the prisoners prior to their release to prisons in or near the counties to which they will return will allow prison mental health staff and parole officers to liaise more effectively with local mental health service providers to guard against the prisoner falling through the cracks. Discharge planning efforts should begin months prior to a seriously mentally ill prisoner's release. Corrections agencies should also establish procedures by which prisoners with mental illness will have access to Medicaid immediately upon release rather than having to wait for months to have the paperwork completed. States and counties should increase the number of programs providing housing and assisted living facilities for newly released prisoners with mental illness.

III.   BACKGROUND

"By default, we get forced to be a pseudo[mental] hospital."
Michael Mahoney, warden, Montana State Prison[6]

"On any given day, at least 284,000 schizophrenic and manic depressive individuals are incarcerated, and 547,800 are on probation. We have unfortunately come to accept incarceration and homelessness as part of life for the most vulnerable population among us."
Congressman Ted Strickland[7]

"We are literally drowning in patients, running around trying to put our fingers in the bursting dikes, while hundreds of men continue to deteriorate psychiatrically before our eyes into serious psychoses…"
Unnamed prison psychiatrist[8]

A staggering number of persons with mental illnesses are confined in U.S. jails and prisons — somewhere between two and four hundred thousand or more, according to expert estimates. The causes of this massive incarceration of the mentally ill are many, but corrections and mental health professionals point primarily to inadequate community mental health services and the country's punitive criminal justice policies. While mental health hospitals across the country were shut down over the last couple of decades as part of the process of "deinstitutionalization," the community-based health services that were supposed to replace them were never adequately developed. As a consequence, many of the mentally ill, particularly those who are poor and homeless, are unable to obtain the treatment they need. Ignored, neglected, and often unable to take care of their basic needs, large numbers commit crimes and find themselves swept up into the burgeoning criminal justice system. Jails and prisons have become, in effect, the country's front-line mental health providers.[9]

Most of the mentally ill who end up in prison are initially incarcerated in jail as pretrial detainees. By all accounts, jails across the country are even less able to care for mentally ill prisoners than prisons. Absent adequate mental health screening and services in jails, the prison systems inherit exacerbated mental health problems when the pretrial detainees suffering from mental illnesses are ultimately sentenced and moved from jail into prison.

Indeed two of the largest mental health providers in the country today are Cook County and Los Angeles County jails, both of them urban entry points into the burgeoning prisons systems of

---

[6] Jennifer McKee, "Mental Illness Behind Bars, Part II: 'We're all kind of strange.' -- inmate," *The Montana Standard,* June 29, 2003.

[7] Congressman Ted Strickland speaking to the House Subcommittee on Crime, Oversight Hearing on "The Impact of the Mentally Ill on the Criminal Justice System," September 21, 2000.

[8] Unnamed prison psychiatrist, cited by California Treatment Advocacy Coalition, *Fact Sheet: "People Suffering from Mental Illness Should be in Treatment No Jail,"* available at: http://www.psychlaws.org/StateActivity/California/factsheet2.htm, accessed on August 27, 2003.

[9] "Jails are not designed as care facilities for those with mental disorders, but in fact many jails today are the largest inpatient mental health institutions in the United States." Martin Drapkin, *Management and Supervision of Jail Inmates with Mental Disorders* (Civic Research Institute, New Jersey, 2003), p.1-1. See Nahama Broner, et al., "Arrested Adults Awaiting Arraignment," 30 Fordham Urb. L.J. 663 (2003) (discussing people with mental illness in the beginning of the criminal justice process).

Illinois and California respectively.[10] Based on a sample of Cook County jail inmates, Northwestern University psychology professor Linda Teplin reported in 1990 that over 6 percent of inmates were actively psychotic, a rate four times that found in the outside population.[11]

Rates of Incarceration of the Mentally Ill

Persons with mental illness are disproportionately represented in correctional institutions. While about 5 percent of the U.S. population suffers from mental illness, a 1998 reported noted that "studies and clinical experience indicate that somewhere between 8 and 19 percent of prisoners have significant psychiatric or functional disabilities and another 15 to 20 percent will require some form of psychiatric intervention during their incarceration."[12] In 2000, the American Psychiatric Association reported research estimates that perhaps as many as one in five prisoners were seriously mentally ill, with up to 5 percent actively psychotic at any given moment.[13] Given the current U.S. prison population, this means there may be approximately 300,000 men and women in U.S. prisons today who are seriously mentally ill, and 70,000 who are psychotic.[14] The National Commission on Correctional Health Care issued a report to Congress in March 2002 in which it presented the following prevalence estimates:

> On any given day, between 2.3 and 3.9 percent of inmates in State prisons are estimated to have schizophrenia or other psychotic disorder, between 13.1 and 18.6 percent major depression, and between 2.1 and 4.3 percent bipolar disorder (manic episode). A substantial percentage of inmates exhibit symptoms of other disorders as well, including between 8.4 and 13.4 percent with dysthymia, between 22.0 and 30.1 percent with an anxiety disorder, and between 6.2 and 11.7 percent with post-traumatic stress disorder.[15]

---

[10] According to "Treatment Not Jail" *Sacramento Bee*, March 17, 1999, "on any given day, Los Angeles County Jail holds as many as 3,300 seriously mentally ill" people. See also Noah Adams, "A Danger To Self And Others," *National Public Radio*, July 6, 1999 (referring to Cook County Jail as having over one thousand prisoners in mental health treatment on any given day).

[11] Linda Teplin, "The Prevalence of Severe Mental Disorder Among Male Urban Jail Detainees: Comparison with the Epidemiologic Catchment Area Program," *American Journal of Public Health*, vol. 80, no. 6 (June 1990.) Teplin's sample consisted of 3,654 free world individuals in a five-city catchment area and 627 jail inmates. It was conducted between November 1983 and November 1984.

[12] Jeffrey L. Metzner, et al., *Treatment in Jails and Prisons*, in Robert M. Wittstein, ed., *Treatment of Offenders with Mental Disorders* (The Guilford press, New York, 1998), p.211. Dr. Metzner also provides a summary of research on the prevalence of mental disorders in jails and prisons, pp.230-233. NAMI (formerly known as the National Alliance for the Mentally Ill) and the Center for Mental Health Services estimate that 5.4 percent of U.S. adults have some form of serious mental illness. Information compiled in a NAMI fact sheet, updated in January 2001. Available online at: http://www.nami.org/helpline/factsandfigures.html, accessed on June 20, 2003. This number is based on 1998 research by R.C. Kessler, published in *Mental Health, United States,* edited by R. W. Manderscheid and M.J. Henderson. (Center for Mental Health Services, 1999).

[13] American Psychiatric Association, *Psychiatric Services in Jails and Prisons,* 2nd Ed. (Washington D.C., American Psychiatric Association, 2000), introduction, p. XIX.

[14] Based on a population of 1,361,258 in state and federal prisons. See Paige M. Harrison and Allen J. Beck*, Prisoners in 2002* (Washington, D.C.: U.S. Department of Justice, Bureau of Justice Statistics, July 2003). Available online at: http://www.ojp.usdoj.gov/bjs/pub/pdf/p02.pdf, accessed on August 26, 2003.

[15] National Commission on Correctional Health Care, "The Health Status of Soon-to-be-Released Inmates, A Report to Congress" (March 2002), vol. 1, p 22. The cited data is based on Bonita M. Veysey and Gisela Bichler-Robertson, "Prevalence Estimates of Psychiatric Disorders in Correctional Settings," vol. 2 of "The Health Status of Soon –to-be Released Inmates (April 2002). Volume 1 is available online at: http://www.ncchc.org/pubs/pubs_stbr.vol1.html, and Volume 2 at: http://www.ncchc.org/pubs/pubs_stbr.vol2.html, both accessed on August, 25, 2003.

In 1999, the federal Bureau of Justice Statistics, drawing on a survey in 1997 of adult prisoners, estimated that 16 percent of state and federal adult prisoners and a similar percentage of adults in jails were mentally ill.[16] This prevalence rate translates into an estimated 230,505 adults with mental illness confined in U.S. prisons, and another 106,476 in its jails.[17] The Bureau of Justice Statistics has also reported that nearly one in ten prisoners are taking psychotropic medications, with that number increasing to nearly one in five in Hawaii, Maine, Montana, Nebraska, and Oregon.[18]

As these numbers suggest, prisons have become warehouses for a large proportion of the country's men and women with mental illness. In September 2000, Congressman Ted Strickland informed his colleagues on the House Subcommittee on Crime that between 25 and 40 percent of *all* mentally ill Americans would, at some point in their lives, become entangled in the criminal justice system. According to the American Psychiatric Association, over 700 thousand mentally ill Americans are processed through either jail or prison each year.[19] In 1999, NAMI (formerly known as the National Alliance for the Mentally Ill) reported that the number of Americans with serious mental illnesses in prison was three times greater than the number hospitalized with such illnesses.[20]

Individual prison systems report high percentages of mentally ill offenders. For example, the California Department of Corrections estimated that as of July 2002, 23,439 prisoners were on the prison mental health roster, representing over 14 percent of the California prison population.[21] The Pennsylvania Department of Corrections estimates that 16.5 percent of its prisoner population, or approximately 6,500 people, are on the mental health caseload, of whom 1,537 are so ill that their ability to function on a day-to-day basis has been dramatically limited.[22] Eleven percent of New York's sixty-six thousand prisoners receive mental health services. In Kentucky, 14.6 percent of the state prison population is on the mental health caseload, and in Texas the figure is 11.6 percent.[23]

---

[16] Paula M. Ditton, *Mental Health and Treatment of Inmates and Probationers* (Washington D.C.: U.S. Department of Justice, Bureau of Justice Statistics, July 1999), p. 3. Available online at: http://www.ojp.usdoj.gov/bjs/abstract/mhtip.htm, accessed on June 20, 2003. Prisoners were identified as mentally ill if they met one of two criteria: they reported a current mental or emotional condition, or they reported an overnight stay in a mental hospital or treatment program.

[17] Based on a population of 1,361,258 in state and federal prisons and 665,475 in local jails. See Paige M. Harrison and Allen J. Beck, *Prisoners in 2002* (Washington, D.C.: U.S. Department of Justice, Bureau of Justice Statistics, July 2003). Available online at: http://www.ojp.usdoj.gov/bjs/pub/pdf/p02.pdf, accessed on August 26, 2003.

[18] Allen J. Beck, Ph.D. and Laura M. Maruschak, *Mental Health Treatment in State Prisons, 2000* (Washington D.C.: U.S. Department of Justice, Bureau of Justice Statistics, July 2001.) Available online at: http://www.ojp.usdoj.gov/bjs/abstract/mhtsp00.htm, accessed on September 10, 2003.

[19] American Psychiatric Association, *Psychiatric Services in Jails and Prisons,* 2nd Ed. (Washington D.C., American Psychiatric Association, 2000), Introduction, p. XIX, 2000.

[20] NAMI, "Criminalization of the Mentally Ill," prepared for the NAMI 2001 Annual Convention, p. 1. Available online at: http://www.nami.org/Content/ContentGroups/Policy/criminalization2001.pdf, accessed on September 15, 2003.

[21] Information contained in chart produced by the Health Care Services Division of the California Department of Corrections titled: "Combined Mental Health Population Per Institution." The figures were last updated July 25, 2002. According to the Monthly Report of Population for July 2002, the total California Department of Corrections population was 157,514. State of California, Department of Corrections, Data Analysis Unit, "Monthly Report of Population," July 31, 2002, accessed from http://www.cdc.state.ca.us/OffenderInfoServices/Reports/Monthly/TPOP1A/TPOP1Ad0207.pdf, on June 18, 2003.

[22] Human Rights Watch telephone interview with Lance Couturier, chief psychologist, Pennsylvania Department of Corrections, January 23, 2003.

[23] Data on Kentucky comes from a Human Rights Watch telephone interview with Dr. Rick Purvis, director, Division of Mental Health Services, Kentucky Department of Corrections, August 13, 2003. According to information provided by Dr. Purvis, there are 2,333 inmates on the mental health caseload. Kentucky has a total prison population of 15,933. Data on Texas comes from an email correspondence to Human Rights Watch from Tati Buentello, administrative

There are no national statistics on historical rates of mental illness among the prison population. Some states, however, report a significant increase in recent years in the proportion of prisoners diagnosed with serious mental illnesses. For example, the mental health caseload in New York prisons has increased by 73 percent since 1991, five times the prison population increase.[24] In Colorado, the proportion of prisoners with major mental illness was 10 percent in 1998, five to six times the proportion identified in 1988.[25] Between 1993 and 1998 the population of seriously mentally ill prisoners in Mississippi doubled and in the District of Columbia it rose by 30 percent.[26] In Connecticut, the number of prisoners with serious mental illness increased from 5.2 percent to 12.3 percent of the state's prison population.[27] Indeed, nineteen of thirty-one states responding to a 1998 survey by the Colorado Department of Corrections reported a disproportionate increase in their seriously mentally ill population during the previous five years.[28] While most mental health professionals we interviewed believe that there has been some increase in the proportion of prisoners who are mentally ill, they caution that the dramatic increases noted above may also reflect improvements in the mental health screening and diagnosis of prisoners.

Deinstitutionalization, Crime and Punishment, and the Rise in the Mentally Ill Prisoner Population

Fifty years ago, public mental health care was based almost exclusively on institutional care and over half a million mentally ill Americans lived in public mental health hospitals. Beginning in the early 1960s, states began to downsize and close their public mental health hospitals, a process called "deinstitutionalization." Many factors precipitated the process. The first generation of effective anti-psychotic medications were developed, which made successful treatment outside of hospitals a real possibility. Litigation increased due process safeguards in mental hospital involuntary commitment and release procedures, which meant far fewer people could be committed or kept in the hospitals against their will. Today, fewer than eighty thousand people live in mental health hospitals and that number is likely to fall still further.[29] In 1955, the rate of persons in mental

---

associate, Texas Department of Criminal Justice, August 18, 2003, which indicated the total number of prisoners on the mental health caseload was 18,823. The Texas prison population is 162,003.

[24] Mary Beth Pfeiffer, "Mental care faulted in 6 prison deaths," *Poughkeepsie Journal*, June 28, 2003.

[25] Colorado Department of Corrections, *Offenders with Serious Mental Illness*, A Multi-Agency Task Group Report to the Colorado legislature Joint Budget Committee, November, 1998; on file at Human Rights Watch. The report includes the results of a survey of prison mental health directors, including their responses to questions regarding the proportion of prisoners with serious mental disorders.

[26] Colorado Department of Corrections, *Offenders with Serious Mental Illness*, 1998.

[27] National Institute of Corrections (NIC), "Provision of Mental Health Care in Prisons" (U.S. Department of Justice, February 2001), table 1, p. 3. Available online from the NIC Information Center at: http://www.nicic.org/pubs/2001/016724.pdf, accessed August 25, 2003. According to the report, eighteen of twenty-five states that responded to the NIC survey reported increases in the size of prison population with mental illness; many of the states, however, did not specify particular percentage increases.

[28] Colorado Department of Corrections, *Offenders with Serious Mental Illness*, 1998.

[29] Numbers calculated by the Council of State Governments, *Criminal Justice/Mental Health Consensus Project* (Council of State Governments, New York, June 2002). The report reflects two years of collaborative work between over one hundred lawmakers, police chiefs, sheriffs, District Attorneys, public defenders, judges, mental health advocates, victim advocates, correctional officials, substance abuse experts, and clinicians on the topic of the mentally ill and criminal justice. In "Some Perspectives On Deinstitutionalization," *Psychiatric Services*, vol. 52, no. 8 (August 2001). Richard Lamb and Leona Bachrach quoted data generated by the National Institute of Mental Health indicating the number of mental hospital beds nationally had fallen to 57,151 by the end of 1998.

hospitals was 339 per one hundred thousand; by 1998, it had declined to twenty-nine per one hundred thousand.[30]

Deinstitutionalization freed hundreds of thousands of mentally ill men and women from large, grim facilities to which most had been involuntarily committed and in which they spent years, if not decades or entire lives, receiving greatly ineffectual, and often brutal, treatment. Proponents of deinstitutionalization envisioned former mental health hospital patients receiving treatment through community mental health programs and living as independently in the community as their mental conditions permitted. This process was catalyzed by passage of the federal legislation providing seed funding for the establishment of comprehensive mental health centers in the community. Unfortunately, community mental health services have not been able to play the role the architects of deinstitutionalization envisioned. The federal government did not provide ongoing funding for community services and while states cut their budgets for mental hospitals, they did not make commensurate increases in their budgets for community-based mental health services. Chronically underfunded, the existing mental health system today does not reach and provide mental health treatment to anywhere near the number of people who need it.

On July 22, 2003, the President's New Freedom Commission on Mental Health sent its final report to President George W. Bush.[31] The Commission found that:

> Mental health delivery system is fragmented and in disarray…lead[ing] to unnecessary and costly disability, homelessness, school failure and incarceration…In many communities, access to quality care is poor, resulting in wasted resources and lost opportunities for recovery. More individuals could recover from even the most serious mental illnesses if they had access in their communities to treatment and supports that are tailored to their needs.[32]

As the Commission's Chairman, Michael F. Hogan, stated in his cover letter with the report:

> Today's mental health care system is a patchwork relic — the result of disjointed reforms and policies. Instead of ready access to quality care, the system presents barriers that all too often add to the burden of mental illnesses for individuals, their families, and our communities.

The Commission also found that minority communities were particularly underserved in or inappropriately served by the current mental health care system. It noted that "significant barriers still remain in access, quality, and outcomes of care for minorities….[They are] less likely to have

---

[30] Richard Lamb and Linda Weinberger, "Persons With Severe Mental Illness in Jails and Prisons: A Review," *Psychiatric Services*, vol. 49, pp. 483-492, 1998. In Richard Lamb and Leona Bachrach, "Some Perspectives on Deinstitutionalization," *Psychiatric Services*, August 2001, vol. 52, no. 8, the authors estimated the number of occupied state hospital beds had fallen as low as 21 per 100,000.

[31] The Commission was created by President Bush on April 29, 2002, with a mandate to produce an interim report by October 2002 and a final report in April 2003.

[32] President's New Freedom Commission on Mental Health, *Achieving the Promise: Transforming Mental Health Care in America*, p.3. Available online at: http://www.mentalhealthcommission.gov/reports/FinalReport/toc.html, accessed August 26, 2003.

access to available mental health services; are less likely to receive needed mental health scare; often receive poorer quality care; and are significantly under-represented in mental health research."[33]

According to the 2002 report of the Criminal Justice/Mental Health Consensus Project, coordinated by the Council of State Governments:

> The professionals in the [mental health] system know much about how to meet the needs of the people it is meant to serve. The problem comes, however, in the ability of the system's intended clientele to access its services and, often, in the system's ability to make these services accessible. The existing mental health system bypasses, overlooks, or turns away far too many potential clients. Many people the system might serve are too disabled, fearful, or deluded to make and keep appointments at mental health centers. Others simply never make contact and are camped under highway overpasses, huddled on heating grates, or shuffling with grocery carts on city streets.[34]

Because of the problems plaguing community mental health systems and the limitations on public funding for mental health services,[35] all too many people who need publicly financed mental health services cannot obtain them until they are in an acute psychotic state and are deemed to be a danger to themselves or others.[36] While some of the mentally ill are fortunate to have families with sufficient financial resources to get them private treatment, many of the mentally ill are impoverished. According to NAMI (formerly known as the National Alliance for the Mentally Ill), one in twenty persons with a severe mental illness is homeless.[37] People with serious mental illnesses are over-represented among the homeless population, which comprises the poorest of America's residents: experts estimate than anywhere from 20 to 33 percent of the homeless have serious mental illnesses. People with serious mental illnesses have greater difficulty escaping homelessness than other people; many have been living on the streets for years.[38]

---

[33] Ibid., pp. 49-50.

[34] Council of State Governments, *Consensus Project* (2002), p. 7.

[35] For example, federal funding of community-based mental health services is greatly diffused, spread across numerous mandatory and discretionary programs. Within Medicaid, community-based mental health services run through more than six separate optional service categories. Moreover, the complicated federal scheme relies on numerous state and local funding streams. The inevitable result is a complex, confusing patchwork of programs, with fragmented services at the community level - a system that is especially difficult for Medicaid recipients with mental illness. See NAMI, Medicaid Funding of Mental Illness Treatment, http://web.nami.org/policy/wherewestand/medicaid02.html, accessed on August 9, 2003.

[36] Because of the restricted access to community services, the phenomenon of "mercy arrests" has arisen in which police officers arrest manifestly psychotic individuals because they know that it is easier to channel them into treatment once they enter the criminal justice system than it is to find them hospital space, or even counseling at a community service institution.

[37] Federal Task Force on Homelessness and Severe Mental Illness, *Outcasts On Main Street: A Report of the Federal Task Force on Homelessness and Severe Mental Illness* (Washington, D.C.: GPO), 1992. Cited by NAMI, accessed on June 11, 2003, from http://www.nami.org/helpline/factsandfigures.html.

[38] Data on homeless who are mentally ill obtained from The National Resource Center on Homelessness and Mental Illness, operated by the Center for Mental Health Services of the Substance Abuse and Mental Health Services Administration. See http://www.nrchmi.com/facts/default.asp, accessed on June 10, 2003, and NAMI, accessed from http://www.nami.org/Template.cfm?Section=Issue_Spotlights&Template=/TaggedPage/TaggedPageDisplay.cfm&TPLID=5&ContentID=2069, on June 23, 2003.

When poor persons with mental illness are able to get treatment, it is typically short-term. People who are hospitalized are often kept for only short periods, until they are stabilized, and then they are released, where they again face limited access to treatment in the community. Persons with mental illness who have prior criminal records or histories of violence have a particularly difficult time getting access to treatment; many mental health programs simply will not take them. According to Richard Lamb, Professor of Psychiatry, Law and Public Policy at the University of Southern California, "it used to be the State Hospital couldn't turn down anybody. Now the state hospitals can and do… It used to be the state hospital was the facility of last resort; and today the jails and prisons are the facilities of last resort."[39]

Community mental health services are especially likely to fail to meet the needs of mentally ill persons with co-occurring disorders. The federal Substance Abuse and Mental Health Services Administration has estimated that 72 percent of mentally ill individuals entering the jail system have a drug-abuse or alcohol problem.[40] Mental health programs are often reluctant to treat persons with substance abuse problems — because of the fear that addicts will prove particularly disruptive and also may try to bring drugs into the programs — and many community mental health staff are not trained to diagnose and treat persons with co-occurring disorders.[41] And, substance abuse programs are often reluctant to take persons who are mentally ill. Despite the prevalence of substance abuse among the mentally ill, few communities have integrated mental health and substance abuse treatment programs.

Deinstitutionalization resulted in the release of hundreds of thousands of mentally ill offenders to communities who could not care for them. At about the same time, national attitudes toward those who committed street crime — who are overwhelmingly the country's poorest — changed markedly. Both the federal and state governments adopted a series of punitive criminal justice policies that encouraged increased arrests; increased the likelihood that conviction for a crime would result in incarceration, including through mandatory minimum sentencing and "three strikes" laws; increased the length of time served, by increasing the length of sentences and reducing or eliminating the availability of early release and parole; and increased the rate at which parolees are returned to prison. The U.S. rate of incarceration soared, becoming the highest in the world: 701 prisoners per one hundred thousand U.S. residents, or one in every 143 residents.[42] Championed as protecting the public from serious and violent offenders, the new criminal justice policies in fact yielded high rates of confinement for nonviolent offenders. Nationwide, nonviolent offenders account for 72 percent of all new state prison admissions. Almost one-third of new admissions are nonviolent drug offenders.[43]

Most of those swept into the criminal justice system are poor, many are homeless, many have substance abuse problems, and many would be good candidates for alternatives to incarceration.[44]

---

[39] Human Rights Watch interview with Richard Lamb, Los Angeles, California, January 31, 2003.

[40] Department of Health and Human Services, Substance Abuse and Mental Health Services Administration (SAMHSA), *The Prevalence of Co-Occurring Mental Illness and Substance Use Disorders in Jails,* Spring 2002. The report sources its information to Abram, K.M. and Teplin, L.A., "Co-Occurring Disorders Among Mentally Ill Jail Detainees," *American Psychologist*, vol. 46, no. 10 (1991), pp. 1036-1045. Equivalent data for the prison population is not provided.

[41] See National Center for Mental Health and Juvenile Justice, GAINS Center For People with Co-Occurring Disorders in Contact with the Justice System, accessed on June 23, 2003 from: http://www.ncmhjj.com/projects/gains.asp.

[42] BJS, *Prisoners in 2002,* p. 2.

[43] Human Rights Watch, "Punishment and Prejudice," *A Human Rights Watch Report*, vol. 12, no. 2 (May 2000).

[44] See, e.g., Marc Mauer, *Race to Incarcerate* (New York: New Press, 1999).

Many of them are also mentally ill. In making America's response to crime and drug use more punitive throughout the 1980s and 1990s, state and federal lawmakers inadvertently contributed to the imprisonment of greater numbers of mentally ill citizens. The percentage of America's mentally ill population either living in prison, or having recently come out of prison, increased dramatically.[45]

"Criminalizing the Mentally Ill"
There is a direct link between inadequate community mental health services and the growing number of mentally ill who are incarcerated. As the Criminal Justice/Mental Health Consensus Project noted:

> Law enforcement officers, prosecutors, defenders, and judges — people on the front lines every day — believe too many people with mental illness become involved in the criminal justice system because the mental health system has somehow failed. They believe that if many of the people with mental illness received the services they needed, they would not end up under arrest, in jail, or facing charges in court. Mental health advocates, service providers, and administrators do not necessarily disagree. Like their counterparts in the criminal justice system, they believe that the ideal mechanism to prevent people with mental illness from entering the criminal justice system is the mental health system itself — if it can be counted on to function effectively. They also know that in most places the current system is overwhelmed and performing this preventive function poorly.[46]

The President's New Freedom Commission found that across the country the mental health "system's failings lead to unnecessary and costly disability, homelessness, school failure, and incarceration."[47] Every state across the country has its own experience with the "criminalization of the mentally ill."[48] For example, a committee appointed by the state legislature in Maine reported that:

> Community mental health services, though very good, are, due to lack of resources, inadequate to meet the needs of persons with mental illness. This has resulted in some persons with mental illness falling through the treatment services net and into the criminal justice system. The lack of community mental health resources also impairs the ability of law enforcement, courts and corrections facilities to divert persons with mental illness away from the criminal justice system and into more appropriate treatment settings.[49]

---

[45] American Psychiatric Association, *Psychiatric Services in Jails and Prisons,* 2nd Ed. (Washington D.C., American Psychiatric Association, 2000), introduction, p. XIX.

[46] Council of State Governments, *Consensus Project* (2002), p. 26.

[47] President's New Freedom Commission on Mental Health, *Interim Report of the President's New Freedom Commission on Mental Health,* October 29, 2002, p. 1. Available online at: http://www.mentalhealthcommission.gov/reports/Interim_Report.htm, accessed on June 23, 2003.

[48] H. Richard Lamb, M.D. and Linda E. Weinberger, Ph.D., "Persons With Severe Mental Illness in Jails and Prisons: A Review," *Psychiatric Services,* vol. 49, no. 4, April 1998, pp. 483-492. According to Lamb and Weinberger, the term "criminalization of the mentally ill" was first coined in Abramson M.F., "The criminalization of mentally disordered behavior: possible side-effect of a new mental health law," *Hospital and Community Psychiatry,* vol. 23, 1972, pp. 101-105.

[49] State of Maine, 120th Legislature, *Final Report of the Committee to Study the Needs of Persons with Mental Illness Who Are Incarcerated,* December 19, 2001, introduction, p. ii, accessed from http://www.state.me.us/legis/opla/incarrept.PDF, on June 23, 2003.

Thousands of mentally ill are left untreated and unhelped until they have deteriorated so greatly that they wind up arrested and prosecuted for crimes they might never have committed had they been able to access therapy, medication, and assisted living facilities in the community. Mental health professionals told Human Rights Watch that it is next to impossible to get their clients admitted to hospitals or treatment programs until after they have deteriorated to such a point that they have already committed a crime.

The relationship between deinstitutionalization and incarceration is not that of a direct population shift from hospitals to prisons. As described by Pennsylvania psychiatrist Dr. Pogos Voskanian, who works with ex-prisoners in an after-prison program called Gaudenzia House, "deinstitutionalization has created not so much a problem for people who have been deinstitutionalized, but for people who can't get into institutions in the first place."[50] Michael Thompson, lead author of a Criminal Justice/Mental Health Consensus Project report on mental illness in the criminal justice system,[51] agrees that people who might in the past have benefited from publicly provided mental health services are now left untreated until their mental illness deteriorates to the point where they commit a criminal offense and are sent to prison.[52] Some experts use the term "transinstitutionalization" to refer to this problem of persons with mental illness being left untreated until they end up institutionalized within correctional settings.[53]

Mental health professionals also believe the growing number of mentally ill persons in jails and prisons reflects the difficulty of obtaining court orders committing persons with serious mental illness to mental health hospitals. Unless a person poses a clear danger to him or herself or to others, courts will not issue orders for involuntary commitment.[54] In addition, they point to the increased difficulty of obtaining court rulings that mentally ill persons are incompetent to stand trial or of securing verdicts of "not guilty by reason of insanity."[55] As a result persons who are extremely ill, even psychotic, end up in prison.

---

[50] Human Rights Watch interview with Pogos Voskanian, psychiatrist, Gaudenzia House, Philadelphia, Pennsylvania, August 13, 2002.

[51] Council of State Governments, *Consensus Project* (2002). Coordinated by the Council of State Governments, the Project produced a 432-page report which grew out of a two-year effort to prepare recommendations for improving the criminal justice system's response to people with mental illness. The Steering Committee was made up of representatives from The Council of State Governments, the Police Executive Research Forum, the Pretrial Services Resource Center, the Association of State Correctional Administrators, the National Association of State Mental Health Program Directors, the Bazelon Center for Mental Health Law, and the Center for Behavioral Health, Justice & Public Policy.

[52] Human Rights Watch interviews with Mike Thompson, New York City, New York, April 29, 2002, June 13, 2002. Thompson generously shared much of the CSG's ongoing research with Human Rights Watch.

[53] See, e.g., Jolynn E. Hurwitz, *Mental Illness and Substance Abuse in the Criminal Justice System* (The Health Foundation of Greater Cincinnati), September, 2000: "Deinstitutionalization became 'transinstitutionalization' as police resorted to arresting individuals with mental health disorders when the local mental health systems were unresponsive." The authors quote E.F. Torrey & Zdanowicz, M. *Deinstitutionalization: A deadly debacle, 2000*, and S.P.M. Harrington, *New bedlam: Jails—not psychiatric hospitals—now care for the indigent mentally ill*, The Humanist (May-June, 1999), pp. 9-13.

[54] Prior to the 1970s, many mentally ill persons were involuntarily committed to mental hospitals with minimal protections for their right to liberty and personal autonomy. Since then, substantial case law and new legislation have significantly increased procedural and substantive safeguards for the civil liberties of the mentally ill.

[55] A public furor erupted when John Hinkley was found "not guilty by reason of insanity" in his 1982 trial for the attempted assassination of President Reagan. In the four years following, Congress and half of the states enacted changes in the insanity defense that limited defendants' ability to use this defense. Nine states limited the substantive test of insanity; seven states shifted the burden of proof to the defendant; twelve states created specific "guilty but mentally ill" verdicts; and Utah, Montana, and Idaho completely abolished their existing insanity defenses.

Economic incentives may also encourage states to channel seriously mentally ill offenders into prisons rather than state hospitals. "State hospitals cost $90-$100,000 per year per patient," said Dr. Fred Maue, chief of clinical services, Pennsylvania Department of Corrections. "In prison, a seriously mentally ill individual is imprisoned and treated for around $35,000. Prison isn't the best place for a mentally ill person to be. But it's better than to just be homeless in the community."[56] Departments of correction have also been better able to protect — and even increase — their budgets in recent years than state agencies with responsibility for social and mental health services. As Mike Robbins, former acting mental health director for the Washington Department of Corrections, told Human Rights Watch:

> The mental health agencies of the DHSS [Department of Health and Social Services] have received budget cuts impacting their service. It feeds the mentally ill into the Department of Corrections. It's still cheaper to house the mentally ill in prison than in a state hospital. As money is harder to come by for the DHSS, plans for handling that person, providing services to that person, may not take place. And it's then not unlikely for us to see that person with our system.[57]

Just as it is poor and homeless mentally ill individuals who have the greatest difficulty obtaining the mental health treatment they need, so it is poor and homeless mentally ill individuals who are disproportionately incarcerated. According to the National Resource Center on Homelessness and Mental Illness, the homeless who are mentally ill are twice as likely as other people who are homeless to be arrested or jailed, mostly for misdemeanors.[58] Reproduced in table 1 are figures from the federal Bureau of Justice Statistics (BJS) reflecting the rates of homelessness and unemployment among mentally ill and other prison and jail inmates.

Table 1: Homelessness, Employment, and Sources of Income of Inmates, by Mental Health Status[59]

	State Prison		Federal Prison		Local Jail	
	Mentally Ill Inmates	Other Inmates	Mentally Ill Inmates	Other Inmates	Mentally Ill Inmates	Other Inmates
Homeless						
In Year Before Arrest	20.1%	8.8%	18.6%	3.2%	30.3%	17.3%
At Time of Arrest	3.9	1.2	3.9	0.3	6.9	2.9
Employed in Month Before Arrest						
Yes	61.2%	69.6%	62.3%	72.5%	52.9%	66.6%
No	38.8	30.4	37.7	27.5	47.1	33.4

---

[56] Human Rights Watch interview with Dr. Fred Maue, chief of clinical services, Pennsylvania Department of Corrections, Gaudenzia House, Philadelphia, Pennsylvania, August 13, 2002. In 2002, the *New York Times* published an editorial reporting that the annual cost to New York State of maintaining a person in a psychiatric hospital in New York was $120,000. "New York's Mentally Ill Deserve Better," *New York Times,* Editorial, October 9, 2002.

[57] Human Rights Watch interview with Mike Robbins, former acting mental health director, Washington Department of Corrections, Olympia, Washington, August 19, 2002.

[58] National Resource Center on Homelessness and Mental Illness, *Get the Facts*, March 17, 2003, accessed from http://www.nrchmi.com/facts/facts_question_3.asp, on June 10, 2003.

[59] This table reproduced from data compiled by the Bureau of Justice Statistics, *Mental Health and Treatment of Inmates and Probationers*, 1999, table 7, accessed from http://www.ojp.usdoj.gov/bjs/pub/pdf/mhtip.pdf on June 23, 2003.

The BJS figures in table 1 suggest higher rates of employment than those arrived at in other surveys. According to the President's New Freedom Commission on Mental Health for example, about one out of every three adults with mental illness are employed. A survey by NAMI of its members revealed that 17 percent of consumers of mental health services were employed part-time and only 14 percent full-time.[60]

The BJS also provides data on the crimes which have sent the mentally ill to prison and jail. According to the BJS, 47.1 percent of mentally ill prisoners confined in state prison and 69.7 percent of mentally ill prisoners in jails committed property, drug, or public order offenses.[61] A higher percentage of mentally ill prisoners committed violent offenses than other offenders (52.9 percent compared to 46.1); similarly, a higher percentage of mentally ill jail inmates committed violent offenses than other inmates (31.3 percent compared to 26.0 percent).[62]

Diversion

Incarceration is an excessive, unnecessarily costly, and even counterproductive response to low-level nonviolent crimes, particularly when committed by persons who have substance abuse problems and/or are mentally ill. Growing public recognition of the human, social, and financial costs of the country's experiment in mass incarceration has prompted the development of efforts to divert certain low-level offenders from jail and prison. Across the country, drug courts have burgeoned to divert low-level drug offenders into substance abuse treatment programs.[63] Because of the high percentage of mentally ill offenders who also have substance abuse problems, the diversion of drug offenders into treatment programs should help preclude incarceration of some mentally ill offenders.[64]

Although the effort is only nascent, momentum is also developing to divert low-level nonviolent offenders who are mentally ill to mental health treatment rather than jail.[65] There are approximately ninety mental health courts currently operating in twenty-two states.[66] For example, Brooklyn, New

---

[60] Written communication to Human Rights Watch from Ron Honberg, director of legal affairs, NAMI, September 9, 2003.

[61] BJS, *Mental Health and Treatment of Inmates and Probationers*, 1999, table 5.

[62] Ibid.

[63] United States General Accounting Office, *Drug Courts: Better DOJ Data Collection and Evaluation Efforts Needed to Measure Impact of Drug Court Programs* (Washington, D.C.: April 2002), available online at: http://www.gao.gov/new.items/d02434.pdf, accessed on June 10, 2003. Drug abuse counselors and mental health staff inside prisons repeatedly told Human Rights Watch they believed that the true percentage of mentally ill prisoners with substance abuse histories was actually far higher, since many seriously mentally ill people used alcohol and illegal drugs as a form of self-medication.]

[64] 58.8 percent of state prisoners with mental illness and 64.6 percent of jail inmates with mental illness were using alcohol or illegal drugs at the time of their offense. BJS, *Mental Health and Treatment of Inmates and Probationers*, 1999, table 10. Among non-mentally ill inmates, 51.23 percent of those in state prison and 56.5 percent of those in jail reported drug or alcohol use at the time of their offenses.

[65] See, e.g., John S. Goldkamp and Cheryl Irons-Guynn, "Emerging Judicial Strategies for the Mentally Ill in the Criminal Caseload" (Bureau of Justice Statistics, April 2000). Human Rights Watch visited the mental health court operating in Broward County, Florida in September 2001. See also Center for Crimes, Communities and Culture, *Mental Illness in US Jails: Diverting the Nonviolent, Low-level Offender*, Research Brief, Occasional Paper Series, no. 1 (New York: The Open Society Institute, November 1996), accessed online at: http://www.soros.org/crime/research_brief__1.html, on June 10, 2003.

[66] Human Rights Watch interview with Ron Honberg, director of legal affairs, NAMI, September 4, 2003. NAMI is working with the National GAINS Center for People with Co-Occurring Disorders in Contact with the Justice System, the Council of State Governments, and other organizations to compile a complete list of mental health courts in each

York, recently started using a mental health court to divert non-violent mentally ill offenders into mandated treatment programs.[67] In some places, regular criminal courts are able to divert some mentally ill defendants into treatment programs. Connecticut has a program in which its courts can send certain categories of offenders who are deemed to be seriously mentally ill into mental health treatment programs. Although relatively new, these diversion efforts appear to reduce recidivism and are cost-effective as well. A study in Connecticut, undertaken as part of a national study by the federal Substance Abuse and Mental Health Services Administration (SAMHSA), found the average costs of offenders who were diverted into drug treatment programs in Connecticut were about one-third of those who were not.[68]

As this report reveals, for many persons with mental illness, prison can be counter-therapeutic or even "toxic." Nevertheless, we recognize the tragic irony that, for many, prison may also offer significant advantages over liberty. For some mentally ill offenders, prison is the first place they have a chance for treatment. For those who are poor and homeless, given the problems they face in accessing mental health services in the community, prison may offer an opportunity for consistent access to medication and mental health services. Realizing this opportunity depends, of course, on whether the prisons provide the necessary services. Depending on the quality of the facility in which mentally ill offenders are confined, prison may be less dangerous, less chaotic, less troubling than, for example, life as a homeless person on the street or as a misfit living on the fringe of society. "I have been to prison four times: three times for three years, once for two years," 40-year-old E.V. stated, rocking back and forth non-stop as she talked, a year and a half after her release from a women's prison in California.[69] E.V. was shot in the cheek and shoulders in 1986 during a robbery; she claims she was in a coma for two months following this attack, that she began taking drugs afterwards in order to fight off severe depression, and that at night she hears voices — she thinks of the people who shot her — threatening her well-being. Her most recent stints in prison, she said, were the first times she ever had routine access to mental health services. Yet, she stated, if she needed to see a counselor, she'd "have to make like it was an emergency. Get an attitude, conflict. Argue with the C.O.s, stuff like that. Then they'd take you out and give you a ducat [referral] to see someone." Now diagnosed as being borderline developmentally disabled, as well as suffering from acute anxiety, depression, the side-effects of a fifteen-year cocaine addiction, and needing outpatient mental health care, E.V. is an example of the kind of patient, suffering

---

state. Mental health courts are defined as courts that are criminal courts, have a separate docket dedicated to persons with mental illness, divert criminal defendants from jail to treatment programs, and that monitor the defendants and have the ability to impose criminal sanctions on their failure to comply with the terms of their diversion. Lucille Schacht, Ph.D., "Mental Health Courts and Diversion Programs Supported by State Mental Health Authorities: 2001," NASMHPD Research Institute, Inc., under contract with the Substance Abuse and Mental Health Services Administration (SAMHSA), June 2002. Florida created the first mental health courts in 1998; in 1999, Arkansas and Wyoming created courts; in 2000, Georgia, North Carolina, New Hampshire, and Ohio started their courts; in 2001; Alabama, Montana, Nevada, Pennsylvania, Tennessee, and Vermont joined in; and in 2002, New York followed suit. The American Psychiatric Association states that Indiana and Alaska also operate mental health courts. Human Rights Watch visited the mental health court for Broward County, Florida in September, 2001.

[67] The Brooklyn Mental Health Court began as a pilot program in March 2002. In September 2002, it was formally integrated into Brooklyn's court system. It is aimed at non-violent offenders, and the district attorney's office has to agree before a case can be moved to the mental health court. See Leslie Kaufman, "Court for Mentally Ill Defendants Will Start Today," *The New York Times*, October 1, 2002.

[68] These numbers are quoted in Albert Solnit, *The Costs and Effectiveness of Jail Diversion: A Report to the Joint Standing Committee of the General Assembly* (Hartford, CT: The Department of Mental Health & Addiction Services, February 1, 2000).

[69] Human Rights Watch interview with E.V, ex-prisoner, Sober Living Facility, Los Angeles, California, May 17, 2002.

simultaneously from multiple disorders whom the prison system is increasingly being called upon to treat.[70]

---

[70] Documented in E.V.'s prison medical records.

C.X., New York, July 28, 2002

I've been in the S.H.U. [secure housing unit] for over 6 ½ years where I've been locked in a cell for 23 to 24 hour a day 7 days a week. In March of 2002 I had a mental breakdown because of being in S.H.U. and I attempted suicide by swallowing 150 pills. I was saved and sent to Central New York Psychiatric Center for treatment where I stayed for about 7 weeks. I was then discharged and sent to Wende Correctional Facility.... Upon my arrival at Wende I was put in an observation cell in the mental health unit where I was kept for 25 days in a strip cell. I was mistreated and denied everything. There was no heat in the place. I was put in a dirty, bloody cell. I was jumped and assaulted by correctional officers, and was left unattended to by the mental health staff. In the time I was there I continually requested to be sent back to CNYPC for further treatment because I went into a relapses and could not bare being locked in a cell 24/7 again. Instead the mental health staff took me off my mental health anti-depression medication and told me that they was not going to send me back to CNYPC no matter what I did or said. In the course of the 25 days I spent in M.H.U. I attempted suicide 3 times. Twice I was rushed to Erie County Medical Center for treatment and sent back to Wende where I was again placed in M.H.U. and left without any kind of further medical or mental health care. I told the head mental health staff that I can't stay locked in a cell 24/7 anymore and that if they sent me back to S.H.U. that I'll kill myself. They said I'll just have to do that and they sent me back to S.H.U. and was taken to E.C.M.C. for treatment again and then sent back to Wende and back in S.H.U. Right now I don't know what more to do. I'm writing this letter in hopes that someone will do something about the way these people in the mental health department here treats people, after I'm gone because I simply cannot carry on no more like this I hope that my death will bring about some good, if not at least I'll finally find some peace.

IV.   WHO ARE THE MENTALLY ILL IN PRISON?

"I am a commander of Star Wars SS. We have been practicing nuclear allimators stronger than the Russians. If I'm killed it's going to burn stars and the world at the same time. If we don't watch it, people will burn and I will go into a different dimension. So I'd like to keep my single cell as long as possible. I write to Berlin, to Red China, they don't send me no package."[71]
- D.O.T., California State Prison, Corcoran.

The mentally ill in prison, as in the world outside prison, suffer from a wide array of mental disorders serious enough to require psychiatric treatment. The symptoms of some prisoners with serious mental illness are subtle, discernable only by clinicians. This is particularly true for prisoners suffering serious depression, who may just appear withdrawn and unsociable to other prisoners and staff. But the serious mental illness of some prisoners is easily identified even by the layman: they rub feces on themselves, stick pencils in their penises, bite chunks of flesh from their bodies, slash themselves, hallucinate, rant and rave, mumble incoherently, stare fixedly at the walls. While many of the mentally ill in prison do not suffer major impairments in their ability to function, some, like the above-quoted prisoner, are so sick they live in a world entirely constructed around their delusions.

Not only is the number of prisoners with mental illness growing, but more persons are being incarcerated whose illnesses fall at the most severe end of the mental illness spectrum. According to Dave Munson, lead psychologist at Washington State's McNeil Island Correctional Center, "the severity of the mental illness of those coming in is increasing. People are no longer going to state hospitals. The prisoners often have no idea how they ended up here."[72] In Oregon, the administrator for counseling and treatment services reported that in the last five years the prison system has begun receiving prisoners who have been in mental health group homes since childhood.[73] Gloria Henry, warden of Valley State Prison for Women, California's largest prison for female prisoners, also points to the severity of the mental conditions of incarcerated women:

> I don't know how [some of these women] were sentenced to prison. They have no understanding of why they are in prison. I don't know what purpose it serves. To some degree the services will be limited, because this is a prison, not a state hospital. We're having to adjust and make changes to accommodate mental health — and it's difficult.[74]

Overview of Mental Illness
Mental disorders include a broad range of impairments of thought, mood, and behavior. The degree of impairment can vary dramatically from individual to individual. Also, some individuals with mental illness have periods of relative stability during which symptoms are minimal, interspersed

---

[71] Human Rights Watch interview with D.O.T., California State Prison, Corcoran, Enhanced Outpatient Program, California, July 11, 2002.

[72] Human Rights Watch interview with Dave Munson, head psychologist, McNeil Island Correctional Center, Washington, August 22, 2002.

[73] Human Rights Watch telephone interview with Gary Field, administrator for counseling and treatment services, Oregon Department of Corrections, June 24, 2002.

[74] Human Rights Watch interview with Gloria Henry, warden, Valley State Prison for Women, California, July 17, 2002.

with incidents of psychiatric crisis. Other individuals are acutely ill and dramatically symptomatic for prolonged periods.

In this report, we use the term serious mental illness to refer to diagnosable mental, behavioral, or emotional disorders of sufficient duration to meet diagnostic criteria specified in the Diagnostic and Statistical Manual of Mental Disorders of the American Psychiatric Association, (generally referred to as DSM-IV)[75] and that result in substantial interference with or limitations on one or more major life activities.[76] The DSM-IV defines a mental disorder as:

> a clinically significant behavioral or psychological syndrome or pattern that occurs in an individual and that is associated with present distress (e.g. a painful symptom) or disability (i.e., impairment in one or more important areas of functioning) or with a significant increased risk of suffering death, pain, disability, or an important loss of freedom.[77]

The DSM-IV classification for mental disorders includes serious mental illness (Axis 1) and serious personality disorders (Axis 2). In prisons, the category of serious mental illness is typically limited to such conditions as schizophrenia, serious depression, and bipolar disorder. Schizophrenia is a frightening, complex, difficult, and debilitating disease which may include disordered thinking or speech, delusions (fixed, rigid beliefs that have no basis in reality), hallucinations (hearing or seeing things that are not real), inappropriate emotions, confusion, withdrawal, and inattention to any personal grooming. Among the subtypes of schizophrenia is "paranoid schizophrenia" with characteristics of delusions of persecution and extreme suspiciousness. Even if a person with schizophrenia is described as recovered or in remission, quite likely he or she is neither ill nor well, but will usually have a great deal of difficulty adjusting to life situations, and can be driven over the edge by overwhelming demands.[78] Serious or clinical depression, which can be experienced episodically or chronically, usually includes, among other symptoms, profound feelings of sadness, helplessness, and hopelessness. It can also be accompanied by psychotic features, including hallucinations and/or delusions. Clinical depression, which is far more common among women than men, is a significant suicide risk factor. Bipolar disorder (previously called manic-depressive disorder) is characterized by frequently dramatic mood swings from depressions to mania. During manic phases some people may be psychotic and may experience delusions or hallucinations.

Wholly apart from ensuring adequate mental health treatment, the incarceration of thousands of persons with these illnesses poses extremely difficult management challenges for correctional staff trying to ensure prison safety and security. For example, serious depression puts people at risk of suicide. Persons with schizophrenia may experience prison as a peculiarly frightening, threatening environment that can result in inappropriate behavior including self-harm or violence directed toward staff or other prisoners. Persons with bipolar disorder in a manic phase can be disruptive,

---

[75] American Psychiatric Association, *Diagnostic and Statistical Manual of Mental Disorders*, 4th ed. (Washington D.C.: American Psychiatric Association, 1994).

[76] This is the definition used by The President's New Freedom Commission on Mental Health, "Achieving Promise: Transforming Mental Health Care in America," p. 2 (July 23, 2003), available on line at: http://www.mentalhealthcommission.gov/reports/FinalReport/toc.html, accessed on August 26, 2003.

[77] Ibid., xxi-xxii.

[78] Hans Toch and Kenneth Adams, *Acting Out: Maladaptive Behavior in Confinement* (Washington D.C.: American Psychological Association, April 2002), p. 16

quick to anger, provocative, and dangerous.[79] Prisoners with serious mental illness, particularly if the illness has psychotic features, may find it next-to-impossible to abide by, or, in more extreme cases, even to understand, prison regulations. According to correctional mental health expert and clinical professor of psychiatry at the University of Colorado's Health Sciences Center Dr. Jeffrey Metzner, "A small percentage [of prisoners] don't understand the rules. They're the ones who are psychotic. More common is that prison rules don't mean much to someone hearing voices — that's the least of their problems." A person with paranoid schizophrenia, said Metzner, may, on a literal level, understand a rule but nevertheless view a request to abide by that rule as being part of a conspiracy directed against him. "It's less of not understanding and more of acting on distortions."[80]

It is not uncommon for persons who end up in jail or prison to have Axis 2 personality disorders which result in serious problems in thinking, feeling, interpersonal relations, and impulse control. When these disorders are associated with significant functional impairments they constitute serious mental illnesses. According to the DSM-IV, personality disorders are "an enduring pattern of inner experience and behavior that deviates markedly from the expectations of the individual's culture, is pervasive and inflexible, has an onset in adolescence or early adulthood, is stable over time, and leads to distress or impairment."[81]

Perhaps the most prevalent personality disorders among jail and prison inmates are anti-social personality disorder (ASPD) and borderline personality disorder. The essential feature of the former is "a pervasive pattern of disregard for, and violation of, the rights of others."[82] Persons with antisocial personality disorder, typically men, can be particularly difficult to manage in a correctional setting. They can often be manipulative, volatile, disruptive, and likely to engage in aggressive, impulsive "acting out" behavior which can include assaults on others, self-mutilation and/or suicide attempts. Epidemiological research shows that only 15 percent to 20 percent of prisoners have bona fide ASPD, if the diagnosis is made using the criteria in the DSM-IV. Yet, according to psychiatrist Dr. Terry Kupers, who has examined mental health services in many prisons, correctional mental health staff have a tendency to over-diagnose the presence of ASPD, essentially using it as a default diagnosis for anyone who seems to have mental problems of some sort but does not have an obvious Axis I illness. A diagnosis of ASPD becomes, in fact, a moral rather than clinical judgment; prisoners with APSD are "bad" not "mad."[83]

According to the DSM-IV, borderline personality disorder is marked by "patterns of instability in interpersonal relationships, self-image and affects, and marked impulsivity that begins in early adulthood." People with borderline personality disorder often have volatile and extreme emotions, are prone to depression, and can be difficult and manipulative. Many resort to self-mutilation at some point. Borderline personality disorder can also include episodes of psychotic decompensation. Research suggests that childhood trauma — particularly sexual and physical abuse — is one of the

---

[79] See Martin Drapkin, *Management and Supervision of Jail Inmates With Mental Disorders* (New Jersey, Civic Research Institute, 2003), ch. 4, which provides an excellent overview of the nature of and correctional implications of various mental diseases and disorders.

[80] Human Rights Watch telephone interview with Dr. Jeffrey Metzner, clinical professor of psychiatry, University of Colorado Health Sciences Center, April 2, 2003. Dr. Metzner is a nationally recognized psychiatrist and correctional mental health expert who has provided evidence on prison mental health conditions in dozens of cases.

[81] *Diagnostic and Statistical Manual of Mental Disorders*, 4th ed. (Washington D.C.: American Psychiatric Association, 1994), p. 629.

[82] *Diagnostic and Statistical Manual of Mental Disorders*, 4th ed. (Washington D.C.: American Psychiatric Association, 1994).

[83] Email communication from Dr. Terry Kupers to Human Rights Watch, May 29, 2003.

causal factors for the disorder. About 70 to 77 percent of people diagnosed with this disorder are women.[84] Some psychiatrists, such as Harvard University's Dr. Judith Herman, believe that many, if not most, women diagnosed as borderline are in fact suffering from what Herman calls, "complex posttraumatic stress disorder." The multiple traumas cause psychological disorganization and emotional dyscontrol that look very much like borderline personality disorder. If the diagnosis, however, is of borderline personality disorder, the complex posttraumatic stress disorder is ignored and, all too often, the women are considered just plain difficult and not amenable to or in need of treatment.[85]

Although people with personality disorders may appear "normal" — just obnoxious or difficult — these mental disorders are very real and drive those who have them to behave the way they do. Unlike Axis 1 mental illnesses, personality disorders are not believed to be caused by abnormality of brain chemistry or other organic problems, but are rooted in life histories, such as childhood traumas and neglect, and perhaps genetics. For that reason, they do not generally respond to medications and are thus harder to treat and contain. Personality disorders can and often do co-exist with Axis-1 mental illnesses, further complicating the diagnosis and treatment of both.

It is a convention in correctional psychiatry to identify as serious mental illnesses only certain serious Axis I disorders such as bipolar disorder, major depression, and schizophrenia, and to limit mental health treatment to prisoners with those disorders. It is a convention in part created by the shortage of mental health staff: absent sufficient numbers to treat everyone, the determination of who warrants treatment is restricted to the most deeply troubled individuals and also those who are more likely to respond to the primary treatment modality offered in prison — medication. Correctional mental health staff are particularly reluctant to expend treatment time on prisoners with personality disorders. The judgment of correctional mental health staff about the seriousness of a non-psychotic mental condition may also be colored by their concerns that prisoners may be malingering or seeking secondary gains. It is also a convention that survives under constitutional jurisprudence that has failed to clarify the boundaries of the "serious mental illness" for which mental health services are required.

Nevertheless, individuals who suffer from other illnesses not on the short list of Axis I disorders can be equally distressed and disabled. Some personality disorders can include episodes of psychotic decompensation and several of the personality disorders can result in severe disability. For example, an individual suffering from a severe generalized anxiety disorder with panic attacks might spend all of her time terrified, incapable of acting productively, and cringing in her cell. Someone with severe obsessive-compulsive disorder might spend all his time cleaning his cell or counting cracks in the wall and be completely incapable of undertaking other activities. A person with a dysthymic disorder (a less severe form of depression than a major depressive disorder) might successfully commit suicide.

---

[84] Sartx, Blazer, George & Winfield, "Estimating the Prevalence of Borderline Personality in the Community," *Journal of Personality Disorders*, vol. 4, no. 3 (1990), pp. 257-272; Nehls, "Borderline Personality Disorder: Gender Stereotypes, Stigma, and Limited System of Care," *Issues in Mental health Nursing*, vol. 19 (1998), pp. 97-112. Some mental health professionals believe the diagnosis of borderline personality disorder has become a demeaning "wastebasket" category into which difficult women are lumped. Email communication from Dr. Terry Kupers to Human Rights Watch, May 20, 2003.

[85] Email communication from Dr. Terry Kupers to Human Rights Watch, May 20, 2003. See also, Judith Herman, M.D., *Trauma and Recovery* (New York: Basic Books, 1997).

Failure to diagnose and properly attend to prisoners' personality disorders can lead to inappropriate responses by correctional staff that aggravate the prisoners' conduct and heighten the incidence of self-mutilation and suicide attempts. The clinical diagnosis of personality disorders should be followed with useful therapeutic interventions, such as individual and group talk therapy and cognitive skills and anger management training. Medication cannot address the fundamentals of personality disorders but can alleviate frequently concomitant symptoms, such as depression and anxiety. Mental health interventions can not only make life in prison more tolerable both for the prisoners and the staff who have to deal with them; they also can provide the prisoners with life-skills — such as personal hygiene, education, anger management, and an ability to recognize the signs of an approaching mental health crisis — that will serve them well when they are released from prison.

Examples of Mentally Ill Prisoners

To provide a sense of the nature and degree of serious mental illness from which some prisoners suffer, we note below some descriptions, many of which were made by mental health experts and courts who had access to complete mental health records:

- "Prisoner 1 is a 25-year-old who was transferred to [Wisconsin's] Supermax in February 2001. He has a history of serious mental illness beginning at age 11. According to a [1995] entry in his clinical file…he was diagnosed with Paranoid Schizophrenia. Prisoner 1 experiences command hallucinations, which are voices that tell him to do bad things. Prisoner 1's charts list medication orders dating back to 1995 that include the antipsychotic medications Thorazine, Haldol, Quetiapine, Seroquel, Loxitane, Risperdal and Olanzopoine. On the Mental Illness Screening Tool in his file, Prisoner 1 was assigned a diagnosis of "Chronic paranoid Schizophrenia vs. Major Depression with Psychotic Features." Prisoner 1 told Dr. Kupers [plaintiffs' expert] that he hears voices constantly that command him to kill himself or hurt others….Prisoner 1 told Kupers that he cannot sleep because he "sees things," including "demons moving around the floor and climbing on my bed" all night. Prisoner 1 told Kupers that he has paranoid thoughts that the guards are out to get him. He paces in his cell. Prisoner 1 continues to experience auditory hallucinations and massive anxiety despite his strong psychotropic medications…[86]

- Psychologist Craig Haney painted a harrowing picture of some of the prisoners with mental illness he encountered in Texas prisons:

  - I'm talking about forms of behavior that are easily recognizable and that are stark in nature when you see them, when you look at them, when you're exposed to them. In a number of instances, there were people who had smeared themselves with feces. In other instances, there were people who had urinated in their cells, and the urine was on the floor…. There were many people who were incoherent when I attempted to talk to them, babbling, sometimes shrieking, other people who appeared to be full of fury and anger and rage and were, in some instances, banging their hands on the side of the wall and yelling and screaming, other people who appeared to be simply disheveled, withdrawn and out of contact with the circumstances or surroundings. Some of them would be huddled in the back corner of the cell

---

[86] *Jones 'El v. Berge*, 164 F. Supp.2d 1096, 1108 (W.D. Wis., 2001).

and appeared incommunicative when I attempted to speak with them. Again, these were not subtle diagnostic issues. These were people who appeared to be in profound states of distress and pain.[87]

o [A Texas prisoner was]...a 45 year old man with chronic paranoid schizophrenia found in a decompensated psychotic state. His thinking was grossly disorganized and his speech was irrelevant. He appeared confused, agitated, and paranoid. The medical record indicated that his antipsychotic medication had been discontinued...due to refusals. There could be no question that his decompensation was long and tortured.... A 28 year old man with schizoaffective disorder and mental retardation...he appeared floridly psychotic and deteriorating. His left arm was severely mutilated from multiple self-inflicted lacerations.[88]

• "John Doe #117 was charged with 'being untidy' because he smeared feces on his cell door...[A] psychological report found that John Doe #117 was 'mentally limited and often psychotic...not able to control his behavior and...not in good touch with reality'...[A subsequent psychological evaluation] determined that John Doe #117 was 'cognitively limited,' 'schizophrenic' and 'not completely in control of his behavior.'"[89]

• "Inmate [V.Y.A.] is a 40-year-old Black male with a history of chronic, Paranoid Schizophrenia with a positive response to anti-psychotic drug therapy. Inmate [V.Y.A.] initially reported auditory hallucinations, lack of sleep, and concerns about possible effects of blood pressure medication. His mental status deteriorated and regressed considerably while in the infirmary, including alternatively claiming to be Jesus and denying he was Jesus. His affect was often intense, agitated and paranoid threatening. Thought process was disorganized, grandiose, and delusional, with auditory hallucinations at times reported but at other times denied. Decompensation continued until Inmate [V.Y.A.] became compliant with medication regime...Assessment Diagnosis: Axis I: Schizophrenia, Paranoid, Chronic with acute exacerbation."[90]

• "[V.R.] is delusional and thought disordered; his speech is disorganized and tangential, with loose associations. He believes that he is 'attached to an alien affiliation' and that he has been forced to commit treason against the Untied States. He also claims that he is a woman, but 'they haven't found his vagina yet.' He said that he shot his mother when he was three years old, but does not know if she died or not. He also reported that he believes that there is a radio in his nerves that is broadcasting. He often picks at his ear to see if the receiver is

---

[87] *Ruiz v. Johnson*, 37 F. Supp. 2d 855, 909 (S.D. Tex., 1999).

[88] Letter from Keith Curry, Ph.D. to attorney Donna Brorby, March 19, 2002, pp. 19-20; on file at Human Rights Watch. Brorby was the lead attorney in *Ruiz v. Johnson*, a lawsuit over Texas prison conditions, and Curry visited the prisons on behalf of the plaintiffs.

[89] *New Jersey Prison System Report of Dr. Dennis Koson, C.F. v. Terhune*, Civil Action No. 96-1840 (D.N.J., September 8, 1998), on file at Human Rights Watch. The trial court approved the parties' settlement of the case on July 30, 1999. *D.M. v. Terhune*, 67 F. Supp. 2d 401 (D.N.J., 1999).

[90] Mental health evaluation of V.Y.A. by Illinois Department of Corrections, December 31, 1998; on file at Human Rights Watch.

in there but can't find it. He still believes it is there. He also gets messages through 'federal codes' in his cell."[91]

- "D.R. has been on psychiatric medication since the age of ten years old for hearing voices and what he calls 'psychological illusions.' He has had several previous psychiatric hospitalizations. He describes visual hallucinations of seeing ghosts, animals, people and things move. Auditory hallucinations are outside of his head, they are sometimes about Jesus, they take up to 500 different forms and talk to each other. They sometimes command him to kill himself although he has not made any previous suicide attempts. He is obviously severely mentally retarded and appeared to be blithely indifferent to his conditions.[92]

- "Mr. BF is a forty year old black man who has been incarcerated since July 1994. [He] has a history of severe mental illness. During the period of incarceration preceding his arrival at Attica, he was psychiatrically hospitalized at CNYPC [Central New York Psychiatric Center] a total of seven times and was in and out of MHUs in the facilities where he was housed. On each occasion that he was transferred to CNYPC, he presented with symptoms of a highly agitated, confusional psychosis with some suicidal features. His clinical presentation has also included a great deal of agitated, bizarre and inappropriate behavior, including sexual preoccupations, grandiose ideation of being a rock star, and a fixation with princess Diana of Britain. At times he experienced visual and auditory hallucinations, and sometimes carried on loud conversations with the voices he heard. He was observed to be hearing voices and seeing strange people who were not there, and became preoccupied with spacecraft, aliens, voodoo, and the singer Mariah Carey. At times, he was observed to be overtly confused and disoriented, mumbling incoherently.... At times he was quite floridly ill, while at other times, he appeared to be reasonably coherent. His behavior was often grossly bizarre and inappropriate…[H]e was observed to have inserted a lighter, cigarettes, and pictures into his anus. On at least one occasion, he inflicted multiple lacerations on both sides of his face….He smeared feces on his cell wall — even using his excrement as a paint to write words on the walls. At times he was suicidal.[93]

- "[A prisoner in Illinois] reports he hears voices of dead people: his brother…his own victim(s); voices usually happen at night. No visual, olfactory, gustatory or tactile hallucinations…. States that cutting his arms and legs helps him to relax. Sometimes it is intended to be lethal. Has no recollection of trying to eat his own flesh except as told to him by correctional staff…diagnostic formulation: Long-standing history of psychiatric treatment/psychiatric hospitalization(s) for depression and SSDI for physical and mental disorder. [While in prison] diagnoses of depression, dysthymic disorder, cyclothymia,

---

[91] Human Rights Watch, *Cold Storage: Super-Maximum Security Confinement in Indiana* (New York: Human Rights Watch, 1997), pp. 36-37. The prisoner was examined by psychiatrist Terry Kupers, who served as a consultant to Human Rights Watch.

[92] Ibid., p.37. Psychiatrist Terry Kupers also examined this prisoner.

[93] Dr. Stuart Grassian, Second Site Visit to the Attica SHU, Mental Health Care, *Eng v. Goord*, Civ 80-385S (W.D. New York, October 1999) (redacted copy). In his report, Dr. Grassian provides detailed descriptions of the conditions, behavior and medical history of eight seriously mentally ill inmates incarcerated in the secured housing unit at Attica. His report also documents in detail the failure of the mental health staff to provide proper treatment for these inmates and the deterioration of their conditions accompanying prolonged incarceration in segregation. Dr. Stuart Grassian, Second Site Visit to the Attica SHU, Mental Health Care, *Eng v. Goord*, Civ 80-385S (W.D. New York, October 1999) (redacted copy), p. 40.

adjustment disorder, adult attention deficit disorder, PTSD, impulse control disorders, atypical psychosis and personality disorders…Differential diagnosis includes: Major depressive disorder, recurrent, with psychotic features; Schizophrenia, undifferentiated type; Borderline personality disorder; Schizotypal personality disorder.[94]

- Y.R. is an prisoner on Virginia's death row. He was convicted of a triple-murder carried out when he was eighteen years old. Although he underwent a psychiatric evaluation conducted by a state expert, he was never given a mental health competency hearing, despite his lawyers believing him to be incompetent to stand trial.[95] Y.R., who three psychiatric experts believe developed schizophrenia aged about sixteen, sometimes believes himself to be an incarnation of famous rap stars. At other times, he declares that he is God and that the Bible was written about him. He believes that when he is executed he will immediately return to earth, bringing with him all his dead relatives. When he acts out, bangs on the walls, or floods his cell, guards have, at least twice, placed him into four point restraints; because he is so ill, he cannot write to his attorney. She only finds out about these events when other prisoners on death row contact her and tell her what has been happening to her client.[96]

- During our research, Human Rights Watch interviewed numerous other prisoners also identified by mental health staff, family members, or correctional staff as seriously mentally ill and whose illness was patent. For example, we interviewed a prisoner, V.P., at Corcoran State Prison, California who was incarcerated for murdering his wife because she had cheated on him. He told Human Rights Watch that he'd been playing a game called "no murder." "I hear my wife. She talks about game playing. No Murder. She says she's sorry she fooled around….. I think about game 'no murder.' I want to go home." V.P. also said that his wife and her father had also killed him several times, but that he hadn't died; and that the whole family had been playing this game for two thousand years.[97]

---

[94] Mental Status Evaluation of an inmate [name withheld] by Katherine Burns, M.D. dated April 3, 1999; on file at Human Rights Watch.
[95] Human Rights Watch telephone interview with Jennifer Givens, attorney, Virginia Capital Representation Resource Center, October 2, 2002.
[96] Ibid.
[97] Human Rights Watch interview with V.P., Corcoran, California, July 11, 2002.

V.   MENTAL ILLNESS AND WOMEN PRISONERS

"I have been superintendent of the Bedford Hills Correctional Facility in New York State for 17 years. During that period of time, I have seen the number of mentally ill women entering the prison system rise precipitously. Where once mental institutions kept patients for long periods in back wards, today the burden of providing for mentally ill people who have committed crimes has shifted to the correctional system. It is clear that prisons must adapt by creating more appropriate environments for these inmates – as long as society believes that is where mentally ill inmates should be maintained."[98]
- Elaine Lord, superintendent, Bedford Hills Correctional Facility, New York

While serious mental illness is epidemic amongst both male and female prisoner populations, the statistics for female prisoners are particularly stark. A national study in 1999 by the Bureau of Justice Statistics based on a survey of prisoners, found that "[t]wenty nine percent of white females, 20 percent of black females and 22 percent of Hispanic females in State prison were identified as mentally ill. Nearly four in ten white female inmates aged twenty-four or younger were mentally ill."[99]

Striking as they are, the Bureau of Justice Statistics (BJS) figures may not fully represent the extent of mental illness among incarcerated women. In New York, for example, 26 percent of incarcerated women are on the active mental health caseload (compared to 11 percent of men).[100] In Pennsylvania, 37.7 percent of female prisoners are on that state's mental health caseload.[101] In the late 1990s, the Colorado Department of Corrections estimated that 27.9 percent of the women in the Colorado Women's Correctional Facility had severe mental health needs.[102] While women made up only 5.7 percent of the state's total number of prisoners, they made up a startling 16.3 percent of the correctional system's most seriously mentally ill prisoners.[103] Georgia estimates that 33 percent of its female prisoners are mentally ill.[104] In Vermont, of the forty-five prisoners at Dale Women's Correctional Center, thirty-six were on the mental health roster as of September 2002.[105] Arkansas's deputy director of Health and Correctional Programs, Max Mobley, estimates twice as high a percentage of female prisoners are seriously mentally ill as are males.[106] In Oregon, 47 to 49 percent of female prisoners are on the mental health caseload.[107]

---

[98] Elaine Lord, "Prison Careers of Mentally Ill Women," in Hans Toch and Kenneth Adams, *Acting Out*, 2002, p. 368.

[99] BJS, *Mental Health and Treatment of Inmates and Probationers*, 1999, p. 3.

[100] Figures as of 2000, from Lord, "Prison Careers of Mentally Ill Women," p. 369.

[101] Human Rights Watch interview with Lance Couturier, Ph.D., mental health director, Pennsylvania Department of Corrections and Fred Maue, Ph.D., chief of clinical services, Pennsylvania Department of Corrections, Gaudenzia House, Philadelphia, August 13, 2002.

[102] Colorado Department of Corrections, *Adult Inmate Profile*. Numbers accurate as of June 30, 1998.

[103] Ibid.

[104] Figure provided by Michael Hitchcock, Program Development Division, Georgia Department of Corrections, in response to Human Rights Watch survey, June 24, 2002.

[105] Human Rights Watch interviews, Dale Women's Correctional Center, Vermont, September 26, 2002. Information on the mental health roster was provided by the chief psychiatrist for the Vermont Department of Corrections, and by Matrix, the mental health care provider with whom the Vermont Department of Corrections contracts for services.

[106] Written communication to Human Rights Watch from Max Mobley, director of mental health, Arkansas Department of Corrections.

[107] Human Rights Watch telephone interview with Gary Field, administrator for counseling and treatment services, Oregon Department of Correction, June 24, 2002. Oregon DOC also provided written answers to a Human Rights Watch survey.

Imprisonment may be even harder for women than for men. One crucial difference is that women prisoners are more likely to have dependent children who were living with them prior to incarceration.[108] The separation from children because of incarceration — and particularly when, as if often the case, the prison is located far from the children — takes an enormous psychological toll on women. In addition to the grief, emptiness, anger, bitterness, guilt, and fear of loss or rejection that women prisoners who are mothers may experience, all women prisoners must cope with the stresses that are inherent in incarceration. Indeed, those stresses may be greater because facilities for women often lack the diversity and extent of educational, vocational, and other programs that are available (albeit typically in insufficient quantity and quality) in facilities for men.

Like men, women with mental illness can find themselves unable to adapt to and cope with prison life, with the result that they end up accumulating histories of disciplinary infractions. An analysis of data from the Bureau of Justice Statistics' 1986 *Survey of Inmates at State Correctional Facilities* showed that women who currently or in the past had utilized mental health services had significantly greater disciplinary problems in prison; female prisoners currently on psychotropic medications had annual infraction rates that were twice that of other women prisoners — and, indeed, had higher infraction rates on average than male prisoners who were also on medication.[109] As Superintendent Elaine Lord has written, mental illness "impacts [women's] performance and even her participation in programs... [it affects their] ability to abide by the rules and routine of an institution that is styled on military protocols for following orders and establishing routines"[110] At Bedford Hills Correctional Facility, a New York prison for women, 80 percent of the "Unusual Incident Reports" (staff documentation of incidents involving serious threat to facility safety or security) involved prisoners who were on the active mental health caseload. Although women prisoners are typically less violent than men — and mentally ill women less violent than mentally ill men — they can and do cause injuries to themselves and others. Superintendent Lord observes:

> Obviously, one of the dangers of having seriously mentally ill women in prison is that they are a source of violent acts within the inmate community that are very difficult to prevent because they are tied to mental illness; they simply make no sense. Just as the public has difficulty comprehending why a mentally ill person pushes someone off a train platform, so, too, prisoners and correction staff have difficulty comprehending seemingly random acts of violence perpetrated within a prison.[111]

Although the rate at which women are incarcerated has soared in the past decade, in great part because of the war on drugs, they still represent a small segment of the prison population.[112] Most prison systems still have not developed adequate facilities for women at different security levels and

---

[108] Christopher J. Mumola, *Incarcerated Parents and Their Children*, Bureau of Justice Statistics, August 2000, table. 4: 64.3 percent of state female parents and 84 percent of federal female parents lived with their children prior to incarceration, compared to 45.3 percent of state male prisoners and 55.2 percent of federal male prisoners. Available online at: http://www.ojp.usdoj.gov/bjs/pub/pdf/iptc.pdf, accessed on August 26, 2003.

[109] Richard C. McCorkle, "Gender, Psychopathology, and institutional Behavior: A Comparison of male and Female Mentally Ill Prison Inmates," *Journal of Criminal Justice*, vol. 23, no. 1, 1995, pp. 53-61.

[110] Lord, "Prison Careers of Mentally Ill Women," p. 375.

[111] Ibid., p. 381

[112] According to the Bureau of Justice Statistics, at the end of 2002, women made up 6.8 percent of the state and federal prison population. BJS, *Prisoners in 2002*, p. 1.

do not offer women prisoners the range of programming and services that are available to men. Prison medical care for women is particularly deficient, including mental health care.

In New York State, women who are seriously mentally ill must be confined at Bedford Hills Correctional Facility, a maximum-security prison, even if their security level is minimum or medium, because it is the only prison for women in the state with intensive mental health services. Over half of the population at Bedford Hills is on the active mental health caseload; and half of those cases fall within the two highest need categories for mental health services. Twenty-two percent of the prisoners on the mental health caseload were diagnosed with schizophrenia, 21 percent with depressive disorders, and an additional 13 percent were diagnosed as psychotic, not otherwise specified.[113]

In 1997, researchers from Northwestern University's Psycho-Legal Studies Program investigating jail conditions found that "because there are relatively few female inmates, the per capita cost is too high to provide them with comparable services" to the specialized mental health treatment available in an increasing number of male institutions.[114] Focusing on a random sample of 1,272 female arrestees, the researchers found that "less than one quarter of female jail detainees who had severe mental disorders and needed services received them while they were in jail."[115] The lack of services affects not only women in jail pending trial or serving short jail sentences, but also women serving longer prison sentences in the six states which house prison and jail inmates in the same facilities.[116]

In Vermont, the Chittendon Community Correctional Center is the intake jail in Burlington that deals with 40 percent of all intakes in the state. In the fall of 2002, between eighty and ninety women were there on any given day out of a total population of 197 prisoners.[117] Based on the numbers diagnosed with serious mental illness, jail Superintendent Susan Blair believes that the female prisoners should be assigned three to four times the number of hours of mental health services provided to male prisoners; yet, because of scarce resources, they end up being provided with only double the amount allocated the men.[118] "The women are a much needier group," Blair told Human Rights Watch. "It's more challenging for the staff here to deal with some of these folks."

Even in states which make an effort to provide adequate mental health services for their prisoners, women are often short-changed. For example, U.C., a one-time prisoner in Pennsylvania's prison system, told Human Rights Watch that in Muncie women's prison, Pennsylvania, there was:

> very little mental health care. I was devastated. I hated it there. I saw the psychiatrist every three months and a counselor once in a while. There was nobody to talk to. They told me to go to church — that that would help me…. I remember

---

[113] Lord, "Prison Careers of Mentally Ill Women," p. 374.

[114] Linda Teplin, Karen Abram, and Gary McClelland, "Mentally Disordered Women in Jail: Who Receives Services?" *American Journal of Public Health*, vol. 87, no. 4, April 1997. As a further reference on this subject, the authors footnote a book by C. Feinman, *Women in the Criminal Justice System* (Westport, Conn., 1993).

[115] Ibid., p. 607.

[116] BJS, *Prisoners in 2002*, p. 11

[117] Human Rights Watch visited Chittendon Jail, Burlington, Vermont, September 26, 2002. Intake numbers provided by Superintendent Susan Blair.

[118] Human Rights Watch interview with Susan Blair, superintendent, Chittendon Community Correctional Center, Burlington, Vermont, September 26, 2002.

trying so hard to remain in contact with reality before they put me back on Haldol. It took a week to see the psychiatrist and get put back on Haldol. They said "you'll just have to wait till he gets around to you."

After Muncie, U.C. was moved to Cambridge Springs Prison.

I still had to wait four or five days to see the psychiatrist if I needed anything. I was doing good the first four years. Then I became incoherent again. They had me in a padded cell about a week. Then I improved. They put me on more medicine. I've been doing good since.[119]

Wisconsin Coalition for Advocacy attorney Todd Winstrom, who has represented mentally ill clients at Taycheedah women's prison, told Human Rights Watch that there are lower mental health staffing levels at Taycheedah than in men's prisons in the state and there is less access to drug and alcohol programming. Although men's prisons have had specialized mental health units for several years, Taycheedah only opened its mental health unit in 2001.[120]

In 1993, prisoners at the Washington Corrections Center for Women (WCCW), brought a class action lawsuit, *Hallett v. Payne*, challenging the quality of medical, dental and mental health services at the facility. Under a 1995 consent decree, prison administrators agreed to develop a comprehensive plan to significantly upgrade delivery of medical, dental, and mental health care services to meet minimal constitutional standards.[121] The court in *Hallett* mandated an unspecified "adequate staffing" level, to be determined by an independent monitor; upgrades in the prison's information management system; the creation of a more streamlined method for delivering medications; and the presence of mental health staff available for evaluation and treatment five days per week.[122] —

In 1999, hearings were held to determine whether federal court jurisdiction over mental health services at WCCW should continue.[123] The plaintiffs presented evidence that the facility continued to lack enough mental health staff to meet the serious mental health needs of the prison population; that programming and treatment remained unduly limited and inconsistent; that prisoners were given disciplinary tickets for self-harm behavior even if it was a result of mental illness; that mentally ill prisoners were inappropriately placed in segregation unit to control their behavior and that prisoners in need of intensive psychiatric care were kept at WCCW even though it could not provide the services necessary for them. While the court concluded it had concerns about the staffing and state of mental health services, it was persuaded that substantial efforts had been made to improve the delivery of mental health care at WCCW and that overall care did not fall below constitutional standards. It therefore ruled that the prospective-relief provisions of the Prison Litigation Reform Act barred it from granting plaintiffs' motion to extend the court's jurisdiction. In its decision, it pointed out that most of "the medical experts and staff expressed the opinion that WCCW was 'coping' with its mental health issues, but that its resources for delivering care were operating at full

---

[119] Human Rights Watch interview with U.C., Philadelphia, Pennsylvania, August 13, 2002.

[120] Human Rights Watch telephone interview with Todd Winstrom, attorney, Coalition for Advocacy, June 5, 2002.

[121] ACLU of Washington Annual Report 1999-2000, Available online at: http://www.aclu-wa.org/pubs/1999.2000.Annual.Report.html, accessed on September 8, 2003.

[122] Human Rights Watch telephone interview with David Fathi, Esq., ACLU National Prison Project, April 2, 2003.

[123] Under the terms of the agreed order settling the case, federal court jurisdiction would expire in four years unless extended upon a showing of defendants' non-compliance. The prisoners moved to extend jurisdiction; the defendants moved to vacate the judgment under the Prison Litigation Reform Act.

capacity, with little or no margin for planning, innovation , or increasing care for individual inmates." [124]

When Human Rights Watch visited WCCW in August 2002, it was in the process of expanding the number of full-time psychologists from five to eight. It had also hired a risk management specialist.[125] Superintendent Stewart was committed to boosting mental health services to the maximum extent possible within budget constraints. "Uncontrolled, it [mental illness] would wreak absolute havoc on this institution," she explained. "As sick as some of the women are. I'd like to see the ability to do better transitioning. When inmates leave here, all our great work goes to hell if they go out and there's no support for them. I'd also like better training for staff. What we have now is decent, but we need to do more — or else we can become part of the problem."[126]

Case Study: R.M. and Seriously Mentally Ill Women Prisoners in Vermont

Because Vermont's prison system is so small, the state has not built a specialized mental health unit for its women prisoners. Prisoners and outside observers acknowledge that the mental health services provided at the Dale Women's Facility are excellent. But if women become unmanageable at Dale (which is an open-plan prison in which prisoners are free to wander the facility and intermingle during the day) they are transferred to the administrative segregation unit at the Chittendon Community Correctional Center in Burlington, Vermont, which is also operated by the state Department of Corrections.[127] While most of the Chittendon Community Correctional Center's prisoners are either pre-trial or serving time for misdemeanor convictions, the facility thus also holds women serving longer prison sentences. Chittendon's mental health staff, however, is limited to a part-time psychiatrist and two counselors. Prisoners with mental health needs have no access to group therapy, infrequent access to counselors, and many report they are routinely provided ample opportunity to self-mutilate. "We need to have a mental health unit," Chittendon Superintendent Susan Blair stated. "We might get services — a full-time clinician who would give more attention to the folks."[128] In addition, because the correctional center was not built to deal with seriously mentally ill prisoners, it does not have any specially designed observation cells for female prisoners in need of around-the-clock constant observation. Thus, when a prisoner gets to the point where they need non-stop observation, they have to be placed in the grimy holding cells that are usually reserved for those brought into the jail for the night to sleep off drinking binges.[129]

R.M. was twenty years old when Human Rights Watch interviewed her at Chittendon where she was being held in an administrative segregation cell. Inside the facility, R.M., who is a heroin addict and who was severely sexually abused as a child, hurts herself on a regular basis. Her arms are criss-crossed with raw, red cuts. One of her legs, on the day Human Rights Watch met her, had a big, bloody, open wound. R.M. stated that she jabs pencils into her limbs, that she cuts herself with razors, and that she sticks staples, retrieved from the bindings of magazines, into her open wounds.

---

[124] Report and Recommendation, *Hallett v. Payne*, Case No. C93-5496FDB, September 3, 1999. The court's findings with regard to mental health services were affirmed on appeal. *Hallett v. Morgan*, 296 F.3d 732 (9th Cir., 2002).

[125] Human Rights Watch visit August 21, 2002. Information on the mental health system and employee numbers was provided by Superintendent Belinda Stewart and program clinical manager Dr. Rob Newell.

[126] Human Rights Watch interview with Superintendent Belinda Stewart, August 21, 2002.

[127] Dale prison for women holds approximately forty-five inmates, and has no separate, secure area for inmates who are acting out so violently that they cannot be around other inmates.

[128] Human Rights Watch interview with Susan Blair, superintendent, Chittendon Community Correctional Center, Burlington, Vermont, September 26, 2002.

[129] Human Rights Watch was shown these holding cells during our September 26, 2002 visit.

She also smashes her head against the walls of her cell when she gets agitated. Ill with serious diabetes, R.M. confided her desire to kill herself by depriving herself of needed diabetes medications. "I'm going to kill myself here and they don't care," she told Human Rights Watch. "I know how to do it. I can. I swallowed a pencil the other day. That was fun. I shove things in my legs all the time and they don't care." R.M. expressed a desire to return to the state mental hospital. "I wish I could," she says, pouting like a child. "They don't have enough staff. It's ok. If they don't take me, I'm going to kill myself."[130]

Although the mental health staff do not think that R.M. has an axis-1 disorder, they do believe she has one of the most severe cases of borderline personality disorder they have ever seen; they believe she will never be able to function normally in a prison's general population, or, for that matter, out in the community.[131] The mental health evaluation notes for R.M. list a "long hx [history] of severe behavioral disturbance, borderline personality, PTSD, Hx of drug abuse, diabetes." It also records that she has a history of being seriously abused. Over the period of her involvement with mental health services at Chittendon, she has been listed as being agitated, angry, irritable, depressed, and as needing anti-depressant medication, mood stabilizers, and antipsychotics.

R.M.'s story is not one that revolves around indifferent correctional staff. The staff at Chittendon, and, indeed, the mental health teams throughout the state's prison system, devote weekly meetings to R.M.'s case. But the Vermont prison system lacks the resources to provide adequate services to seriously mentally ill individuals, particularly those like R.M. who belong in a hospital. Faced with the behavioral outbursts of R.M., security staff have believed they have no alternative but to isolate her from other prisoners and keep her locked in her cell twenty-three hours a day. In a period of under a year, R.M. has picked up nearly fifty disciplinary reports, for offenses including the use of obscene language, flooding her cell, defacing state property, and assault.[132] She has been placed on suicide watch periodically and is routinely written up for acts of self-harm.

The mental health team at Chittendon informed Human Rights Watch that despite repeated requests to the state mental hospital to take R.M. in, and despite the hospital's promises that it would develop a plan on how to admit and treat her, it has continuously dragged its feet. The team suspects the hospital's reluctance to admit R.M. may be connected to the fact that when R.M. was previously at the hospital she threatened to stab her psychiatrist. When interviewed, R.M. was serving six-to-eighteen months on charges of possession of heroin, unlawful mischief, and disorderly conduct. Because the hospital was taking so long to develop a plan for her, it is likely that her sentence would be up before she was ever removed into a hospital setting. A typical memo written by mental health staff following one of the weekly team meetings reads as follows:

> [A staff member from the Vermont State Hospital] updated the team that they are short on staffing resources and there were some directive issues that Dr. F. wanted resolved prior to R.M. going to VSH [Vermont State Hospital.] She was unable to give any time line as to when these pieces would be resolved. There is vagueness in

---

[130] Human Rights Watch interview with R.M., Chittendon Community Correctional Center, Burlington, Vermont, September 26, 2002. At the time, R.M. was scrubbing her walls clean of the graffiti she'd spent the previous days covering her cell with.

[131] Human Rights Watch interviewed mental health team at Chittendon Jail, Burlington, Vermont; and John Holt, mental health director, Matrix Health Systems, Northwest State Correctional Facility, Vermont, September 26, 2002.

[132] Human Rights Watch obtained a copy of R.M.'s disciplinary report from the Vermont Department of Corrections; on file at Human Rights Watch.

what exactly needs to be put in place to receive R.M..... R.M. appears to be regressing through this process and is convinced that VSH is playing games so as not to take her. She believes they do not want her.[133]

It is, as the staff freely admit, a far from happy situation. The Vermont prison system's chief psychiatrist, Dr. Michael Upton, told Human Rights Watch that "this is not therapy. This is management. It's trying to keep the symptoms few."

Human Rights Watch also interviewed mentally ill women at the Dale prison who had also spent time at Chittendon. One prisoner, J.F.D. has bounced back and forth between Dale prison and Chittendon jail for three years. Describing conditions at the jail she said "I'd put a slip in on Sunday night for suicidal thoughts. They'd get it Monday and it'd be three weeks before they see you." Inside the jail, this prisoner slit her wrists several times, slammed sharpened pencils into her arms, and even carved her son's initials into her left arm. "They'd just look at you like 'that's dumb,' and not give you any mental health counseling," she recalled.[134] Another Dale prisoner, V.O., stated that she was at the jail for five and a half months. "You don't get to see your caseworkers. The doctor only comes in once a week. Sometimes they put you on the wrong medications."[135] A third, Q.F., stated that access to mental health at the jail "was hit or miss. I never knew when I was going to see my mental health counselor." All of these women said that at Dale prison, unlike at Chittendon, the mental health services were superb and the staff extremely respectful. It appeared, therefore, unlikely that these women were simply malcontents.[136]

---

[133] This memo is contained in R.M.'s mental health files, obtained by Human Rights Watch after receiving a signed release from R.M. This particular memo refers to a meeting held September 17, 2002.

[134] Human Rights Watch interview with J.F.D., Dale Women's Facility, Vermont, September 26, 2002.

[135] Human Rights Watch interview with V.O., Dale Women's Facility, Vermont, September 26, 2002.

[136] Human Rights Watch interview with Q.F., Dale Women's Facility, Vermont, September 26, 2002.

Y.O., New Jersey, October 15, 2002

Some of our problems…are, but not limited to: physical abuse by staff and custody, verbal abuse, by staff and custody. We are denied adequate clothing for the weather. We have not been issued winter coats, or thermo underwear. I've witness state officials beat mentally ill inmates up who were and is incapable of defending themselves for no reasons. The nurse often give us inmates the wrong medications, and have our tier officer threaten or even jump on us if we speak up concerning the matter. It's currently 43 degrees outside and our housing officer is going to make us stand outside in the cold. We are all sick with flu-like sintums. No one comes to our aid. We get prescribed medications that we never receive. We have no heat. The unit is filthy and stinks.

L.I., Illinois. [letter undated]

I was placed in an situation where I've lost a peace of mind within fear frustration depression, the feeling of being helpless I've picked up a selfharm behavoir of cutting myself to where I need 5 to 14 stitchies at a time. Or smearing feces over my body to keep officers not wonting to touch me as they always cause me harm, stumping my feet or bending my hand causen pain to my risk, ramming my head to the walls smacking me on my butt after stripping me nude, standing on my arms when I'm strapped down on my back in restraints. Jump on leaven my face and eye swold up. Bouncing on the back of my legs with legcuffs on me cutting my ankles open, when was laid down on my stomatch as my butt was spanked say I sound like a lady bitch from screaming. I've been stripped out nude continually that made me loose control of my own actions by security or mental health staff. I've been harassed, retaliated on, tortured physically to where it have effected me mentally and physically.

V.K., New York, August 12, 2002

I am a active mental health patient and I was just discharge from CNYPC [Central New York Psychiatric Center]…. I am not getting no treatment, I'm only given medication and punishment in the special housing unit. I want help, but no one wants to help me.

VI. SYSTEMS IN TRANSITION

U.S. prison systems, at present, face two key forces for change which are often at odds: on the one hand, litigation to induce reform of mental health services, which prison officials are otherwise slow to undertake; and on the other hand, funding pressures and cutbacks that make implementation of reforms more difficult.

Reform through Litigation

While it should not take the threat of a lawsuit to get correctional systems to improve their mental health services, in practice, litigation or the threat of it, is the prerequisite for systematic improvements in mental health services. The earlier lawsuits challenged the utter lack of mental health services in prisons. More recently, litigation has sought improvements in existing systems.

Class action lawsuits have led to improvements in prison mental health care in a number of states, including Alabama, Arizona, California, Florida, Indiana, Iowa, Louisiana, Michigan, New Mexico, New Jersey, New York, Ohio, Texas, Vermont, Washington, and Wisconsin. Lawsuits have led to consent decrees and court orders instituting reforms and the court appointment of masters and monitors to oversee compliance. Considering the needs of today's mentally ill prisoners, the progress to date is far from enough. Viewed from the perspective of where prison mental health was two decades ago, the progress has been momentous.

- In Ohio, for example, Dr. Reginald Wilkinson, the director of the Ohio Department of Rehabilitation and Correction, was confronted with a devastating expert assessment of Ohio's mental health services developed after prisoners brought suit in 1993 claiming the services were so poor as to be unconstitutional. After receiving this assessment, Wilkinson engaged in a remarkable collaboration with correctional mental health experts, plaintiffs' attorneys, and other stakeholders to develop the blueprint for a major overhaul of the state's prison mental health services. The suit ended in a settlement without extensive adversarial proceedings, and the department has remained committed to providing quality mental health services. Within three years of the settlement, full-time equivalent staff providing psychiatric services increased from sixty-one to 284; the number of hospital beds had increased dramatically; and the percentage of prisoners on the psychiatric outpatient caseload had increased from 7.4 percent of the prison population to 12.2 percent.[137]

- In California, for example, a class action brought on behalf of all prisoners in the state prison system who suffered a serious mental illness resulted in a comprehensive court order addressing the state's grossly deficient mental health services, including lack of screening and inadequate staffing, personnel qualifications, access to care, supervision of psychotropic medication, use of restraints, medical records, and suicide prevention efforts.[138] Numerous changes were instituted in California prisons as a result of the litigation, including the establishment of Enhanced Outpatient Programs offering intensive mental health

---

[137] *Dunn v. Voinovich*, C1-93-0166 (S.D. Ohio, July 10, 1995). A description of the process by which the consent decree was reached is provided by Fred Cohen and Sharon Aungst, "Prison Mental Health Care: Dispute Resolution and Monitoring in Ohio," *Criminal Law Bulletin*, July-August 1997, pp. 299-327. Cohen served as an expert in the pre-settlement *Dunn* process and subsequently served as the court-appointed monitor.

[138] *Coleman v. Wilson*, 912 F. Supp. 1282 (E.D. Cal., 1995).

programming and monitoring, in separate housing units, for the most seriously mentally ill prisoners in thirteen prisons; and enhanced access to evaluation and services for thousands of less severely ill prisoners living in general population.

- In 1999, New Jersey settled a class action lawsuit brought by mentally ill prisoners and agreed to invest an additional $18 million a year to improve the state's correctional mental health services.[139] The settlement followed in the wake of a report prepared by correctional mental health expert Dr. Dennis Koson, who found:

> The treatment of mentally ill inmates in the [New Jersey Department of Corrections to be] among the worst I have seen.... The extensive shortcomings identified in mental health treatment services, the lack of any special facilities for mentally ill inmates, and the harsh disciplinary practices have the net effect of causing significant injury to seriously mentally ill inmates.[140]

Among other provisions of the settlement, New Jersey agreed to higher staffing levels, improved staff-patient ratios, better training for staff, and the provision of more specialized services.[141]

Successful litigation does not necessarily translate quickly into actual improvement. Some directors of correctional agencies accepted on-paper compliance with court decrees as a substitute for real, durable reforms. Faced with court orders or consent decrees mandating improved mental health services, some correctional authorities resist putting reforms in place. The reluctance can stem from institutional inertia, bureaucratic obstacles, failure to understand the importance of adequate mental health services, or the lack of funding. For example:

- Nineteen years after a federal court ordered major improvements in mental health services in Texas prisons, the court, "was deeply disconcerted by the inadequate and negligence [sic] medical and psychiatric treatment" that still existed.[142] The court found that the Texas prisons' psychiatric care systems were, "frequently grossly wanting, and that plaintiffs may have in fact shown deliberate indifference in individual cases or institutions."[143]

- In 1990, a prisoner filed a lawsuit alleging constitutional violations in connection with conditions at Iowa State Penitentiary (ISP), particularly with regard to disciplinary practices.

---

[139] *D.M. v. Terhune*, 67 F. Supp. 2d 401 (D.N.J., 1999).

[140] *New Jersey Prison System Report of Dr. Dennis Koson, C.F. v. Terhune*, Civil Action No. 96-1840 (D.N.J., September 8, 1998), p. 4, on file at Human Rights Watch. Human Rights Watch successfully sued the New Jersey Department of Corrections to secure public release of the Koson report. The settlement is reported at: *C.F. et al. v. Terhune et al.*, 67 F. Supp. 2d 401 (D. N.J., 1999).

[141] *D.M. et al v. Jack Terhune et al.* 67 F. Supp. 2d 401 (D. N.J., 1999.) The voluntary settlement committed the New Jersey Department of Corrections (DOC) to seek $16 million per year in additional mental health funding, and $2 million in construction funds to pay for new mental health facilities. The agreement is to remain in place until such time as the DOC has been found to be compliant with the terms of the settlement for one full year. Because it is a voluntary settlement, rather than one imposed by a federal court, it is not subject to the limiting time-constraints imposed by the Prison Litigation Reform Act. Human Rights Watch was not able to obtain permission from New Jersey Department of Corrections to visit any of its facilities or to interview officials concerning mental health services.

[142] *Ruiz v. Johnson*, 37 F. Supp. 2d at 907.

[143] Ibid.

The case became a class action in 1995. In 1997, a federal district court ruled certain practices at the prison were unconstitutional. The court's 118-page order describes shocking conditions, including prisoners sentenced arbitrarily to egregiously long sentences in lock-up cell houses from which they were unable to extricate themselves, the lack of evaluation for mental illness after the initial intake screening, the failure to consider mental illness in the determination of punishment for infractions, and the confinement of mentally ill prisoners in segregated disciplinary housing — a unit described as pandemonium and bedlam — where they received almost no treatment at all for their illnesses. The court ordered the Iowa Department of Corrections (IDOC) to develop a plan to remedy the constitutional violations.[144] It took two years (and four tries) for the Iowa Department of Corrections to come up with a plan that was acceptable to the court and to obtain funding from the Iowa legislature to pay for it. Among the IDOC plans the court approved in August, 1999, was the construction of a new two hundred-bed special needs unit at ISP for the mentally ill. The IDOC represented to the court that architectural plans were being drawn and that construction was scheduled to begin in late 1999 and operation expected in late 2000. The court accepted the new two hundred-bed unit as "virtually fait accompli." The court also ordered the IDOC to maintain funding for three psychologists, including one doctorate level psychologist, and gave the IDOC until December to fill all those positions.[145] At oral argument in 2000 during an appeal of the district court's decision, IDOC officials assured the appellate court they were moving forward with the new unit which currently consisted of a "hole in the ground."[146] Nevertheless, in October 15, 2001, the district court issued an unpublished opinion in which the judge noted that completion of the new special needs unit had been delayed until August 2002, that instead of 200 beds, the unit would initially consist of only forty; additional beds up to 200 would be constructed at a later time.[147]

- A federal court in 1977 found that a grossly inadequate system of medical care, including psychiatric care (no psychiatrists or psychologists were employed nor was there any prearrangement to provide psychiatric treatment for prisoners who needed it), was part of unconstitutional conditions at the Rhode Island Adult Correctional Institutions.[148] Nine years later, in 1986, the court found, among many remaining problems, that the psychiatric staffing remained insufficient, there was inadequate monitoring of prisoners on psychotropic medications, and deficient suicide prevention practices.[149]

---

[144] *Goff v. Harper*, Findings of Fact and Conclusions of Law, No. 4-90-CV-50365 (S.D. Iowa, June 5, 1997) (unpublished).

[145] *Goff v. Harper*, 59 F. Supp. 2d 910 (S.D. Iowa, 1999).

[146] *Goff v. Harper*, 235 F. 3d 410 (8th Cir., 2000).

[147] Fred Cohen, "Iowa Struggles to Provide Constitutionally Acceptable Mental Health Care: Promises Made?" *Correctional Mental Health Report*, July/August 2003, p. 19.

[148] *Palmigiano v. Garrahy*, 443 F. Supp. 956 (D.R.I., 1977), remanded on issue of deadlines, 599 F. 2d 17 (1st Cir. 1979); defendants found in contempt of court, 737 F. Supp. 1257 (D.R. I. 1990). The court ordered defendants to hire an adequate number of mental health professionals to diagnose, treat, and care for those prisoners who have mental health problems. It also ordered defendants to bring the health care delivery system into compliance within six months with the minimum standards of the American Public Health Association, the United States Public Health Service, and the Department of Health, State of Rhode Island.

[149] *Palmigiano v. Garrahy*, 639 F. Supp. 244 (D.R.I., 1986). The court noted that:

> In the nigh on to nine years that have elapsed since the publication of *Palmigiano* there has been an endless stream of motions and hearings; virtually all have concerned the state's failure to comply with the 1977 Order. The repetitive lament offered by the state was its inability to accomplish the ordered

The Problem of Funding Mental Health Services in Prisons

One of the major impediments to adequate mental health services in prison is, quite simply, their cost — providing mental health care is expensive. For example, in Pennsylvania, the average prisoner costs $80 per day to incarcerate. Yet if an prisoner is mentally ill, the added costs of mental health services, medications, and additional correctional staff boost the average daily cost to $140.[150] We have not been able to find figures for total national expenditures on prison mental health services.[151] Many individual prison systems Human Rights Watch contacted indicated they were unable to calculate the portion of their medical budgets devoted to mental health services. Nevertheless, data on prison mental health services budgets from some states illustrate the sums involved, as well as reveal significant differences in the resources allocated to mental health. The differences reflect both decisions on quantity and quality of care to provide as well as regional differences in salaries for mental health professionals.

Table 2: Fiscal Year 2003-2004 Mental Health Care Budgets in State Departments of Corrections (DOC)[152]

State DOC	Budgeted Amount in Dollars	Prison Population[153]	Per Capita Expenditure in Dollars
California[154]**	245,598,000	162,317	1513
Georgia[155]**	24,956,358	47,445	526
Michigan[156]	83,992,600	50,591	1660
Minnesota[157]	4,719,000	7,129	662

changes within the established time frames. And with patient confidence the Court bowed, with the same leitmotiv, continuing the matter to another day.

Palmigiano, 639 F. Supp. at 246.

[150] U.S. Senate Judiciary Committee, Statement of Dr. Reginald Wilkinson, director, Ohio Department of Rehabilitation and Correction, "Mentally Ill Offender Treatment and Crime Reduction Act of 2003," S. 1194, 108th Congress, July 30, 2003.

[151] The average national daily cost per inmate for health care – medical and mental health care – in 2001 was $7.39. Camille G. Camp and Camp, George M., *Corrections Yearbook 2001: Adult Systems* (Connecticut: Criminal Justice Institute, 2002), p. 106. A breakdown for mental health services alone was not provided.

[152] Caution must be used in comparing budgets because of differences in how state agencies calculate budgets.

[153] BJS, *Prisoners in 2002*, table 3.

[154] Human Rights Watch telephone interview with Terry Thornton, spokesperson, California Department of Corrections, June 16, 2003; California Legislative Analysts Office, *Analysis of the 2000-2001 Budget Bill*, accessed online at: http://www.lao.ca.gov/analysis%5F2000/crim%5Fjustice/cj%5F2%5Fcc%5Fmentally%5Fill%5Fanl00.htm. According to the analysis: "[t]he number of CDC inmates receiving such treatment has grown primarily because of court rulings requiring that the state to do a better job of identifying mentally ill offenders and a better job of providing services to those it has identified as needing treatment."

[155] Figures provided in electronic correspondence to Human Rights Watch from Peggy Chapman, public relations and information specialist, Georgia Department of Corrections, June 12, 2003 and from Georgia Health Services, Overview, Fiscal Year 2002. Although the amount budgeted rose from $24 million in 2001, the number of mentally ill prisoners increased by 500, resulting in a net decrease in the amount per prisoner. A portion of the state's funding for mental health services comes from kickbacks from prisoners collect phone calls provided by the telephone service provider to the Department of Corrections. Human Rights Watch telephone interview, Bill Kissell, director of health services, Georgia Department of Corrections, February 5, 2003.

[156] Human Rights Watch telephone interview with Tori Ellison, budget analyst, Michigan Department of Corrections, June 12, 2003.

New Jersey[158]**	23,651,000	27,891	848
Rhode Island[59]**	974,231	3,520	277
Texas[160]**	67,156,018	162,003	415
Washington[161]**	14,935,244	16,062	930

** Includes amounts budgeted for contracted out mental health services.

The fiscal crisis currently gripping the fifty U.S. states has led to financial belt-tightening and budget cut-backs, including in prison budgets. Prison mental health services have not been spared. In Georgia, for example, the most recent mission statement published by the Office of Health Services boasts of having "reduced psychiatrists and psychologists staffing by 30% with significant budget savings." The same report declares that, despite the risk of "moderate to significant medical and legal risk," the department has decided, as a money-saving gesture, to abandon a plan to open a psychiatric unit at Johnson State Prison, even though this "will limit options for referrals of inmates in mental health crisis and inmates will have to be transported greater distances to access beds." The department also decided to fill only 85 percent of vacant mental health counseling positions.[162]

In Florida, mental health director Roderick Hall told Human Rights Watch that it was impossible to estimate the amount of money spent by the correctional system on mental health services because "it's not tabulated that way. The state budgets money for health care. The accounting structure doesn't break down between mental health, physical health, and dental health."[163] However, despite the lack of specific numbers, the evidence suggests that Florida's mental health services have also been impacted by budget tightening: a March 2001 Correctional Medical Authority committee meeting detailed Florida's plans to cuts dollars from its correctional mental health expenditures through "cost saving efforts with psychotropic medications including reduction in the use of liquid psychotropics and limitation of formulary SSRIs [selective serotonin reuptake inhibitors] to two drugs." The meeting also detailed how medications would be distributed only "twice [per day] in most places where possible due to limited resources."[164]

In Michigan, a state that in recent years has made dramatic improvements to its system of mental health service provision within prisons, budget cuts took $5 million from the $72 million-hospital

---

[157] Human Rights Watch telephone interview with John Calabrese, assistant finance director, Minnesota Department of Corrections, June 12, 2003.

[158] Human Rights Watch telephone interview with Barbara Kutrzyba, manager II, Fiscal Resources, New Jersey Department of Corrections, June 12, 2003.

[159] Electronic correspondence to Human Rights Watch from Richard Frechette, associate director/CFO, Rhode Island Department of Corrections, June 13, 2003.

[160] Electronic correspondence to Human Rights Watch from Celeste Byrne, budget director, Texas Department of Criminal Justice, July 21, 2003; Human Rights Watch telephone interview with Celeste Byrne, August 18, 2003.

[161] Electronic correspondence to Human Rights Watch from Trenton Howard, budget manager, Washington Department of Corrections, June 13, 2003.

[162] In 2002, Georgia spent $9.60 per day per inmate on health services (mental and physical); Alabama spent $4.13. Data provided in Georgia Department of Corrections, Office of Health Services, *Georgia Department of Corrections, Health Services Overview for 2002*, available online at: http://www.dcor.state.ga.us/pdf/hsovrFY03.pdf, accessed on July 1, 2003. The numbers are from p. 9; the quote is from p. 40.

[163] Human Rights Watch telephone interview with Roderick Hall, mental health director, Florida Department of Correction, April 14, 2003.

[164] Minutes from Correctional Medical Authority Mental Health Committee Meeting, March 23, 2001.

and prison mental health services in 2002 and fifty mental health service positions were slashed.[165] According to the Director of Bureau of Forensic Mental Health Services in the Department of Community Health, Roger Smith, this has resulted in the number of treatment hours per patient in the intensive residential treatment programs being reduced from approximately twenty to twenty-three per week, down to sixteen.[166] Tony Rome, clinical director of the Michigan Bureau of Forensic Mental Health Services, asserted that so far basic outpatient programming in Michigan's prisons has not been cut. But, Rome acknowledged, the system is tightening up it criteria for outpatient eligibility.[167]

In Iowa, the corrections budget for fiscal year 2003 was cut 4.2 percent with proportionate cuts befalling the already-strapped mental health services.[168] Massachusetts has also recently implemented significant cuts in its mental health programs for incarcerated offenders.[169] And in South Carolina, the Department of Mental Health, responsible for administering mental health services to the state's prisoners, recently lost $31 million in state funds, and $20 million from the federal government, and is facing another 5 percent cut to its budget.[170]

---

[165] Human Rights Watch telephone interview with Roger Smith and Tony Rome, director and clinical director, Michigan Bureau of Forensic Mental Health Services, June 19, 2002.

[166] Human Rights Watch telephone interview with Tony Rome, clinical director, Michigan Bureau of Forensic Mental Health Services, June 19, 2002. In a subsequent telephone interview, February 10, 2003, Tony Rome told Human Rights Watch that the number of treatment hours per week was being cut to twelve hours.

[167] Human Rights Watch telephone interview with Tony Rome, April 21, 2003.

[168] Human Rights Watch telephone interview with Harbans Deol, medical director, Iowa Department of Corrections, April 2, 2003.

[169] Human Rights Watch telephone interview with Dr. Thomas Conklin, medical director, Hampden County Jail, October 9, 2002. Hampden County Jail deals with low-level state prisoners as well as county inmates, ibid.

[170] Editorial, "Deplorable Conditions," *Greenville News*, December 8, 2002.

E.N.X., Illinois, January 24, 2000

I am on the mental health wings. I've seen some bizarre acts on these wings. Self-mutilation. Attempted suicides. All types of crisises. The last D.T.Q. self-mutilation were he told the officer he wanted to see mental health or he was going to cut on himself and the c/o replied "so what." Then thought I was lying to him that D.T.Q. cut himself. It was ten minutes before c/o came down to D.T.Q.'s cell. Another guy had a crisis and was banging his head on the cell door, busting his forehead open. These guards don't give a damn. Staff crisis member don't make it a priority to go see inmates who request to see them.

O.D., Indiana, August 22, 2002

I am writing on behalf of several other offenders who are mentally ill and very unstable in my opinion, but these correctional employees at the long term supermax secured housing unit say all they want is attention. The first inmate names is E.L.M., a black male age 22 to 24, has self-mutilation, cut himself on several times on his arms, but also have cup open his sack that holds his nuts, balls or family jewels several different occasion in which require immediately medical emergency attention had to be transported by ambulance.... Inmate D.Y.E. has been on strip cell status for 24 hours on suicide watch just came off today and is on 15 minute watch. This white male inmate has had no suicide watch blanket for over 24 hours, and no mattress either for over 24 hours to sleep on. This inmate is force to lay on concreat with only pair of boxers on, with cold air conditioner 24 hours a day.... U.D., white male is mentally ill inmate that set his cell on fire on May 12, 2001, and received 2nd to 3rd degree burns all over his body, lost al finers on both hands and one thumb. This inmate has been brought back to SHU even after had some skin grafts, he has open wound on his right upper thigh, approx. one foot long, by 4 inches wide and approx. 1 ½ deep infected, is not covered by any bandages at all. Also still has open wounds from the fire burns. He doesn't have no way to write.... Also has 2nd to 3rd degree burns on his back as well from neck down to buttocks, he's burn really bad.... O.Y. has cut all over his body and stabs himself with ink pen, and medical staff will not send him out, so they ask him to remove pen imbedded himself.... D.N.V. been sticking pieces of handcuffs up his penis into blader. Also can't read, spell, write, no education at all. O.D. has been strapped to a bed with metal handcuffs on each arm, 3 set of handcuffs per wrist and laid like this for three days, 72 hours, no breaks to walk at all, in Sept 1999, also 2000, 2001 and 2002.... As for myself, I've been in SHU-max since Dec. 9, 1994, have cut myself over 60 times, needed hospitalization for staples and surgery too.

VII. DIFFICULTIES MENTALLY ILL PRISONERS FACE COPING IN PRISON

Mental health experts have described prisons as a "toxic" environment for the seriously mentally ill.[171] While prison is a challenging environment for all prisoners, it is even harder for those with serious mental illnesses. As psychology professor Hans Toch of the State University of New York, Albany, told Human Rights Watch, "Prisons are not set up for people who have coping competence as limited as it is for some of these folks."[172] They are tense and overcrowded places in which all prisoners struggle to maintain their self-respect and emotional equilibrium despite omnipresent violence, exploitation, and extortion; despite an utter lack of privacy; stark limitations on family and community contacts; and the paucity of opportunities for education, meaningful work, or other productive, purposeful activities. Prisoners with mental illness must survive as best they can in frequently brutal and brutalizing environments that they may be particularly ill-equipped to navigate. Even prisoners with chronic and severe impairments live under the same conditions and subject to the same stresses and rules as other prisoners.

The predominant goals of correctional authorities are ensuring security and safety. As in the outside society, offenders are deemed responsible for their actions, and the actions are assumed to be volitional. Compliance with the rules is achieved primarily through punishment and the deterrence that punishment is supposed to achieve. Few accommodations are made for the needs of mentally ill prisoners, whose symptoms often manifest themselves in violations of prison rules.

Physical Conditions

Except when transferred to acute care or hospital settings, prisoners who are mentally ill are typically confined in the same facilities as other prisoners. Because of the massive prison building campaign many states have undertaken over the past decades to keep up with the soaring prison population, and catalyzed by prisoner litigation challenging conditions of confinement, most prisoners in the United States are confined in at least minimally acceptable physical facilities. That is, by and large, they do not live in filthy, vermin-infested, decrepit and decaying buildings with inadequate sanitary facilities, ventilation, lighting, and water supplies, such as those at a Rhode Island prison which a court ruled were unfit for human habitation.[173]

Nevertheless, thousands of prisoners, including mentally ill prisoners, do still live in greatly overcrowded, poorly ventilated, decrepit, dark, and/or dirty facilities. Severe overcrowding, for example, is a problem in many states.[174] For inmates with mental illness, the risks of serious

---

[171] Human Rights Watch telephone interview with Andrea Weismann, May 30, 2002, former head of the health center for the jails of Washington, D.C., and currently in charge of developing mental health care systems for released inmates in Washington, D.C.

[172] Human Rights Watch telephone interview with Hans Toch, distinguished professor, School of Criminal Justice, State University of New York, Albany, November 22, 2002.

[173] In 1977, a federal district court ruled that the lack of sanitation, medical care, lighting, heating, and ventilation, and the noise, idleness, fear, violence, and the lack or inadequacy of programs of inmate classification, education, physical exercise, vocational training, or other constructive activity created a total environment in the Maximum Security Building of the Rhode Island Adult Correctional Institution that was unfit for human habitation, shocking to the conscience of a civilized person and in violation of the U.S. Constitution. *Nicholas v. Garrahy*, 443 F. Supp. 956 (D. R.I., 1977).

[174] In 2002, according to BJS estimates of the capacity of state prison systems, Alabama was operating at 201 percent of its prisoner population capacity (or 101 percent over capacity), Delaware's population represented 216 percent of its

psychological harm resulting from such conditions are particularly onerous. As an expert in a class action lawsuit alleging unconstitutional overcrowding in Alabama's prisons for women noted:

> The absence of privacy adds tension and stress to the daily existence of each inmate. Inmates with serious mental illness have fewer resources with which to cope with added turmoil. Anxious, depressed, psychotic suicidal and homicidal inmates are at increased risk of deteriorating emotionally and of having impaired judgment in such settings. Thus overcrowding ultimately results in a residential setting that puts mentally ill inmates at substantial risk of seriously harming themselves, seriously harming others and of being seriously harmed and/or killed.[175]

- At Mississippi's State Penitentiary at Parchman, mentally ill prisoners in need of water to cool themselves down during summer heat (which is particularly important for persons on psychotropic medications who can have severe, even deadly reactions to heat) reported having to drink from their toilet bowls because of a lack of enough drinking water. "The plumbing is dysfunctional throughout Unit 32," states the complaint in a lawsuit filed on July 12, 2002, by six death row prisoners.

> Almost every cell has a "ping-pong" toilet, which, when flushed, pushes excrement and waste into the bowl in the adjoining cell…. An overwhelmingly strong stench pervades the Unit, some of it from filth on the tier, some of it from a cesspool adjacent to the Unit, some of it from the defective plumbing and ping-pong toilets, some of it caused by flooding, which drenches inmates' cells and soaks their mattresses and bedding with filthy water that is allowed to stand for days at a time. Severely mentally ill inmates throw food and excrement on the floor of their cells and the hallways, which prison staff allow to decompose for days or even weeks.[176]

The lawsuit also alleges that mosquitoes, beetles, and other bugs swarm the prisoners' cells in summer; that the Delta summers turn the tiny cells into "heat boxes" and that seriously mentally ill prisoners housed on the unit "express their suffering and hallucinations in ceaseless raving, screaming, cursing, animal noises, moans, and shrieks…."[177]

A federal district court ruled that these conditions were unconstitutional and ordered extensive remedial actions.[178] During the litigation, the prison cleaned up its cells in

---

lowest reported capacity, and Washington state's prison population was 164 percent of its lowest reported capacity. BJS, *Prisoners in 2002*, p. 7.

[175] Cheryl D. Wills, M.D., *The Impact of Conditions of Confinement on the Mental Health of Female Inmates Remanded to Alabama Department of Corrections, Laube. v. Haley*, Civil Action No. 02-T-957-N (M.D. Ala., 2002); on file at Human Rights Watch. On December 12, 2002, the court granted plaintiffs motion for preliminary injunction finding that inmates at the Julia Tutwiler prison for Women are at a substantial risk of serious harm caused by the facility's " greatly overcrowded and significantly understaffed open dorms…[T]he unsafe conditions] are so severe and widespread today that they are essentially a time bomb ready to explode facility-wide at any unexpected moment in the near future." *Laube. v. Haley*, 234 F. Supp. 2d 1227, 1252 (M.D. Ala., 2002).

[176] *Willie Russell v. Robert Johnson*, Complaint, Case No. 1:02CV261-D-D (N.D. Miss.).

[177] Ibid. p. 7.

[178] *Russell v. Johnson*, 2003 U.S. Dist. LEXIS 8573 (N.D. Miss., May 21, 2003). The state obtained a stay of the court's order while it appeals the decision.

preparation for an effort to obtain accreditation from the American Correctional Association. The court found, however that the evidence showed that prior to the cleanup:

> [I]nmates on Unit 32-C were subjected to cells that were extremely filthy with chipped, peeling paint, dried fecal matter and food encrusted on the walls, ceilings, and bars, as well as water from flooded toilets and rain leaks… that inmates are routinely moved from cell to cell and are forced to clean their new cells that may have been left in horrendous sanitation by the prior occupants, especially if the occupant were mentally ill. Furthermore, adequate cleaning supplies and equipment are not routinely made available for inmates to clean their cells. Several inmates testified they clean their cells with their shower soap, towels and tee shirts. These filthy conditions contribute to the infestation of pests and play a role in the mental well-being of inmates.[179]

The court found that the cells were unreasonably hot during summer months and that "inadequate screening on the cell windows causes the inmates to choose between suffering from the heat or increasing the mosquitoes in their cells" if they open their windows in an effort to cool down. Regarding the "ping-pong" toilets, the court insisted the problem be eliminated: "no one in a civilized society should be forced to live under conditions that force exposure to another person's bodily wastes. No matter how heinous the crime committed, there is no excuse for such living conditions."[180] The court found that the lighting in the cells was "grossly inadequate."[181]

- One correctional expert concluded that the receiving unit at the Holman Correctional Facility in Alabama was so cramped, unventilated, unlit, unsanitary as to "make some men mad and mad men madder."[182] An experts' report prepared in connection with litigation about mental health services in Alabama prisons, noted that the receiving unit was, "medieval," that the cells were "dungeon-like and filthy…. Even with both doors open, there was little illumination within a cell." It was their opinion, "that no person — whether mentally ill or not — should be required to live in the conditions of the receiving unit."[183] Holman is not a specialized mental health facility, but many of its prisoners have serious mental illnesses. The experts also discovered in Alabama prisons the use of, "one-half inch thick rubber or plastic mats used for sleeping." A white foam oozed from some of the mats onto the concrete block which serves as the bed. The experts' report noted that:

> When lifted, the surface in each case was blackened, resembling some type of fungus or mildew. Inmates could actually scoop-up the white foam and display it in their hands. When asked, the inmates said they had no access to

---

[179] 2003 U.S. Dist. LEXIS 8573, at *5.

[180] Ibid., at *8.

[181] The maximum foot-candles obtained by the plaintiffs' expert, Mr. Balsamo, was seven or eight foot-candles, with the typical cell being in the two to four foot-candle range. The court found that twenty foot-candles is the appropriate level of lighting for these cells.

[182] Unpublished, written statement of Fred Cohen provided to Human Rights Watch; on file at Human Rights Watch.

[183] Kathryn Burns, M.D. and Jane Haddad, Psy.D., "Mental Health Care in the Alabama Department of Corrections," *Bradley v. Hightower*, Civ. No. 92-A-70-N (N.D. Ala., June 30, 2000)), pp. 40-41. This document will be posted on the Human Rights Watch website (http://www.hrw.org).

any cleaning materials and claimed that they were being medically affected by the foam and fungus. One inmate displayed a rash over much of his body and said it came from the pad and the fresh mortar used to construct his new bed.[184]

- As of 1997 the cells in the disciplinary detention area at New Jersey State Prison:

    had the non-flushing toilets that were overflowing with feces, paper and cloth. Inmate workers wearing masks were employed to drain these holes with a roto-rooter and then fill them with bleach. The result was a nauseating stench that only added to the general odor of feces throughout the area. Inmates were not given toilet paper and reported gnats or other small insects everywhere, including in their food. There was poor or no lighting in these cold cells. There was no fresh bedding, and inmates generally wore the same clothing for lengthy periods of time.[185]

- A court described the Iowa State Penitentiary in 1997 as follows:

    The bug range [colloquial term for the cell-block] populated with severely ill inmates] is dominated by maddening waves of noise. Some inmates yell at the top of their lungs for no apparent purpose other than to make noise. This behavior often lasts for hours. Other inmates are known as "bangers." These inmates bang on either their cell walls, their cell bars or their stainless steel sink-toilet combinations. They bang with whisk brooms, shoes or whatever else makes the loudest racket. Some inmates bang on the cell walls with their heads…. Still other inmates in the bug range urinate and defecate anywhere other than their [toilets]. Some inmates cover the walls of their cells with feces…some of these inmates also defecate and urinate in the communal shower and cover the walls and fixtures with their excrement.[186]

Vulnerability of Mentally Ill Prisoners to Abuse by Other Prisoners

Corrections and mental health experts acknowledge that mentally ill prisoners are likely to be victims of other prisoners — mentally sound as well as mentally ill. They are vulnerable to assault, sexual abuse, exploitation, and extortion. Their vulnerability is heightened when there are not sufficient correctional staff adequately trained to monitor, supervise, and protect mentally ill prisoners.

Dr. Terry Kupers identifies many of the problems facing the mentally ill in prison:

    For mentally disordered prisoners, danger lurks everywhere. They tend to have great difficulty coping with the prison code — either they are intimidated by staff into

---

[184] Ibid., p. 23.

[185] *New Jersey Prison System Report of Dr. Dennis Koson, C.F. v. Terhune*, Civil Action No. 96-1840 (D.N.J., September 8, 1998). p. 38.

[186] The court ruled subjecting non-mentally ill inmates to such noisy and filthy conditions violated their Eighth Amendment rights. He did not address the rights of mentally ill inmates to be free of such conditions, although in the same decision he ruled that mental health treatment was unconstitutionally inadequate. *Goff v. Harper*, Findings of Fact and Conclusions of Law, No. 4-90-CV-50365 (S.D. Iowa, June 5, 1997) (unpublished).

snitching or they are manipulated by other prisoners into doing things that get them into deep trouble...male and female mentally disordered prisoners are disproportionately represented among the victims of rape.... Many voluntarily isolate themselves in their cells in order to avoid trouble. Prisoners who are clearly psychotic and chronically disturbed are called "dings" and "bugs" by other prisoners, and victimized. [Their] anti-psychotic medications slow their reaction times, which makes them more vulnerable to "blind-siding" an attack from the side or from behind by another prisoner.[187]

Other prisoners share the fears, misconceptions, and erroneous beliefs about mental illness that exist outside the prison walls. "This leads to an unwillingness to associate with persons who have mental illness, and, thus, social isolation of persons with mental illness. The consequences of social isolation are themselves further disabling and stigmatizing."[188] Victor Hassine, a Pennsylvania prisoner who wrote a book about his prison experiences, described mentally ill prisoners as "pathetic and disruptive." He explains, "Their helplessness often made them the favorite victims of predatory inmates. Worst of all, their special needs and peculiar behavior destroyed the stability of the prison system."[189]

An expert retained by plaintiffs in a lawsuit over overcrowding and other conditions in Alabama's correctional facilities for women noted that "several inmates stated that mentally ill inmates are extremely vulnerable to the manipulations of their peers. They seek favors or material goods, in exchange for protection and/or safety. The shortage of correctional officers greatly amplifies the severity of this problem."[190] The Correctional Association of New York found that 54 percent of prisoners in New York's intermediate care units for mentally ill prisoners reported victimization in the general population, including having property stolen and physical and/or sexual assaults. Fifty-seven percent reported not feeling safe in the general population.[191] A mentally ill Montana prisoner housed in a special unit for the mentally ill told a reporter that prisoners who are "different like him are picked on in the rest of the prison. That doesn't really happen [in the special unit] because we're all kind of strange."[192] As the Chief of Clinical Services and the Chief of Psychological Services for the Pennsylvania Department of Corrections have pointed out, "individuals in this special population [with mental illness and/or mental retardation] are at greater risk of being victimized and manipulated by more predatory inmates." [193]

According to a class action complaint against the Georgia Department of Corrections filed by prisoners at Georgia's Phillips State Prison, when:

---

[187] Terry Kupers, *Prison Madness: The Mental Health Crisis Behind Bars and What We Must Do About It* (San Francisco: Jossey-Bass Publishers, 1999), p. 20.
[188] Lisa Callahan, *Evaluation of Specialized Mental Health Training*, Ohio Department of Rehabilitation and Correction, July 1, 2000, p. 4; on file at Human Rights Watch.
[189] Victor Hassine, *Life without Parole: Living in Prison Today* (Los Angeles: Roxbury, 1996), p. 29.
[190] Cheryl D. Wills, M.D., *The Impact of Conditions of Confinement on the Mental Health of Female Inmates Remanded to Alabama Department of Corrections*, prepared for *Laube v. Haley*, Civil Action No. 02-T-957-N (M.D. Ala., 2002), p.16.
[191] Correctional Association of New York, *Mental Health in the House of Corrections*, forthcoming report.
[192] Jennifer McKee, "Mental Illness Behind Bars, Part II," *The Montana Standard*, June 29, 2003.
[193] Lance Couturier, Ph.D. and Frederick Maue, M.D., "Suicide Prevention Initiatives in a Large Statewide Department of Correction: A Full-Court Press to Save Lives," *Jail Suicide/Mental Health Update*, vol. 9, no. 4 (Summer 2000), p. 2.

Prisoner 14 first arrived at Phillips State Prison in 1999, he was raped repeatedly by several prisoners. He was transferred to August State Medical Prison for over a week as a result of the injuries he sustained during this assault. Since this incident, Prisoner 14 has been raped again by other prisoners. In addition, Prisoner 14, who is seriously mentally ill and mildly retarded, feels compelled to exchange sex for commissary items such as cigarettes and coffee because he has no money.[194]

The complaint alleges further that sexual abuse among prisoners is "condoned, ignored or encouraged by prison staff who fail to take adequate steps to reduce or prevent the incidence of abuse."

An Indiana prisoner suffering from schizophrenia told Human Rights Watch that he was constantly being coerced into unwanted sex. Describing his situation, he said:

So one day I goes to the day room going to get my medication there was a big Black guy both of them call me to the back of the day room. They were punking[195] me out. I didn't want to fight them they made me call them daddy, made kept repeating it…these things keeps happening to me…these officers and these inmate they take avantige of the weak give them coffee, cigerrete to make them do things for them…there was a White guy that took advantages of me in prison at another facility…. I don't know my rights or about the law, so I'm hit everytime I go to prison.[196]

Terry Kupers presents the case of "Aaron," a twenty-three-year-old white man who had a long history of severe mental illness prior to his arrest and conviction for child abuse in 1996:

In prison, Aaron, who stands five feet six inches and has a retiring personality, was singled out for abuse. After he was taken off his medications by the prison psychiatrist who had decided he did not need such an expensive drug [Clozaril, a powerful "atypical" anti-psychotic medication], he began to hallucinate again and wrapped T-shirts around his head to protect his brain from hostile rays. His mental deterioration was quickly noted by prison toughs, and he was beaten and raped several times.[197]

A prisoner in Texas wrote to Human Rights Watch about rape in Texas prisons. Addressing the characteristics of prisoners who are sexually abused, he wrote that they are "Mentally ill; primarily white inmates; physically small; inmates who are not emotionally or physically violent in nature (passive people); child molesters/rapists…."[198]

---

[194] *Fluellen v. Wetherington*, First Amended Complaint, Civil Case No. 1:02-CV-479 (JEC) (N.D. Georgia, March 15, 2002), p. 15. On March 21, 2003, the judge denied the motion for class certification in an unpublished opinion.

[195] A "punk" is a derogatory prison term for a male prisoner who has been sexually abused and exploited, and is usually someone who is seen as too weak to defend himself. See *No Escape: Male Rape in U.S. Prisons* (New York: Human Rights Watch, 2001), pp. 90-91, 98.

[196] Letter to Human Rights Watch from B.S., Indiana, June 16, 1999, published originally in Human Rights Watch, *No Escape: Male Rape in U.S. Prisons* (New York: Human Rights Watch, 2001).

[197] Terry Kupers, *Prison Madness*, 1999, pp. 20-21.

[198] Letter to Human Rights Watch from J.F.L., Texas, March 22, 1999, published originally in Human Rights Watch, *No Escape: Male Rape in U.S. Prisons* (New York: Human Rights Watch, 2001).

Improper supervision and treatment can also leave the mentally ill vulnerable to each other. For example, in 2001, two prisoners who were mentally ill died violent deaths at the hands of other prisoners at Phillips State Prison in Georgia: one was beaten to death, and the other was bludgeoned to death by a seriously mentally ill cellmate who had repeatedly warned correctional officers that he was on the verge of snapping. On January 12, 2003, another killing occurred, with both the victim and the person responsible for his death prisoners with mental illness. Several other mentally ill prisoners at Phillips have been assaulted and sustained serious injuries in recent years.[199]

Rule-Breaking by Mentally Ill Prisoners

On March 21, 2003, New York State Department of Correctional Services Commissioner Glenn S. Goord responded in a letter to prisoner families concerned about the care of the mentally ill in prison. He said, "I take exception to your allegation that we punish people because they are sick. Being mentally ill is not now, and never has been, against department rules."[200] Commission Goord's response is disingenuous: while mental illness itself may not technically violate prison rules, a number of the all but inevitable concomitants of mental illness do.

Prisoners with mental illness may find it difficult, if not impossible, to comply consistently with prison rules. Some exhibit their illness through disruptive behavior, belligerence, aggression, and violence. Many will simply — and sometimes without warning — refuse to follow straightforward routine orders to sit down, to come out of a cell, to stand up for the count, to remove clothes from cell bars, or to take showers. Forensic psychologist Keith Curry described the process as follows:

> Once incarcerated, inmates suffering from schizophrenia, schizoaffective disorder, bipolar disorder, and major depressive disorder display predictable deficits in behavioral and emotional control, maladaptive interpersonal styles, social skills deficits, and distorted perceptions of their environments. As a result, they are less able to conform their behavior to the rigid expectations of prison life and often fall into self-defeating patterns of irrational opposition to the demands placed upon them. Seriously mentally ill inmates are thus more prone to disciplinary infractions....[201]

Such rule violations, even if the result of mental illness, are routinely punished.

Numerous studies report that the mentally ill have higher than average disciplinary rates. In 1986, Kenneth Adams, then of the State University of New York at Albany, studied prisoners in Clinton prison and found that "referred inmates [inmates on the mental health roster] have higher infraction rates than nonreferred inmates.... At Clinton, the median annual infraction rate for nonreferred inmates is 3.0. This compares to a median rate... of 5.4 for active service referred inmates."[202] On

---

[199] *Fluellen v. Wetherington*, Plaintiffs' Motion for Preliminary Injunction, Civil Case No. 1:02-CV-479-JEC (N.D. Ala., February 20, 2003). The court never ruled on the motion for a preliminary injunction. Instead, on March 21, 2003 it denied the plaintiffs' motion for class certification. Human Rights Watch telephone interview with attorney Tamara Serwer, August 7, 2003.

[200] Mary Beth Pfeiffer, "Mental Care Faulted in 6 Prison /Deaths," *Poughkeepsie Journal*, June 28, 2003.

[201] Letter from Keith R. Curry, Ph.D. to Donna Brorby, March 19, 2002. Curry had been retained by Brorby, attorney in the *Ruiz v. Johnson* litigation, to survey mental health conditions in Texas prisons.

[202] Kenneth Adams, "The Disciplinary Experiences of Mentally Disordered Inmates," *Criminal Justice and Behavior*, vol. 13, no. 3, September 1986, pp. 297-316.

the other side of the country, a study by researchers in Washington in 1996 found that: "offenders with serious mental illness constitute 18.7% of the prison population but account for 41% of the infractions."[203] In Colorado prisons, an internal prison report showed that:

> As a group, OSMIs [offenders with serious mental illnesses] are more likely than non-OSMIs to be given writeups for disobedience and verbal behavior such as disobeying a lawful order, refusal to work, sexual misconduct, threats, and verbal abuse. It is certainly conceivable that the impairment in social skill and perception found in many mental illnesses contributes to this pattern of conduct.[204]

According to the Bureau of Justice Statistics, mentally ill prisoners in state and federal prisons as well as local jails are more likely than others to have been involved in a fight and also more likely to have been charged with breaking prison rules. For example, 36.7 percent of mentally ill state prison prisoners have been in fights since admission, compared to 24.4 percent of other prisoners. Similarly, 62.2 percent of mentally ill state prisoners have been charged with breaking prison rules, compared to 51.9 percent for other prisoners.[205]

After identifying patterns of disturbed, disruptive, or disturbed-disruptive episodes in their sample of New York prisoners, Hans Toch and Kenneth Adams concluded that "more often than not periods of high disciplinary involvement overlap with symptomatic behavior for seriously disturbed inmates." Among prisoners who have been hospitalized for psychiatric treatment, disturbed-disruptive episodes are the most common. Among prisoners who have received outpatient mental health services, disruptive episodes are the most common and purely disturbed episodes relatively rare.

> These data indicate that disruptiveness is the central feature of maladaptive patterns among outpatients.... Our findings for [prisoners who have been hospitalized while in prison for mental illness] underscore the limitations of viewing custodial and mental health problems as separate and discrete. Temporal coincidence does not necessarily imply causation in the sense that disciplinary problems are always the result of emotional disorders. It does suggest, however, that at some level, different manifestations of coping problems are interrelated.[206]

Discipline for Misconduct

Prison management is predicated on obedience to rules. Rule-breaking is subject to discipline and punishment. When the rules are broken by the mentally ill, punishment remains the default response, although in the past few years some prison systems have begun wrestling with ways to accommodate consideration of the role of mental illness in prompting prisoners to commit infractions.

---

[203] Jemelka, R., Lovell, D., and Wilson, T. (1996). *Prevalence of Psychiatric Disability Among Prisoners.* Cited by Lovell and Jemelka in "When Inmates Misbehave: The Costs of Discipline," *The Prison Journal*, vol. 76, no. 2, June 1996.

[204] Memorandum by Dr. John Stoner, Colorado Department of Corrections, August 26, 2002. The data was compiled in response to a request by Human Rights Watch to Gene Atherton, Colorado Department of Corrections.

[205] BJS, *Mental Health and Treatment of Inmates and* Probationers, 1999, table 13. The same holds true for federal inmates: 41.2 percent of mentally ill federal inmates were charged with infractions compared to 32.7 percent of those who were not mentally ill.

[206] Hans Toch and Kenneth Adams, *Acting Out*, 2002, pp. 106-10, 112.

A federal district court in California ruling in 1995 found that:

> "Mentally ill inmates who act out are typically treated with punitive measures without regard to their mental status."…[and] such treatment was the result of inadequate training of the custodial staff so that they are frequently unable to differentiate between inmates whose conduct is the result of mental illness and inmates whose conduct is unaffected by disease…. There is substantial evidence in the record of seriously mentally ill inmates being treated with punitive measures by the custody staff to control the inmates' behavior without regard to the cause of the behavior, the efficacy of such measures, or the impact of those measures on the inmates' mental illnesses.[207]

Similarly, in 1997, a federal district court found that at the Iowa State Penitentiary, prisoners with mental illness received disproportionately severe sentences. For example, "the inmate who commits the relatively minor misdeed of sloshing cereal on a guard would receive thirty days disciplinary detention, one year in administrative segregation and loss of one year's good time." This is the same punishment given for grave offenses such as hitting a correctional officer. In addition, the disciplinary officer:

> does not review an inmate's mental health status before assigning a punishment. Thus when, for example, [the officer] disciplines Inmate 103 for banging his head against his cell wall to keep his dead father from entering his cell, [the officer] has no idea of the type or magnitude of mental afflictions that inmate suffers. [As mental health staff testified, the officer] cannot tell the difference between inmates who simply act out their frustrations and those patients who are indeed mentally ill.[208]

Deciding upon the proper weight to be given to mental illness in determining whether infractions should be punished, and if so how, is not an easy matter. Indeed, the question of discipline is at the heart of the inherent tension between the security mission of prisons and mental health considerations. Corrections officials have a legitimate need to maintain order — which they believe is best done through punishment for rule breaking, and the deterrent effect they believe it has. Many fear that accommodating mental illness will encourage excuses for misconduct, condone malingering, encourage others to engage in similar misconduct, and promote a general breakdown in order. They assume misconduct is volitional, and they find it difficult to understand the role mental illness can nonetheless play in behavior and the ability to handle the stresses of incarceration.

Dr. Terry Kupers points out that severely disturbed individuals:

> are prone to act bizarrely and inappropriately because of their psychiatric condition. Acting out and rule-breaking can be signs of a mental disorder that is not adequately treated and controlled. For instance, many disturbed prisoners hear voices or "command hallucinations" telling them to commit violence against themselves or others. When a psychotic prisoner loses control and follows the hallucinatory commands, more intensive treatment is needed.[209]

---

[207] *Coleman v. Wilson*, 912 F. Supp. 1282, 1320 (E.D. California, 1995).
[208] *Goff v. Harper*, Findings of Fact and Conclusions of Law, No. 4-90-CV-50365 (S.D. Iowa, June 5, 1997) (unpublished).
[209] Terry Kupers, *Prison Madness*, 1999, p. 81

From a mental health perspective, the disciplinary process all too often ignores the very real impact of mental illness on conduct and ends up punishing individuals for behavior directly connected to their illness. The goal of deterrence is clearly misplaced when individuals have no meaningful control over their conduct. Punishment can also be counterproductive to therapeutic and behavioral goals for those who are mentally ill, particularly when the punishment consists of being locked down in isolation cells.[210] For the person with mental illness who accumulates misconduct reports, "the pattern of custodial routine is an original demand for compliance, and subsequent deprivation and punishment reinforce the original demand, which intensifies the problems by imposing more pressures upon already existing pressures without providing any solution to the original problem."[211] Yet, the formal disciplinary process in most prisons does not offer options other than some form of punishment. It does not include consideration of more constructive, productive, and change-oriented responses that would help contribute long-term to the prisoner's ability to cope better both with his or her illness and with prison life.

Prisoners accused of serious (and sometimes not so serious) infractions have their guilt and punishment determined in prison disciplinary proceedings. Criminal law recognizes that it is fundamentally unfair to try someone incapable of either understanding the charge or presenting a defense, and it is unfair as well as cruel to punish someone for conduct that he cannot appreciate or control. With few exceptions, "incompetence" to participate in disciplinary proceedings and an "insanity" defense are not, however, formal features of prison disciplinary systems. Correctional mental health law expert Fred Cohen has written that the case law does "not require an administrative insanity defense and prison systems would not now easily tolerate it."[212] Human Rights Watch believes, however, that prisoners who are incompetent by virtue of their mental illness should not be subjected to disciplinary proceedings, at least as long as they remain in such a condition. Indeed, we believe that prisoners who are incompetent should be in a hospital setting with institutional responses to their conduct determined solely by mental health staff.

Of course, many prisoners who are seriously mentally ill are "competent" to participate in disciplinary proceedings. But they still present difficult questions regarding the extent to which their mental illness should be factored into findings of guilt and disposition, i.e., to what extent should they be held responsible for their conduct and what should the sanctions be. Prison officials operate disciplinary proceedings with the same reluctance to permit mental conditions to function as an excuse to misconduct that is so evident in criminal trials. They have not taken advantage of the flexibility they have as architects of prison regimes to modulate institutional responses to wrongdoing.

According to correctional mental health expert Dr. Jeffrey Metzner, while many states have come down against insanity defenses during internal disciplinary hearings, most states now do let mental health experts testify during disciplinary hearings.[213] The formal and informal roles played by mental health staff in disciplinary hearings vary as does the willingness of disciplinary hearing officers to

---

[210] For example, in Georgia's Phillips State Prison, mentally ill inmates are typically punished for infractions that often reflect symptoms of mental illness by being locked down in isolation, typically for two or three weeks at a time, but sometimes longer. *Fluellen v. Wetherington*, First Amended Complaint, Civil Case No. 1:02-CV-479 (JEC) (N.D. Georgia, March 15, 2002), p. 22.

[211] Vernon Fox, quoted in Hans Toch and Kenneth Adams, *Acting Out,* 2002, p. 353, footnote 17.

[212] Fred Cohen, *The Mentally Disordered Inmate and The Law* (New Jersey: Civic Research Institute, 2000), p. 13-3.

[213] Human Rights Watch telephone interview with Dr. Jeffrey Metzner, February 12, 2003.

take mental health perspectives into consideration. Vince Nathan, who has been an expert in numerous prison cases, told Human Rights Watch that, "The idea of ceding security authority to mental health personnel is pretty repugnant to most prison administrations."[214] In New York, for example, the law requires the mental health staff present information at a disciplinary hearing if a prisoner's mental state is an issue. According to the Correctional Association of New York, however, attorneys report these safeguards have not been implemented in:

> a manner that protects mentally ill prisoners from being punished for being ill. This failure is due to several factors: mental health staff's overdiagnosis of malingering by mentally ill prisoners, hearing officers' lack of training in mental illness symptomatology, and mental health staff's reluctance to get involved in security issues.[215]

In Ohio, the disciplinary system for misconduct by prisoners incorporates consideration as to whether the prisoner is competent to participate in the hearing because he or she understands the charges and can cooperate in the proceedings.[216] However, insanity — or even a lesser level of mental disorder — is not a defense. Even if an offense could clearly be shown to be caused by or inextricably connected to mental illness, the prisoner can still be found guilty of the infraction. The mental illness is, however, be taken into account in the determination of the sanction for the infraction. The adjudicating body, the Rules and Infractions Board (RIB), consults with mental health staff about the diagnosis, treatment, and needs of prisoners accused of infractions who are on the mental health caseload, and mental health staff may provide input and make recommendations about suitable disposition if there is a finding of guilt. According to Fred Cohen, who is currently a contracted consultant to the Ohio Department of Rehabilitation and Correction, when a prisoner's mental illness is clearly related to his conduct, the RIB will often find guilt, but sentence the prisoner to time served in segregation pending the hearing or will set a sentence of a numbers of days in disciplinary segregation as punishment, but suspend the sentence.[217] But the tension remains between recognition from a mental health perspective that an prisoner was not able to control his behavior in any meaningful sense and the decision nonetheless that he should be punished for it.[218] Director Dr. Reginald Wilkinson explained to Human Rights Watch, "what we cannot do is ignore the disciplinary aspect [of misconduct]. Otherwise, this would lead to faking [of mental illness] by other inmates."[219]

On September 1, 2001 a new Georgia Department of Corrections policy became effective regarding discipline procedures for prisoners who have mental illness (or mental retardation) requiring that they be "screened and evaluated by mental health/mental retardation staff during the investigation phase of the disciplinary process when there is a violation of the institutional/departmental rules."[220] For prisoners with more serious conditions, the procedures prescribed require a determination by mental health staff regarding whether the prisoner at the time of the infraction was responsible for

---

[214] Human Rights Watch telephone interview with Vincent Nathan, March 26, 2003.

[215] Correctional Association of New York, *Mental Health in the House of Corrections*, forthcoming report.

[216] Ohio Department of Rehabilitation and Correction Policy 206-05(D) (July 18, 1999) requires the suspension of disciplinary proceedings if an inmate is incompetent.

[217] Written communication from Fred Cohen to Human Rights Watch, August 28, 2003.

[218] Fred Cohen, *The Mentally Disordered Inmate and The Law* (New Jersey: Civic Research Institute, 2000), p. 13-5.

[219] Human Rights Watch telephone interview with Dr. Reginald Wilkinson, director, Ohio Department of Correction, July 3, 2003.

[220] Georgia Department of Corrections, *Standard Operating Procedures, MH/MR Discipline Procedures*, September 1, 2001.

the conduct. This includes a determination of whether the prisoner "lacks substantial capacity to appreciate the inappropriateness of his/her conduct or to conform his/her conduct to the requirements of the laws/regulations due to mental illness." The regulations further require that if mental health staff determine a mentally ill prisoner can be held responsible for the rule breaking conduct, they must still indicate whether his or her present mental status should preclude use of some regular disciplinary sanctions in favor of alternative sanctions. Such alternatives may include placement in specific therapy or psycho-education groups, individual counseling or therapy or placement in an intensive behavioral therapy unit.

An internal study was done to ascertain whether mental health staff input in fact had any outcome on disciplinary hearings at Georgia's Phillips State Prison. The study, which looked at disciplinary procedures in the months of September and October 2002, found that of ninety-four disciplinary reports issued in September to mental health prisoners, thirteen of the prisoners were found incompetent to participate in the disciplinary proceedings, eight were found competent to participate but had alternate sanctions recommended. In October, of eighty-four disciplinary reports issued to mental health prisoners, twenty-five of the prisoners were found incompetent and four were found competent to proceed but alternate sanctions were recommended. Dr Jeffrey Metzner, who at the behest of the Georgia Department of Corrections has been evaluating mental health services at Phillips State Prison, considered the results to be consistent with "the mental health input having an impact on this process." Discussions he had with staff suggested, however, "possible confusion relevant to the criteria for competency to proceed versus responsibility assessments." [221]

University of California psychiatrist Michael Krelstein surveyed the fifty state departments of corrections and the Federal Bureau of Prisons about their disciplinary systems. In many states prison officials "informally expressed the view that mental health clinicians should neither volunteer to, nor be placed in the position of having to, provide ultimate opinions on disciplinary responsibility."[222] They expressed concerns that having mental health staff involved in determining discipline responses would create a conflict of interest for the mental health teams; could encourage non-mentally ill prisoners to feign illness knowing that this illness might mitigate the prison system's responses to their misbehavior; and could place the clinicians at risk of revenge attacks from patients whom they had assigned punishments. For example, Krelstein found that:

> Under Texas policy, mental health may communicate with custody regarding the disciplinary management of seriously mentally ill inmates, but are prohibited from performing forensic evaluations including sanity at the time of the alleged disciplinary infraction or competence to undergo disciplinary proceedings.[223]

According to Krelstein, Texas justified the state's policy on forensic evaluations on the grounds that "custody [staff] could object to the mental health [staff's] insanity determinations, which excuse an inmate's antisocial or violent behavior, further straining custodial-clinical staff relations."[224] Moreover, he told Human Rights Watch, the mental health staff themselves are generally reluctant

---

[221] Letter from Dr. Jeffrey Metzner, M.D. to John Jones, Office of the Attorney General, State of Georgia, December 18, 2002. The results of the study are included in Appendix 9 to Dr. Metzner's letter.

[222] Michael Krelstein, "The Role of Mental Health in the Inmate Disciplinary Process: A National Survey," *The Journal of the American Academy of Psychiatry and the Law*, vol. 30 (2002), pp. 488-96.

[223] Ibid.

[224] Human Rights Watch telephone interviews with Michael Krelstein, senior psychiatrist, South Nevada Adult Mental Health Services, April 10, 2003 and August 14, 2003.

to go before a disciplinary committee and argue that a prisoner was insane at the time of his misbehavior:

> because that essentially forgives the crime, and that is a slippery slope in terms of what mental health's role ought to be within the prison setting.... There's no precedence for mental health staff to provide the ultimate answer for "yes, you are guilty," or "no, you are not guilty."[225]

Our research for this report uncovered countless examples of mentally ill prisoners being punished for rule-breaking connected to their mental illness. We provide examples throughout this report, and note several below, in an effort to communicate the nature and pervasiveness of an unsolved problem that vexes prisoners, correctional staff, and mental health professionals alike:

- In October 2001, a prisoner at Georgia's Phillips State prison who was mentally ill had had an extensive history of self-mutilation, heard the murder of another prisoner, David Strickland, at the hands of his cellmate in a nearby cell. The prisoner "responded to the stress by cutting himself, and was subsequently given a disciplinary report and placed in an isolation cell for "destruction of state property."[226] The property in question was the prisoner's own body.

- On March 31, 2001, James Mitchell, a mentally ill prisoner who was incarcerated at the Southern Ohio Correctional Facility in Ohio and was assigned to the Residential Treatment Unit, began screaming and kicking his cell door. He subsequently explained that "he was hearing voices and was trying to get someone to tell them that he wanted to see psych." He was charged with destruction of property and creating a disturbance. The Rules Infraction Board stated that it believed the statement by Mitchell, but nonetheless found him guilty and sentenced him to twenty days in disciplinary control.[227]

- "I remember this one woman very clearly, there was a fire drill and they had to evacuate. She was in the middle of a major panic attack, sitting in the bathroom. She couldn't get up," Janet Schaeffer, one-time director of mental health services at the Washington Correctional Center for Women, told Human Rights Watch.

> She was given an infraction for this and put in segregation. It wasn't like she was trying not to follow the rules. She'd done well in prison prior to that. They put her in segregation. She started to do very poorly there. Something triggered them calling me. I went to see her and continued to see her. It turned out this woman was very delusional. She'd gone unnoticed in the prison.[228]

---

[225] Ibid., April 10, 2003.

[226] *Fluellen v. Wetherington*, First Amended Complaint, Civil Case No. 1:02-CV-479 (JEC) (N.D. Georgia, March 15, 2002), p. 23; Email communication from attorney Tamara Serwer to Human Rights Watch, Southern Center for Human Rights, August 12, 2003.

[227] Amended Summary Pursuant to F.R.E. 1006 of Documents Relevant to the Testimony of Plaintiff Mitchell, *Austin v. Wilkinson*, Case No. 4:01-CV-71 (N.D. Ohio) (undated). Human Rights Watch does not know if he actually served this sentence.

[228] Human Rights Watch telephone interview with Janet Schaeffer, former Director of Mental Health Services at the Washington Correctional Center for Women, May 29, 2002.

- Attorney Jane Kahn, who has represented many seriously mentally ill prisoners in California, told Human Rights Watch that her clients are routinely disciplined for acts related to their illness.[229] In some instances, these prisoners are criminally prosecuted for their prison conduct, which in a number of cases has led to them receiving life sentences under California's three strikes law.[230]

  > We see a lot of [mentally ill prisoners] get third strikes — mental health cases with, for example, bipolar disorder. They'd be in a manic state — because the medication delivery is abysmal still. There are shortages of MTAs [medical technician assistants], problems getting prescriptions filled in the pharmacies. Prescriptions run out. Or someone is discharged from a crisis bed or transferred between prisons and their medications don't follow them. There was a guy in Chino. By the time we saw him, he was in Ad Seg [administrative segregation] and had picked up a third strike for assaulting another inmate. His mental illness wasn't picked up at the intake screening. He was on medications in the community — he was a schizophrenic. But the prison didn't pick this up. He became horribly psychotic.[231]

Kahn told Human Rights Watch about the following cases exemplifying the use of punishment in California prisons to respond to conduct connected to mental disorders:[232]

  o One prisoner, diagnosed with paranoid schizophrenia and bipolar disorder, was being housed in the Enhanced Outpatient Program at the Salinas Valley prison. When he responded to news of an unfavorable legal decision by pacing repeatedly up and down his unit, a correctional officer immediately ordered him back to his cell. The prisoner became very upset and threw his legal papers, some of which hit the officer in the leg. He was charged with "battery on a peace officer." According to Kahn, the prisoner is "totally delusional."

  o A seriously mentally ill prisoner kept telling female officers that he loved them. He was charged with threatening the guards and was locked down for thirty days.

  o A bipolar prisoner who was so ill that he had been forcibly medicated after refusing his medications, was locked down in a secure housing unit for throwing food and feces at officers while in a manic state.

  o A delusional prisoner told a clinical psychologist at Salinas Valley during a confidential counseling session that his skin was poisonous and if a correctional officer touched him he would die. The psychologist, who was also a case manager,

---

[229] Human Rights Watch telephone interview with Jane Kahn, attorney, April 8, 2003.

[230] Under California law, if someone has two prior serious felonies on their record, any third felony conviction, even a non-violent one, qualifies that person for a Three-Strikes-And-You're-Out sentence of 25 years-to-life. If inmates with two prior serious felony convictions are convicted of committing a crime inside prison, that conviction qualifies them for a Three Strikes sentence.

[231] Kahn has copies of the disciplinary write-ups, referred to as 115s, in the cases mentioned here. She also has copies of the medical records for these inmates.

[232] Human Rights Watch telephone interviews with Jane Kahn, April 8 and August 19, 2003.

wrote a disciplinary ticket saying the prisoner was threatening to kill a correctional officer. The prison was eventually forced to drop this charge.

- Prison expert Dr. Dennis Koson prepared a report for the plaintiffs in *C.F. v. Terhune*[233] in which he found: "when inmates are seriously mentally ill and not adequately treated, they become increasingly incapable of conforming to institutional rules of conduct and, as a result, often are charged with disciplinary infractions."[234] Koson wrote of one prisoner, John Doe #117, who:

  > was charged with "being untidy" because he smeared feces on his cell door. In the absence of a psychological evaluation, he received a sanction of 60 days loss of commutation time, 90 days administrative segregation, and 15 days detention as well as referral to mental health staff for treatment.

  Later on, the prisoner was charged with flooding his cell, and, following a psychological report that showed he was "often psychotic," the prisoner was again referred to the mental health staff. After that, however, Koson found that:

  > subsequent disciplinary officers… declined even to seek a [mental health] evaluation or ignored its findings when requested. On July 1, 1995, John Doe #117 was again charged with flooding his cell. A psychological evaluation determined that John Doe #117 was "cognitively limited," "schizophrenic," and "not completely in control of his behavior." Nonetheless, he received detention and administrative segregation time.

- At Tamms prison in Illinois, lawyers suing the prison on behalf of mentally ill prisoners, refer in their complaint to H.X.[235] H.X. is a forty-year-old chronic schizophrenic, who has a documented record of serious mental illness going back to his childhood. According to the complaint:

  > Several times [H.X.] has tried to harm himself or his surroundings at Tamms on account of his active psychosis, and he has been punished for his actions. For example, twice after he attempted suicide by swallowing a piece of his mirror, he was found guilty of damaging or misusing state property. When guards found him with a homemade rope around his neck attempting to hang himself, they gave him a ticket for destroying the sheet he had torn to make a rope; the Adjustment Committee found him guilty and ordered him to pay restitution for the torn sheet.

- In 1997, a court in Iowa found that the prison administrator in charge of hearing discipline cases at the state penitentiary "does not check closely to see if the inmates he is punishing have psychological problems when he presides over the administrative hearing." The court referred to the case of one prisoner who was found guilty of 185 violations between 1984

---

[233] *New Jersey Prison System Report of Dr. Dennis Koson, C.F. v. Terhune*, Civil Action No. 96-1840 (D.N.J., September 8, 1998), p. 38.
[234] Ibid., p. 4.
[235] *Boyd v. Snyder*, Amended Complaint, No. 99 C 0056 (N.D. Illinois, February 25, 1999).

and 1988 and who had, as a result, spent the past eight years in isolation. Another prisoner had been punished for painting his cell walls with his own blood.[236]

- In 2003, Harbans Deol, medical director of the Iowa Department of Corrections reported to Human Rights Watch that correctional officers tend to refer prisoners to the disciplinary process even when the prisoners "might be having behavioral problems that are a symptom of their illness." Because he believes this to be counterproductive, his office is working to create better training programs for the correctional officers in the Iowa prison system. "We try to teach [correctional officers] if someone is acting out it might be a symptom of their illness. Some correctional officers might actually poke fun [at the mentally ill.] That escalates into a worsening of his condition. He'll say something to the C.O. and be disciplined for it." Because mental health staff in Iowa have no mandated role in disciplinary hearings, whether or not an prisoner's mental status is taken into account during a hearing is left to the discretion of the individual administrative law judges appointed by the prison administration who conduct the hearings. Deol told Human Rights Watch that there have been instances in which prisoners in the final stages of cirrhosis of the liver have begun acting strangely due to the accumulation of ammonia that builds up in the body as a result of liver malfunction and that can lead to hallucinations and delirium. Instead of responding to the behavior through administering appropriate medications, some judges, Deol reported, have disciplined prisoners for these actions.[237]

- In Wisconsin, according to Coalition For Advocacy attorney Todd Winstrom, who was involved in investigating the treatment of the mentally ill at Oshkosh Correctional Institution, the correctional system recently amended its administrative code to exclude mental illness as a defense in disciplinary hearings. The Wisconsin Department of Corrections did not return repeated phone calls from Human Rights Watch requesting information on, and clarification of, this policy. The effects of the mentally ill picking up disciplinary tickets for their behavior are varied. Sometimes, it results in prisoners losing their prison jobs; other times it results in parole being denied. Frequently it results in prisoners being sent into segregated housing. Winstrom reported that one female prisoner at Taycheedah Correctional Institution was twice punished by 180 days in segregation for slitting her throat.

Misconduct reports can lead both to an prisoner being placed in restrictive housing (discussed below, chapter IX), to loss of good time, and ultimately, to mentally ill prisoners serving most or all of their maximum sentence. "I'll be honest with you," Superintendent Vaughn, of Graterford Prison, Pennsylvania, told Human Rights Watch. "Most mental health cases, if they get five-to-ten end up doing the max, because they don't adjust well…."[238] Indeed, the Pennsylvania Department of Corrections reports that prisoners with serious mental illness are three times as likely as other prisoners to serve their maximum sentence.

---

[236] *Goff v. Harper*, Findings of Fact and Conclusions of Law, No. 4-90-CV-50365 (S.D. Iowa, June 5, 1997) (unpublished), pp. 33-34.
[237] Human Rights Watch telephone interview with Harbans Deol, medical director, Iowa Department of Corrections, April 2, 2003.
[238] Human Rights Watch interview with D. Vaughn, superintendent, Graterford Prison, Pennsylvania, August 12, 2002.

Ill-Equipped

According to the Bureau of Justice Statistics, mentally ill prisoners in state prison serve more time on average than other prisoners. Mentally ill offenders average a total of 103 months in prison, fifteen months longer than other offenders. The largest differences in time served were among violent and property offenders. The mentally ill serve an average of at least twelve additional months for violent and property offenses.[239] Because of their disciplinary records — as well as concerns about their mental illness itself — mentally ill prisoners are also at greater risk than others of being denied parole when brought before a parole board. As Superintendent Vaughn pointed out to Human Rights Watch, parole boards "don't want to chance it on releasing them."[240] Dr. Reginald Wilkinson, Director of the Ohio Department of Rehabilitation and Correction also pointed out in testimony to Congress that mentally ill prisoners serve more time before getting parole, or never get parole but simply max out of their sentence, because the lack of adequate community services makes it difficult for the parole board to develop an effective community treatment and supervision plan.[241]

---

[239] BJS, *Mental Health and Treatment of Inmates and Probationers*, 1999, p. 8.
[240] Human Rights Watch interview with D. Vaughn, superintendent, Graterford Prison, Pennsylvania, August 12, 2002.
[241] U.S. Senate Judiciary Committee, Statement of Dr. Reginald Wilkinson, director, Ohio Department of Rehabilitation and Correction, "Mentally Ill Offender Treatment and Crime Reduction Act of 2003," S. 1194, 108th Congress, July 30, 2003.

I.J., NEW YORK

The case of I.J., a schizophrenic prisoner incarcerated at various correctional facilities in New York State, illustrates the repetitive cycle of misbehavior and discipline that many mentally ill prisoners go through. We have quoted below the detailed description of I.J.s history in the complaint filed by Disability Advocates Inc. alleging inadequate mental health services and inappropriate punitive segregation for New York state prisoners.[242]

> I.J., a diagnosed schizophrenic with borderline intellectual functioning, has been committed to CNYPC [Central New York Psychiatric Center] on twenty-nine separate occasions since his incarceration in 1981. He has a history of being suicidal when he is mentally decompensated. His admissions to CNYPC have been precipitated by depressed and sometimes self-abusive behaviors, as well as regressive behaviors such as defecating and urinating on the floor of his cell and becoming withdrawn and mute.
>
> I.J. frequently suffers from hallucinations which are paranoid and persecutory, and which command self-harm. On numerous occasions from 1993 through 1996, he became severely decompensated, experienced paranoia and auditory hallucinations, and was admitted to CNYPC. I.J. has extreme behavioral problems, likely precipitated by his mental illness, and, as a result, has spent a large portion of his incarceration housed in twenty-three hour isolated confinement in SHU [special housing unit.] He has repeatedly suffered serious psychiatric deterioration in SHU.
>
> During the occasions that he has been hospitalized at CNYPC or housed in an OMH [New York State Office of Mental Health] Satellite Mental Health Unit and has accepted medication, he has not presented behavioral problems and has functioned markedly better than in isolated confinement.
>
> In May 2000, while housed in the ICP [Intermediate Care Program] at Great Meadow C.F. [Correctional Facility], I.J. was again suffering a period of serious psychiatric deterioration. During that period, I.J. was sentenced to 180 days SHU time for two incidents of use of abusive language with no testimony from mental health staff requested or proffered at the disciplinary hearings.
>
> I.J. was transferred to SHU where his deterioration escalated. According to a misbehavior report issued on May 24, 2000, I.J. refused to obey orders to turn the light on in his cell or to remove his jumpsuit from the cell gate; he reportedly began yelling threats at the corrections officer, ripped the light bulb from his wall and smashed it against the sink and toilet in his cell.
>
> The misbehavior report indicates that OMH staff were notified and came to speak to I.J. after which he was escorted without incident to the OMH Satellite Mental Health Unit for observation.

---

[242] Case study excerpted from the complaint filed by Disability Advocates Inc., et al., *Disability Advocates Inc., v. New York State Office of Mental Health, et al.*, No. 02 CV 4002, (S.D.N.Y., May 2002), pp. 28-33.

On the date of his hearing, June 8, 2000, I.J. again was transferred to an observation cell in the OMH Satellite Mental Health Unit due to agitated behavior and smearing feces. He was reportedly exhibiting delusional thinking, refusing to eat and refusing medication.

I.J. did not appear at the hearing regarding the May 24 incident. OMH was not consulted by the hearing officer and did not testify at the disciplinary hearing. I.J. received one year in SHU for destroying state property, refusing a direct order, and using threatening language.

Shortly after his June 8 admission to an OMH observation cell, I.J. was returned to SHU from the observation cell at his request. He was transferred back to twenty-three hour isolated SHU confinement without having accepted medication and without any indication that his condition had stabilized. No efforts to encourage compliance with medications or to consult with CNYPC are recorded in his mental health record.

I.J. continued to psychiatrically deteriorate in SHU. In August 2000, he was admitted again to the OMH Satellite Mental Health Unit for observation. His behavior was described as being loud and yelling, he reported that he was hearing voices, seeing ghosts, and that he was experiencing suicidal ideation.

Despite the OMH-observed and recorded paranoia and delusions for the two days following his admission to the OMH Satellite Mental Health Unit, I.J. was transferred back to his SHU cell on August 7, 2000. He was not seen again by OMH until September 21, 2000 when DOCS [New York State Department of Correctional Services] staff requested OMH intervention.

On September 21, 2000, DOCS staff referred I.J. to mental health staff due to his "strange behavior." No description of his behavior was recorded, and I.J.'s OMH record does not document any intervention by OMH staff.

I.J. was subsequently seen by OMH staff approximately every two to three weeks during rounds in SHU.

In October 2000, OMH noted that I.J. was compliant with his medications and that he requested an increase in medication because he was seeing ghosts.

The following month, I.J. began to suffer severe psychiatric deterioration again. He became medication non-compliant and refused to leave his cell to meet in private with OMH staff.

On November 9, 2000, I.J.'s medication orders were discontinued because he had been refusing to take medication. No efforts to encourage compliance with his prescribed medication regime are recorded in his OMH record.

In December 2000, a month after the medication orders were discontinued, I.J. began to smear feces in his cell and became very agitated.

On December 6, 2000, I.J. refused to leave his cell to be transferred to an observation cell in the OMH Satellite Mental Health Unit. He was forcibly extracted from his SHU cell by DOCS staff utilizing a form of tear gas and an extraction team. After the extraction he was placed in an observation cell in the OMH Satellite Mental Health Unit.

Just two days later, on December 8, 2000, I.J. was returned to isolated confinement in SHU. In SHU, he deteriorated to the point where he refused to shower, refused to turn his light on, was paranoid, delusional, fearful and suspicious, and believed others to be possessed.

On January 4, 2001, I.J. finally was removed from SHU due to his beliefs that his food was being poisoned and that others were possessed, and due to his refusal to bathe. He was again taken to an observations cell in the OMH Satellite Mental Health Unit.

On January 10, 2001, I.J. was committed to CNYPC after remaining in an observation cell for six days where he continued to express paranoid beliefs and suspicions.

There is no indication in I.J.'s OMH records from June 2000 through January 2001 that I.J. was ever evaluated for psychiatric hospitalization prior to January 8, 2001.

On March 23, 2001, I.J. was discharged from CNYPC to the SHU at Clinton C.F. His discharge plan included a combination of medications, and an indication that he "will need observation, counseling and encouragement to take medications."

I.J. was not seen in SHU by OMH staff between April 10, 2001 and May 1, 2001. On May 1, he was observed to be paranoid, and he stated that he did not fell well and that he felt confused. He informed OMH staff that he had stopped taking his medications two weeks earlier.

OMH did not take any action to remove I.J. from SHU; he was not transferred to an observation cell in the OMH Satellite Mental Health Unit. He was in fact not seen by OMH staff again for two weeks. At that time, it was noted that his paranoia had increased; he reported that he believed that corrections officers were tampering with his food. The response of OMH staff was to discontinue all of his medications because he had not taken them, and to permit DOCS to continue to house him in SHU. Despite his noted deteriorating mental condition, mental health visits were reduced to a monthly basis.

By June 2001, I.J.'s mental status had further deteriorated. He was loud and disruptive and had begun to throw feces around his cell. His behavior resulted in disciplinary charges.

OMH mental health staff reported their view that I.J. was "manipulative" and they arranged for his transfer to the Attica C.F. [Correctional Facility] SHU. OMH staff did not arrange for more intensive mental health treatment, nor did they consult with CNYPC.

On June 20, 2001, I.J. was transferred to Attica C.F. in an agitated and paranoid state. He refused to comply with a strip search at Clinton C.F. during the transfer procedure and was given an additional disciplinary ticket for this behavior.

I.J. was sentenced to two years of SHU time and 18 months loss of good time for refusing the strip search and he received six months of SHU time for throwing feces and urine at an officer.

At the Attica C.F. SHU, I.J. has continued to receive tickets for hostile and agitated behavior, and now faces nearly six years of SHU with no appreciable mental health treatment for his schizophrenia.

I.J. is scheduled to remain in SHU through July 2006 — a date more than a year beyond the maximum expiration date of his sentence.

On May 16, 2002, I.J. was transferred from the Attica SHU to CNYPC.

P.F., New Jersey, July 20, 2002

I have a lot to say about the condition that mental ill prisoner got to go throught in here meaning being assault by correction officers because we on psych medication or they feel like beating on a prisoner to bring him to his sence. Sir, you got prisoners who got very bad mental problems and we need help not being beat on by officers. See sir I been in and out of psychiatric hospital from youth. By trying to kill myself and being locked up I'm not receiving the help I need.

C.I., Illinois September 24, 1999

Bad news, the tact unit just split F.R.'s head open. Here's what happened. At 5:00pm c/o [U.] gave him a dinner tray and he said it had metal in it. So at 8:00pm nurse [P.N.]. came with his medication. He refused it saying they was trying to poison him. At 8:20, Captain K. tried to talk him into taking his medication, he refused. Oops, at 8:10, Dr. [F.] and Nurse [P.N.] also tried to talk to him also, he refused. At 8:40, c/o [E.] came with the video camera because they were suiting up the tact unit to force him to take his medication. At approximately 8:55 the tact unit came to his cell, gave the 3 direct orders then mased him. When they entered the cell I could hear them punching on him and they slammed his head on the floor. They just brought him back in and put him in a hot shower with his head split open and said he has to get stitches in the back of his head.

VIII. INADEQUATE RESPONSES AND ABUSES BY CORRECTIONAL STAFF

Correctional officers, the front line custodial staff who interact on a daily basis with prisoners, have a difficult job in the best of circumstances. Working in insufficient numbers, they are asked to exercise power over and maintain control of prisoners crowded into facilities that are often no more than warehouses, devoid of opportunities to keep their inhabitants productively and peacefully engaged. The difficulties and frustrations of work as a correctional officer are compounded when prisoners have mental illness. The at times aggressive, bizarre, or repellent behavior of mentally ill prisoners can try the patience of anyone, even mental health professionals. But few correctional officers have the training in and understanding of the nature of mental illness that would help them cope better with the challenges posed by offenders with severe illnesses. They come to their jobs with the fears and prejudices of the general population towards the mentally ill. The correctional culture of order, obedience, and discipline in which they were trained leaves them further ill-prepared for handling prisoners whose behavior is either chronically or episodically ruled by their mental illness.

The Mental Health Role of Correctional Staff
Correctional staff experience prisoners at close quarter twenty-four hours a day. They come to know patterns of prisoner behavior and can detect changes in them sometimes better, if not more rapidly, than mental health staff whose interactions with prisoners may be more sporadic. In most prisons, mental health staff do not regularly monitor the mental health condition of prisoners who are not on the mental health caseload either because they were not identified as ill during the initial prison in-take screening process or because they developed mental illness or emotional crises while imprisoned. Since correctional officers have the most contact with prisoners, they can notice unusual behavior or changes that may signal a mental disorder.

Correctional officers are in a position to notice if a prisoner has suddenly become extremely withdrawn and incommunicative or if one has started to act bizarrely. They are the source of many referrals to mental health staff of prisoners, alerting mental health staff of a prisoner's need for attention. They have the opportunity to develop a relationship with them, and if a prisoner begins acting out, they can talk to the prisoner and help calm them down. On evenings and weekends there may be no mental health professionals present at all in the prison. Correctional officers find themselves in situations in which they must assess a prisoner's conduct and make judgment calls about whether mental health professionals should be summoned; whether to remove a prisoner from his or her cell and into an observation cell or mental health unit; whether prisoners are merely acting out for attention, or whether they are in need of an immediate mental health intervention.

Understanding the nature and symptoms of mental illness enhances the ability of correctional officers to respond appropriately to mentally ill prisoners, an ability which has become increasingly important as the number of prisoners with mental illness has grown. If correctional officers view acting out as volitional, deliberate misbehavior, if they do not realize a prisoner who is mumbling to himself is hallucinating, if they don't realize that huddling in the corner of a cell may be a sign of crippling depression, they will not call for mental health staff.

For example, a team of experts who reviewed a series of issues relating to psychiatric services in Massachusetts prisons, found that officers were under-referring prisoners for medical services.

Officers had a threshold for referrals that precluded attention for many prisoners. "Correctional officers informed us that if an inmate develops a serious mental disorder, it is not likely to result in officers' requests for mental health attention to the inmate as long as the inmate is clean, quiet, and obedient. "Bizarre behavior" is not likely to result in a referral as long as it is not disruptive."[243] In the case of John Salvi, an prisoner who was not on the mental health caseload at the time he committed suicide, the evaluation team found there was substantial evidence that Salvi "was suffering from serious thought disorder and manifested some unusual behaviors…but he did not attract enough attention to reach the relatively high threshold that staff typically use as signals for mental health services referrals." The evaluation team also noted that "[a]ll of the correctional officers we interviewed felt that they did not have enough training in recognizing mental illness in inmates and in making decisions about referring inmates for mental health services."[244]

Training for correctional officers in mental health issues can also help overcome a common assumption that security staff and mental health staff are worlds apart in views, concerns, and methods of handling prisoners. Stereotypes also impede collaboration between custodial and mental health staff. Correctional officers often believe mental health professionals coddle their patients, are duped by manipulative prisoners, and don't sufficiently appreciate security needs. Mental health professionals may view correctional officers as blind to anything but regimentation, control, and punishment. Better mental health training for correctional officers and more collaboration between custodial and mental health staff could overcome such stereotypes and redound to the benefit of the mentally ill offenders under the control and supervision of both.

Mental Health Training for Custodial Staff

Correctional and mental health professionals interviewed by Human Rights Watch agreed on the importance of mental health training for correctional officers. They pointed out that training on the signs of and nature of mental illness will not only enable correctional officers to better respond to problems that emerge with prisoners, but that it will also enable them to better assist mental health staff. "They need more training to give a better idea of how to identify and deal with individuals with mental health issues," Warden Gloria Henry, of California's Valley State Prison for Women told Human Rights Watch. "When you're trained in security, to have people comply with rules and regulations, that's what your expectations are. When you're dealing with people with mental health problems, you need to know how to approach them."[245]

Nevertheless, such training is sorely lacking. In 2001, according to a survey by the National Institute of Corrections, forty states claimed to provide some mental health training to correctional officers, but mostly the training was minimal. Ten prison systems claimed to include roughly four hours of mental health classes in their basic training package for new correctional officers, thirteen admitted to providing fewer than four hours, and only seven stated that they provided more than four hours of training.[246]

In Texas, in connection with litigation about inadequate treatment of mentally ill prisoners, the Texas Department of Criminal Justice (TDCJ) markedly increased mental health training for

---

[243] Kenneth Appelbaum, et. al, *Report on the Psychiatric Management of John Salvi in Massachusetts Department of Correction Facilities 1995-1996*, submitted to the Massachusetts Department of Correction, January 31, 1997, p. 35; on file at Human Rights Watch.

[244] Ibid., p. 39

[245] Human Rights Watch interview with Gloria Henry, warden, Valley State Prison for Women, California, July 17, 2002.

[246] National Institute of Corrections, *Provision of Mental Health Care in Prisons*, 2001, p. 9.

correctional officers. In December 2001, the TDCJ noted that the department was providing, "increased training in the recognition of and the appropriate referral of the psychotic as well as potentially suicidal patient."[247] It also noted:

> A concerted effort was made to provide 20 hours of specialized training for all on-hand correctional staff statewide over the last two years. In addition, the pre-service training curriculum has been revised and incorporates an extensive block of training related to mental health issues. This training has included descriptions of the most common types of psychiatric symptoms, including symptoms associated with psychotic disorders.... The training includes specific reinforcement to the policies and practices governing the placement and monitoring of offenders in segregated status. Correctional staff are instructed to inform the mental health staff of any segregated offender who exhibits symptoms of mental illness. Emphasis is placed on the role that correctional officers can play in identifying offenders who are at risk of deterioration in mental status and managing offenders with mental health needs.[248]

We were not able to ascertain the extent of annual follow-up, or mental health in-service training for correctional officers. The National Institute of Corrections (NIC) report found that a total of forty hours of annual mandated in-service training for correctional officers was the norm.[249] But the report did not provide a breakdown on the content of the in-service training and to what extent it includes mental health components.[250]

A 1999 report commissioned by the California Commission on Correctional Peace Officer Standards and Training reviewed in-service training in a number of states. According to the report, California provides a three-hour course on "unusual inmate behavior." No other state reported a similar course. Ohio and Tennessee each offered a course, lasting two and three hours, respectively, titled "managing manipulative inmate behavior." Arizona, Nebraska, and Nevada provided officers with a course titled "con games." Tennessee offered a three and a half-hour course in "psychological testing." Under courses on health and welfare, only eight states — Arizona, Georgia, Hawaii, Michigan, New Mexico, Ohio, Pennsylvania, and Utah — offered courses specifically on "mental health issues/special needs inmates." While Michigan claimed to offer a rather extensive sixteen hours of training in this area, the others ranged from between one hour and forty-five minutes to six hours.[251] "We have not had a good success rate in training correctional officers. We don't have a formal training program to raise sensitivity," Harbans Deol, medical director for the Iowa Department of Corrections, told Human Rights Watch.[252]

The Colorado Department of Corrections claims that it provides correctional officers with an eight-hour in-service course on mental health issues. Qualifications necessary for teaching this course are,

---

[247] State of Texas, "Intervention Plan for Seriously Mentally-ill Offenders in Administrative Segregation," *Ruiz. v. Johnson*, Civil Action H-78-987, December 15, 2001.

[248] Ibid.

[249] Miki Vohryzek-Bolden, Ph.D., Center for Health and Human Services, California State University, Sacramento, *Overview of Selected States' Academy And In-Service Training for Adult and Juvenile Correctional Employees*, Conducted for the California Commission on Correctional Peace Officer Standards and Training, June 30, 1999, table 14a., p. 83.

[250] National Institute of Corrections, *Provision of Mental Health Care in Prisons*, 2001, p. 9.

[251] Vohryzek-Bolden, *Overview of Selected States*, 1999, table 9a, pp. 53-61.

[252] Human Rights Watch telephone interview with Harbans Deol, medical director, Iowa Department of Corrections, June 14, 2002.

however, limited. "Instructors for this course should be knowledgeable about human behavior and have good communication skill," the October 2001 instructor's guide advised.[253]

Providing adequate training in mental health issues to correctional staff is complicated by the educational level of most correctional officers. According to the National Commission on Correctional Healthcare (NCCHC), most correctional officers lack a university education. "Nationally, the level of a correctional officer's education is high school," Harbans Deol told Human Rights Watch. "That creates a problem: how do you educate these people medically?"[254]

Few states provide formal additional training to guards volunteering to work in mental health units within the prisons. In responses to a National Institute of Corrections survey, only Delaware, the District of Columbia, Louisiana, New Hampshire, New Jersey, New York, Ohio, and Oregon reported that they provided special training to guards on these units.[255] Nevertheless, in some prisons or units that have a special therapeutic mandate of trying to treat and rehabilitate mentally ill offenders, correctional staff do work more closely with mental health staff and receive more training. The Washington Department of Corrections developed a "mobile consultation team" to help the system deal with prisoners who are particularly difficult and disruptive. Team members include not only mental health professionals, but experienced corrections officers. The team works with prison staff who have requested consultation and together they engage in joint problem solving.[256] Professor Hans Toch praises innovative programs that:

> provide officers with noncustodial human-service responsibilities that resemble those of traditional mental health professionals. At the same time, the programs create a collegial relationship among the officers and mental health workers who are attached to the programs. The staff of innovative programs come to function as inclusive interdisciplinary teams.[257]

Toch argues strongly, and in our judgment cogently, for mental health training for correctional officers that goes beyond "a diluted psychology-101-type lecture format." Instead, he believes officers should receive hands-on training that presents officers with real symptoms being experienced by real prisoners in the prisons in which the officers work and that integrates those officers into the mental health teams and case conferences in which prisoners' mental health needs are discussed.[258]

Correctional Officers' Use of Excessive Force

Dangerous situations can and do arise in prisons in which the use of force may become necessary to protect staff, prisoners, or property from injury and to maintain or reestablish control. The type and extent of force used, however, should always be proportionate to the need, and force should never be used as punishment or reprisal against a prisoner. The Eighth Amendment of the U.S. Constitution is violated when force is maliciously and sadistically used against a prisoner to cause

---

[253] Colorado Mental Health Training Course for Law Enforcement and Corrections Officers. Instructor's Guide, prepared by Richard K. Sherman, MS, October 2001, p. iv.

[254] Human Rights Watch telephone interviews with Harbans Deol, June 14, 2002 and April 2, 2003.

[255] National Institute of Corrections, *Provision of Mental Health Care in Prisons*, 2001, p. 9.

[256] Hans Toch and Kenneth Adams, *Acting Out*, 2002, p. 357.

[257] Ibid., p. 407.

[258] Human Rights Watch telephone interview with Hans Toch, February 18, 2003.

harm, rather than in a good faith effort to maintain and restore discipline.[259] In addition, the constitution prohibits officials from using force that is greater, in amount or kind, than what is needed to maintain or restore order, or when force is used without any legitimate penological purpose.

International standards mandate that "officers who have recourse to force must use no more than is strictly necessary."[260] Instruments of restraint, such as four-point restraints (a process in which the prisoner is fastened to his or her bed by the feet and wrists) or strait jackets, should only be used on medical grounds by direction of a medical officer, or by order of the prison director "if other methods of control fail, in order to prevent a prisoner from injuring himself or others or from damaging property; in such instances the directors shall at once consult the medical officer."[261] The American Correctional Association's "use of force" policy calls on correctional authorities to seek to reduce or prevent the necessity of the use of force, to authorize force only when no reasonable alternative is possible, to permit only the minimum force necessary, and to prohibit the use of force as a retaliatory or disciplinary measure. It emphasizes the importance of operating procedures and staff training to "anticipate, stabilize, and diffuse situations that might give rise to conflict, confrontation, and violence"; and the provision of "specialized training to ensure competency in all methods of use of force, especially in methods and equipment requiring special knowledge and skills such as defensive tactics, weapons, restraints and chemical agents…."[262]

There are no national statistics on the use of force by staff against prisoners, nor independent research assessing how well use of force practice in any given state correctional system conforms to appropriate standards. Information about use of force typically becomes public in the context of criminal prosecutions or civil litigation addressing staff abuse of prisoners that resulted in serious injuries. Human Rights Watch was unable to determine whether mentally ill prisoners are more likely to be in situations involving use of force by staff than other prisoners or whether the force used against mentally ill prisoners is more likely to be excessive than in situations involving prisoners who are not mentally ill.

Nevertheless, some correctional experts believe that correctional officers may be too quick to resort to force and to use excessive force particularly when dealing with mentally ill prisoners. Lacking adequate training in mental illness and in conflict de-escalation, often also poorly trained in the use of force in general, their efforts to control mentally ill prisoners have led, in some cases, to prisoner deaths or other serious injuries. In the past five years, Steve Martin, a well known corrections consultant and use of force expert, has investigated over twenty cases of sudden in-custody death and numerous others of serious injuries, the majority of which involved prisoners with mental health histories. Martin describes a pattern of escalating force typical in these cases:

---

[259] *Hudson v. McMillian*, 503 U.S. 1 (1992), at 6-7.

[260] Standard Minimum Rules for the Treatment of Prisoners, adopted Aug. 30, 1955 by the First United Nations Congress on the Prevention of Crime and the Treatment of Offenders, U.N. Doc. A/CONF/611, annex I, E.S.C. res. 663C, 24 U.N. ESCOR Supp. (no. 1) at 11, U.N. Doc. E/3048 (1957), amended E.S.C. res. 2076, 62 U.N. ESCOR Supp. (no. 1) at 35, U.N. Doc. E/5988 (1977), article 54(1).

[261] Standard Minimum Rules, Rule 33.

[262] American Correctional Association's (ACA) public correctional policy on use of force, as published in Craig Hemmens and Eugene Atherton, *Use of Force: Current Practice and Policy* (American Correctional Association, 1999), pp. vi-vii. Specific standards governing the use of force in corrections are contained in the ACA's Standards for Adult Correctional Institutions, and Standards of Adult Local Detention Facilities.

> Once you're into the actual application of force, you have a "death escalation cycle."
> As the inmate is subject to a greater level of force, he develops a greater level of
> anxiety, his resistance escalates accordingly, which in turns requires a greater
> escalation of force.[263]

According to Martin, the strange, often violent, and irrational behavior of agitated mentally ill
prisoners, and their protracted struggling against being restrained, can scare correctional officers into
acting more aggressively than they should during a restraining process. "What is very evident in
these cases is the officers are simply frightened of the detainee. You can see [on the videotapes of
the incidents] they perceive the detainee as an utter immediate threat to their physical well-being.
It's a dynamic created almost from the get-go." In one jail Martin recently investigated, the name of
which he is prevented from revealing by the terms of his contract, he investigated ninety-three cases
of force used against mentally ill prisoners in a twelve-month period. "I'd estimate half of these
could have been avoided altogether if you'd had some health care intervention," Martin stated.

Martin told Human Rights Watch of an event that occurred in the Los Angeles County Jail in 1999.
A man, G.M., with a long history of chronic mental illnesses, who was also wheelchair-bound as a
result of having cerebral palsy, was brought into the jail. He was homeless and hungry; and a jail
official at some point decided to give him a sandwich. Shortly afterwards, another correctional
officer decided to take the sandwich away. The action enraged G.M., who jerked his arm backwards
and struggled to keep a hold on his food. This was seen as him resisting an officer and several other
guards immediately joined the fray, subdued the prisoner (who was still in his wheelchair), and
rushed him off to a room where he could be restrained. "Three-to-five minutes into the event, he
expired," Martin told Human Rights Watch. Not only were no mental health personnel present to
explain to G.M. why his sandwich was being confiscated, no mental health staff were present to
advise the security officials during the restraint itself. Instead of calling in the mental health team,
guards converged on the man's wheelchair and began aggressively restraining him. Martin's
investigation found that G.M. was manhandled out of his wheelchair and placed face up on a bed.
Several correctional officers jumped on top of him to begin attaching the restraints; only after the
restraints were in place and the officers got off of G.M.'s body did they realize that he had stopped
breathing. The subsequent medical examiner's report found that G.M. had suffocated after his
airwaves were restricted by the weight of the guards atop his body. Martin told Human Rights
Watch that G.M.:

> died from a classic case of positional asphyxia. A mental health team could have
> intervened by saying it was inappropriate to place him in four-point restraints. There
> should have been a mental health professional there, on-site, when they were
> bringing him in, in a wheelchair, to where they were going to restrain him. The
> security personnel really had no knowledge of this guy's history. They weren't even
> aware he had cerebral palsy.[264]

Martin reported several other cases of mentally ill prisoners involved in altercations with correctional
officers who restrained them and the prisoners died from positional asphyxiation, which is caused by
an inability to breathe because of being placed in a prone position, with the arms behind the back,
making it impossible for the respiratory muscles to work properly. The inability to breathe is

---

[263] Human Rights Watch telephone interview with Steve Martin, attorney, Austin, Texas, October 1, 2002.
[264] Ibid., April 11, 2003.

aggravated, and a fatal outcome is likely, when the prisoner is overweight or obese and when one or more officers kneel, sit, or stand on him. For example, an overweight prisoner with a history of chronic mental illness, was acting out in his cell, yelling, and carrying on. He reacted violently when a group of officers tried to remove him from his cell. One of the officers then sprayed the prisoner with O.C. pepper gas in his face, which made the prisoner even more agitated. The officers ultimately got him down on his stomach and restrained him. He died of asphyxiation.[265]

- In the case of Larry Frazier, a combination of mental illness, physical illness, and excessive use of force by prison staff proved a lethal cocktail. Frazier, a fifty-year-old diabetic and schizophrenic was moved from Connecticut to Virginia's Wallens Ridge prison as a part of a prison space leasing deal. At Wallens Ridge, Frazier went into diabetic shock, and began convulsing. He struggled with corrections officers and was stunned several times with an Ulton II stun gun, which delivers fifty thousand volts of electricity as correctional officers restrained him to a gurney. Frazier went into a coma and died five days later of heart failure.[266] A doctor brought in to investigate his death concluded the use of the stun gun may have contributed to Frazier's fatal heart attack. The lawyer representing Frazier's estate in a suit against the Virginia Department of Corrections told Human Rights Watch he believes it possible that because of Frazier's mental illness he had an antagonistic relationship with the guards and they therefore were more ready to assume he was disobeying their orders when he did not follow their orders to stop moving.[267]

- In Nevada's Ely prison in November 2002, according to a written statement by prisoners who witnessed the incident, P.T., a mentally ill prisoner on psychotropic medications, was shot in the groin by guards after they ordered him to stop talking with another prisoner and he refused. According to the statement:

> One of the officers grabbed him to restrain him, [P.T.] evaded their attempts and shrugged off their efforts, and was trying to get away from them. One guard tripped over his own feet and fell as [P.T.] was successful in evading them. At this point a warning shot was fired…. After the first shell was fired, the officers again attempted to restrain the inmate. [P.T.] again was able to shrug off their attempts without attacking them, and walked away from the guards as the second round was fired directly at the inmate's groin area making a direct hit. The guards were then able to get him to the ground without further resistance.[268]

The Nevada Department of Corrections (DOC) confirmed that correctional officers shot a prisoner at Ely in November. According to Glen Wharton, the Assistant Director of Operations for the DOC, the officers used bird shot, which he called "pellets." The officers did not shoot directly at the prisoner, but shot at the floor to lessen the impact. The

---

[265] Ibid.

[266] Frazier died on July 4, 2000. Prison officials suspended the use of the stun gun after Frazier's autopsy. Jen McCaffrey, "Doctor: Repeated use of stun gun at prison may have led to death," *The Roanoke Times*, July 26, 2003.

[267] Details on Frazier's case were provided to Human Rights Watch by Connecticut attorney Antonio Poinvert. Human Rights Watch telephone interview with attorney Antonio Poinvert, February 10, 2002.

[268] The affidavit was dated November 23, 2002, and was sent to prisoners' rights activist Mercedes Maharis. Maharis forwarded it to Human Rights Watch on February 25, 2003.

prisoner was hit by the ricochet of the shot and was not seriously injured. According to Wharton, this technique is commonly used at Ely to subdue violent prisoners and causes minimal injury.[269]

- Prisoners in Louisiana have alleged in a lawsuit that guards at the Louisiana State Penitentiary would routinely conduct cell-extractions on seriously mentally ill prisoners. The complaint stated that prisoners would be assaulted "by a number of guards wielding electric shields and batons, that lead to an inmate being jolted with currents of electricity and beaten severely." The guards are also alleged to have used pepper spray and gas spray during these extractions.[270]

A number of mentally ill prisoners have died in recent years after being placed in restraining chairs. Most of the deaths occurred in jails. For example:

- In 1997, Michael Valent, a mentally ill prisoner in Utah, died of blood clots after spending sixteen hours strapped nude in a restraining chair.

- In 1997, a mentally ill man in a jail in Osceola County, Florida, died after being placed in a restraining chair and having his head snapped back so violently that he suffered fatal injuries to his brain stem.

- In a jail in Jacksonville, Florida, in 1999 a twenty-year-old mentally ill man died, reportedly after guards choked him while he was in a restraining chair.[271]

Other Abuses and Inappropriate Responses by Correctional Officers

"Certain correctional officers, if they don't like you they won't do nothing for you. This morning, I got up and got out the door at 8.15. The C.O. [correctional officer] wouldn't let me get my meds. If you don't follow their orders, you lose your job, get a ticket, go to Seg [administrative segregation custody]. A kid the other night was real upset, and talking about committing suicide. The C.O. just didn't care. Finally the kid erupted, started slamming on the door. Then they handcuffed him, put him in Seg. Then they took him to the Intensive Mental Health Unit."
— Y.E., a prisoner at Garner Correctional Institution, Connecticut.[272]

Some correctional officers respond not just with professionalism, but with compassion and sensitivity to mentally ill prisoners. Some do not. Our research uncovered numerous allegations of correctional officers working with the seriously mentally ill who have taunted them, deliberately provoked them, physically mistreated them, used force maliciously against them, turned a blind eye to abuses against them by others or responded with indifference to their needs. For example:

- According to a federal court, evidence presented in the long-running class action litigation against the Texas prison system, "called into question the correctional officers' ability, and

---

[269] Human Rights Watch telephone interview with Glen Wharton, assistant director of operations, Nevada Department of Corrections, June 20, 2003. Human Rights Watch criticized the unnecessary use of firearms by prison officers in "Red Onion State Prison: Super-Maximum Security Confinement in Virginia," *A Human Rights Watch Report*, vol. 11, no. 1(G), May 1999.

[270] *Reickenbacker v. Foster*, Complaint, Civil Action No. 99-910-C-1 (M.D. La., 2002).

[271] Anne-Marie Cusac, "The Devil's Chair," *Progressive Magazine*, April 2000.

[272] Human Rights Watch interview with Y.E., inmate, Garner Correctional Institution, Connecticut, June 10, 2002.

willingness, to recognize psychiatric needs. One inmate, who had a history of self-mutilation, gave unrefuted testimony that a guard provided a razor blade when the inmate threatened to self-mutilate."[273]

- A corrections officer allegedly told a prisoner in the mental health unit at Washington Correctional Center for Women, who had taken a razor to her arm in a failed suicide attempt, "next time do it right," and "arteries in your neck bleed."[274]

- On July 13, 1998, the Washington Department of Corrections fired a correctional officer after its internal investigation established he had her perform oral sex on him on multiple occasions, and threatened to kill her if she told anyone.[275]

- Fred Cohen, who has observed conditions in Alabama prisons in connection with ongoing litigation, told Human Rights Watch that the states' correctional officers commonly regard seriously mentally ill prisoners as malingerers against whom they are quick to use force. He told Human Rights Watch that he encountered seriously mentally ill prisoners:

  > locked up in steel cages that looked like shipping containers. That's where they were locking up discipline cases. What they took to be rebelliousness was a guy who was totally dazed.... I heard from a number of inmates that all kinds of violence was imposed. If they didn't understand a [correctional officer] they might be pulled from a bunk, kicked around, hit with batons.[276]

- A February 2001 class action complaint by mentally ill prisoners at Phillips State Prison in Georgia, alleges a pervasive culture of guard brutality at the prison. Lawyers for the Southern Center for Human Rights, which filed the case for the prisoners, have interviewed over two hundred prisoners. "We discovered they've taken 300 of the most seriously mentally ill men in the system and segregated them into Phillips," Lisa Kung, an attorney at the Southern Center for Human Rights, told Human Rights Watch.

  > They were supposed to be provided with adequate mental health care and treatment. Instead, the place had become this sort of madhouse — of systemic guard brutality. There was no sense of the setting being anything close to a hospital setting. It was much worse than any other prison, because the guards considered the mental illnesses security threats. The level of brutality was above and beyond beating people up. A typical example would be you're unhappy with your medications and can't get a psychiatrist to come down and see you; so you bang on the doors. The guards are pissed off, so they come in, beat you up, write up a ticket and throw you in the hole. This had become a culture of brutality.[277]

---

[273] *Ruiz v. Johnson*, 37 F. Supp. 2d. 855, 904 (S.D. Texas, 1999) (internal citations omitted)

[274] Declaration of [Prisoner name withheld], December 17, 1999, contained in excerpted record submitted with plaintiff's Revised Opening Brief, *Hallet v. Payne*, No. 00-35098 (9th Cir., June 29, 2000).

[275] Washington Department of Corrections letter to [correctional officer's name withheld] contained in excerpted record submitted with plaintiff's Revised Opening Brief, *Hallet v. Payne*, No. 00-35098 (9th Cir., June 29, 2000).

[276] Human Rights Watch telephone interview with Fred Cohen, attorney and monitor, February 17, 2003.

[277] Human Rights Watch telephone interview with Lisa Kung, attorney, Southern Center for Human Rights, June 13, 2002.

The complaint against Phillips lists fifteen incidents which are alleged to typify the abuse at the hands of correctional officers to which mentally ill prisoners at Phillips State Prison are subjected . One of the examples is the following:

> On or about May 31, 2001, Prisoner 2, who is mentally ill, spit on a counselor in the presence of a lieutenant. In response, the counselor and lieutenant both spit on Prisoner 2. The lieutenant then entered the cell, Pushed Prisoner 2 and kicked his feet out from under him, put his knee in prisoner 2's back, grabbed his head and bashed it against the floor. After placing Prisoner 2 in handcuffs and leg shackles, the lieutenant walked Prisoner 2 through the sallyport gate. He then put Prisoner 2 in a headlock and dragged the prisoner in leg shackles on a forced run to the second gate, about 75 feet away. At the infirmary, Prisoner 2 was put in five-point restraints and shot with Haldol.[278]

Jason Freeman, a mentally ill prisoner at Phillips, submitted an affidavit to support plaintiffs' motion for a preliminary injunction in which he testified that in January 2003, after his cellmate set fire to their cell, Freeman:

> pounded on the door and called for help.... It took about ten minutes before the officers would open the cell door. When the officers got to our cell, they placed [both inmates] in handcuffs. There was so much smoke that I was choking. When I was coming out of the cell I slipped because there was water all over the floor [where his roommate] had flooded the cell. When I was on the floor, Officer Santos kicked me in the head until the lieutenant told him to stop. As Officer Santos escorted me down the stairs, I slipped because I was disoriented and couldn't breathe because there was smoke all over the unit. When I tried to stand up, the officer hit me in the face, and I spit at him.[279]

Tamara Serwer, another attorney with the Southern Center for Human Rights working on the case, told Human Rights Watch that after the complaint was filed, a cadre of officers who had been particularly brutal were transferred. A new warden, who has a mental health background, took over at Phillips shortly before the lawsuit began and recognized, according to Serwer, that the culture at the facility needed to be changed.

- An ex-prisoner, U.F., in Philadelphia told Human Rights Watch:

> I've been suffering from mental illness for thirty years. Since I was fourteen. I had a breakdown. A blackout for eighteen months. I just snapped. I was in and out of hospitals. Always on medications. Acute schizophrenic paranoia. Post-traumatic stress. I got raped in Graterford [prison] by five

---

[278] *Fluellen v. Wetherington*, First Amended Complaint, Civil Case No. 1:02-CV-479 (JEC) (N.D. Georgia, March 15, 2002), p.11.
[279] Declaration under Penalty of Perjury of Jason Freeman, *Fluellen v. Wetherington*, Civil Case No. 1:02-CV-479-JEC (N.D. Georgia, February 13, 2003).

guys. I was in the shower. The guards had to have seen it. It's not the best of places. Too many people. The guards ain't no good. They turn their heads on things. If they don't like you, they don't intervene, no matter what happens.[280]

- According to an Indiana prisoner, correctional officers look on and laugh or joke when a fellow prisoner self-mutilates. "The Sergeant came back onto this range at 1.00 p.m. to collect [food] trays," the prisoner wrote.

  > Officer M [name deleted] also came onto the range and I got them to look into W.'s cell and they both saw that W. had stuck the pen into his neck. They continued to pick up trays on this range and then on Six Range. Sergeant E. [name deleted] and the other Sergeant working stood and laughed at [the prisoner] and then exited the range laughing.[281]

  Four years earlier, a different prisoner asserted how yet another prisoner, "has been beaten repeatedly by the guards here. The man obviously has some psychological problems because he defecates and rubs the feces all over his body. The guards think it is funny and continue to harass him daily."[282]

- In Pelican Bay State Prison, a supermax prison found by a federal court to have violated the Eighth Amendment rights of its prisoners, prisoner-guard dynamics were so poisoned in the 1990s that officers routinely resorted to violence (e.g., beatings and unnecessary as well as excessively violent cell extractions) against prisoners, including many who were mentally ill.[283] In one incident, correctional officers dragged a seriously decompensating African-American prisoner, Vaughn Dortch, who had covered his body in feces, to a tub full of scalding water, dumped him into the water, and, while screaming racial epithets, promised to scrub him down until his skin turned white. The water was so hot that the skin was literally burnt off Dortch's legs.[284]

- A California prisoner, on medication for his mental illness, recently told Human Rights Watch that correctional officers in some of the prisons he has been in:

  > are not equipped to deal with people with psychiatric problems. They misinterpret when a person is sick compared to what a person is being an idiot. Sometimes I get sick and they don't understand what is going on. They think you're playing with them. Since you're in general population they'll try and provoke you. Because if they think you're sane, they'll think

---

[280] Human Rights Watch interview with D.S., ex-prisoner, Gaudenzia House, Philadelphia, Pennsylvania, August 13, 2002.

[281] The prisoner's letter was sent to the Alliance for the Mentally Ill, June 21, 1999. It was then forwarded to Human Rights Watch.

[282] Written statement by James Wilson, April 2, 1995 (copy on file at Human Rights Watch).

[283] The evidence of excessive and malicious use of force at Pelican Bay lead to a court ruling that it violated the Eighth Amendment. *Madrid v. Gomez*, 889 F. Supp. 1146 (N.D. California, 1995).

[284] This incident was one of many examples of extreme violence perpetrated by Pelican Bay correctional officers that Judge Henderson detailed in his January 1995 opinion in the *Madrid v. Gomez* case. *Madrid v. Gomez*, 889 F. Supp. 1146 (N.D. California, 1995.) The water temperature for Dortch's bath was estimated at 125 degrees Fahrenheit.

you're just being an asshole. Then they'll really provoke you, put you up against a wall, put you down, grab your scrotum real hard. If you do anything, they'll mace you.[285]

- A prisoner told Dr. Dennis Koson, who was evaluating New Jersey prison conditions for plaintiffs in *C.F. v. Terhune*,[286] that he:

    saw correctional officers taunt John Doe #81 by breaking his cigarettes after promising him a light. This made John Doe #81 angry. Several hours later, John Doe #81 hung himself.... John Doe #124 also said correction officers might skip mentally ill inmates' meals out of spite.[287]

- "Nothing short of some major cultural change is going to alter the situation," Janet Schaeffer, one-time Director of Mental Health Services for the Washington Correctional Center for Women, at Purdy, subsequently Director of Outpatient Mental Health Services, and currently employed at Berk County Jail, Pennsylvania, told Human Rights Watch. "The culture views prisons as places to shut people away and to punish them."[288] As a result, Schaeffer has come to believe, the correctional officers often seemed to act as if they had carte blanche to torment their prisoners. "Mentally ill people, generally, are pretty fragile individuals. They're more vulnerable," Schaeffer asserted.

    If [an inmate walks from her] living unit to the dining room by the same route every day and then all of a sudden they say "you can't walk within ten feet of a building, and you're near a building so we're going to give you an infraction" it fucks with your soul. It really, really does. It's crazy-making. It messes with you. Sometimes it was very painful to see women treated that way. My staff would come to me outraged by this.

---

[285] Human Rights Watch interview with D.F., Corcoran, California, July 11, 2002.
[286] *New Jersey Prison System Report of Dr. Dennis Koson*, *C.F. v. Terhune*, Civil Action No. 96-1840 (D.N.J., September 8, 1998), p. 38.
[287] Ibid.
[288] Human Rights Watch telephone interview with Janet Schaeffer, psychologist and former director of mental health services, Washington Correctional Center for Women, May 29, 2002.

TIMOTHY PERRY, CONNECTICUT

On April 12, 1999, a twenty-one-year-old schizophrenic man named Timothy Perry was found dead in an observation cell hours after he had been placed in four-point restraints. At the time, Perry, who also suffered from schizoaffective disorder, impulse control disorder, borderline personality disorder, major depression, and oppositional defiant disorder, and who was estimated to have an intelligence quotient (IQ) of seventy-six, was in restraints, strapped to a bed in a cell in the mental health unit of Connecticut's Hartford Correctional Center.[289]

Perry had suffered from mental illness for many years, had been treated in several Connecticut state facilities, and in the months preceding his death had been a resident of Cedarcrest Regional Hospital. At the end of March, following violent actions against staff at the hospital, and after the state's forensic mental health facility at Whiting had refused to admit him, Cedarcrest called in the police to arrest Perry. Following his arrest, he was sent to the correctional center, a local detention facility under the control of the Department of Correction. In prison, Perry continued to act bizarrely and aggressively. On the evening of April 12, correctional officers decided to put him in restraints.

Perry was carried by several officers to a holding cell. They placed him face down on a mattress, attached leg irons, and held a towel over his mouth and face. Over the telephone, a department of corrections psychiatrist ordered that Perry be sedated and restrained. As a result of this phone call, the staff picked Perry up again and carried him to a cell equipped with four point restraints. After he was restrained, they injected his body with powerful sedatives.

According to a forensic doctor's review of the evidence about the events leading to Perry's death, the placement of Perry:

> face down in a prone position with his hands restrained behind his back and his legs restrained, and with a towel held over his mouth, placed [him] at a significant risk of death. It is further my opinion that these actions were more likely than not indeed the cause of his death. Such a position inhibits chest wall motion and compromises breathing.[290]

According to the Complaint for Damages filed by Perry's family after his death:

> The Defendants' use of excessive force against Timothy rendered Timothy unconscious, comatose, dying or dead at or near the time that he was in cell 10 [the

---

[289] R. *Bartley Halloran Administrator of the Estate of Timothy Perry v. Armstrong et al.*, Complaint for Damages, 3: 01 CV 582 (AVC) (Hartford Federal Court, April 11, 2001), p. 14. Information on the Perry case was also gained from internal Connecticut Department of Correction memos and letters, forensic reports, investigations into Perry's death carried out by the Office of Protection and Advocacy for Persons with Disabilities, and the videotape filmed by Hartford Correctional Center correctional officers in the run-up to, and discovery of, inmate Perry's death.

[290] See Letter from Barbara C. Wolf, M.D. to Susan Werboff, Director, Connecticut Office of Protection and Advocacy for Persons with Disabilities, October 23, 2000. Dr. Wolf provided Ms. Werboff with an analysis of the events leading to and causes of Mr. Perry's death based on her review of the autopsy, police investigative reports and other records.

first cell] and after the time that the Defendants moved him to cell 24 [the cell equipped with the restraints].[291]

In cell 24, where the officers' actions were videotaped, officers continued to restrain the now-naked Perry and to use pain compliance techniques against him. They even accused him of continuing to resist, despite the fact that, as established by subsequent investigations, he was either already dead at this stage, or, at the very least, comatose. The autopsy report indicated the injected sedatives pooled near the point of injection, suggesting his blood circulation had all-but-ceased by the time they were administered.[292] Turning the unresponsive Perry onto his back, tied down by his wrists and ankles, the officers left the cell.

Two hours later, a nurse looked through the windows of the cell and noticed that Perry's feet had become discolored and that he was completely still. When she had the cell door opened, the nurse found that Perry had no pulse, that his body was cold and that he had been dead for some time.

Perry's death received wide publicity. The circumstances of the case were so egregious and the correctional officers' and medical staffs' flouting of prison policies so pronounced that the state was compelled to settle the lawsuit. Perry's guards had failed to follow protocols on how to restrain a prisoner safely; they had applied too much weight to his prone body; they had blocked his air passages; they had failed to notify the treating psychiatrist that he was being restrained; they had failed to follow a strict fifteen minute observation routine for Perry; they had failed to check his vital signs; and the nurse who injected him with medications had somehow injected Thorazine into his body, despite the fact that his charts indicated he was allergic to the drug. Once it was clear that he was not breathing, they had also failed to immediately call in medical assistance. In the largest wrongful death settlement ever paid out by the State of Connecticut in the death of a single man without children, Perry's estate was awarded $2.9 million.[293]

---

[291] R. Bartley Halloran Administrator of the Estate of Timothy Perry vs. Armstrong et al., Complaint for Damages, 3: 01 CV 582 (AVC) (Hartford Federal Court, April 11, 2001), p. 14.

[292] According to the lawyer for Perry's family, Antonio Poinvert, the prison videotape of Perry's last moments clearly shows correctional officers saying Perry was still resisting them even though Perry's naked body was motionless and unresponsive, and he had no reflexes even after officers push his feet back hard against his Achilles tendons. Human Rights Watch interview with Antonio Poinvert, attorney, Greenwich, Connecticut, May 10, 2002.

[293] Information provided by the Perry estate's attorney, Antonio Poinvert. Human Rights Watch interview with Antonio Poinvert, attorney, Greenwich, Connecticut, May 10, 2002.

Y.D., CALIFORNIA

Y.D. is a twenty-six-year-old African-American woman currently living in Los Angeles.[294] When she was a child, her mother and her mother's boyfriends beat and sexually abused her. She told Human Rights Watch that her mother later abandoned her and her brother, and that county social services found them living in a chicken coop. She has been in and out of psychiatric institutions since she was nine years old and is a methamphetamine addict. Since 1996, Y.D. has been in and out of prison almost continually. Most recently, she was released from prison in March 2002, after serving time for a parole violation. She currently lives in a private re-entry home run by an ex-prisoner in the Watts area of Los Angeles, California. On her forehead is a large, jagged scar, the product of a suicide attempt while behind bars. She has been diagnosed with several bi-polar disorders and schizophrenia.

> I lived in Napa State Hospital from aged 9 to 13. I don't know why. They had me on all kinds of medications. They used to strap me to the bed and give me shots in the ass. I lived on the streets after I got out till I went to prison for assault and battery in 1996 [she attacked another homeless woman and seriously injured her.] I have violent outbursts. I'm taking soroquil, prozac, and nuratin.

Because of her violent outbursts and her sometimes-bizarre behavior, she has regularly found herself at odds with those assigned to guard her.

> The first time in prison, [at Valley State Women's Prison] a Correctional Officer and a Sergeant made me stand on the wall by the cafeteria on tiptoes for a long time. The whole time, they talked shit to me, told me I was a crack head, would amount to nothing. They were trying to get me to hit them, so they could lock me up. They made me stand for hours. When the shift ended, another officer came and I had to keep standing there.

> [Another time] A C.O. [correctional officer] named [name withheld from publication] would mess with me. He wouldn't let me out of my room. When they'd pop the doors, he wouldn't pop mine. He put me on lockdown. Every time I came out of the room, I'd get in trouble. He'd make me feel bad, tell me I was stupid, that I can't do nothing right. He said I was crazy. I was being super-impulsive and couldn't do simple, basic things.

In 1999, Y.D. was sentenced to three more months in prison, on a parole violation. She got written up so many times for disruptive behavior that she ended up serving nearly a year. During this time, the psychologist who was counseling her began intervening with the correctional officers to try to stop them picking on her. In 2002, while in jail on another charge, she jumped through a window and slashed open her head.

---

[294] Human Rights Watch interviews with Y.D. and several other seriously mentally ill ex-inmates, Sober Living Facility, Los Angeles, California, May 17, 2002. Y.D.'s testimony was largely corroborated by her caseworkers.

> I was freaking out. I do stupid shit sometimes. I don't take my medication when I'm just out there, I don't go to the doctor, so I have bad days. I cried for almost a month straight. I freaked out. The county jails wouldn't accept me because I had to get 60 stitches and was freaking out. They took me to prison and put me in the suicide room. They left me there for 60 days. The floor was super-dirty. I didn't want to lie on it because I didn't want to get my head infected. But it got infected anyway. My stitches got infected. I had to take antibiotics. They wouldn't let me take a shower for six days. They were messing with me. They'd come by and kick the door. I freaked out and started banging my head against the door. I opened my stitches again. They took me to the hospital.

After returning from the hospital, she was placed in the mental health crisis unit at Chowchilla prison. There, she recalls, she was treated well, and, for the first time in her prison experience, she felt comfortable. The mental health crisis beds, however, are mainly designed to stabilize prisoners and then return them to the general population. And so, Y.D. was returned to Valley State, part of the unfortunately common cycle of mentally ill prisoners within prisons between crisis units and the general population.

> I still had my stitches in. The C.O.s don't treat you good. They just harass you. I'm super-impulsive. One time we were walking in line to a meal. I stepped out of line — not on purpose. The C.O. started screaming at me, and pulled me out of line and made me walk with him step by step. I couldn't do it. I started crying. When I took a step that wasn't with him, he'd stop walking and make me start over again. Then another C.O. made him stop and said I could go back to the unit.

MARK EDWARD WALKER, MONTANA

Mark Edward Walker, a Montana resident, was charged in 1994 with felony forgery, arson, and criminal mischief; sentenced to probation; violated the terms of his probation and then absconded to Colorado during his probation revocation proceedings. In 1997, he was arrested in Colorado on a criminal charge, and was confined for eleven months in the Colorado prison system in 1998 and then extradited to Montana, where he was ultimately confined in the Montana State Prison (MSP) in February, 1999. While incarcerated in Colorado, he was diagnosed with hebephrenic schizophrenic disorder, a diagnosis that was later changed to bipolar disorder, for which he was prescribed lithium. While on lithium, he did not receive any major disciplinary write-ups.[295]

On February 5, 1999, on his intake at Montana State prison, Walker indicated that he had been diagnosed as bipolar and had been taking lithium. On February 10, he notified the staff psychiatrist that he was experiencing stomach pains from the lithium, and shortly thereafter stopped taking his medication. The staff psychiatrist did not evaluate Walker until March 11, 1999. That evaluation lasted thirty minutes. The psychiatrist "discontinued prescribing Lithium for Walker without reviewing Walker's medical records and without completing any psychological testing. He concluded that Walker did not have a serious mental illness, but rather an antisocial personality with narcissistic traits."

Over the next year, Walker became increasingly disruptive; whereas he averaged only two severe disciplinary infractions a month in his first six months at MSP, in the next six months he averaged eleven. In August, 1999, he was transferred into the maximum security unit after he broke a showerhead and claimed to have swallowed it. According to correctional officer, he went from being a timid quiet prisoner into an "excited, belligerent, hostile, disruptive and suicidal inmate." He yelled and screamed for hours on end, spit on officers, covered his cell with ketchup mustard and mayonnaise, refused to comply with direct orders from officers. He also made three suicide attempts on October 8, Walker tried to hang himself with a sheet. Four days later, he tried to hang himself with his prison overalls.

Rather than receiving psychiatric or psychological treatment, Walker's behavior was treated as purely a disciplinary matter. He received more than one hundred disciplinary write-ups and was placed in disciplinary detention, or "lock down" for six months. While in lock down, he was also placed on the A-block for five separate "behavioral management plans"(BMPs). According to Walker and numerous other prisoners, the A-Block cells were filthy, with blood, feces, vomit, and other debris in them. One prisoner testified he had bloodied a cell by smashing his head against the wall. Walker inhabited that cell for a while. After Walker was removed, and the original prisoner returned, the blood streaks and the words he had written in blood on the wall remained unchanged.

BMPs consisted of withholding all "privileges from an inmate, and then returning them based on conduct." They are not designed to be therapeutic, but are a tool to help manage dangerous behavior. Prisoners on BMPs are housed in a detention unit designed for disciplinary punishment; the cells are windowless, sparsely furnished and prisoners are allowed no time in the recreation yard. While on BMP, Walker was kept twenty-four hours a day in the cell. He was stripped of all his

---

[295] All of the facts in this case study come from *Walker v. Montana*, 2003 MT 134 (Supreme Court of Montana, April 29, 2003).

clothing, spending his days and nights naked. He was not permitted to have bedding or a pillow, but had to simply sleep on the concrete slab that served as a bed. The water to his sink and toilet were turned off (with guards turning it on at regular intervals). He was given a "space" or "suicide" blanket. He was not given hot meals, only slices of meat and cheese served with bread. Through "good behavior" Walker would then "earn" back pieces of clothing, a mattress, hot meals, etc. Although BMPs are supposed to last twenty-four to forty-eight hours, Walker's first BMP lasted five days; his second BMP lasted eleven; his third six days (ending because he had a court date); his fourth lasted two weeks; and his fifth nearly three weeks, ending on March 1, 2000. MSP officials acknowledged that Walker did not respond well to the BMPs; indeed, his behavior grew progressively worse. While on a BMP in January 2000, Walker filed a pro se petition with the court asserting violations of the state constitution. He had to dictate it to a neighboring prisoner, because he did not have any paper or writing implements.

Throughout the year, the mental health staff at MSP continued to claim that Walker was not bipolar, although they recognized he was at chronic risk for self-harm. They also believed he was manipulating, in order to be reassigned to a less restrictive setting. At the request of Walker's court-appointed attorney, a private psychiatrist specializing in forensic and correctional psychiatry, Dr. William Stratford, evaluated Walker in February 2000 and administered several mental evaluation tests, reviewed all of Walker's medical records and interviewed Walker's family. Basic on his evaluation, Stratford concluded that Walker suffered from bipolar disorder as well as a mixed personality disorder which severely hampers his social and occupational functioning. He further concluded that Walker had been properly treated his mental illness while imprisoned in Colorado, but that he was neglected while at MSP.

According to Dr. Stratford, MSP's treatment of Walker had fallen so far below the standard of care that it was negligent and scandalous. He said MSP officials were too eager to label Walker as a bad person rather than seriously mentally ill. Because he was not treated, but merely disciplined, Walker "got worse and worse." Dr. Terry Kupers also reviewed Walker's records and interviewed him. Dr. Kupers concluded it was "absolutely clear" that Walker suffered from a serious mental illness, most likely bipolar disorder, and he testified it was "inexcusable" that Walker was not on medications, particularly since they were effective in the past. Indeed, he testified that the diagnosis by MSP mental health staff that Walker did not have a mental illness was "preposterous" and fell below medical ethical standards.

A Montana state district court denied Walker's claim that he was the victim of cruel and unusual punishment in violation of the Montana constitution while incarcerated at MSP. The Supreme Court of Montana reversed this finding. On April 23, 2003, the court held that Walker's treatment constituted an affront to the inviolable state constitutional right of human dignity possessed by the prisoner; it also concluded that the BMPs and living conditions on the A-block, to the extent they exacerbated his conditions, constituted unconstitutional cruel and unusual punishment.

M.C., New Jersey, August 1, 2002

My mental illness is said to be bipolar disorder. My medications are depicote and elavil. As for a general history in prison, I can generally say that "I have seen it all." Everything from receiving what I think is the best medical care to covering myself with pheasis with the hope that corrections officers would be discusted to beat me simply because I am a special needs inmate. Being a special needs inmate is ok from the hrs of 8.00 am till 5.00 pm as long as there are doctors on the wing then police (DOC) will treat special needs inmates with respect. However any time doctors are not on the wing then the DOC begins to treat all special needs inmates less than human at the least. After the doctors leave this prison the DOC has a cornival-type attitude towards special needs inmates by making fun of them even until an inmates becomes upset and untamed. Maybe even to the point that the DOC officer will write the inmate a charge even though the officer excited the problem to begin with.

U.L., Nevada, June 3, 2002

From July 2001 until December 2001 I attempted to see a psychiatrist and a medical doctor. They refused to see me for months. I had to file 2 grievances and over 7 requests just to see them. The medical unit here in Nevada is a sub-contractor, very inefficient, only concerned about the quick fix and charge you $4.00 per visit plus $2.00 for prescriptions. On the street I had tried several medications. The only one that helped was Xanax or Valium. Zoloft and Prozac made me crazy and even more anxious, that I had to stop taking them after 30 days. So what do they give me here? Zoloft. I almost lost it and had to go see the psyc Dr. on an emergency situation because I hadn't slept in almost a week. If I'm let out of doors regularly I'm fair for a while. Right now I've been in lock down for 120 days for the offense of spilling milk at breakfast and the officers beat me up and gave me a year in the hole. To be specific, the access to mental health professional is terrible at best and needs to be looked into badly. I put in a kite to the psych Dr. 4 weeks ago and I've yet to see the Dr. I've been refused my medication and my special diet (I'm lactose intolerant) since being in the hole on March 19th.... There is *no* respect for anyone healthy or mentally handicapped, trust me.

IX.   INADEQUATE MENTAL HEALTH TREATMENT IN PRISONS

The goal of mental health services in prison, as in the community, should be to facilitate recovery and to build the resilience and coping skills needed to improve independence and quality of life. Unfortunately, prison mental health services are focused primarily on managing mental health crises and managing symptoms. Strapped for funding and operating within a public climate that emphasizes the punitive purpose of prisons, correctional agencies have not taken advantage of the opportunity they have to make significant long-term differences in the lives of their mentally ill prisoners. Many prisons, indeed, do not even provide adequate basic mental health treatment.

Over the past decade, organizations such as the National Commission on Correctional Health Care (NCCHC), individual correctional mental health experts, court decisions, and settlement agreements have produced detailed guidelines on the necessary components of mental health care inside prisons. Prisons must have procedures for screening and identifying mentally ill prisoners; a range of mental health treatment services, including appropriate medication and other therapeutic interventions; a sufficient number of mental health professionals to provide adequate services to all prisoners suffering from serious mental disorders; adequate and confidential clinical records; protocols for identifying and treating suicidal prisoners; procedures to ensure timely access by prisoners to necessary mental health services; and different levels of care, from emergency psychiatric services and acute inpatient wards, to intermediate levels of care, to "outpatient" services.

Our research suggests, however, that no prison system provides all of these components. While many have carefully developed protocols and policies, implementation often lags far behind and appropriate services are not available for all the prisoners who need them. As the court reviewing the constitutionality of psychiatric care in Texas prisons noted, in a conclusion that is applicable to many prison systems, the Texas prison system's "carefully developed policies and procedures notwithstanding, it is determined that the plaintiffs' experts' assessment of poor implementation of those policies and procedures is both substantially credible and a matter of extreme concern. Simply stated, large numbers of inmates throughout the TDCJ [Texas Department of Criminal Justice] system are not receiving adequate health care."[296]

Other than litigation, mechanisms for ensuring adequate mental health services are scant. According to Judy Stanley, director of accreditation for the NCCHC, only 231 of the nation's approximately 1,400 prisons have received NCCHC accreditation, meaning that they adhere to NCCHC guidelines and submit themselves to monitoring by the organization. The NCCHC does not monitor the actual quality of the care provided to prisoners. Most state correctional systems do not have procedures for independent review of the quality of the mental health services they provide. Our research also suggests that even internal quality control mechanisms are typically ineffective.

In this chapter, we look at a few specific mental health service problems that are particularly salient across the country and which suggest the magnitude of the problem confronting corrections.

---

[296] *Ruiz v. Johnson*, 37 F. Supp.2d 855, at 906 (S.D. Texas, 1999).

Understaffing

Effective mental health services are staff intensive. A range of mental health professionals are needed — including psychiatrists, psychologists, counselors, nurses, recreational/occupational therapists — if individuals with serious mental illness are to receive the individualized mental health interventions required to address their psychiatric needs. All of the correctional officials and mental health experts Human Rights Watch interviewed while researching this report stated that the single most important requirement for good mental health services is adequate staffing levels. At the same time, almost every one of them also asserted that understaffing is the most critical problem facing prison mental health systems.

As of January 2001, according to the 2001 Correctional Yearbook, forty-nine correctional agencies reported having a total of 17,640 mental health and counseling staff.[297] Of these, 18.4 percent are psychiatrists or psychologists. Counselors, who typically need no mental health degree or training and "others" accounted for 58.6 percent of the total.

There are no hard and fast rules for how many mental health professionals, and of what kind, are needed for each prison — or within a prison system. "The fundamental policy goal should be to provide the same level of mental health services to each patient in the criminal justice process that should be available in the community," stated a 2000 report by the American Psychiatric Association.[298] In this report, the authors wrote that in prisons the caseload of each full-time psychiatrist or equivalent should be no more than 150 patients on psychotropic medication.[299] Experts recently hired by the state of Washington to generate long-term mental health proposals for the prison system, advocated ratios of one psychiatrist for every two hundred offenders with outpatient mental health needs; one supervising psychologist per institution; one mental health professional for every seventy-five seriously mentally ill prisoners, and one mental health nurse per one hundred patients.[300] Caseloads in this range, the experts believed, would allow mental health specialists adequate time with each patient to properly diagnose them and develop individualized treatment plans. Experts we consulted indicated that few correctional institutions nationwide meet these staffing levels.

Iowa, for example, has a prison population of over eight thousand, of whom, 1,800 to two thousand are mentally ill.[301] The entire Department of Corrections has only thirty psychologists, most of whom, according to medical director Harbans Deol, have only a bachelor's degree. In addition, there are three psychiatrists for the entire prison population. To meet appropriate staffing ratios, Deol said the prison system would have to hire eight more psychiatrists. But, he continued, "we don't have the money for it. And it's very hard to attract psychiatrists to the Department of Corrections."

---

[297] Camille G. Camp and George M. Camp, *Corrections Yearbook 2001: Adult Systems*, "Snapshot: Mental Health and Counseling Staff on January 1, 2001" (Connecticut: Criminal Justice Institute, 2002), p. 177.

[298] American Psychiatric Association, *Psychiatric Services in Jails and Prisons*, 2nd Ed. (Washington D.C., American Psychiatric Association, 2000), p. 6. The APA points out that this goal "is deliberately higher than the 'community standard' that is called for in various legal contexts."

[299] Ibid., pp. 7-8.

[300] *State of Washington Department of Corrections Final Report Health Care Facility Master Plan*, DLR Group in association with Pulitzer/Bogard & Associates, L.L.C., 2000.

[301] Human Rights Watch telephone interview with Harbans Deol, medical director, Iowa Department of Corrections, June 14, 2002.

The mental health director for Arkansas's Department of Corrections, which has almost fourteen thousand prisoners, informed Human Rights Watch that the department employed four full-time psychiatrists.[302] Unlike most states, which have found that somewhere in the region of 8 to 15 percent of their prisoner population suffers from a serious mental illness, Arkansas estimates that only 4.7 percent of its prisoners are on psychotropic medications and on the mental health caseload. This would suggest an acceptable psychiatrist/patient ratio of one to 164. However, it is likely that the startlingly low number of mentally ill on the mental health caseload is more a product of under-diagnosis than it is a genuine reflection of the mental health status of Arkansas's prisoners. Assuming that Arkansas prisoners in fact are as statistically prone to mental illness as the rest of the country's prison population, it is likely that the four psychiatrists are actually working in a system housing closer to 1,500 mentally ill prisoners.

The Department of Justice, which conducted an investigation in 1998 of conditions at Wyoming State Penitentiary pursuant to the Civil Rights of Institutionalized Persons Act, found that the prison had a psychiatrist on the premises only two days per month. "The psychiatrist sees approximately 25 inmates per month, but cannot keep up with the number of new mental health referrals," they wrote. In one three-month period, ninety-five new cases were referred to the mental health team, but:

> WSP [Wyoming State Penitentiary] administered only six psychiatric diagnostic evaluations during this time period. Due to inadequate staffing, if seen at all, most inmates in need of crisis psychiatric intervention were seen by an infirmary physician rather than by a trained mental health care provider.[303]

A New York State Office of Mental Health Taskforce report in 1997 on prison mental health services found that:

> Outpatient staffing has remained relatively constant at approximately 215 in the last four years, while the demands, in terms of evaluations, admissions, treatment, commitments, discharges, and linkages has risen. Similarly, satellite outpatient mental health resources have not kept pace with the changes in and volume of the correctional population.... New York has lower per capita inpatient beds than all other states of comparable or smaller DOC population with the exception of New Jersey.... New York has clearly not kept pace, per capita, with the rise in this state's prison population and has not had resources increased, in some cases, in many years.[304]

Inadequate mental health staffing occurs because prison systems are funded for too few positions and the funding has not increased to keep pace with the burgeoning prison population. In addition, prison administrators have a difficult time filling mental health positions because the pay offered prison staff is often too low, the work environment is often unpleasant, prisons are frequently situated in out-of-the-way places, and working in corrections has historically been seen as "low

---

302 Questionnaire was answered by Arkansas Department of Corrections' mental health director Max Mobley.
303 Letter to Wyoming Governor James Geringer from Bill Lann Lee, acting assistant attorney general, Civil Rights Division, U.S. Department of Justice, June 29, 1999.
304 New York State Office of Mental Health, Task Force on the Future of Forensic Services, *Report of the Subcommittee on Prison Mental Health Services*, pp. 9-11, January 31, 1997.

status." In Florida, the Correctional Medical Authority (CMA), the oversight body responsible for ensuring the delivery of medical and mental health care in Florida prisons, discussed in 2001 the proposition that mental health staffing ratios should "reflect available resources." According to the minutes of the CMA meeting:

> Discussion ensued about the appropriateness of that approach with several members expressing the belief that the plan should contain two sets of ratios: one based on what is clinically appropriate and one based on available resources. [305]

One doctor present pointed out "that with caseloads [for psychologists] of 60-to-80, psychotherapy will not occur to the extent necessary."[306]

The director of mental health for the Maine Department of Corrections complained that it was hard to keep psychiatrists working for the department, and told Human Rights Watch that psychologists were paid up to $20,000 a year less in prison than in community settings.[307] In Virginia, a starting salary for a psychologist working within the correctional system is only $31,935.[308] This is lower than the starting salary for psychologists offered by the Northern Virginia Training Center residential facility six years ago. In 1997, starting salaries for psychologists there ranged from $34,943 to $54,500.[309] It is also significantly lower than the starting salary offered school psychologists — in August 2003, York County advertised a position for a school psychologist paying $35,186.[310]

Understaffing also reflects high rates of turnover in mental health staff — itself caused by the pay and quality of work considerations noted above and the consequent difficulty of recruiting replacements. The turnover of mental health staff adversely affects mental health services: new staff are not as familiar with prisoners mental health histories and behavior, and staff changes disrupts the development of the prisoner confidence and trust which is crucial to effective therapeutic relationships.

Randall Berg, an attorney representing seriously mentally ill prisoners in Florida's highest security prisons, told Human Rights Watch that he believed as many as one quarter of mental health positions in these prisons were vacant. "There's a significant staff turnover," he stated. "So there's no continuity of care."[311] At the Washington Correctional Center for Women (WCCW), "since 1996, there have been six different mental health supervisors, and a slew of other key mental health staff have quit — many in frustrated desperation."[312]

---

[305] Minutes from Florida Correctional Medical Authority Mental Health Committee Meeting, March 23, 2001.
[306] Ibid.
[307] Human Rights Watch telephone interview, Joe Fitzpatrick, clinical director, Maine Department of Corrections, March 28, 2003.
[308] Job Announcement advertised by the Virginia Department of Corrections Human Resources division.
[309] Job listing posted on http://www.geocrawler.com. Available online at: www.geocrawler.com/archives/3/1131/1997/6/100/3123487/, accessed on September 15, 2003.
[310] York County School Division, Human Resources Department, Yorktown, Virginia. August 2003.
[311] Human Rights Watch telephone interview with Randall Berg, attorney, Miami, Florida, April 21, 2003.
[312] Tara Herivel, "Wreaking Medical Mayhem in Washington's Prisons," *Prison Legal News*, September, 1999. Herivel's source for this was a deposition by Alice Payne, warden, Washington Correctional Center for Women, in the context of the lawsuit, *Hallet v. Payne.*

Following a court ruling that California's deficient mental health services violated the Eight Amendment,[313] the state's budget for mental health services has grown considerably. Indeed, just between 2001 and 2003, the budget has increased 20 percent, even though the prison population has been relatively stable.[314] The state's per capita expenditures for mental health services are reputed to be among the largest in the country.[315] Yet, even in California, mental health services at many prisons are understaffed. At the California Medical Facility, California, prison psychiatrist Radu Mischiu told Human Rights Watch that "turnover is huge," and asserted that the average stay for mental health staff in the prison was a mere six months.[316] In December 1998, the Office of the Special Master appointed under *Coleman* reported that while the prison was funded for 8.5 full time psychiatrists, because of staffing turnover the prison only had 5.5 of the positions filled.[317] In April 2002, the Special Master reported that positions for two psychiatrists, five psychologists, a half-time psych tech, and an office assistant were vacant at Pelican Bay. At Pleasant Valley State Prison, the chief psychiatrist's position had been vacant almost a year. At Wasco State Prison, six psychologist positions were unfilled. And at Avenal, the one full-time psychiatrist was found to only be working thirty-six hours per month.[318] In October 2000, the Special Master appointed by the Court in the wake of the *Madrid* case wrote about the Psychiatric Services Unit (PSU) at Pelican Bay State that "the PSU has suffered chronic staffing shortages, including psychiatrist shortages and a long-term problem with inadequate numbers of psychiatric technicians. The direct result of this shortage is the PSU's failure to provide adequate out of cell structured therapy."[319]

Low staffing levels combined with the high rates of turnover have contributed to the mental health crisis behind bars in many states. For example, in Maine, external auditors monitoring mental and medical health services noted that between 2000 and 2001 all three of the state's prisons had experienced:

> notable slippage in the quality of care delivered…. Factors contributing: turnover of key health administrators, vacancies in PA [Physicians Assistants] and Psychiatrist positions, time on move to new facility takes away from day to day administration, emphasis on cost containment by medical director.[320]

---

[313] *Coleman v. Wilson*, 912 F. Supp. 1282 (E.D. California, 1995).

[314] The California Department of Corrections mental health services budget has grown from $204,725,000 in 2001 to $245,598,000 in 2003. Human Rights Watch telephone interview with Terry Thornton, spokesperson for the California Department of Corrections, June 16, 2003. California's prison population was 163,001 in 2000, and declined slightly to 162,317 in 2002. BJS, *Prisoners in 2002*, p. 3; and Allen J. Beck, Ph.D. and Paige M. Harrison, *Prisoners in 2000* (Washington D.C.: Department of Justice, Bureau of Justice Statistics, August 2001), p. 3.

[315] See table 2 above, Fiscal Year 2003-2004 Mental Health Care Budgets in State Departments of Corrections (DOC). For fiscal year 2003-2004, $245,598,000 is budgeted .Human Rights Watch telephone interview with Terry Thornton, June 16, 2003.

[316] Human Rights Watch interview with Radu Mischiu, MD, psychiatrist, Administrative Segregation EOP, California Medical Facility, California, July 19, 2002.

[317] Dr. Jeffrey Metzner, Memorandum, to Special Master J. Michael Keating, Office of the Special Master, December 11, 1998.

[318] J. Michael Keating, Ninth Monitoring Report of the Special Master on the Defendants' Compliance with Provisionally Approved Plans, Policies and Protocols, *Coleman v. Davis*, No. CIV S-90-0520 LKK JFM P, April 24, 2002.

[319] *Special Master's Report Re Status of PSU and EOP Compliance with Health Services Remedial Plan*, p. 5. Filed October 17, 2000.

[320] The quote is taken from a summary of the audits published in the *Report on the Current Status of Services for Persons with Mental Illness in Maine's Jails and Prisons: 2002*, Attachment One, The Citizen's Committee on Mental Illness, Substance Abuse, and Criminal Justice and the National Association for the Mentally Ill, Maine, September 2002.

While Joe Fitzpatrick, clinical director for the Maine Department of Corrections, told Human Rights Watch that the vacant positions had been filled since the audit was conducted, he also reported that, because of budget constraints, a bill to improve the mental health services offered to incarcerated individuals was recently trimmed of all additional financial obligations. Currently none of the prisons, including the one housing a small, specialized mental health unit, has a full-time psychiatrist. Instead, two prisons have a psychiatrist assigned two days a week and one has no psychiatrist but does have access to the nearby state mental hospital.[321]

The qualifications, training, and competence of prison mental health staff should be equal to community standards.[322] But the hiring of under-qualified, and thus lower-paid, staff is one way in which prisons lower their mental health costs. Throughout our research, questions arose concerning the qualifications of the mental health staff that work in prisons. A 1988 nationwide survey found that 40 percent of mental health staff in prisons had less than a Master's degree.[323] Human Rights Watch was unable to find updated data on this. Nevertheless, there have continued to be periodic reports of states utilizing under-qualified counselors and psychologists, or staff whose licenses to practice in the free world have been suspended.[324] Dr. Jeffrey Metzner told Human Rights Watch that in many of the prison systems he has visited, unlicensed psychologists are inadequately supervised by licensed practitioners. "They frequently have supervision on paper only," Metzner asserted. "I've seen counselors with a B.A. in home economics."[325] Oftentimes, Metzner also noted, for-profit companies brought in to deliver correctional mental health services employ licensed clinical directors and fill the rest of the psychologists' and case workers' positions with unlicensed practitioners whom they can pay less. "Many of the companies do that to one extent or another." In Rhode Island, mental health director Frederick Friedman told Human Rights Watch that four of the system's five psychologists are unlicensed.[326] In Iowa, only two of the eighteen psychologists have PhDs, the rest having either Bachelor's or Master's degrees.[327] In 1997, the mental health staff at Indiana's Maximum Control Facility's (MCF) consisted of a behavioral clinician with a Master's degree in counseling psychology, who also served as the superintendent's administrative assistant.[328]

---

[321] Human Rights Watch telephone interview with Joe Fitzpatrick, clinical director, Maine Department of Corrections, February 6, 2003.

[322] Jeffrey Metzner, Cohen, F., Grossman, L.S., Wettstein, R.M: "Treatment in Jails and Prisons." In: Wettstein, R., Ed.: *Treatment of Offenders with Mental Disorders* (New York: Guilford Press, 1998), pp. 211-264. Mental health professionals in the community typically face licensure, certification, or registration requirements.

[323] Dr. Jeffrey Metzner quotes this study in his article "Guidelines for Psychiatric Services in Prisons," *Criminal Behavior and Mental Health* (1993), vol. 3. Dr. Metzner sources this information to I.D. Goldstrom, R.W. Manderscheid, and L.A. Rudolph, in their essay "Mental Health Services in State Adult Correctional Facilities," *Mental Health, United States* (Washington D.C.: U.S. Government Printing Office, 1992).

[324] In May 2000, a *Prison Legal News* investigative piece by Mark Sherwood and Bob Posey reported that 30 percent of Florida Department of Correction doctors have negative marks on their record.

[325] Human Rights Watch telephone interview with Dr. Jeffrey Metzner, April 2, 2003.

[326] Human Rights Watch telephone interview with Frederick Friedman, mental health director, Rhode Island Department of Corrections, April 2, 2003.

[327] Human Rights Watch telephone interview with Harbans Deol, mental health director, Iowa Department of Corrections, April 2, 2003.

[328] One of the clinician's tasks was to screen inmates to make sure mentally ill prisoners had not been transferred to the MCF. His screening consisted of asking inmates a few questions at their cell door, e.g., whether they had thoughts of suicide. He did not review their medical and psychiatric records prior to meeting with them and did not do a formal mental status exam or a thorough psychiatric history with the inmates. Nor did he monitor the mental health of inmates on segregation, another one of his responsibilities. He acknowledged to Human Rights Watch that he rarely referred inmates to a psychiatrist. Human Rights Watch, *Cold Storage: Super-Maximum Security Confinement in Indiana* (New York:

In some prisons Human Rights Watch visited, senior mental health staff, including some psychiatrists, appeared to have serious problems conversing in English. Human Rights Watch doubted some of these employees could easily communicate with many of their prisoner-patients. In other settings, we found prisons reliant on staff who likely did not have the licenses that would allow them to practice in the private marketplace. In Graterford Prison, Pennsylvania, for example, large-scale investments have been made in mental health care over the last few years, and Human Rights Watch found the staff to be uniformly dedicated and caring individuals. Nevertheless, of the fourteen psychologists employed at the prison, not a single one had a PhD, and only three of the fourteen were licensed psychologists. Louis Mariani, chief psychologist at Graterford, told Human Rights Watch that the advantage of hiring unlicensed psychologists was that they were cheaper than their licensed peers. "I don't know if the Commonwealth of Pennsylvania would let us hire licensed psychologists — because they'd have to pay them [more]."[329] The counselors there "can have a Bachelor's degree in just about anything," Mariani asserted, and don't need any formal mental health training. In Mississippi, according to the University of Mississippi Medical Center's Linda Powell, none of the too-few psychologists employed within the system have PhDs.[330] In South Carolina, investigators from the Legislative Audit Council published a report in March 2000 severely criticizing the quality of medical and mental health care in the state's prisons, especially in those prisons that had contracted out their services to a private company named Correctional Medical Services (CMS), which is the largest private corrections health care provider in the country. The investigators found that "inmate counseling staff at both CMS and SCDC [South Carolina Department of Corrections] sites did not meet the minimum qualifications for their positions."[331]

The downside of such a practice is obvious. As Judy Stanley, director of accreditation for the National Commission on Correctional Health Care, points out, it means under-trained, and under-qualified personnel end up making clinical decisions about appropriate treatment strategies and crisis interventions for seriously mentally ill prisoners.[332] For example, plaintiffs' expert Dr. Roberta Stellman, testified in the Texas prison litigation that nurse practitioners made serious diagnosis and prescription decisions.[333]

Mental health intervention decisions are also made — or not made — by untrained personnel because mental health staff typically do not work weekends or evenings in prisons. Correctional and security staff are left to respond to the needs of mentally ill prisoners. Indeed, mental health crises apparently happen more frequently on the weekends and evenings.

Human Rights Watch, 1997), pp. 75-77. Since the time of our research, Indiana has increased the mental health staff at MCF.

[329] Human Rights Watch interview with Louis Mariani, chief psychologist, Graterford Prison, Pennsylvania, August 12, 2002. The numbers were provided by Mariani.

[330] Human Rights Watch telephone interview with Linda Powell, director of utilization review and case management, University of Mississippi Medical Center, May 1, 2003.

[331] South Carolina Legislative Audit Council, *A Review of Medical Services at the South Carolina Department of Corrections*, March 2000. Report summary, p. 4. Available online at: http://www.state.sc.us/sclac/, accessed on July 2, 2003.

[332] Human Rights Watch telephone interview with Judy Stanley, director of accreditation, National Commission on Correctional Health Care, January 22, 2003.

[333] *Ruiz v. Johnson*, 37 F. Supp. 2d 855 (S.D. Texas, 1999).

Poor Screening and Tracking of Mentally Ill Prisoners

The identification of prisoners with mental illness is the necessary predicate for mental health treatment. U.S. courts have repeatedly noted that the U.S. Constitution requires adequate screening and monitoring for mental illness.[334] Nevertheless, in many prison systems screening and tracking of mentally ill prisoners is problematic. Prisoners with mental illness are not identified upon entry into prison and are left untreated. If they are identified after screening and placed on mental health caseloads, prison data management systems often are inadequate to track services provided, or to ensure that the prisoners' records follow them when they are transferred to different prisons. In addition, prisoners who develop mental health problems after admission are often not identified and placed on the mental health caseload in a timely manner.

Initial screening occurs when a prisoner is admitted for the first time to a facility — either in the transfer to prison from jail or, in some systems, when a prisoner is transferred between institutions. The screening typically consists of a questionnaire which prisoners answer. If a good questionnaire is used, the administrative staff need not have much or any mental health training. If the screening questionnaire is adequate and properly administered, such personnel will probably have a fairly good rate of referring intake prisoners for more in-depth evaluations.

According to the Consensus Project, effective screening should enable a determination of prisoners in need of immediate mental health attention within twenty-four hours or within a brief reasonable time frame of three to seven days. If the screening suggests the prisoner is in need of mental health treatment (e.g., if the prisoner indicates that he or she has been receiving medication for a mental illness, or has been previously hospitalized for mental illness), the prisoner should receive a more comprehensive examination that includes an inquiry into mental health histories, an interview with the prisoner by qualified mental health staff, and review of health care records and other pertinent information. Unfortunately, staff conducting the initial screening as well as more comprehensive examinations usually do not possess the results of prior psychiatric assessments, even assessments made during the prisoner's pre-trial incarceration or psychiatric diagnoses undertaken as part of trial competency or insanity defense proceedings. Such prior psychiatric workups may, indeed, never make it to the prison. [335]

The Michigan Bureau of Forensic Mental Health Services has created a comprehensive prison screening infrastructure. Nevertheless, officials believe that they miss, at intake, between six and eight seriously mentally ill prisoners per month, according to Director Roger Smith. These individuals are identified during subsequent follow-up screening processes. Using computerized databases, the system has the capacity to identify the individual prison clinicians who are repeatedly failing to identify these mentally ill prisoners, and can put them under a more intensive supervision regimen.[336] Connecticut is another state that has invested in the creation of a sophisticated mental health care database.

Most states, however, do not have such databases in place, and in these states mentally ill prisoners not identified during intake-screening are at risk of going without needed treatment throughout their

---

[334] *Ruiz v. Estelle*, 503 F. Supp. at 1336.

[335] See, e.g., Kenneth Appelbaum, et. al, *Report on the Psychiatric Management of John Salvi in Massachusetts Department of Correction Facilities 1995-1996*, submitted to the Massachusetts Department of Correction, January 31, 1997; on file at Human Rights Watch.

[336] Human Rights Watch telephone interview with Tony Rome, clinical director, Bureau of Mental Health Services, February 10, 2003.

stay behind bars. "Those systems that are suffering," Smith believes, "are those that don't have the ability to monitor on a regular basis what is going on in their system. If you can't do that, things can get out of control pretty quickly."[337]

Some states, such as Alabama, have barely begun computerizing *any* aspect of their correctional mental health systems.[338] In Wisconsin, a 2001 legislative audit found that the Department of Corrections had no way of determining the total number of seriously mentally ill prisoners in its system.[339]

In Wyoming, investigators from the Civil Rights Division of the U.S. Attorney General's office concluded that:

> WSP [Wyoming State Penitentiary] provides virtually no diagnostic assessments utilizing past treatment records and diagnoses, multi-disciplinary treatment planning, or aftercare planning.... WSP's erratic mental health care documentation exacerbates these problems. The prison often fails to document services rendered, mental health records do not contain physicians' orders, and the records have large gaps during periods of critical care.[340]

In California, Doug Peterson, chief deputy clinical services and head of health care at California State Prison, Sacramento, readily admitted that his prison's database is "horrible as a management tool, which affects inmate care. It's harder to monitor whether they're getting what they're supposed to be getting."[341]

Protocols developed by the American Correctional Association, the National Commission on Correctional Health Care, and through litigation recommend that prisoners be monitored, at regular intervals, for emerging mental illness throughout their stays in prison. Prisoners whose initial intake screening does not reveal a serious mental illness do not need to be seen by mental health staff as regularly as do those so identified. But, they do still need some access to, and regular monitoring by, mental health staff. Because many people first develop serious mental illnesses while in their late teens and twenties — the age group that makes up the bulk of incoming prisoners — the fact that an initial intake-screening process finds an individual to be free of mental illness is no guarantee that they will remain healthy throughout their sentence. "It is almost impossible," said Toch, "to predict which of the vulnerable inmates you put into these settings are going to fall apart in them."[342] This observation is made more urgent by the fact that prisons are high-stress environments, particularly likely to trigger mental health problems amongst individuals vulnerable to such sicknesses. And yet, as Fred Cohen pointed out, because they are already overworked, "prison mental health staff aren't looking for business, for more customers."[343] In many prisons, there is no routine monitoring of

---

[337] Human Rights Watch telephone interview with Roger Smith, director, Bureau of Mental Health Services, June 19, 2002.
[338] Human Rights Watch telephone interview with Fred Cohen, December 12, 2002.
[339] Wisconsin Legislative Audit Bureau, *Prison Health Care, Department of Corrections: An Evaluation*, May 2001.
[340] Letter to Wyoming Governor James Geringer from Bill Lann Lee, acting assistant attorney general, June 29, 1999, available online at: http://www.usdoj.gov/crt/split/documents/wyofind.htm, accessed on September 2, 2003.
[341] Human Rights Watch interview with Doug Peterson, chief deputy clinical services and head of health care, California State Prison, Sacramento, California, July 18, 2002.
[342] Human Rights Watch telephone interview with Hans Toch, November 22, 2002.
[343] Human Rights Watch telephone interview with Fred Cohen, December 10, 2002.

mental health of prisoners who are not on mental health caseload, even when the prisoners are in notoriously stressful settings such as segregation that can prompt mental health crises. (See chapter XII below.) Prisoners who are not on mental health caseloads only obtain mental health services either through self-referrals, the referrals of other prisoners, or the referrals made by security staff.

The following example from Texas reveals how extremely impaired prisoners can remain outside the prison mental health system. Forensic psychologist Keith Curry, reporting on a site visit to Smith prison on behalf of plaintiffs in the *Ruiz* litigation, wrote of:

> a 39 year old man admitted to Smith [prison] from Coffield on September 19, 2001 where he had been treated with a dose of antipsychotic medication for the diagnosis of Psychotic Disorder NOS. Since the patient's medication was discontinued shortly before transfer, the nurse at Smith did not pick up on the psychiatric history upon chair review. This occurred despite descriptions of extensive prior treatment and an impatient admission for bizarre behavior and psychotic decompensation as recently as January 22, 2001. As a result, no referral was made to mental health. The inmate was observed on rounds by the psychiatric nurse on October 1 and 11, 2001 after custody staff commented upon the inmate's bizarre behavior. The nurse noted that the inmate was, "delusional, disorganized, agitated, labile, with rapid speech, flight of ideas, and loosening of associations." Despite this, she noted that he was in, "no apparent distress." She nonetheless suggested that he see the physician's assistant for a medication evaluation. However, the inmate declined this offer and no further mental health notions were made in his medical record. [On the day of Curry's visit in mid-March, 2002] the inmate was highly agitated with prominent paranoid delusions. He was grossly disoriented with rapid speech, loosening of associations, clang associations, and apparent responses to internal stimuli. This inmate would stand out as severely impaired on any psychiatric inpatient unit, but was receiving no mental health services while being locked in a windowless box 24 hours a day for six months.[344]

Ruling on mental health conditions in Iowa State Penitentiary in 1997, a federal district court found a lack of repeated follow-up evaluations for prisoners. Testimony at trial revealed that "inmates who develop problems after entering the system or inmates whose problems do not manifest themselves until they have been in the system for a while are often left undiagnosed. These are the inmates most likely to end up in the lockup cellhouse....."[345]

Lack of Timely Access to Mental Health Staff

As the American Psychiatric Association (APA) points out, "[t]imely and effective access to mental health treatment is the hallmark of adequate mental health care."[346] It has concluded, however, that in prison such access is impeded by delays in transmitting prisoners' oral or written request for care; permitting unreasonable delays before patients are seen by mental health staff or outside consultants; and the imposition of fees that prevent or deter prisoners from seeking care.[347] Indeed, one of the

---

[344] Keith Curry, Ph.D. letter to the law offices of Donna Brorby, March 19, 2002, p. 28.
[345] *Goff v. Harper*, Findings of Fact and Conclusions of Law, No. 4-90-CV-50365 (S.D. Iowa, June 5, 1997) (unpublished), p. 90.
[346] American Psychiatric Association, *Psychiatric Services in Jails and Prisons*, 2nd Ed. (Washington D.C., American Psychiatric Association, 2000), p. 4.
[347] Ibid.

most frequent complaints voiced by mentally ill prisoners is that they have to wait days, weeks, and even months to see mental health staff after they request a meeting or to have their medications altered. Based on testimony and information Human Rights Watch collected during research for this report, we believe that this lack of access is a product both of understaffing and of a prison culture that tends to view prisoners as inherently manipulative and thus not truly in need of mental health interventions.

- In Georgia's Phillips State Prison, a psychiatrist's review of prisoner treatment documents indicated that, "[e]ssentially all inmates are seen by the psychiatrist at one month intervals regardless of their clinical condition. There were multiple instances in which records documented a worsening of symptoms (psychosis, thought disorganization, behavioral manifestations of mental illness, depression, weight loss, etc.) with no plan to schedule the inmate for a psychiatric appointment before the next regularly scheduled appointment or to provide any other type of intervention. This practice promotes needless suffering and worsening of psychiatric illness."[348]

- In 1994, Gregory Stampley, a prisoner with a long history of schizophrenia, died in Minnesota's Stillwater prison. According to a newspaper report based on evidence presented during a subsequent lawsuit brought by his family, Stampley spent the last days of his life:

  > in a small concrete cell soiled by his own excrement, babbling incoherently, drinking water scooped from a toilet and refusing to accept prescribed medication from his guards. Twice, guards tried unsuccessfully to arrange for a prison psychologist to go to Stillwater to examine Stampley.[349]

  A year later, the state prison ombudsman wrote that the Department of Corrections had often failed to provide treatment for mentally ill inmates in a timely manner.[350] She also concluded that the guards had unnecessarily kept Stampley in a restraint board to control his behavior. In the lawsuit, Stampley's mother claimed the prison system failed to give her son adequate care and accused the staff of neglect and abuse. The state denied the charges but nonetheless agreed to pay Stampley's family $168,500 and to make psychologists available twenty-four hours a day, either in person, or via telephone, to consult with guards.[351]

- A 1998 investigation by the U.S. Department of Justice into conditions at the Wyoming State Penitentiary found that the mental health staffing was so inadequate that out of ninety-five people referred to mental health services in a three-month period, only six were actually given psychiatric evaluations. "Due to inadequate staffing," a report to Governor James Geringer noted, "if seen at all, most inmates in need of crisis psychiatric intervention were seen by an infirmary physician rather than by a trained mental health care provider." In the administrative segregation unit of the prison:

---

[348] Declaration of Kathryn A. Burns, M.D., M.P.H., November 6, 2002, *Attached to Plaintiffs Motion for Preliminary Injunction, Fluellen v. Wetherington*, Civil Case No. 1:02-CV-479-JEC (N.D. Georgia).

[349] Patrick Sweeney, "State, Inmate's Family Settle Suit," *Saint Paul Pioneer Press*, April 23, 1996.

[350] Jim Adams, "Report Raps Mental Health Treatment in State Prisons," *Star Tribune*, April 29, 1995.

[351] Patrick Sweeney, "State, Inmate's Family Settle Suit," *Saint Paul Pioneer Press*, April 23, 1996.

Inmates who had been receiving mental health services outside of administrative segregation experienced discontinuity in care once assigned to the unit. For example, we discovered numerous instances of inappropriate cessation of long-standing mental health medications. Likewise, inmates widely complained of and our chart reviews confirmed a general lack of responsiveness to mental health services requests from administrative segregation unit inmates.[352]

In their report, the investigators referred to one case in which "an inmate with a history of state hospitalization requested mental health assistance. Mental health personnel, however, did not see this individual for over a month, waiting until he attempted to commit suicide by slashing his wrists."[353]

- Experts investigating mental health services in Alabama prisons found that:

> Outpatient services for inmates identified as experiencing serious mental illness are provided by CMS [Correctional Medical Services] mental health staff who may be present in a particular facility only one or two days per week. The ADOC [Alabama Department of Corrections] psychologists are not responsible for the monitoring and treatment of inmates with serious mental illness. Inmates who experience emergencies on days when a CMS mental health staff member is not present are routinely placed on watch in isolation until the CMS staff member's next scheduled day. Isolation alone, particularly under the conditions previously described, is inadequate treatment for mental health emergencies and exacerbates the inmate's distress and suffering.

> On days when a CMS mental health staff member is on-site, the number of outpatient inmates requiring just routine monitoring is so great that it results in these inmates receiving little more than a brisk, "How are you doing?" Any hope of facilitating an inmate's adjustment to correctional living and enhancing treatment compliance through education is not achieved.[354]

- Because of the above-mentioned poor mental health coverage in Mississippi's prisons, seriously mentally ill prisoners in the three state prisons have only minimal access to mental health staff. According to Linda Powell, at Mississippi State Penitentiary at Parchman, prisoners only see their psychiatrist every ninety days and only have contact with their psych assistants — the staff who are supposed to be on the lookout for mental health problems — once a month.[355]

---

[352] Letter to Wyoming Governor James Geringer from Bill Lann Lee, acting assistant attorney general, Civil Rights Division, U.S. Department of Justice, June 29, 1999.

[353] Ibid.

[354] Kathryn Burns, M.D. and Jane Haddad, Psy.D., "Mental Health Care in the Alabama Department of Corrections," *Bradley v. Hightower*, Civ. No. 92-A-70-N (N.D. Ala., June 30, 2000)), p. 66.

[355] Human Rights Watch telephone interview with Linda Powell, May 1, 2003.

Diagnoses of Malingering

Many prisoners with serious mental illness go untreated or are under treated because staff dismiss their symptoms as faking or manipulation. According to Fred Cohen, a high incidence of diagnosis of "malingering" mental records is a "sign of a system in disrepair."[356]

There are no obvious criteria for determining whether or when an prisoner's behavior reflects mental illness or not. "Disruptive or violent conduct may be a manifestation of illness or just orneriness. Quiet, seemingly introspective behavior may be just that or it may be evidence of decompensation."[357] But the ability to make just such determinations is, after all, "part of the mental health clinician's art, inside or outside prison walls."[358] Security staff, who lack mental health training, are often quick to assume that prisoners are acting volitionally or manipulatively when they act out.

Unfortunately, some correctional mental health staff are also too quick to see malingering or manipulation and to overlook mental illness. Prisoners can, of course be manipulative, feigning mental illness for numerous reasons — to gain a transfer, change housing assignments, seek attention, or to improve their legal situation. But manipulation is not inconsistent with mental illness. Behavior such as self-mutilation can be manipulative. But it can also — and simultaneously — be a symptom of a major psychiatric disorder or a self-reinforcing behavior that requires a psychiatric response. In facilities in which the staff lack either the time or the inclination to pay close attention to prisoners, the only option left to a prisoner seeking mental health attention is to manipulate in some way — for instance by creating a disturbance or exaggerating his pain. The less attentive or present the staff, on average, the more manipulative prisoners have to be to get attention, and this is as true for prisoners who are suffering from serious medical or psychiatric ailments as it is for those who are not ill but merely want attention. In other words, seriously mentally ill prisoners are also frequently "manipulative" to get the care they need.

Absent careful evaluation through diagnostic work-ups, it is impossible to determine whether a self-mutilating individual has genuine psychiatric problems — for instance, he might be commanded by hallucinatory voices to cut himself — which, in turn, he may be exaggerating in order to receive needed help. Unfortunately, in some facilities, the "prevailing apprehension among custody and clinical staff [is] of being manipulated into delivering psychiatric services.... The suspicion of malingering and its accompanying withholding of services are particularly acute in the management of self-mutilation and explosive disorders."[359] Diagnoses of malingering or manipulation too often reflect issues of available resources, security concerns, and belief in prisoner pursuit of secondary gains rather than the result of careful objective evaluations.

- In Texas, as part of the *Ruiz* litigation, plaintiffs' experts presented examples of misdiagnosis to suggest the ongoing poor quality of psychiatric care in Texas prisons. Dr. Jeffrey Metzner indicated that system-wide deficiencies included "not recognizing or minimizing symptoms indicative of major mental illnesses by either over-diagnosing malingering or 'no Axis I

---

[356] Written communication from Fred Cohen to Human Rights Watch, August 28, 2003.

[357] Jeffrey Metzner, et al., "Treatment in Jails and Prisons" (1998), p. 220.

[358] Terry Kupers, *Prison Madness*, 1999, p. 87.

[359] National Commission on Correctional Health Care (NCCHC), *Prison Health Care: Guidelines for the Management of an Adequate Delivery System* (Chicago: NCCHC, December 3, 1990), p. 148 (quoting from correspondence from Walter Y. Quijano).

diagnosis.'"[360] Dr. Metzner described the case of a prisoner who was initially diagnosed as schizophrenic, and who had a history of smearing himself with feces, complaining of auditory and visual hallucinations, and claiming to be the Messiah. However, a Dr. Taylor later determined the prisoner was malingering and expressed interest in whether in the future he would consume his feces or just smear them. Another prisoner:

> entered the system with a history of suicide attempts, self-mutilations, hallucinations, and hospitalizations. His medications were discontinued and he was diagnosed as having no Axis I illness. After a brief visit to Skyview [an in-patient psychiatric facility] he was discharged with Dr. Tchokoev recommending no medication and heavy work in the field. The same day he returned to Beto [a prison unit], he cut himself and then attempted to hang himself. He is now in a vegetative state.[361]

- In yet another example, a prisoner went to Skyview after a long history of psychiatric treatment for a number of Axis I and Axis II diagnoses, both in the free world and the Texas Department of Criminal Justice. Once there, Dr. Taylor discontinued his medication and asserted, "[t]his patient has a history of acting out at this facility when he is 'found out' and is aware of the fact that he will be returned to his unit of assignment." By the end of the month, he had returned to Crisis Management and received two more, different Axis I diagnoses.[362]

- In New York, psychiatrist Stuart Grassian made a site visit to Attica one year after a successful lawsuit ended concerning mental health services in that prison. Dr. Grassian found that appropriate mental health treatment for prisoners remained frustrated by "the inappropriate and long-standing preoccupation of Attica OMH [mental health] staff with rooting out malingering…. The records that I have reviewed demonstrate that there is a persistent over-reliance on 'malingering' and 'manipulating' — sometimes even in the face of a lifetime of illness."[363]

- Similarly, in New York, a mental health clinician with over thirty years of forensic and community mental health care experience in New York State told the Correctional Association:

> Sometimes the [forensic mental health hospital] will say that a patient [sent from special housing units (SHU)] isn't mentally ill, he is a manipulator, and they send him/her back to the prison, back to SHU. To me, labeling someone a "manipulator" is pretty useless. If there is a secondary gain issue, our job is to talk about it, to find out what's really going on. There are clinicians who will tell you that eating feces isn't a mental illness but a behavior problem (in some cases). Well, to me, eating feces certainly isn't

---

[360] Dr. Metzner's testimony is quoted by the court in *Ruiz v. Johnson*, 37 F. Supp. 2d 855, 902 (S.D. Texas, 1999)(internal citations omitted).

[361] *Ruiz*, 37 F. Supp. 2d at 903 (internal citations omitted).

[362] Ibid. (internal citations omitted).

[363] Dr. Stuart Grassian, Second Site Visit to the Attica SHU, Mental Health Care, *Eng v. Goord*, Civ 80-385S (W.D. New York, October 1999) (redacted copy), p. 40.

normal behavior. Our job is to find out why the inmate is acting abnormally and how to best treat him/her from a clinical perspective.[364]

- A prisoners' lawsuit filed against the Georgia Department of Corrections in March 2002, alleges abuse and neglect of seriously mentally ill prisoners at the high security Phillips State Prison.[365] Among the allegations, prisoners claim the prison has systematically ignored the mental health issues of prisoners who engage in acts of self-mutilation, tending to view self-mutilation as a gesture by manipulative prisoners seeking attention, or looking to be removed from the unpleasantly harsh environment of a maximum security prison, rather than as a symptom of bona fide mental health problems. In addition, the lawsuit alleges that prisoners are routinely disciplined for their acts of self-mutilation. The Georgia Department of Corrections did not return phone calls from Human Rights Watch requesting a response to the allegations contained in the lawsuit.

- In 1997, the behavioral clinician at Indiana's Maximum Control Facility responsible for screening prisoners requesting a meeting with the prison psychiatrist, routinely refused to refer the prisoners because he believed that they were malingering. Thus, for example, he ignored a written request to see a psychiatrist by a prisoner who stated that he had a history of schizophrenia and needed to be put back on his medications because he was becoming increasingly suicidal and psychotic. Without ever having met with the prisoner or reviewing his records, the clinician told Human Rights Watch that he thought this prisoner was malingering and was not a schizophrenic.[366]

- The complaint in the *Reickenbacker v. Foster* lawsuit in Louisiana alleges that prisoner D.N. "was written up by a social worker for violation of the aggravated malingering rule… because the social worker did not think his condition was 'life threatening.'" The complaint alleges that at Hunt Prison, "manifestations of mental illness, such as repeated shouting or screaming or throwing objects in a cell are mistakenly and deleteriously diagnosed as 'behavioral problems' which are addressed by imposing discipline, not treatment."[367]

- In Washington, Janet Schaeffer told Human Rights Watch of how one prisoner at the Washington Correctional Center for Women was on the mental health roster, and was known to bounce between extremes of depression and mania. The mental health staff began treating her and counseling her. "The treatment was going very well," Schaeffer told Human Rights Watch.[368] "She started to lose weight, which was important because she was a diabetic. She came out of a very deep depression." But then, Schaeffer continued, the prisoner witnessed some aggressive behavior between two other prisoners which triggered memories of her own crime — she was in prison for harming one of her children — throwing the prisoner back into an extremely deep depression. At that point, the prison's

---

[364] Correctional Association of New York, *Mental Health in the House of Corrections*, forthcoming report.

[365] *Fluellen v. Wetherington*, First Amended Complaint, Civil Case No. 1:02-CV-479(JEC) (N.D. Georgia, March 15, 2002).

[366] Human Rights Watch, *Cold Storage: Super-Maximum Security Confinement in Indiana* (New York: Human Rights Watch, 1997), p. 78. Dr. Terry Kupers visited facilities with Human Rights Watch and interviewed a number of seriously mentally ill prisoners.

[367] *Reickenbacker v. Foster*, Complaint, Civil Action No. 99-910-C-1 (M.D. Louisiana).

[368] Human Rights Watch telephone interview with Janet Schaeffer, psychologist and former director of mental health services, Washington Correctional Center for Women, April 29, 2003.

mental health teams were rejigged, and the prisoner was assigned a new therapist. The new therapist, lacking knowledge of the prisoner's history, immediately determined that she was faking her symptoms. "She was seen as somebody who was more dramatic than she needed to be, playing up her symptoms, or somebody who just needed to snap out of it," Schaeffer stated. "The women [in the prison] were generally seen as manipulative as a group. Very few were really seen as mentally ill. The culture is 'you're being manipulated.'" Shortly after being assigned to the new, skeptical therapist, the prisoner set herself on fire.

A clinical bias toward assuming prisoners are manipulating or malingering may be the product of working too long without enough support in a professionally difficult environment. In his book *Prison Madness*, Dr. Terry Kupers suggests that many correctional mental health staff suffer from "burnout;" they feel exhausted, cynical, ineffective, and wish they could find work elsewhere. The more burned out staff become, the harder it is to be caring and conscientious. Kupers believes staff morale is weakened because mental health services are underfunded, understaffed, and "sadly lacking," compared to the huge number of prisoners with serious mental health needs. He also points to the difficulty many competent mental health staff have with being subordinate to security staff, and having security decisions override and undercut their treatment efforts. Dr. Jeffrey Metzner suggests that continuing education and training of prison mental health staff will not only assist professional growth, but help prevent burnout. He also notes that the "use of part-time consultants can decrease the negative aspects of institutionalization, such as less creative thinking and decreased use of common sense impacting full-time staff."[369]

Medication as the Sole Treatment

To facilitate recovery and the alleviation of symptoms of mental illness, mental health treatment in prison, as in the community, should include a variety of mental health therapies, should be multidisciplinary and eclectic in nature, and should be provided in a manner consistent with generally accepted mental health practices.[370] The treatment should reflect an individualized written treatment plan for each mentally ill offender, taking into account life history, psychiatric diagnoses (before and after incarceration), and other factors. It should not be limited to simply alleviating immediate symptoms through psychotropic medication. Yet, "staff at many correctional facilities have overrelied on the use of psychotropic medications and, in many cases, sedative-hypnotic medications, simply to pacify and to control inmates with mental illness and others believed to be disruptive."[371] The court in *Ruiz v. Estelle* expressly noted that simply providing medication did not suffice to meet prison obligations to provide mental health treatment.[372] The American Psychiatric Association includes among the essential services that should be provided as part of prison mental health treatment: "[s]upportive and informative verbal interventions, in an individual or group context as clinically appropriate;" and "[p]rograms that provide productive, out-of-cell activity and teach necessary psychosocial and living skills."[373]

The need for varied therapeutic and life-skills enhancing interventions depends, of course, on the individual's symptoms and diagnosis. A report on mental health by the U.S. Surgeon General's

---

[369] Jeffrey Metzner, et al., "Treatment in Jails and Prisons" (1998), p. 229.

[370] Ibid.

[371] Council of State Governments, *Consensus Project* (2002), p. 136.

[372] *Ruiz v. Estelle*, 503 F. Supp. 1265, 1336 (S.D. Tex., 1980), *aff'd in part*, 679 F.2d 115 (5th Cir., 1982), *cert. denied*, 460 U.S. 1042 (1983).

[373] American Psychiatric Association, *Psychiatric Services in Jails and Prisons*, 2nd Ed. (Washington D.C.: American Psychiatric Association, 2000), p.46.

office, for example, argued that for schizophrenia, a multifaceted treatment approach is essential. "Effective treatment of schizophrenia extends well beyond pharmacological therapy: it also includes psychosocial interventions, family interventions, and vocational and psychosocial rehabilitation."[374] While many prison systems have begun implementing diverse approaches for treating mental illness, most still over-emphasize medication. They do not provide sufficient resources for non-medication therapy, counseling, and a range of supportive structures for prisoners who do not need (or no longer require) hospitalization. In failing to do so, prison mental health staff fail to address the prisoners' needs. They also miss an important opportunity to serve the public interest by taking advantage of the time prisoners are in prison to provide them with the cognitive and life skills enhancement that will increase the likelihood of a successful reentry into society following release from prison.

As Metzner told Human Rights Watch, the problem with most prison mental health services comes after mentally ill prisoners have been identified.

> What do they do with them? That's a common problem across states. Most psychiatrists' roles are limited to medication management due to resource issues. The amount of psychotherapy available is very limited. There aren't enough qualified people, or you might have a bunch of mental health clinicians without proper qualifications.[375]

Prisoners suffering from schizophrenia or other illnesses with psychosis, in particular, are unlikely to receive the intensive interventions necessary to help them learn how to better function in society, or even how to take care of their most basic personal hygiene and everyday living needs. "Although medication has a significant role to play in controlling psychotic symptoms, it cannot teach a patient the skills to acquire friends or a job, or to live in the community," wrote Marnie Rice and Grant Harris, of the Pentanguishene Mental Health Center. "Nor can it teach patients how to take it [the medication] consistently and regularly. Other forms of rehabilitation, such as behavior therapy, skills teaching, and family therapy, are necessary in combination with medication." [376] In other words, while medicating prisoners suffering from schizophrenia is likely to control their most obvious symptoms, it is unlikely to help those individuals learn to live, and cope, with their illnesses over the long-term either in prison or outside the prison walls.

According to Kupers:

> The adequacy of mental health services cannot be measured solely in terms of staffing levels or the number of prisoners who receive mental health treatment, with or without medications. Adequate mental health treatment requires the availability of a trained clinician to develop a trusting relationship with a patient in a setting that permits privacy, where confidentiality is respected so that very personal themes can be explored and worked through. Adequate mental health treatment requires a variety of treatment modalities, including but not limited to crisis intervention;

---

[374] Office of the Surgeon General of the United States of America, *Mental Health: A Report of the Surgeon General*, 2002, ch. 4.

[375] Human Rights Watch telephone interview with Dr. Jeffrey Metzner, November 26, 2002.

[376] Marnie Rice and Grant Harris, "The Treatment of Mentally Disordered Offenders," *Psychology, Public Policy and Law* (March 1997), vol. 3, pp. 126-183.

psychotropic medications as needed; the availability of a certain number of group activities such as group therapy, psycho-educational groups, facilitated socialization or recreational activities, and psychiatric rehabilitation groups that involve psycho-educational programs, training in the skills of daily living and medication compliance; admission to an acute psychiatric hospital as needed; social work outreach to family members as needed; and after-care planning so that the disturbed individual is not returned to the environment that caused a breakdown but rather is provided with the ongoing care and social supports needed to sustain his mental health. [377]

Kupers observed that suicidal prisoners at Wisconsin's supermax prison in Boscobel were often treated solely with medication, and that "the most often prescribed type of medication in suicidal crises — i.e., antidepressants — take between two and three weeks to reach full effect, so that they are not very useful in the acute situation."

There is scant information publicly available that addresses the nature and quantity — much less quality or effectiveness — of the mental health services prisoners receive nationwide. The Bureau of Justice Statistics (BJS) reported that as of June 30, 2000, one in ten state prisoners receives psychotropic medications, and one in eight were in mental health therapy or counseling programs. While these data might be interpreted to suggest that more prisoners receive non-medication treatment than medication, they are too summary to provide useful insight into the nature, quantity, and length of time of the mental health counseling services purportedly provided. We are aware of no data that provide for any prison system a breakdown of the kinds of non-medication therapy provided, the amount of time that prisoners spent in such different therapy modalities over a given period of time how many prisoners had access to such therapy in given period of time, reasons why prisoners left the mental health caseloads, etc. For example, a complaint Human Rights Watch has received in every supermax we have ever visited and which has been raised in virtually every lawsuit filed by supermax prisoners addressing mental health services, is that "therapy" or "counseling" consists of no more than a mental health professional passing by the cell front periodically, asking a prisoner with a mental illness how he or she is doing and then proceeding down the row. Yet states may well include such prisoners among their statistics about how many prisoners receive counseling.

Our research suggests that in many prisons, access to mental health interventions other than medication is extremely limited in quantity and quality. This is especially true regarding long-term psychosocial interventions for seriously mentally ill prisoners living in the general prison population. "It's commonly not available to all the people who need it," Dr. Jeffrey Metzner reported to Human Rights Watch. "If you're in general population, a small percentage will need it, but it's limited. The limitations have to do with space and with staff resources — whether you have enough mental health clinicians."[378] In specialized residential treatment units and other intermediate care programs, there is far more access to modalities of treatment beyond medication, but such programs typically can serve only a very small number of prisoners. (See discussion below, chapter X).

- Dr. Kathryn Burns, a psychiatrist with extensive correctional experience, reviewed mental health treatment records of prisoners at Phillips State Prison in Georgia at the request of plaintiffs in *Fluellen v. Wetherington*. Although the prisoners she reviewed were classified as

---

[377] Testimony of Dr. Terry Kupers, *Jones 'El v. Berge*, Civil Case 00-C-0421-C (W.D. Wisconsin, 2001).
[378] Human Rights Watch telephone interview with Dr. Jeffrey Metzner, February 12, 2003.

requiring and receiving residential unit treatment and crisis stabilization services, the records revealed a:

> dearth of structured therapeutic activities [which are] a hallmark of residential mental health care in correctional facilities. Mental health treatment is more than simply the prescription of psychotropic medication. Participation in therapeutic activity permits inmates with serious mental illnesses the opportunity to improve their socialization and communication skills, develop additional coping skills, and engage in meaningful activity which is otherwise often unavailable to them in prison because of their illnesses. At Phillips State Prison, recreational and therapeutic activities were provided less often than twice weekly rather than several times daily for five or more days per week. In addition, often when activities were conducted, the inmate files frequently contained a notation that the inmate could not participate as he was on "lock down status."[379]

- State investigators from the Indiana Department of Mental Health studied mental health services at Putnamville Correctional Facility. They found that eight of twelve prisoners whose health records they examined were taking psychotropic medications but had no individualized treatment plans. The investigators found that the prison psychiatrist routinely prescribed medications over the phone without first examining his patients, and discovered one prisoner with toxic levels of the prescribed drug lithium in his bloodstream.[380]

- In the final report issued in July 1999 by the Special Master overseeing the New Mexico prison system, the monitor reported that, while the state appeared to be in compliance on most issues, "in only 21 (62%) of the files in which activity levels were addressed…did the staff implement the prescribed activity level."[381] In other words, in practice, the state was failing to implement its own recommendations regarding programming for seriously mentally ill prisoners. The report also found that between August 1998 and January 1999, the number of activities available to prisoners actually *decreased* from 16 to 13.[382]

- In Pennsylvania, despite good mental health protocols having been developed in recent years, seriously mentally ill prisoners housed in what are termed the Special Needs Units are supposed to be offered thirty-five hours of programming per week. However, prison administrators include two hours per day of regular exercise, meal times, and the time prisoners are out of the cells working prison jobs as part of the "programming." If these hours are excluded, it turns out that seriously mentally ill prisoners in fact receive only about four or five hours of actual mental health therapy and group programming per week.[383]

---

[379] Declaration of Dr. Kathryn Burns, attached to Plaintiffs' Motion for Preliminary Injunction, *Fluellen v. Wetherington*, Civil Case No. 1:02-CV-479-JEC (N.D. Georgia, February 20, 2003).

[380] Kevin Corcoran, "Prison Mental Health Care: 'Absolutely Atrocious,'" *Indianapolis Times*, September 17, 1997.

[381] Final Report of the Special Master – Mental Health, July 1999, p. 26, *Duran v. Johnson*, Civil Action No. 77-721-JC (N.M., 1999).

[382] Ibid., p. 26, n. 20.

[383] Human Rights Watch interviews, Graterford Prison's Special Needs Unit, Pennsylvania, August 12, 2002.

- In Mississippi's enormous Parchman prison (officially known as the Mississippi State Penitentiary), one part-time psychiatrist and two university psychiatrists put in a total of forty hours per week of psychiatric coverage, much of it tele-medicine-based. The prison also has five psych-assistants and four case managers. Its one psychologist position was, as of May 2003, vacant. This paltry staff is responsible for the mental health needs of a prison population of well over five thousand prisoners spread across buildings and land that take up a massive eighteen thousand acres.[384] The university psychiatrists never visit the prisoners in person, and have sessions via teleconferencing about once every three months, for about ten minutes. Other than medications, few prisoners have any access to counseling or therapy, and if they do it is usually for only a few minutes a month. Psychiatrist John Norton admitted to never having seen the facilities at most of the institutions for which he does tele-medicine.[385] Norton's patients are, he told Human Rights Watch, "medication only. A chronic schizophrenic who's doing well on meds may never go to counseling." Like many of the more cash-strapped prison systems, Mississippi does not mandate that seriously mentally ill prisoners have access to a minimum numbers of hours of counseling per week. The state's other prisons have equally low levels of staffing and equally poor access to counseling and group therapy: at Central Mississippi Penitentiary, 2,500 prisoners are serviced by thirty-two hours a week of psychiatric coverage, one non-Ph.D.-level psychologist and ten lower level case managers, psychiatric evaluators and psych assistants. Meanwhile, the Southern Mississippi Penitentiary currently has no psychiatric coverage at all. If prisoners are deemed to need anything beyond medication, they have to be bussed to the Central Mississippi facility.[386] Linda Powell, director of utilization review and case management at the University of Mississippi Medical Center, which provides medical and mental health services inside the prisons, stated to Human Rights Watch that Mississippi's prisoners "have very little group therapy."[387]

- In Hawaii, a state in which almost 20 percent of the prisoners are on psychotropic medications, the Bureau of Justice Statistics found that fewer than 6 percent of prisoners were receiving any form of therapy or counseling.[388]

- At the Washington Correctional Center for Women, many of the prisoners complain that they have only minimal access to therapy and regular group programs, but that they are medicated at the drop of a hat. Prisoner O.T. told Human Rights Watch:

  > They need to hire more counselors and more therapists and not [use] so much medication. They med people up. If they counseled them, they might

---

[384] The mental health staffing levels were provided by Linda Powell, director of utilization review and case management, University of Mississippi Medical Center, the organization contracted with the Department of Corrections to provide medical and mental health services in the state's prisons. Human Rights Watch telephone interview with Linda Powell, May 1, 2003. The inmate numbers and size of the prison are numbers generated by the Mississippi Department of Corrections.

[385] Human Rights Watch telephone interview with John Norton, associate professor of psychiatry and neurology, University of Mississippi, July 24, 2002.

[386] Human Rights Watch telephone interview with Linda Powell, May 1, 2003.

[387] Ibid.

[388] BJS, *Mental Health Treatment in State Prisons, 2000,* 2001 appendix table B, p. 6.

not need the medication. But they don't have the funding for it. People walk around zoned out. They're just not there.[389]

Many other prisoners echoed her views. While Human Rights Watch recognizes that patients are not clinical experts on appropriate dosages of medications, the fact that many prisoners complained of being powerfully medicated without adequate counseling leads us to believe that this should be an area of ongoing concern within the prison system. This problem was also referred to by Mike Robbins, Washington's former Acting Mental Health Director, who acknowledged that in a prison mental health setting too often the psychiatrist (the doctor who medicates) serves as the primary responder to, and care-giver for, mental health needs rather than the psychologist (the clinician who offers therapy and counseling). In essence, this means that mental illness is dealt with first and foremost, and oftentimes exclusively, through medication.

Lack of Confidentiality

Lack of confidentiality during prisoner meetings with mental health staff is widespread. In a prison context, confidentiality is defined as sound privacy rather than visual privacy, in other words, whether a prisoner can talk to mental health staff without being overheard by correctional officers and other prisoners. The lack of confidentiality is particularly acute in facilities or units where prisoners are kept in their cells twenty-four hours a day.

In numerous facilities that Human Rights Watch visited while researching this report, locked-down or segregated prisoners stated that their main contact with caseworkers and psychologists was in the form of cell-front visits. Because of the lack of adequate numbers of security staff needed to move such prisoners from their cells into settings in which such private counseling can take place, and because of a tendency of prison mental health staff to downplay the importance of confidentiality, all-too-often these prisoners are provided with cell-front sessions that can be overheard by everyone on the block. Many prisoners have told us that their conversations with mental health staff are limited to cell-front exchanges in which they refuse to say anything personal because of the lack of privacy.

"It's a common problem," Dr. Jeffrey Metzner told Human Rights Watch. "It's easy to become institutionalized as a mental health provider. I go to lots of prisons where we make it an issue because they don't have adequate sound privacy."[390]

For example, in October 2000, the National Commission on Correctional Health Care wrote an accreditation report on the supermax prison in Wisconsin and found that:

> Officers are with the inmates during all examinations. Many of the PA [physician assistant] and physician sick call visits are done through the cell door. The officers do step back from the door; however, other inmates on that range can hear the exchange of information. Neither auditory nor visual privacy is maintained. The Standard [regarding confidentiality] is not met.[391]

---

[389] Human Rights Watch visited Washington Correctional Center for Women, August 21, 2002.

[390] Human Rights Watch telephone interview with Dr. Jeffrey Metzner, February 12, 2003.

[391] The National Commission on Correctional Health Care, *Accreditation Report*, October 27, 2000, p. 6.

According to a federal district court, on Unit 32 of Parchman Prison in Mississippi, "[w]hat mental health services are provided generally take place at the inmate's cell within hearing of other inmates and guards. This results in the failure of inmates to tell the mental health specialists anything of substance."[392] The court ordered the Mississippi Department of Corrections to ensure that, "All inmates receiving mental health counseling or evaluation shall meet with the mental health professionals in a private setting."[393]

> Those inmates diagnosed with psychosis and severe mental health illnesses shall be housed separately and apart from all other inmates. The medication levels of all inmates receiving psychotropic medications shall be monitored and assessed in accordance with appropriate medical standards.

Medication

The development of powerful drugs for the treatment of mental illness has enabled a revolution in mental health care in the United States, including in U.S. prisons. The newer types of psychotropic medications have increased the alleviation of symptoms and increased the prospects of recovery for people with mental illness and with far fewer and less debilitating side effects than older medication. Because they increase the likelihood that the prisoner will adhere to a treatment plan, they can reduce long-term mental health treatment costs. Yet many prisons systems limit use of the newer medications because of their cost. The unique context of prisons imposes certain constraints on the delivery and monitoring of medications.

Proper Medication

In some states, because of inadequate mental health staffing, medication is prescribed without an adequate evaluation of the prisoner and the development of an individualized treatment plan. For example, experts examining mental health care in Alabama prisons noted:

> Anyone receiving prescription medication must be assessed by the prescribing psychiatrist on a regular basis to determine the effectiveness or lack thereof and potential side effects. There are numerous instances throughout the Alabama prison system in which psychiatrists prescribe medications for periods of up to three months without any face-to-face contact with the recipient. The nursing staff are medical/surgical type nurses and do not document inmate response to prescribed psychotropic medications.... [M]ental health records reveal instances in which inmates experiencing psychiatric difficulties are prescribed psychotropic medication by a psychiatrist in a remote location who has never seen the inmate. A nurse, with no experience or training in the signs or symptoms of mental illness, relays the information on which the psychiatrist bases his prescription decision. There is no documentation as to the effectiveness of the prescribed medication and no planned follow-up.[394]

---

[392] *Russell v. Johnson*, 2003 U.S. Dist. Lexis 8573 (N.D. Miss. May 21, 2003). Although the court was only addressing the conditions of death row inmates housed on Unit 32, experts for plaintiffs told Human Rights Watch that the conditions are the same throughout Unit 32, including appalling levels of mental health treatment.
[393] Ibid.
[394] Kathryn Burns, M.D. and Jane Haddad, Psy.D., "Mental Health Care in the Alabama Department of Corrections," *Bradley v. Hightower*, Civ. No. 92-A-70-N (N.D. Ala., June 30, 2000)), pp. 81-83.

The Department of Justice's investigation of mental health care in the Wyoming State Prison uncovered many deficiencies, including inappropriate medication. Medication was sometimes inappropriately withheld; prisoners were regularly denied access to mental health staff; prisoners in administrative segregation routinely failed to receive prescribed medications; and psychotropic medications were often prescribed by physicians lacking mental health expertise. This, "resulted in incorrect or dangerous choices of medications, inappropriate polypharmacy, improper and abrupt discontinuances of addicting psychotropics and occasional inappropriate use of emergency medications."[395]

New and more effective medications, such as selective serotonin reuptake inhibitors (anti-depressants) and the atypical antipsychotics are now available for the treatment of mental illness. Unfortunately, these medications are usually much more expensive than older ones. Because of their costs, the "[n]ewer medications…are not used as frequently in prisons and in jails as they are in the general community."[396] Some prison systems have open formularies, allowing psychiatrists to prescribe the most up-to-date medications.[397] But others, such as Mississippi's, still mainly prescribe older medications to their seriously mentally ill prisoners; they cut costs by prescribing the more expensive atypical drugs to only a minority of their seriously mentally ill prisoners.[398] Some very effective drugs such as Chozaril are rarely used in prisons because they require expensive work-ups and continual blood monitoring.

According to Patricia Perlmutter, the lead attorney representing plaintiff prisoners in a lawsuit about New Jersey's prison mental health services, until the state agreed to settle the case in 1999, "the more modern medications weren't available. The prisoners would suffer side effects, then they would refuse their medications."[399] Dr. Dennis Koson plaintiffs' expert in the New Jersey case, reported that:

> Continuity of care is compromised when inmates arrive in the system on "non-CMS [Correctional Medical Services, the private correctional health care provider] formulary" drugs and are taken off them. For example, after many drug trials and a very turbulent psychiatric history in administrative segregation, John Doe 137 was hospitalized at the Forensic Hospital and finally stabilized on Olanzapine, a new and very effective antipsychotic agent that is off-formulary. He stabilized very quickly on the drug and was returned to the prison system on July18, 1997. An on-call psychiatrist was called and, in a telephone order, discontinued the Olanzapine without examining the patient. John Doe 137 became increasingly psychotic and resistant to medication treatment (although he was taking it) which culminated in the use of the involuntary medication process in January 1998.[400]

---

[395] Letter to Governor James Geringer from Bill Lann Lee, acting assistant attorney general, Civil Rights Division, U.S. Department of Justice, June 29, 1999.

[396] Council of State Governments, *Consensus Project* (2002), p. 137.

[397] This is similar to the Medicaid formulary, which gives mentally ill Medicaid patients access to the latest generation of anti-depressants and anti-psychotics.

[398] Human Rights Watch telephone interview with Dr. Terry Kupers, February 7, 2003. In Mississippi, Kupers has found that the newer atypical medications are available, but only on a limited basis.

[399] Human Rights Watch telephone interview with Patricia Perlmutter, attorney, May 13, 2002.

[400] *New Jersey Prison System Report of Dr. Dennis Koson, C.F. v. Terhune*, Civil Action No. 96-1840 (D.N.J., September 8, 1998). p. 62.

Attorney Perlmutter told Human Rights Watch that Koson's findings indicated that "the failure to keep the patient on the more effective and expensive medication led to this patient's decompensating and requiring more intensive services, with a cost both to the patient's health and to the prison's management of the inmate."[401] Under the settlement in the case, monitors now approve the formulary so it is no longer restricted to the older generation of drugs.

Limited access to newer medications was among the problems cited by medical and psychiatric experts reviewing mental health services in Texas prisons in 1998 and 1999. As one expert noted:

> Medication when administered is in many cases inadequate as patients I interviewed on the active caselog demonstrated or complained of on-going symptoms or signs of mental illness or medication-induced movement disorders. Given the armamentarium of medication available including the newer atypical anti-psychotics, I would expect to find the patients having more symptom amelioration than was the case. The medications in use were mainly of the older and less expensive variety. Newer medications such as Risperidone, Olanzapine and Clozaril are not on the formulary and, although the physician can request permission to use an off-formulary drug, there are factors at work which obviously dissuade use of these drugs...In the face of the poor response of a number of the patients to the formulary — approved medications, I believe good medical practice would call for clinical trials of alternate medication, at a minimum. If the goal of the managed care system is to save money, it is doing so at the cost of rendering inadequate and potentially harmful care to the patients.[402]

Delivery

Prisons have their own unique rules for how and when medications can be delivered; rules which may not designed to meet the needs of patients. To prevent hoarding of medications and to ensure the medication is in fact taken, most prisons deliver medication to prisoners in single doses. In many prisons, prisoners must spend an hour or more standing in line two or three times a day to receive their medicine — an inconvenience which deters many from continuing with their medication regime. Some prisons have separate lines for psychotropic medication, which identifies the prisoners in those lines as mentally ill. Some prisoners refuse to take medication because they do not wanted to be identified as "bugs" — prison slang for prisoners who have mental illness.

Some prisons require prisoners to take medication in the early evening that should be taken just before a patient goes to sleep. Taking the medications early either causes the patient to fall asleep in the late afternoon, or to remain awake, and increasingly anxious, before the medication takes effect. At the California Institute for Women, in the southern California town of Corona, a psychiatrist at the prison told Human Rights Watch that if prisoners are given medications at five-thirty p.m., they are likely to still be awake two or three hours later, and that these medications, at high dosage, if not

---

[401] Email correspondence from Attorney Perlmutter to Human Rights Watch, July 15, 2003.
[402] Letter from Dennis M. Jurczak, M.D. to Donna Brorby, Esq., re: *Ruiz v. Scott*, January 19, 1999, p.2; on file at Human Rights Watch. See also, letter from Dr. Jeffrey L. Metzner, to Donna Brorby, Esq. re: Texas Department of Criminal Justice, December 31, 1998, p. 10: " Psychopharmacological treatment was problematic due to a formulary which did not include atypical antipsychotic medications and only one SSRI medication." (referring to mental health treatment at the Estelle Unit prison complex).

followed by sleep, can cause patients to suffer considerable levels of anxiety.[403] "There are no night-time [medication deliveries]," a psychologist at the prison reported. "There should be. A lot of psychiatrists write prescriptions for drugs to be taken just before they go to sleep. But they're taking their meds at 5 or 6 o'clock — and then they fall asleep at 7 o'clock and wake up at 3."[404]

In most prison systems, trained nurses distribute the medications; but in some, correctional officers with no medical background are given this responsibility. Todd Winstrom, an attorney with the Wisconsin Coalition for Advocacy, told Human Rights Watch that in some Wisconsin prisons, guards, rather than nurses, both distribute medications and are responsible for re-ordering the medications when a prisoner's supplies run low.

> That's their policy. It's standard procedure. It's spoken of as an article of faith that guards don't like doing this. They don't regard it as their job. Between low interest and lack of training, errors are pretty common. Sometimes they just allow the medications to run out. It's very common to see a lapse before refills are ordered.[405]

Winstrom believes that the problems would be minimized if nurses were in charge of the medications. "They understand the importance of this and they have the training. Nurses would be afraid of the consequences to their professional license."[406] In Mississippi, prison psychiatrist John Norton told Human Rights Watch that "specially trained guards," rather than nurses, distribute psychotropic medications to prisoners.[407]

Distribution of medications by correctional officers is troubling for other reasons. It raises both privacy concerns (non-medical personnel gaining access to confidential medication information on prisoners) and also heightens the risk of inappropriate delivery (medically untrained staff may unknowingly distribute the wrong medication, or the wrong dosage, or distribute it at the wrong time, not realizing that many drugs must be administered at roughly the same time every day). Such practice is in clear violation of procedures developed by the National Commission on Correctional Healthcare (NCCHC), the American Correctional Association (ACA) and other accreditation organizations.

Medication Discontinuity

The sudden removal of a person from strong anti-depressants or anti-psychotic medications can lead to serious withdrawal effects, including changes in blood pressure and heart rate, irritation, anxiety, sleep-disorders, nausea, paranoia, even, at times, psychosis. Mental health care providers in the free world take care to wean their patients off of these medications slowly. "If you don't," psychiatrist Dr. Terry Kupers explained to Human Rights Watch:

> they can get neuro-physiological rebounds: with the anti-depressant Paxil, they get dizziness, seizures, faintness, agitation, insomnia, anxiety and panic attacks. When

---

[403] Human Rights Watch Interview with Surya Edpuganti, staff psychiatrist, California Institute for Women, California, July 15, 2002.
[404] Human Rights Watch interviews with mental health teams, California Institute for Women, California, July 15, 2002.
[405] Human Rights Watch telephone interview with Todd Winstrom, attorney, Coalition for Advocacy, April 1, 2003.
[406] Ibid.
[407] Human Rights Watch telephone interview with John Norton, associate professor of psychiatry and neurology, University of Mississippi, July 24, 2002.

someone is on anti-psychotic medication, if you discontinue that precipitously they're very likely to have a relapse of the psychotic condition.[408]

In prison, however, the sudden withdrawal from powerful medications is not uncommon. When prisoners are moved from jail to prison, or from one prison to another, any medication they were on will usually be discontinued and they must see a new psychiatrist to have a decision made as to what medications they will receive. In under-staffed correctional mental health systems with few resources devoted to record-keeping and the tracking of mentally ill prisoners, prisoners can wait days, even weeks, to see a psychiatrist in the new institution and to be placed on medication again. Security can also disrupt medication delivery: for example, entire units or wings of prisons are placed for days or weeks under lock-down because of a disturbance. The lockdown means prisoners cannot stand in line for their medication — yet, the prison may not have systems in place for ensuring delivery of medications to individuals in their cells.

Examples of problems in timely delivery of correct medication include the following:

- In South Carolina, investigators found that prisoners at Lee Correctional Institution routinely had to wait days for needed medications. "Medications were considered timely if they were available within two days of when the inmate needed them," they reported. "Approximately 46% (24 of 52) of the medications that we reviewed were not administered within these time periods; three of these medications appeared not to be administered at all."[409]

- In Mississippi, Dr. John Norton, a University of Mississippi psychiatrist contracted to provide a few hours a week of psychiatric services for the Department of Corrections, states that prisoners frequently wait a week or more to be put back on medications after having been withdrawn from the medications when they were removed from their previous institution. "I'll see them within a few days," he asserted. "There definitely can be a gap in medications of a few days. If they come in over the weekend, there'll definitely be a gap. I haven't seen many go without meds for over a week. It's not optimal. But the volume is huge."[410]

- Todd Winstrom, an attorney with Wisconsin's Coalition for Advocacy, described to Human Rights Watch some of the medication problems at specialized mental health unit at Taycheedah women's prison. Over the Labor Day weekend in 2001, Winstrom's clients told him that the prisoners did not receive prescribed Benzodiazepine-category drugs such as Lorazapam. "Supplies had been allowed to run out," Winstrom asserted. "And new ones had not been ordered. I've looked at other cases and I've found that this isn't uncommon." Abrupt withdrawal from this medication, he stated:

---

[408] Kupers was contacted several times during the research for this report. This quote is from a telephone interview on October 10, 2002.

[409] *A Review of Medical Services at the SC Department of Corrections*, Legislative Audit Council, March 2000, report summary, p. 4. Synopsis available online at: http://www.state.sc.us/sclac/Reports/2000/SCDC.htm, accessed on September 8, 2003.

[410] Human Rights Watch telephone interview with John Norton, M.D., July 24, 2002.

can cause serious medical problems — convulsions, seizures, episodes of delusions and dementia, changes in blood pressure and heart rate. In extreme cases it can be fatal. One woman exhibited these symptoms. Non-medical staff made the decision she was malingering and placed her in isolation.[411]

Winstrom also alleged that medical charts for this woman indicate that in a one-month period she was denied 40 percent of her medications. As a result, her behavior worsened, and she began accumulating disciplinary tickets. In another instance, Winstrom told Human Rights Watch that medical records indicate a female prisoner received only 50 percent of her prescribed medications over a twelve-month period.[412]

- In California, mentally ill prisoners who are housed in the general population reported interruptions in their medication. For example, one prisoner, D.F., at Corcoran State Prison stated that he " didn't get [his] medications for six days," after he was transferred to the prison from another one. D.F. alleged that the medical discontinuities occurred every time he was transferred from one facility to another. "They take your medication," he explained. "At the new institution you have to go through the medical thing to get your medication. You wait up to five to seven days to get your medication. By then you're too far gone to know anything. By then, man, it's not cool."[413] At California State Prison at Sacramento, another prisoner, J.G., told Human Rights Watch that in the general population he'd sometimes miss his medications for a couple days after his prescription had expired.[414]

Abrupt withdrawal from medication can also lead to prisoners acting out and becoming disruptive. According to an investigation into Wyoming State Penitentiary by the Department of Justice:

In several cases we reviewed, inmates in general population predictably became problematic after [Wyoming State Prison] inappropriately and suddenly withheld long-standing dosages of benzodiazapines. The discontinuation of medication resulted in irritability, which led in turn to charges of threats and abusive language, and resulted in punitive detention placements in administrative segregation....[415]

Inadequate Monitoring of Medication Side Effects
The first generation of anti-psychotics, including drugs such as Thorazine and Haldol, which are still commonly used in prisons, can cause a Parkinson's-like illness known as Extra Pyramidal Syndrome (EPS). Patients placed onto these drugs can develop the symptoms of EPS almost immediately: excessive saliva, a powerful clamping of the mouth, severe back and neck cramping, and spasms.[416] The syndrome can be treated by the use of Cogentin and Artane medications. A more serious side effect associated with early anti-psychotics is Tardive Dyskinsia, essentially a degenerative muscle-tic and tremor that begins in the face and spreads throughout the entire upper body. There are no

---

[411] Human Rights Watch telephone interview with Todd Winstrom, attorney, Coalition for Advocacy, June 5, 2002.
[412] Ibid., February 12, 2003.
[413] Human Rights Watch interview with D.F., Corcoran, California, July 11, 2002.
[414] Human Rights Watch interview with J.G., California State Prison, Sacramento, July 18, 2002.
[415] Letter to Governor James Geringer from Bill Lann Lee, acting assistant attorney general, Civil Rights Division, U.S. Department of Justice, June 29, 1999.
[416] Information on the side effects of these medications provided by Dr. Terry Kupers, Human Rights Watch telephone interview, October 10, 2002.

medicines to counter this condition. In many prison systems that still prescribe the earlier and cheaper anti-psychotics, severely ill prisoners are put in the uncomfortable position of having to choose between getting their illness under control, but developing Tardive Dyskinsia, or opting not to take the anti-psychotics and thus risking a psychotic break. More recent anti-psychotics, while not producing Tardive Dyskinsia in patients, nevertheless have their own host of side-effects. Atypical anti-psychotics such as Xyprexa, Resperdal, and Seroquel can cause obesity, impotence, heart problems, and passivity. Newer anti-depressants can cause headaches, tremors, and even confusion.[417]

All of these symptoms need to be carefully monitored. Our research suggests, however, that in many prisons the monitoring effort falls far short. For example:

- In Alabama, outside experts who evaluated the state's prison system reported that:

  > [T]here are several psychotropic medications which require periodic blood level monitoring and laboratory studies to check on liver, kidney and thyroid functioning to ensure the medications are not causing damage to those organs. [Yet blood] work is not routinely ordered on ADOC [Alabama Department of Corrections] inmates. Serum levels are not checked to ensure the inmate is receiving an appropriate dosage of medication. Subsequently, behaviors are attributed as being willful or manipulative rather than understood as symptomatic of untreated or improperly treated mental illness.[418]

- In New Jersey, Dr. Dennis Koson reported that :

  > Inspections and chart reviews uncovered inmates experiencing anything from mild to sometimes severe side effects of their medications that went unaddressed for significant periods of time. John Doe #136, for example, was on various psychotropic medications that resulted in dry mouth, dizziness on standing, and urinary retention. Similarly, John Doe #1, was prescribed intramuscular Prolixin, an antipsychotic medication, and noticed tremors which were a side effect of the medication. His psychiatrist then prescribed oral Prolixin, the very drug which had caused the problems. Some side effects I noted were severe and also represented irreversible neurological syndromes.[419]

- When the autopsy results came back on Timothy Perry after he had died in a Connecticut prison (see above case study on Perry), they showed that he had Thorazine in his blood,

---

[417] Ibid.

[418] Kathryn Burns, M.D. and Jane Haddad, Psy.D., "Mental Health Care in the Alabama Department of Corrections," *Bradley v. Hightower*, Civ. No. 92-A-70-N (N.D. Ala., June 30, 2000), p. 82.

[419] *New Jersey Prison System Report of Dr. Dennis Koson, C.F. v. Terhune*, Civil Action No. 96-1840 (D.N.J., September 8, 1998), p. 62.

despite the medical record indicating that he was both asthmatic and allergic to Thorazine, and that he was at risk of having a central nervous system shut-down if given the drug.[420]

- In the segregation unit at Robertson prison in Texas, forensic psychologist Keith Curry found a:

> 37 year old man with chronic paranoid schizophrenia...in a floridly psychotic state despite receiving long-lasting injectable antipsychotic medication once a month. He presented with severe Parkinsonian side-effects from his medication. He reported that mental health staff conducted cursory rounds once a month, but did not inquire about medication side-effects.... Two other inmates taking antipsychotic medications appeared to be psychiatrically stable, but presented with moderate to severe Parkinsonian side-effects that were not being adequately addressed. These side-effects are painful and debilitating, requiring immediate medical attention.[421]

Protecting Prisoners on Medication from Heat Reactions

Heat related illnesses occur when the body's temperature control system is overloaded and body temperatures rise. The risk of heat related illnesses increases when air temperatures exceed ninety degrees, especially with high humidity. Persistent heat stress may lead to heat stroke — a severe medical emergency that can damage the brain and other vital organs, and causing death or permanent disability of emergency treatment is not provided. Many commonly prescribed psychotropic drugs, including Thorazine and Haldol, as well as certain anti-depressants, render patients particularly sensitive to hot weather conditions and heat stroke. They limit the body's ability to cool itself down by sweating and suppress the brain's ability to perceive temperature changes, preventing the patient from initiating compensatory behavioral changes.[422]

Prisoners on psychotropic medication are at particular risk of heat-related illness because most live in prisons that are not air-conditioned and have poor ventilation. Although air-conditioning can be a lifesaver, not a luxury, in its absence prisoners must have access to fans, showers at least once a day, ample supplies of drinking water at all times, and ice. These basic and humane precautions — important for all prisoners — are especially important for prisoners on certain medications. However, some prisons ignore them.

- In the prison at Parchman, Mississippi, the only way to keep hordes of bugs from infesting prison cells is to shut the windows. Closing the windows during the sweltering summer months in the Mississippi Delta creates intense heat in the concrete cells in which mentally ill — as well as non-mentally ill — prisoners live. Prisoners at Parchman are denied adequate supplies of water during the summer months, leading, in some extreme cases, to prisoners drinking water from out of their toilet bowls in attempts to cool themselves down. One

---

[420] Letter from Barbara C. Wolf, M.D. to Susan Werboff, director, Office of Protection and Advocacy for Persons with Disabilities, October 23, 2000; on file at Human Rights Watch.

[421] Keith Curry, Ph.D. letter to the law offices of Donna Brorby, March 19, 2002, p. 20.

[422] This is known as an anticholinergic effect, and is caused by the medications slowing the brain's firing of the nerves that cause sweating, and by causing blood vessels in and under the skin to dilate, thus interfering with the body's ability to cool itself through sweating and through peripheral vasodilation. They also suppress the center in the brain where temperature change is perceived and compensatory behavior initiated.

mentally ill prisoner on the medication Remeron, T.Y., told an outside expert on heat stroke that in late June 2002:

> We were just without any water on the Unit for almost a week. The sewage has been backed up in every cell and people started to throw their wastes out into the hall.... I tried to stay hydrated with the water they bring at meals, but that's the only liquid we got all day: a cup of coffee at breakfast; a small glass of juice at lunch; and a small glass of water at dinner. It wasn't enough for me to take my medicine. And it wasn't enough to live on, especially in this heat. I felt myself drying out and getting weaker. My mouth was cracked and my throat was rough.[423]

An emergency medicine expert, Dr. Susi Vasallo, visited Parchman on behalf of plaintiffs in a class action lawsuit to render an opinion concerning risks of heat-related illness on Unit 32, the death row at the prison.[424] She found that all of the death row prisoners have one or more high risk factors for heat stroke. Nevertheless, the physician serving Unit 32 was "surprised to learn of the risks of heat illness" and had never considered whether the medication the prisoners were taking put them at great risk for heat related illness.

Dr. Vasallo, who describes herself as a Texan who loves the heat, entered one of the prisoner cells when the afternoon sun was shining on it and described it as the same "as getting into a car parked in the hot Texas sun and sitting with the windows rolled up." She found many of the prisoners had no access to fans, infrequent access to showers, and sometimes even limited access to water. They were not allowed to shade their cell windows from direct sunlight, and in the outdoor exercise pens, there was no shade from the sun.

In May 2003, a federal district court found that the ventilation in Unit 32-C:

> is inadequate to afford prisoners a minimal level of comfort during the summer months. While temperatures obviously run high during the summer months in Mississippi, inmates on lockdown status, such as the inmates on Death Row, must rely on the Mississippi Department of Corrections for minimal relief. The probability of heat-related illness is extreme at Unit 32-C, and is dramatically more so for mentally ill inmates who often do not take appropriate behavioral steps to deal with the heat. Also, the medications commonly given to treat various medical problems interfere with the body's ability to maintain a normal temperature.[425]

---

[423] This quote was taken from the plaintiffs' application for a temporary restraining order and/or preliminary injunction allowing plaintiffs' counsel and experts to tour death row on August 8, 2002. *Willie Russell v. Robert Johnson*, 210 F. Supp. 2d 804 (N.D. Miss., 2002). Until the judge granted this order, Mississippi had refused to allow the ACLU or any of its medical experts into the prison to view conditions first-hand.

[424] Dr. Vassallo, is a board-certified physician in Emergency Medicine and Medical Toxicology on the faculty of the New York School of Medicine/Bellevue Hospital Center. Susi Vassallo, M.D., "Report on the Risks of Heat-Related Illness and Access to Medical Care for Death Row Inmates Confined to Unit 32, Mississippi State Penitentiary, Parchman, Mississippi, for the National Prison Project of the American Civil Liberties Union, September 2002.

[425] *Russell v. Johnson*, 2003 U.S. Dist. Lexis 8573 (N.D. Miss., May 21, 2003). The Department of Corrections sought a stay of the court's order while it appealed the decision.

The court ordered prison officials to take heat measurements several times daily from May through September and ordered them to ensure each cell has a fan, and that prisoners have access to ice water and can take daily showers when the heat index is ninety degrees or above. Alternatively, the officials could simply provide fans, ice water, and daily showers during those months without taking heat measurements.

- At the California Institute for Women, in the desert climate of Southern California, one forty-five-year-old prisoner, D.O.F., currently taking lithium and Resperidal to stop her from hearing voices and acting on those internal stimuli, reported that while she had good access to counselors and to psychiatrists:

  > the only thing I'd ask is that we get our heat fans back. I get sick. I feel faint, light, nauseous, listless. I can't operate, I can't function. It happens every day as long as it is hot. It gets hot. Sweat just pours down your face, your body.[426]

- Another seriously mentally ill woman at the same prison, E.F., has been in-and-out of correctional settings since 1980, when she hit a stranger over the head with a bottle in San Francisco's Chinatown. "I thought I'd tell China they shouldn't mess with the United States," she said in explanation. She is currently serving life without parole for a crime she committed while in a psychotic state. For her, too, the heat is one of her biggest concerns. "At first they gave everybody fans because it was so hot," she recalls.

  > And then they never gave anybody fans and people would faint and get sick. It's so hot sometimes you can't bear it. Without a fan in the cell, it's like a boiler house. People get faintish, nauseous, get dizzy, become irritable, don't want to take their medications.[427]

- According to the recent findings of a federal district court, the Julia Tutwiler Prison for women in Alabama, some of whose prisoners are mentally ill and taking psychotropic medication, is "extremely hot in the summer, and lacks needed ventilation, creating a stuffy, stagnant climate."[428] There is no air conditioning. The warden put large floor fans on some dorms, but the effect was "simply to move hot air around." Other measures provided little relief from heat. Although there are ice calls twice a day, ice was sometimes not available at mid-day when the heat is at its hottest. There were no instruments to monitor the heat, so there was no way for officials to determine when the temperature exceeded ninety degrees and therefore, according to prison protocols, prisoners were entitled to additional ice, opportunities to shower, and increased access to drinking water. In disciplinary segregation,

---

[426] Human Rights Watch interview with D.O.F., California Institute for Women, California, July 15, 2002.

[427] Human Rights Watch interview with E.F., California Institute for Women, California, July 15, 2002.

[428] *Laube v. Haley*, Civil Action No. 02-T-957-N, Order (M.D. Ala., December 2, 2002), p. 23. Denying plaintiffs' motion for a preliminary injunction, the court ruled that plaintiffs did not show a substantial likelihood of proving these conditions rose to a level of a constitutional violation, because of insufficient evidence in the record. It asked plaintiffs to provide more specific information on the temperature, humidity, and opportunities for inmates to gain relief from the heat.

the climate was "like a desert." There are only five fans for the seventeen cells in segregation.[429]

- Dr. Jeffrey Metzner, a psychiatric expert retained by plaintiffs in connection with the *Ruiz* litigation in Texas, reviewed reports relevant to prisoners experiencing heat-related illnesses as part of his audit of Texas mental health care. He reported that between June 10 and July 30, 1998, at least sixteen prisoners experienced significant symptoms related to hyperthermia, three of whom died. One-fourth of the prisoners were receiving psychotropic medication and had a history of mental illness. One of the prisoners was a forty-seven-year-old man with a history of paranoid schizophrenia who was receiving Haldol and Congentin, when he died because of hyperthermia. Another prisoner who Dr. Metzner identified as having experienced heat-related problems exacerbated by psychotropic medications was sent to the hospital in June, 1998 with a 107 degree temperature. He had a complicated medical history including multiple sclerosis, diabetes, asthma, and schizophrenia. Like other Texas prisoners, he lived in a unit without air-conditioning, despite the one-hundred degree temperatures to which Texas summers soar.[430]

Inadequate Efforts to Ensure Medication Compliance

One of the most frustrating manifestations of serious mental illness is that frequently very ill individuals believe themselves to be fine, and often believe those who encourage them to take medications are involved in some form of conspiracy against them. Many also stop taking their medications because they are experiencing unpleasant side effects and their medications have not been adjusted in a timely manner. Mental health treatment providers in the community work constantly with their clients to ensure they continue their medication and to educate them about the importance of the medication. Yet, because prison mental health resources are stretched so thin, little effort is devoted to explaining the need for and nature of medication to prisoners.

When prisoners refuse to take their medications, little effort is devoted to coaxing them to change their minds. At most mental health staff may visit a prisoner's cell front and briefly try to convince him or her to take their medications. If a prisoner who stops medications seriously decompensates and becomes a danger to himself or others, he may be involuntarily medicated on an emergency basis and may be sent to the prison's mental health hospital or acute care unit where mental health staff can continue to administer medication involuntarily if certain legally-mandated administrative steps are followed. Yet, even in instances where involuntary medication is actually necessary because a prisoner is refusing to take or his or her medications and has, as a result, become dangerously psychotic, sometimes prison officials do not take the time to seek legal permission for this procedure. "I've seen it happen in Washington, and it happens for reasons that apply in other systems as well," said David Lovell, of the University of Washington. "Lack of staffing can result in not having a routine, systematic, involuntary medication practice. Prisoners will simply vegetate or be put in Ag Seg [administrative segregation] or special housing."[431]

---

[429] Ibid.

[430] Letter from Dr. Jeffrey L Metzner to attorney Donna Brorby, December 31, 1998 regarding the Texas Department of Criminal Justice.

[431] Human Rights Watch telephone interview with David Lovell, professor, University of Washington, October 18, 2002.

Mental health staff may simply ignore prisoners who refuse medication or remove them from the mental health roster. For example, according to Patricia Perlmutter, the attorney who represented plaintiff prisoners in a suit against the New Jersey Department of Corrections:

> If a prisoner refused medication, rather than try to reengage them in treatment, or offering alternative medicines or psychotherapy, the system was so short-staffed they would just strike your name from the mental health caseload. So the most seriously mentally ill wouldn't show up on the caseload.[432]

Florida attorney Randall Berg told Human Rights Watch that between fifty and one hundred seriously mentally ill prisoners at Florida State Prison (FSP) stopped taking medications after the state decided to concentrate its most seriously ill offenders at that prison, and to move those not on medications to other (reportedly better) prisons.[433] Prison mental health staff at FSP did not increase their monitoring of the seriously ill prisoners. Instead, when the prisoners stopped taking their medications, their status was downgraded from "S-3" to "S-2," meaning that a psych specialist stopped by their cell only once a month instead of every week, and that they were seen by a psychiatrist only every ninety days instead of every thirty. Berg asserted that several prisoners decompensated and had to be transferred to crisis units to be stabilized after dropping their medications.

The problem of seriously mentally ill prisoners choosing to withdraw from their medication regimens is exacerbated in states which exclude prisoners on the mental health caseload from desirable programs. For example, in California, prisoners on medication for mental illness do not qualify for work furlough programs. According to social worker Marilyn Montenegro, who works with mentally ill women coming out of prison, "[work furlough] is a very desirable program, so the inmates stop taking their medications and a lot come to the program and the staff realize there's something going on there. And the women say: that's what I did to come here."[434] Sue Burton, executive director of a small re-entry home for mentally ill women leaving prison in California also stated that "the women will deny themselves medical treatment, because they have to be medically cleared to get work-furlough."[435] Rick Jordan, the community involvement officer for Washington's McNeil Island prison, sees a similar problem. "We have zero pre-release camp beds for people on psychotropic medications," Jordan explained to Human Rights Watch. "It's counterproductive to tell people you can go there if you're not taking medications. People stop taking their medications in a usually vain attempt to get there. Then their behavior deteriorates."[436]

---

[432] Human Rights Watch telephone interview with Patricia Perlmutter, May 13, 2002. The settlement is reported at: *D.M. v. Terhune*, 67 F. Supp. 2d 401 (D.N.J, 1999).

[433] Human Rights Watch telephone interview with Randall Berg, attorney, Miami, Florida, April 21, 2003.

[434] Human Rights Watch interview with Marilyn Montenegro, social worker, Los Angeles, California, May 17, 2002.

[435] Human Rights Watch interviews with Sue Burton, et. al., New Way of Life, a re-entry home in Watts, Los Angeles, California, May 17, 2002.

[436] Information provided during Human Rights Watch telephone conference call with senior Washington Department of Corrections officials, February 28, 2003 and Human Rights Watch interview with Rich Jordan, community involvement officer, McNeil Island, Washington, August 22, 2002. McNeil Island's mental health program is run as a pilot program, with the Washington Department of Corrections having contracted out much of the work to the University of Washington.

E.M., Illinois, August 18, 2002

When I was transferred to Joliet Correctional Center the psychiatrist locked me in a glass windowed cell on suicide watch. Then I was prescribed more medication in higher doses. And after seven months I was transferred to Menard Correctional Center where I was locked in a freezing cold glass windowed cell naked with nothing on suicide watch. But, I couldn't cope with being froze naked, so I was released out into cell-house population. The psychiatrist changed my medication and continued to suggest higher doses. Eventually, I began to feel sick with headaches, dizziness, cold sweats, lower back pains and chest decongestion. Then I began having reoccurrences of lockjaw and small type seizures from the medication. I was sent over to the hospital and the psychiatrist stated, 'oh it's nothing.' Sometimes I have episodes of deep depression and frustration and need to be seened by the Crisis Team, but the nurse that occasionally brings my medication says, 'it's a Friday night, nobody here is going to see you!' I spoke to the psychiatrist about the neglect of the nurse and how my depression has become worst from being here. He says, 'I just think your momma babied you too much.' After my father died I fell off into a deeper state of depression and swallowed as many cold pills as I could and tried to cut my throat. The med tec (male nurse) stated, 'you should have swallowed more pills if you want to kill yourself.' I've been written disciplinary reports for acting out when the nurses play games don't bring me the medication.

X.   INSUFFICIENT PROVISION OF SPECIALIZED FACILITIES FOR SERIOUSLY ILL PRISONERS

Prison mental health services typically includes at least three general levels. Acute care or round-the-clock hospital level service is for prisoners whose symptoms of psychosis, suicide risk, or dangerousness justify intensive care and even intrusive measures such as forced medication. Sub-acute care is typically provided outside of hospital settings for prisoners suffering from severe and chronic conditions that require intensive case management, psychosocial interventions, crisis management, and psychopharmacology in a safe and contained environment. Outpatient care is provided in the general population for prisoners who can function relatively normally. It can involve medication, psychotherapy, supportive counseling, and other interventions for prisoners whose illness is either not very severe or for chronically mentally ill prisoners whose symptoms are either under control or have gone into remission and they are essentially asymptomatic.

Most prisoners who receive mental health treatment live in the prison system's general population.[437] As Ohio Department of Rehabilitation and Correction Director Dr. Reginald Wilkinson told Human Rights Watch, "general population is to prison what the community is to a community mental health system."[438] That is, in Ohio, as in many other states, the goal of the prison mental health staff is to enable prisoners with mental illness to live in the general population. In Ohio, for example, 80 percent of prisoners on the mental health caseload live in general population facilities. The rest are in residential treatment units, special crisis units or a psychiatric hospital.

Our research suggests that, as a general rule, prison systems lack sufficient "beds" or places for mentally ill prisoners other than in the general population. There is a shortage of acute care and hospital beds as well as long-term intermediate care. As a result, prisoners are often removed from acute care settings simply to free up beds for other prisoners, not because they no longer need intensive services. Moreover, many states lack intermediate care facilities — long-term residential facilities that provide more extensive mental health and social services — to house prisoners who cannot cope in the general prison population. Where intermediate care facilities exist, they typically only serve a fraction of the population who could benefit from settings that provide a full menu of therapeutic and rehabilitative services.

Crisis Care

Short-term crisis care is essential in a prison setting. Most prisons have either an acute-care facility or the option of sending prisoners to a psychiatric hospital or forensic center. Once the prisoners are stabilized, they are returned to the general population. Correctional and mental health experts across the country have told Human Rights Watch that in-patient beds and acute care facilities are too few in number for the prisoners who need them. Prisoners cycle repeatedly back and forth between prisons, where they do not receive sufficient treatment, and inpatient facilities, where they are permitted to stay for only a short while. Once returned to regular prison setting, as Dr. Jeffrey Metzner told Human Rights Watch, such prisoners frequently "decompensate or clinically deteriorate."[439]

---

[437] BJS, *Mental Health Treatment in State Prisons, 2000*, 2001, p. 4.
[438] Human Rights Watch telephone interview with Dr. Reginald Wilkinson, July 3, 2003.
[439] Human Rights Watch telephone interview with Dr. Jeffrey Metzner, April 2, 2003.

- In New York State, the Central New York Psychiatric Center (CNYPC) is a 206-bed maximum-security hospital that provides the only in-patient psychiatric beds for a prison system with sixty-six thousand prisoners. According to the Correctional Association of New York, the facility is bright, clean, orderly, and calm. There are no cells or bars, even for prisoners who have been brought there from disciplinary lockdown. The facility offers extensive treatment services and therapeutic activities.[440] Throughout the 1990s, New York mental health officials believed that CNYPC should be expanded, noting in 1997 that the facility had not increased its capacity since 1981, even though the prisoner population in New York had more than doubled. Although New York had a lower number of in-patient beds per capita than other states of comparable or smaller size, the facility was never expanded. Instead, New York developed and expanded its Residential Crisis Treatment Programs (RCTPs), which are now located in the Mental Health Satellite Units of twelve maximum-security prisons. These RCTPs contain observation cells for prisoners on suicide watch and between six and ten dormitory beds.[441]

Disability Advocates Inc., a New York protection and advocacy agency, has filed a lawsuit on behalf of prisoners with mental illness in New York State that alleges that there are insufficient treatment opportunities and access to programs for the state's prisoners with mental illness. Among the claims in its complaint are that the number of in-patient beds at CNYPC are insufficient; that prisoners are frequently held in observation cells while they wait for days or even weeks to be admitted to CNYPC; and that the lack of in-patient beds has been so "severe that at times CNYPC has operated at or above capacity on a 'one-for-one' basis, wherein a facility must take a prisoner back from CNYPC in order to send one in."[442] Disability Advocates also alleges that many prisoners with mental illness are returned prematurely from CNYPC, even though they have a continuing need of inpatient care to stabilize their illness and to ensure they remain stabilized. It also claims that:

> Acute care is rarely offered to prisoners with mental illness unless they are deemed to be an imminent danger to self or others. Severely disabled prisoners may be gravely ill and suffering, exhibiting extreme paranoia, experiencing depression or delusions, but until they actively engage in behavior to injure themselves or pose an imminent threat to others, they often are not even evaluated for admission to CNYPC or are denied admission despite their serious medical need.[443]

- According to Roderick Hall, director of mental health at the Florida Department of Corrections, the entire prison system of 75,210 prisoners has only fifty-one acute care beds for those whom a court has ordered to be hospitalized; 184 crisis stabilization beds for

---

[440] Correctional Association of New York, *Mental Health in the House of Corrections*, forthcoming report.

[441] Research by the Correctional Association of New York indicates that the RCTPs are "woefully lacking." As their report notes, "Despite the fact the RCTP's are designed to provide critical mental health evaluation and triage services within the prison system, it is…corrections officers who police the units and enforce their own rules. 'I've known officers who will give tickets to patients on suicide watch for behavior that is obviously related to their mental illness,' says [a former mental health clinician]." Correctional Association of New York, *Mental Health in the House of Corrections*, forthcoming report.

[442] *Disability Advocates, Inc. v. New York State Office of Mental Health*, Complaint, No. 02 CV 4002 (S.D. N.Y., May 28, 2002).

[443] Ibid.

decompensating prisoners; and 323 "intermediate care" beds.[444] None of these beds are intended to be long-term housing options.

- Mississippi sends its most acutely psychotic prisoners to the privately run prison of East Mississippi Correctional Facility. However, for the three thousand remaining mentally ill prisoners on the state system's mental health roster, the state has only fourteen suicide-watch/acute care beds at Parchman, and a six-bed crisis-stabilization infirmary at the Central Mississippi Penitentiary.[445] Human Rights Watch contacted East Mississippi Correctional Facility, run by the private corporation of Wackenhut, to obtain information on its staffing levels and acute-care services. Wackenhut representatives declined to provide any information.[446]

Specialized Intermediate Care Units

Some states have created specialized assisted living units for seriously mentally ill prisoners who do not need acute care services but, who cannot function in the general population. By creating such units, "80 percent of their mental health problem is solved," Dr. Jeffrey Metzner told Human Rights Watch.[447] "It's a crucial component. These housing units can provide more of a therapeutic milieu. When you mix the non-mentally ill and the mentally ill you don't get a therapeutic milieu; you frequently get an abusive milieu." The specialized units also, "attract correctional officers with a particular interest in working with the mentally ill."[448] Unfortunately, too few states have invested adequately in this aspect of their correctional mental health systems. Those who have such units do not have enough relative to the need; others do not have any at all.

Texas, for example, has allocated approximately 1,500 acute care beds for mentally ill prisoners who have become psychotic or otherwise entered into crisis. "Frankly, it's probably more than enough. It has more than average beds per capita for in-patient care," attorney Donna Brorby told Human Rights Watch. But, Brorby continued, the Texas Department of Criminal Justice has failed to invest in sub-acute care long-term residential units. "There is little to no sub-acute care," she stated. Because of the lack of sub-acute care residential units, many seriously mentally ill prisoners end up spending much of their sentences in administrative segregation units because they prove so difficult to control in general population. "If a system doesn't have mental health care, where you find the seriously mentally ill is in segregation."[449]

Dr. Jeffrey Metzner told Human Rights Watch that he believes California, Michigan, Ohio, Georgia, New York, Vermont, New Jersey, Puerto Rico, Colorado, and Kansas have all taken steps towards creating networks of sub-acute care facilities.[450] Washington State has also created an innovative intermediate-care facility at the McNeil Island prison. A study published in 2001 by the National Institute of Corrections found that while thirty-three states operated separate long-term housing

---

[444] Human Rights Watch telephone interview with Roderick Hall, director of mental health, Florida Department of Corrections, April 13, 2003; BJS, *Prisoners in 2002*, p. 3.

[445] Human Rights Watch telephone interview with Linda Powell, director of utilization review and case management, University of Mississippi Medical Center, May 1, 2003.

[446] Human Rights Watch telephone interview with Eastern Mississippi staff, May 1, 2003.

[447] Human Rights Watch telephone interview with Dr. Jeffrey Metzner, November 26, 2002.

[448] Ibid., April 2, 2003.

[449] Human Rights Watch telephone interview attorney Donna Brorby, August 5, 2002. Brorby was a lead attorney in the *Ruiz v. Johnson* litigation in Texas.

[450] Human Rights Watch telephone interview with Dr. Jeffrey Metzner, November 26, 2002.

units of one sort or another for seriously mentally ill prisoners, most of these were designed only to house psychotic prisoners. Only five states provided units that provided what the NIC termed "'sheltered,' 'supportive,' 'partial care,' or 'assisted housing,' for mentally ill inmates who need it."[451]

In 1995, in *Coleman v. Wilson*, the court agreed with prisoners that California's prison mental health services were unconstitutionally deficient.[452] The decision prompted dramatic changes and improvements, including the development of the Enhanced Outpatient Program (EOP), a specialized intermediate care program for mentally ill prisoners. *Coleman* "drove a lot of the funding," Mule Creek prison warden Mike Knowles told Human Rights Watch.[453] "It happened quicker. It probably would have evolved anyway as a need. The numbers had grown. But *Coleman* assisted us in getting the staffing we needed." The EOPs, which operate in thirteen prisons statewide, provide comprehensive psychiatric and counseling services to between one and two percent of the total state prison population.[454] The EOPs are intended to provide intensive and extensive mental health resources for the most needy sub-acute cases (those needing intensive intervention but not hospitalization) within the prison system. Prisoners in the EOPs are supposed to have round-the-clock access to mental health staff. They should be seen by psychiatrists and psychologists on a regular basis; staff are to develop an individualized treatment plan for each prisoner; and a broad array of group therapy and programming options should be available.

The relatively small number of EOPs, however, does not meet the demand. As a result, the programs are seriously overcrowded. According to internally generated California DOC data, as of July 2002 the EOP system, which was designed to hold 2,481 prisoners, was catering to 3,179.[455] In some prisons, the overcrowding within EOP programs is particularly severe. San Quentin's EOP is operating at 385 percent of its design capacity, the EOP at Valley State Prison for Women is at 156 percent.[456] In Mule Creek, the EOP is funded for 180 prisoners, yet has 230.[457] Prisons without EOPs are supposed to transfer prisoners deemed to need intensive services into an EOP program within thirty days of the mental health staff having recommended a transfer. But, because of the shortage of EOP bedspace and the slow pace of administrative decision-implementation most administrators acknowledge transfers can be delayed far longer than thirty days. The warden at Mule Creek also told Human Rights Watch the problem of overcrowding is compounded by the fact that psychiatric social workers and psychologists at the prison are paid lower salaries than correctional officers; the low pay for mental health staff makes it harder to recruit and retain them.[458]

---

[451] U.S. Department of Justice, National Institute of Corrections, *Provision of Mental Health Care in Prisons*, February 2001, p. 6. The report does not identify the states.

[452] *Coleman v. Wilson*, 912 F. Supp. 1282 (E.D. Cal., 1995), *cert. denied*, 520 U.S. 1230 (1997).

[453] Human Rights Watch interview with Mike Knowles, warden, Mule Creek State Prison, California, July 19, 2002.

[454] Prisons in California listed as having the capacity to house EOP inmates are: California Correctional Facility for Women (CCFW), California Institute for Women (CIW), California Medical Center (CMC), California Medical Facility (CMF), Corcoran (COR), Los Angeles County (LAC), Mule Creek State Prison (MCSP), Pelican Bay State Prison (PBSP), R. J. Donovan (RJD), California State Prison at Sacramento (CSP-SAC), San Quentin (SQ), Salinas Valley State Prison (SVSP), and Valley State Prison for Women (VSPW).

[455] California Department of Corrections, Health Care Placement Unit, "EOP Population by Security Level," population chart created on July 25, 2002; on file at Human Rights Watch.

[456] California Department of Corrections, Health Care Placement Unit, "Mental Health Adseg/SHU/PSU," population chart created on July 25, 2002.

[457] Human Rights Watch interviews, Mule Creek State Prison, California, July 19, 2002. Numbers provided by Warden Mike Knowles.

[458] Ibid.

In Washington State, the large McNeil Island prison includes a seventy-five bed medium-security living unit as well as over twenty segregation beds for seriously mentally ill prisoners. Within this facility, mentally ill prisoners have daily access to an array of mental health staff and psycho-educational classes ranging from anger management to relapse prevention. University of Washington researchers brought into the prison to monitor the success of the facility have found that "participants were substantially less symptomatic when they left the program than when they entered."[459] Human Rights Watch visited McNeil Island in the summer of 2002 and found that staff and prisoners appeared to have a far less antagonistic relationship than was the case in most prisons we have visited.

New York State has eleven Intermediate Care Programs (ICPs) located in maximum security prisons. The ICPs are residential treatment units for prisoners who have significant psychiatric histories who are victim-prone or unable to cope with life in the general population. According to the Correctional Association of New York:

> ICPs provide intensive therapeutic care in a safe and structured environment. Inmates reside in cell blocks with programming, recreation and therapeutic areas that are separated from the rest of the correctional facility. They also have their own staff of correctional and mental health professionals as well as energetic Inmate Program Assistants who help organize activities and serve as big brothers and mentors to the inmates with mental illness. While some of the men reside on the unit and work in programs with general population inmates, one step away from integrating back into the large prison community, others spend their time solely on the unit, participating in programs such as daily living skills, personal hygiene and medication compliance. ICP inmates pass through four functional levels to complete the program and some may transfer back to the prison "community." The average length of stay in an ICP is approximately two years.[460]

Through surveys and interviews with prisoners, staff, and corrections officers, the Correctional Association found that the ICPs offered therapeutic safe environments and provided prisoners with access to a range of mental health services and intensive treatment programs. The staff was reportedly compassionate, committed, and enthusiastic.[461]

Although placement in an ICP is supposed to be temporary (the Correctional Association reports an average stay of twenty-six months) staff acknowledge that some residents will never be able to go back into the general prison population.

The existing ICP units are, however, insufficient for the number of mentally ill prisoners who might benefit from the protection, treatment, and care they provide. According to the Correctional Association, the 518 ICP beds can only accommodate one-third of the prisoners who have been classified as being the most severely mentally ill in the system, and clinicians, superintendents, correctional officers, and prisoners have emphasized the need for more ICP beds.[462] In addition, the

---

[459] David Lovell, David Allen, Clark Johnson (University of Washington) and Ron Jemelka (Texas Health Quality Alliance), "Evaluating the Effectiveness of Residential Treatment for Prisoners with Mental Illness," *Criminal Justice and Behavior*, vol. 28, no. 1, February 2001, pp. 83-104.

[460] Correctional Association of New York, *Mental Health in the House of Corrections*, forthcoming report.

[461] Ibid.

[462] Ibid.

ICPs choose to exclude certain mentally ill prisoners, typically those who have engaged in predatory behavior, who have anger/impulse control disorders, anti-social personality disorder or borderline personality disorders. These prisoners remain in the general population, typically end up in punitive segregation, and receive adequate mental health treatment only if they decompensate and end up being sent to the forensic mental health hospital.

In Ohio, as part of the dramatic reconstruction of correctional mental health services that began after the class action lawsuit *Dunn v. Voinovich* was filed in 1993, the state has developed a series of residential treatment units (RTUs) for prisoners with serious mental illness who do not require hospitalization but who are not able to be maintained in the general population. The goal of the RTUs is to treat and stabilize those with mental illness sufficiently so that they can eventually move back into the general population. The RTUs have a level system built into them based on mental health considerations. As prisoners move up the levels, they have increased out of cell time in which they interact with other prisoners and engage extensive programmed activities as developed by the mental health staff. The treatment teams at the RTUs include the case manager, psychiatrist, psychologist, nurse, and correctional officers. Prisoners are supposed to participate in the development of their treatment plans and decision regarding changes in the plan. By participating in treatment team sessions, each prisoner has a voice in his fate. Our research suggests that this is an extremely rare example of prisoners being able to participate actively in decisions concerning their treatment.

Expansion of Specialized Care Facilities
States that have created intermediate care facilities view them as temporary steps on the way to returning prisoners to the general prison population. As mentioned above, the prevailing correctional view is that the general population is seen as the "community," in which prisoners with mental illness should be housed whenever possible. But this use of the rationale of deinstitutionalization and the community mental health model is somewhat problematic in the prison context. One obvious difference is that, unlike mentally ill persons in the community, prisoners have already lost their liberty by virtue of their conviction and prison sentence; correctional authorities have nearly unlimited authority to determine how and where prisoners will be confined. It may be that more prisoners with serious mental illness should spend more of their prison time in intermediate care units (except when hospitalization is needed). If they did so, those prisoners, as well as prisoners without mental illness, staff, and prison systems as a whole might well benefit.

There seems little doubt that prisoners with serious mental illness would benefit from longer-term access to the array of mental health and rehabilitative services provided in such units. The data are not available to determine whether prisoners with mental illness who have been in intermediate care facilities are able to sustain the benefits of that experience over time in the general prison population or whether they are better able to protect themselves from victimization.[463]

Not surprisingly, seriously mentally ill prisoners seem to prefer living in intermediate facilities or even forensic mental health hospitals. Prisoners typically have more freedom, programming, and human interaction in such facilities than in the segregation facilities. What may be treated as an

---

[463] See, e.g., David Lovell, David Allen, Clark Johnson & Ron Jemelka, Evaluating the Effectiveness of Residential Treatment for Prisoners with Mental Illness, Criminal Justice and Behavior, vol. 28, no. 1 (American Association for Correctional Psychology, 2001).

infraction or rule violation in prison can be seen as acting out behavior in therapeutic settings that is not responded to within a punitive framework. As Fred Cohen pointed out during his testimony as a witness for the Department of Rehabilitation and Correction in a class action lawsuit against Ohio's supermaximum security prison, hospitals "can be a fairly comfortable place for some inmates…it becomes a complicated jousting sometimes between inmates who really need it and inmates who don't really need it but want to stay there."[464] Also perhaps not surprisingly, infraction rates and misbehavior by mentally ill prisoners seem to decline in hospital or intermediate care settings. For example, the Correctional Association of New York found that the prisoners had considerably lower rates of infractions overall and rates of violent infractions dropped considerably when they were in the ICP compared to rates prior to ICP admission.[465] The lower rates of infractions may reflect the availability of more extensive treatment services and more programming options, the greater respect with which prisoners are treated, the development of better prisoner-staff relations, the availability of more social and sociable interactions with other prisoners, and/or a staff practice of not using the prison disciplinary system to respond to misconduct.

One of the arguments for trying to "mainstream" mentally ill prisoners in the general prison population is that there is more access to educational, vocational, and recreational programs there and the mentally ill will better prepared for the outside world upon release. But prisoners in intermediate care units who have higher levels of functioning could access general population programs while remaining in the units, as in New York's ICPs.

There are other arguments in favor of expanding the number of specialized living facilities for long-term housing of the seriously mentally ill prisoners. Such a policy would allow prisons to concentrate their mental health resources in a more rational manner. Specialized facilities can be operated to minimize the typical conflict between security and mental health considerations in general population prisons, by, for example, bringing correctional officers into individual treatment teams. Such facilities can be operated to maximize mental health treatment and social rehabilitation skills. Correctional staff who work in such facilities can be specially trained and chosen for the unique nature of the facility. Finally, longer-term use of special facilities would reduce the current pattern in which mentally ill prisoners repeatedly cycle between general population settings in which they decompensate and crisis units in which they are housed temporarily while they are being stabilized.

---

[464] Testimony of Fred Cohen, Transcript of Proceedings before the Honorable James Gwin, Preliminary Injunction hearing, *Austin v. Wilkinson*, Case No. 4:01 CV 0071 (N.D. Ohio, September 24, 2001), pp. 34-35.

[465] Correctional Association of New York, *Mental Health in the House of Corrections*, forthcoming report. Rates of infractions dropped from 67 percent to 51 percent, and many of those were for smaller infractions such as smoking. Rates of infractions for violence dropped from 38 percent to 16 percent.

XI.   CASE STUDY: ALABAMA, A SYSTEM IN CRISIS

In 1990, a psychologist at West Jefferson Correctional Facility, Alabama, wrote to the Director of Mental Health Treatment for the Alabama Department of Corrections (ADOC) about the inability to get prisoners transferred to the system's acute care facility:

> We have six men who have been ordered to Kilby Correctional Facility Psychiatric Ward. One was ordered December 6, 1989, one on December 20, 1989, two on December 29, 1989 and one on January 5, 1990. We are told that Kilby Correctional Facility has no beds.[466]

A month later, the Director of Mental Health Treatment informed the ADOC's Associate Commissioner that "the physical facilities for Mental Health In-Patient Care at Kilby are totally inadequate." At the time, Kilby had only eighteen beds to deal with all the acute psychiatric patients in Alabama's prisons. Based on Department of Justice estimates of the numbers of prisoners in need of in-patient psychiatric care, the Director recommended two hundred more beds be brought on-line by 1995.[467]

The beds were not created. In 1992, two years after this recommendation, the Director of Mental Health Treatment for MBM — the organization subcontracted to provide mental health care at the Kilby facility — informed the Department of Corrections that because of chronic overcrowding and long waiting lists, "we can, therefore, not accept inmates for admission to Mental Health unless the transferring facility accepts, in return, inmates who have been stabilized and released from inpatient status. That is, man for man swaps must be made."[468]

By the early 1990s, the scale of Alabama's failings on mental health services were obvious to all who cared to look. In 1992, the *Bradley v. Harrelson* (the case name subsequently changed to *Bradley v. Hightower*)[469] lawsuit was filed against the ADOC alleging across-the-board failings in the provision of mental health services. Despite the filing of the lawsuit, conditions did not improve.

The year following, in June 1993, the mental health staff at Staton Correctional Facility informed the ADOC that paranoid, self-mutilating prisoners were being held in the prison's isolation cells because of a lack of mental health beds. They also alleged, in an email, that:

> Questcare, the medical contractor for Department of Corrections, has chosen to restrict available medications which are prescribed by the treating psychiatrist. These include major tranquilizers and antidepressants which are essential to treating a number of inmates at all institutions. Dr. Margaret Bok, former psychiatrist at Staton, resigned due in part to her frustration treating inmates without having these medications to prescribe.[470]

---

[466] *Bradley v. Hightower,* Recommendation of the Magistrate Judge, Civ. No. 92-A-70-N (N.D. Ala., April 3, 1997).
[467] Ibid.
[468] Ibid., p. 12.
[469] Ibid.
[470] Ibid.

The *Bradley* lawsuit took five years before any judicial ruling on the merits. Finally, in April 1997, the court found that the above-mentioned swap process delayed necessary transfers and kept acutely mentally ill prisoners separated from urgently needed mental health care.[471] There were also long delays in removing prisoners from Kilby to Taylor Hardin, the state's secure psychiatric medical facility. Surveying the history of delayed treatment, the court wrote that:

> In 1989, the average delay from the filing of the petition for commitment of the inmate to actual transfer of the inmate was 89 days. In 1992, it was 72 days. In 1993, the delay was over six months. In 1994, the delay was still 90 days. During the period time between arrival at Kilby and transfer to Taylor Hardin, inmates were housed in single cells on either the P-1 ward, C-Block, or the West Ward isolation cells. During this period of time, inmates so confined were suffering substantial harm.[472]

A federal court ordered the ADOC to set in place a plan to remedy the constitutional violations in the provision of mental health services. Yet, change was slow in coming, and the plaintiffs continued to argue for further court interventions.

In 2001, when three correctional mental health experts toured the Alabama prison system on behalf of the plaintiffs in connection with the ongoing *Bradley* litigation, they found mental health services still in crisis. It was what one of the experts, Professor Fred Cohen, has scathingly termed a "primitive" mental health system presided over by a director who had had his license suspended in two states, and with only three psychiatrists for a prison population of over twenty thousand.[473]

The final expert report is a detailed and damning assessment of mental health services — or the lack thereof — in the Alabama prison system.[474] It concludes the ADOC's:

> system for identifying, housing, and treating inmates with serious mental illness is grossly inadequate and riddled with systemic deficiencies. This is not to say that all aspects of the system and every facility are equally deficient…. Pockets of minimal acceptability, however, cannot lift an entire system to the level of acceptability.[475]

The experts found that Alabama prison system's "clinical staff is hopelessly thin and often under-qualified."[476] The "seriously deficient" mental health staffing levels:

> do not permit the provision of timely or minimally adequate treatment of inmates with mental illness. Without sufficient staff, inmates identified with mental illness receive grossly inadequate care and follow-up, while other inmates with mental illness remain unidentified…. [Because of inadequate mental health staffing] therapeutic programming is either severely limited or non-existent.[477]

---

[471] Ibid.

[472] Ibid.

[473] Human Rights Watch telephone interview with Fred Cohen, August 8, 2002.

[474] Kathryn Burns, M.D. and Jane Haddad, Psy.D., "Mental Health Care in the Alabama Department of Corrections," *Bradley v. Hightower*, Civ. No. 92-A-70-N (N.D. Ala., June 30, 2000).

[475] Ibid., p. 65.

[476] Ibid., p. 88

[477] Ibid., pp. 65-67.

In the ninety-page document, the experts provide extensive documentation of numerous problems plaguing the system. Their report suggests that just about every problem that might be encountered in a prison mental health system exists in Alabama. We quote below from the report's catalogue of practices that "result in the prolonged and needless suffering of may inmates with serious mental illness:"[478]

1. There is no practical access to hospital-level treatment, and the care that is given this designation at Kilby Mental Health Unit does not approximate hospital care.[479]

2. Inmates with serious mental illness report that they frequently must violate rules, hurt themselves or cause property damage to gain the attention of staff. Often even this destructive behavior does not eventuate in treatment; only further disciplinary action and segregation result.

3. The medical records do not reflect adequate treatment planning or interventions and there is simply no way to determine continuity of care.

4. Acutely psychotic inmates are locked-down for long periods of time with little or no treatment....

5. Medications are administered in a dangerous and unprofessional manner.

6. Therapeutic programs and counseling are wholly inadequate. Some claims as to providing psychotherapy, both in terms of frequency and what this clinical activity entails, are transparently false.[480]

---

[478] Ibid., pp. 4-5.
[479] Kilby is the ADOC facility which is supposed to provide in-patient care equivalent to hospital care. The report finds that with regard to Kilby, there is:

> no evidence that any of the aspects of hospital-level care...are provided.... There is no assessment (admission or otherwise) by a multidisciplinary team, and no multidisciplinary treatment plan which defines the inmate's problems, the planned interventions, the staff responsible, or the goals to be achieved. Treatment consists of brief, non-confidential interactions with the psychologist, irregular participation in limited group sessions, and infrequent psychiatric interaction. The primary mode of treatment is medication – for which consent is neither sought nor granted. Inmates are very often prescribed long-acting injectable antipsychotic medications [which are] contraindicated for management of acute psychiatric illness due to their long duration of action.

Kilby lacks twenty-four hour, seven-day-a-week psychiatric nursing, "a benchmark for hospital care." After discussing many other problems at Kilby, the experts conclude, that the "end result is that the ADOC effectively denies access to inpatient treatment for inmates with acute and serious mental illness...the 'treatment provided on the Kilby MHU consists of little more than seclusion, increased correctional supervision, and coerced psychotropic medication." Ibid., pp. 73-77.
[480] In its conclusion, the report notes that every:

> type of what goes by the name "treatment" or "treatment unit" is seriously deficient in some critical aspect. Rounds that are designed to assess inmates and provide inmates with access are rapid "drive-throughs." Brief encounters at the cell or in a "pill line" are termed "psychotherapy." Inmates with serious mental illness are locked-down under primitive conditions, and, if thought suicidal, are stripped and made to sleep on the floor on a thin plastic mat. Medications are distributed in an

7. Conditions of confinement in some areas housing inmates experiencing serious mental illness are totally unfit for these very vulnerable inmates.

8. Based on inmate reports and medical record documentation, some mental health staff have demonstrated a general distrust of and contempt for individual inmate-patients.

9. The only treatment consistently available is psychotropic medication, but the medication is administered improperly; required monitoring often if not done; and medication is sometimes prescribed without the physician ever seeing the inmate. Medication is not supplemented anywhere we visited by adequate therapy or therapeutic programming….

10. There is little or no evidence of effective training of staff on the rudiments of mental illness and medication.

"Alabama is the worst system I've seen, or ever hope to see," Fred Cohen told Human Rights Watch. The prisoners:

> received unbelievably poor levels of care. In one facility — a residential treatment unit — the water was overflowing. Inmates were verbally harassed, physically harassed. They were pulled out of bed and knocked about by correctional officers…. There were a few correctional officers working in serious mentally ill units who were characterized as particularly brutal. I cross-referenced these allegations. They would just beat these guys. I'd never seen anything like this.[481]

Before the courts could issue a further ruling, Alabama agreed to settle the case and expand its mental health services.

Human Rights Watch attempted to contact the Alabama Department of Corrections on several occasions over a one-year period to ask for their perspective on these findings. The Department repeatedly refused to respond. Finally, the mental health director informed Human Rights watch that the ADOC Commissioner had sent a letter to his staff instructing them not to convey any information to Human Rights Watch.[482]

Mental health care is also inadequate for incarcerated women in Alabama. In 2002, prisoners at Tutwiler, the state's only prison for women, filed a lawsuit charging that overcrowding of prisoner dorms and significant understaffing of security guards in the Alabama state prison system violated prisoners' Eighth Amendment rights.[483] Tutwiler, built in 1942 to house 364 prisoners, was home to

---

unprofessional and dangerous fashion…the 'treatment plans' that exist do not meet the most basic requirements for such plans….
Ibid., p. 88
[481] Human Rights Watch telephone interview with Fred Cohen, August 8, 2002.
[482] Human Rights Watch telephone interview with Ron Kavanaugh, mental health director, Alabama Department of Corrections, March 28, 2003.
[483] *Laube v. Haley*, 234 F.Supp.2d 1227 (M.D.Ala., 2002).

approximately 1017 women at the time of the lawsuit.[484] Chief among the prisoners' complaints was the substandard treatment of mentally ill prisoners.

Due to overcrowding at Tutwiler, many mentally ill women in need of supportive living environments are mixed into the general population.[485] According to the complaint prepared by attorneys from the Southern Center for Human Rights, if a mentally ill prisoner is not considered to be a threat to herself and is not experiencing acute mental health problems, she is placed in the general population regardless of the severity of her illness. Unstable prisoners are "left to roam around the large dormitories talking to themselves and acting in a bizarre and often threatening manner."[486]

In 2002, Cheryl Wills, M.D., toured the Tutwiler facilities as part of a report prepared for the plaintiff prisoners. In her report, Dr. Wills recounts interviews with several prisoners who emphasized the insufficiency of medical and mental health care at the facility. According to the prisoners she interviewed:

- There is no residential mental health program for the prisoners at Tutwiler.

- Psychiatric services are not easily accessible for prisoners that are not acutely ill.

- The easiest way to receive mental health care was to harm oneself, and that strategy was not always successful.

- Prisoners were frequently disciplined for exhibiting symptoms of their mental illness.

All prisoners interviewed by Dr. Wills agreed that the facility was dangerously overcrowded.[487]

After evaluating the plaintiffs' claims of overcrowding, understaffing, and substandard medical and mental health care, federal district judge Myron Thompson held that "these unsafe conditions have resulted in harm and the threat of harm to individual inmates…[and] are essentially a time bomb ready to explode facility-wide at any unexpected moment in the near future."[488] He found that housing of mentally ill prisoners in the general population was dangerous not only to other prisoners, but to the mentally ill prisoners themselves, who were "vulnerable to control and attack at the hands of aggressive inmates."[489]

The Tutwiler Prison Plan developed by the defendants, Governor Riley, Commissioner Campbell, and Warden Deese, includes plans to speed up the parole process for non-violent offenders at

---

[484] Ibid., at 1232.

[485] Southern Center for Human Rights, Second Amended Complaint, *Laube v. Haley*, Civil Action CV-02-T-957-N (M.D. Ala., December 18, 2002), p. 33.

[486] Southern Center for Human Rights, *Women Prisoners file Class Action Lawsuit Against Governor, Department of Corrections*, Press Release, August 19, 2002.

[487] Cheryl D. Wills, M.D., *The Impact of Conditions of Confinement on the Mental Health of Female Inmates Remanded to Alabama Department of Corrections, Laube. v. Haley*, Civil Action No. 02-T-957-N (M.D. Ala., 2002).

[488] On December 2, 2002, Judge Myron Thompson ruled that the prison violated the U.S. Constitution because it was so overcrowded and unsafe. The judge issued a preliminary injunction and ordered the state to come up with a plan to make the prison safer. The injunction expired March 2, 2003.

[489] *Laube*, 234 F.Supp.2d at 1235.

Tutwiler, and reduce the number of Tutwiler prisoners.[490] The plan does not, however, address increased corrections or health care staffing, improved delivery of mental or medical health care services, or the development of more specialized living facilities for seriously mentally ill prisoners.

---

[490] Tutwiler Prison Plan, prepared by defendants in *Linda Laube, et al. v. Donal Campbell*, et al., Civil Action No. 02-T-957-N (M.D. Ala., February 22, 2003). At the writing of this report, more than 300 former Tutwiler inmates are currently being housed at a private prison in Basile, Louisiana, run by Louisiana Corrections Services.

V.K., NEW YORK

Human Rights Watch interviewed several seriously mentally ill prisoners housed in the secure housing unit of New York's Wende Correctional Facility.[491] Of the prisoners interviewed, forty-year-old V.K. appeared the most actively psychotic. Our interview with V.K. took place in a legal visiting room locked from the outside. It was cut short after V.K., a large man with long dreadlocks, wearing blues-brother sunglasses, his front teeth capped with gold, began responding to internal stimuli and, specifically, began talking with an invisible person he called "Peter," a creature V.K. said told him to stab and hurt people.

Because it was outside normal visiting hours, the Human Rights Watch interviewer had to remain in the general visiting area, adjacent to the legal visiting room, for over an hour, waiting to be allowed to leave the prison. During this time, he could see and hear V.K. and the interactions passing officers had with him. V.K. began a rambling conversation with himself, a crazed smile on his face, started rocking back and forth, and then proceeded to take his clothes off. The guards left V.K. in the interview room for nearly an hour without bringing in an escort to return him to his cell. Correctional officers periodically walked past and made snide comments. One said, "four years in the box ain't wearing well with him, eh? He's getting lonely."

V.K. told Human Rights Watch that his first encounter with mental health services was when he was in fourth grade. "My teacher slapped me and I beat him with a baseball bat," V.K. stated. "Broke both his legs, one of his arms and cracked his head open. They sent me for mental health, to a hospital." Whether this childhood memory is based on fact or on fiction is hard to tell, as fantasy and reality seem to blend in V.K.'s mind.

V.K. talked very slowly, stopping at random moments mid-sentence to respond to voices only he can hear. Serving twenty years-to-life for first-degree robbery, he was clearly consumed by fantasies and visions of violence. Because of his extremely violent tendencies, and assaults on prison staff, V.K. has lived in secure housing units since 1998. Inside the special housing unit (SHU), V.K.'s access to mental health services consists of being given psychotropic medications, and occasional cell-front visits from a counselor. V.K. has no out-of-cell counseling, no group therapy, and no mental health programming. Periodically throughout his life he has decompensated to the point where he has had to be removed to a state hospital for the criminally insane after stabbing or threatening to hurt people; from prison, he has also been taken to the Central New York Psychiatric Center. "I was hearing voices," V.K. stated, describing the last time he was removed from the SHU and sent to the Psychiatric Center.

> Telling me to stab the police [a common prison term to describe correctional officers]. Because I'm scared they're going to do something to me. Before they hurt me, I'm going to do something to them. I went [to CNYPC] June 10th and they discharged me June 27th and sent me here. I'm locked in all the time. They wrote me a ticket saying I was masturbating and putting a finger in my a-hole. Now a lot of officers come by and say "are you a homo? Do you suck dick?" It's stressing me

---

[491] Human Rights Watch interviews with R.P., V.K., et al., Wende Correctional Facility, Alden, New York, September 13, 2002.

out. I'm getting tired of this horseshit, man. Verbally abusing me. I've been in the box five years and I'm not the man I used to be.

V.K. claimed that in some of the New York prisons he has been, correctional officers at times have denied him his medications at times. Absent these medications, he said that he gets "very depressed. And sometimes I'm hearing voices; they be telling me to kill police." Because of his violent behavior, V.K. will likely continue to accumulate time in "the box."

J.H., Nevada, June 4, 2002

I'm a Hispanic, grew up poor, and around drugs, and gangs, always did bad in school. As a little child I went through some trauma with my mother, grew up without any mother figure, or any real affection. I was sentenced for attept robbery and was given six years in prison. At that time I was 17 years old. In 1999, while in max I stabbed a correctional officer and in Sept 2001 I was sentenced to four years, and that's what I'm doing now.

My mental illness is depression, poor impulse disorder, and some scizophrenia. I was diagnosed in December of 2001. Now a general history of my time in prison will be kind of long, I want to ingulf you for a moment so you may possibly feel the madness I went through and how I eventually ended up sick and in a mental unit. I came to prison in "1996" when I was 17 years old, at that time there was no programs for young men like there is now, we were put in general population. As I came off the streets with a cholo mentality I brought it with me. So early in my time I got in trouble for beating on a "child molester" and a "rapist." I was sent from medium custody to medium max. It was March 14, 1997. I had been on G.P. [general population]for a month and a ½. A yard stabbing went down, and 10 vatos were sent to segregation. I was one of them. I ended up with two years in disciplinary segregation. After this I never got out of the "hole." Five years in solitary confinement really messed me up. I had no family support, no t.v., radio, or a walkman, and still don't.... I began to get depressed and have angry feelings all the time. At Ely, they would put mentally ill inmate in the "hole" because the nurses didn't want to put up with them, and because Ely has no mental facility.... I have seen officers taunt mentally ill inmates by laughing at them, calling them names, and kicking on their cell doors. Instead of giving them counseling the are put on forced medication which is a shot of "dorisien" once of month. At Ely, in solitary we are divided up into three groups, all living on the same tier. G.P.s, P.C.s [protective custody], mentally ill inmates, all doing "hole time," every day, all day and night, we have to listen to screaming, yelling, shit talking, kicking on doors. This can really hurt a person mentally, such as it did myself. I did four years like that. I began to get angry, depressed, and suicidal all the time, but I kept holding out, until I ended up stabbing an officer. I got beat up that same day, Aug 1, 1999, then on Sept. 24, 1999, I was retaliated on, I was in my cell when officers instigated a situation, and said I refused a shake down. S.Q.U.A.D. was called. They emptied 3 8oz cans of gas into my cell, shot me with a tazer gun, then beat me up repeatedly, and dragged me out of my cell so the nurses could see me, it made no difference because the nurses covered everything up....

It became a constant madness for me, and that's how I became ill, I don't have good social skills, I'm kind of a loner, and I'm scared of the world. I'm going to turn 24 years old in Oct. and all these years without any love, affection or a woman to talk to have kept me depressed. On Nov. 30 2001, I attempted to kill myself. I just couldn't take it.

T.R., Arizona, August 21, 2002

I am a diagnosed paranoid schizophrenia, I was diagnosed as having paranoid schizophrenia back in early 1992. I was seriously mentally ill probably since I was 13 years old. I also suffer from major depression. I never saw a psychiatrist on the streets but I had many problems, I have had taken been prescribed many psychotropic medications to treat serious mental illness, anti-psychotics, anti-depressants and anti-anxiety medications.

I have been housed on Death Row since July of 1995. All of Death Row was moved to SMU II [SMU is the Special Management Unit] on September 4th 1997. SMU II is a supermaximum unit. It is atypical by every means, I am locked in my cell 24 hours a day 7 days a week. I hardly ever get out of my cell.... I have been put on mental health watches around 6 times, wich is inside a small holding cell, striped naked the light is on all the time, no room to lay down for 3 solid days, no sleep nothing. I would prefer death than to live like this. It's basically no one cares.

O.G., Indiana, September 3, 2002

I've been diagnosed with a mental illness since 1988. My mental illness has caused me to go to prison for 12 year sentence. My sentence was 8 do 4 with a 4 year probation when I get out. I robbed bank one with note that had my name signed to the bottom of it. And then turned myself in to the police and gave them all of the money back. I had completed my 8 do 4 with only one writup pending and was scheduled to leave prison this year. When I was sent to I.S.P. for the 4th time that year I sometimes would not get my medication and when I did get it would be the wrong kind. That caused me to dread taking it then the problems got worst for me. The voices I heard kept coming and I could not get any sleep. After I was there for about 2 ½ months I couldn't take it anymore and started getting write ups. For the next 2 ½ months I was fearing for my life and doing anything to make me feel better. In the process of me getting write ups I got 5 battery on officers. I felt that the officers were coming in my cell at night having sex with me. And that I needed to be transfer to a new facility. I threw cold tap water right out of the faucet on officers and voiced my feeling about them having sex with me while I slept. After every one they would put me on the psyche unit for a while then move me right back to population.... I got 6 years segregatio time. And I max out in 4 years. The time that I was on the pcsych unit at Indiana State Prison, they labele me as suicidal and put me in a seclusion cell with no sheet or blanket for days wearing only a pair of short Due to the cold I suffered nerve damage to my feet and could not walk for days. The first time, I also wiped my waste on the wall in population and in the seclusion cell. The third time I went to the pscych unit I was beat for spitting by two officers while handcuffed. The last time I was striped down to my short and taken out of my cell for cleaning and they shocked me for 15 seconds.... I called a officer to my ce and asked him if he wanted to get spit on he told me to take my best shot. He was standing about 15 fee away. I spit out my cell and asked him did I get him he said no. I wasn't trying to hit him. Soon after the two officers came and told me to cuff up so I did. When I got off the range where there is no camera the started hitting me in the face and banging my head against the wall. I went down and they made me get up Then they took me to my cell. I wiped waste on my wall then they came back to take me to see the nurs My face was bleeding and swollen. On the way back from seeing the nurse they did it again. I staye completely naked for two days.... I am a born again Christian and I believe god will see me thru this but am scared to leave my cell. Now I really am getting suicidal they had to rush me to the hospital last week swallowed 100 pain pills.

XII.   MENTALLY ILL PRISONERS AND SEGREGATION

Prisoner Brown [who is confined in a supermax facility in Indiana] has had seizures and psychiatric symptoms since childhood. He has bipolar disorder and a severe anxiety disorder, a phobia about being alone in a cell, and many features of chronic post-traumatic stress disorder. After he has been in his cell for a while, his anxiety level rises to an unbearable degree, turning into a severe panic attack replete with palpitations, sweating, difficulty breathing, and accompanying perceptual distortions and cognitive confusion. He mutilates himself – for example, by inserting paper clips completely into his abdomen – to relieve his anxiety and to be removed from his cell his cell for medical treatment.[492]
— Inmate evaluation by Dr. Terry Kupers, Indiana, July 1997.

When [the mentally ill are] in segregation, if they're not appropriately engaged they continue exhibiting the behaviors that got them there in the first place. If anything, they heighten that activity, which then puts them back before a disciplinary committee, and they get more [segregation] time. So instead of getting out, they wind up staying longer and longer and longer, and they deteriorate.[493]
— Michael J. Sullivan, former director, Wisconsin Department of Corrections, 2001.

If prisons are the end-of-the-line for those who fail to abide by society's rules, the various lockdown, isolation, and segregation units within correctional settings are the end-of-the-line for those prisoners who fail to abide by the internal rules and regulations that govern the prison system. Mentally ill prisoners are disproportionately confined in such settings. Isolated day-in, day-out in tiny, barren cells with scant contact with any other human beings, including mental health staff, prisoners with mental illness are left to suffer cruelly. Mental health care in such units is woefully inadequate. Many prisoners decompensate, becoming so psychotic they are eventually removed for brief hospital stints. Once stabilized, they are returned to the segregation units, where they are likely, over time, to decompensate again.

Overview of Segregation
All prison systems in the United States have "prisons within prisons," harsh solitary punishment cells where prisoners are sent temporarily for breaking prison rules. In the last two decades, however, corrections departments have increasingly chosen to segregate or isolate disruptive, rule-breaking, or otherwise dangerous prisoners for prolonged periods. Many of them are placed in special super-maximum security facilities; others are confined in segregation units within regular prisons.[494] The prisoners may be confined in segregation units administratively — meaning the segregation is an administrative housing or classification decision. Administrative segregation can, and often does, continue indefinitely until the correctional authorities unilaterally decide to release

---

[492] Inmate evaluation by Dr. Terry Kupers, member of a Human Rights Watch research team in July 1997. See Human Rights Watch, *Cold Storage: Super-Maximum Security Confinement in Indiana* (New York: Human Rights Watch, 1997), p. 37.

[493] Testimony of Michael J. Sullivan, former director, Wisconsin Department of Corrections, *Jones 'El v. Berge*, Civil Case 00-C-0421-C (W.D. Wisconsin, September 20, 2001), p.39.

[494] Based on visits to a dozen such facilities and extensive other research, Human Rights Watch has criticized prolonged supermax confinement as being disproportionately severe to legitimate security and inmate management objectives and for imposing pointless suffering and humiliation on prisoners, in violation of international human rights standards. Human Rights Watch, "Out of Sight: Super-Maximum Security Confinement in the United States," *A Human Rights Watch Report*, vol. 12, no. 1(G), February 2000; Human Rights Watch, "Red Onion State Prison: Super-Maximum Security Confinement in Virginia," *A Human Rights Watch Report*, vol. 11, no. 1(G), May 1999; and Human Rights Watch, *Cold Storage: Super-Maximum Security Confinement in Indiana* (New York: Human Rights Watch, 1997).

the prisoner back to the general prison population. Prisoners may also be isolated as punishment for a disciplinary offense. Disciplinary segregation is usually for a fixed term, set by the internal prison hearing process that led to conviction for the offense.

The nomenclature of the new, specialized segregation facilities varies — secure housing units, supermaximum security (supermax) prisons, intensive management units. Human Rights Watch typically refers to them as "supermax" prisons or as segregated confinement. Whatever the name, and despite some variation among prison systems with regard to supermax and segregated confinement, the basic model is a modern day version of solitary confinement. Prisoners typically spend their waking and sleeping hours locked alone in small, sometimes windowless cells, some of which are sealed with solid steel doors.[495] They are fed in their cells, their food passed to them on trays through a slot in the door. Between two and five times a week, they are let out of their cells for showers and solitary exercise in a small enclosed space. Most have little or no access to education, recreational, or vocational activities or other sources of mental stimulation. Radios and televisions are usually prohibited; the number of books or magazines reduced to a bare minimum — if any.[496] They are allowed scant personal possessions. In some prison systems, there are increased "privileges" or programs for administrative segregation prisoners who maintain good behavior for designated periods of time. These privileges, such as in-cell video educational programming, are limited, and typically do not include opportunity for out-of-cell interaction with other people — prisoners, staff, or others. The prisoners are usually handcuffed, shackled, and escorted by two or three correctional officers every time they leave their cells.

In recent years, states have begun incarcerating ever-larger proportions of their prison population in these highly controlled environments. Between 1994 and 2001, according to the Corrections Yearbook 2001, the average percentage of prisoners in segregation and protective custody increased from 4.5 percent to 6.5 percent.[497] The exact number of prisoners held in administrative or disciplinary segregation on any given day is unknown. As of January 1, 2001, thirty-six states reported a total of 49,348 segregated prisoners, excluding prisoners held in protective custody.[498] Individual states vary considerably in the proportion of their prison population that is segregated: Arkansas reported that 15 percent of its prison population was in either administrative or disciplinary segregation; Texas reported 6.8 percent in administrative segregation (and provided no data on disciplinary segregation); New York reported 7.8 percent in disciplinary segregation and none in administrative segregation. As of February 2000, Human Rights Watch's research indicated that more than twenty thousand prisoners were housed in special supermaximum security facilities.[499]

---

[495] A few prison systems, e.g., New York and California, double-cell inmates in segregation.

[496] The punitive restrictions on inmates in segregation can reach the tragically absurd. In Texas, inmates at the lowest levels of segregation were denied regular hygiene products; they had to use an all-in-one soap, a restriction which experts on supermax confinement found astonishing. *Ruiz v. Johnson*, 37 F. Supp. 855 (S.D. Texas, 1999). In Massachussetts, inmates in the Departmental Disciplinary Unit at MCI-Cedar Junction were allowed to have junk novels, but regulations expressly forbade any educational reading material. See *Torres v. DuBois*, 1997 Mass. Super. Lexis 539 (Feb. 10, 1997).

[497] Camille G. Camp and Camp, George M., *Corrections Yearbook 2001: Adult Systems* (Connecticut: Criminal Justice Institute, 2002), p. 38. Protective custody refers to non-punitive segregation of inmates from the general population to protect them from other inmates.

[498] Ibid.

[499] Human Rights Watch, "Out of Sight: Super-Maximum Security Confinement in the United States," *A Human Rights Watch Report*, vol. 12, no. 1(G), February 2000, p. 3. Explaining the trend toward supermax incarceration, the authors of the Human Rights Watch report wrote that:

Mentally Ill in Segregation

[I]n all of the systems that I've studied in one fashion or another, if a prison system has gone bad or is bad...in its provision of mental health care, what you have to do is go to the segregation units and you will find the sickest people locked down, unattended to, and it's the way that a malfunctioning prison system operates to hide their mentally ill [I have found this in]... every system that I've ever looked at and the poorer the system, the more serious the conditions, the close deterioration, terrible nightmare for the inmate."[500]
— Testimony of Fred Cohen, LL.M., LL.B., *Austin v. Wilkinson,* September, 2001.

The mentally ill are disproportionately represented among prisoners in segregation. As discussed earlier in this report, persons with mental illness often have difficulty complying with strict prison rules, particularly when there is scant assistance to help them manage their disorders. Their rule-breaking can lead to increasing punishment, particularly if they engage in aggressive or disruptive behavior. Eventually accumulating substantial histories of disciplinary infractions, they land for prolonged periods in disciplinary or administrative segregation. For example:

- In Oregon, 28 percent of the prisoners in the state's intensive management units (the state's most secure facilities) are on the mental health caseload.[501]

- The New York Correctional Association reports that 23 percent of all prisoners in special housing units (SHUs) are on the mental health caseload.[502] According to its survey of a sample of prisoners in New York's SHUs, nearly one-third of the SHU prisoners on the mental health caseload have had prior psychiatric hospitalizations. Over one-half suffer from depression; 28 percent are diagnosed with either schizophrenia or bipolar disorder. It

---

Thinly staffed, overcrowded, and impoverished facilities breed tension and violence, particularly where prison management has not placed a high priority on promoting staff-inmate and inmate-inmate relations predicated on mutual respect. Many corrections authorities have turned to prolonged supermax confinement in an effort to increase their control over prisoners. They believe that if they can confine all the most dangerous or disruptive inmates in facilities designed specifically for that purpose, they will be able to increase safety and security in other prisons.... A significant impetus for supermax confinement also comes from politicians. Crime and punishment have been central issues in American politics for over two decades, and advocating harsh punitive policies for criminal offenders remains a politically popular position. Elected officials advancing tough-on-crime policies have promoted large supermax prisons for their symbolic message, regardless of actual need. Fearful of being accused of 'coddling inmates' or being 'soft on crime,' few politicians have been willing to publicly challenge supermaxes on human rights grounds.

[500] Testimony of Fred Cohen, Preliminary Injunction Hearing, *Austin v. Wilkinson,* No. 4:01 CV 0071 (N.D. Ohio, September 24, 2001), p. 14.

[501] Human Rights Watch telephone interview with Gary Fields, administrator, Counseling and Treatment Services, Oregon Department of Corrections, June 24, 2002.

[502] Correctional Association of New York, "Mental Health in the House of Corrections," forthcoming publication, p. 14; *Eng v. Coughlin,* 80-CV-385S, 1988 U.S. Dist. LEXIS 18327 (W. D. N.Y., January 29, 1988). In March 1998, the New York Department of Correctional Services agreed to resolve a lawsuit against Attica prison by no longer keeping seriously mentally ill inmates, "or those known to be at substantial risk of serious mental or emotional deterioration," in the special housing unit (SHU) at Attica. The New York Department of Correctional Services did not, however, extend the exclusion of mentally ill inmates from special housing units throughout its system. Judge William M. Skretny of the United States District Court Western District of New York issued a voluntary Stipulation of Dismissal on March 16, 1998, after both parties agreed to the removal of seriously mentally ill inmates from Attica's SHU, speedier mental health screening for incoming inmates, and periodic mental health monitoring of SHU inmates.

also found that the average SHU sentence for mentally ill prisoners is six times longer than that reported for SHU prisoners generally.[503]

- As of July 2002, 31.85 percent of the administrative segregation population in California prisons, or 1,753 prisoners, were on the mental health caseload.[504] In Corcoran State Prison, 423 of the 1400 SHU beds (30.21 percent) and in Valley State Prison for Women, twenty-nine of the forty-four SHU beds (65.91 percent) were inhabited by mentally ill prisoners.[505]

- Dr. Dennis Koson reported in 1998 that in New Jersey:

  > [a]s a result of [the] disciplinary process that all but criminalizes the most common symptoms of mental illness as well as the lack of alternative housing facilities, mentally ill inmates are almost three times more likely to be found in administrative segregation than they are in general population.[506]

  His descriptions of some of the prisoners' conditions were searing. One prisoner in administrative segregation at Eastern Jersey State Penitentiary:

  > stood at the window rocking and staring. His room was incredibly foul, reeking of feces and garbage. There was blood everywhere on the window. He had cut his hand on the edge of the window the day before and was rubbing his hand on the window again. He generally was not responsive to questions, instead just stared at his hand.[507]

- At Indiana's Secure Housing Unit (SHU), in the Wabash Valley Correctional Facility, staff in 1997 acknowledged to Human Rights Watch that somewhere between one-half and two-thirds of the prisoners were mentally ill.[508]

- 29 percent of prisoners in Washington State's intensive management units manifested some mental illness symptoms, with 15 percent qualifying as seriously mentally ill.[509]

- In 1997, a federal court in Iowa found that half of the mentally ill prisoners at Iowa State Penitentiary (ISP) were in disciplinary detention or administrative segregation. The high security Cellblock 220, at ISP, housed so many seriously mentally ill prisoners that it was commonly known as the "bug range." The judge wrote that:

---

[503] Correctional Association of New York, "Mental Health in the House of Corrections," forthcoming publication.

[504] California Department of Corrections, Health Care Placement Unit, "Mental Health Adseg/SHU/PSU," population chart created on July 25, 2002.

[505] Ibid.

[506] New Jersey Prison System Report of Dr. Dennis Koson, C.F. v. Terhune, Civil Action No. 96-1840 (D.N.J., September 8, 1998), p. 6.

[507] Ibid., pp. 81-82.

[508] Human Rights Watch, Cold Storage: Super-Maximum Security Confinement in Indiana (New York: Human Rights Watch, 1997), p. 34.

[509] David Lovell, Kristin Cloyes, David Allen, Lorna Rhodes, "Who Lives in Super-Maximum Custody? A Washington State Study," Federal Probation, vol. 64, no. 2, Dec. 2000.

[I]nmates in the bug range urinate and defecate anywhere other than their stools. Some inmates cover the walls of their cells with feces. Other inmates gather their urine and throw it at anyone who passes by their cell. Some of these inmates also defecate and urinate in the communal shower and cover the walls and fixtures with their excrement.[510]

- In the Special Needs Unit (SNU) for the seriously mentally ill in Pennsylvania prisons, those with discipline problems are channeled into the SNU Disciplinary Custody cells. When Human Rights Watch visited Graterford, eleven of the twenty-three prisoners in SNU 1 were in Disciplinary Custody, where they were kept in their cells twenty-three hours per day.[511]

Impact of Segregation on the Mentally Ill

Mental health records for prisoners in Ohio State Penitentiary, a supermaximum security facility. Psychiatrists' Clinic Progress Note: "At OSP [O.'s] behavior deteriorated precipitously…. The isolation at OSP provoked quite serious decompensation with both self-destructive and aggressive behaviors;" Treatment Team Mental Health Evaluation: "[O.] is not to return to OSP…Apparently at OSP, the confinement at that institution intensified his propensity to become violent, aggressive, and self-destructive…. His mental health problems contraindicate the transfer back to OSP in the future." Treatment Team Progress Note, "Regarding transfer back to OSP, although stable at the present time, it is perhaps to be anticipated that further deterioration and decompensation would occur if [P.] were to be transferred back to that super maximum security prison."
— Plaintiff's exhibits in *Austin v. Wilkinson.*[512]

"It's a standard psychiatric concept, if you put people in isolation, they will go insane…. It's a big problem in the California system, putting large numbers in the [secured housing units, California's supermax confinement facilities]… Most people in isolation will fall apart."
— Sandra Schank, staff psychiatrist, Mule Creek State Prison, California.[513]

Perhaps nowhere in corrections is the contradiction between the paradigm of security and that of mental health more apparent than in supermax settings. Whatever the correctional justification for such facilities, it is clear they were not designed with their mental health impact in mind. Indeed, mental health experts did not participate in the development of such regimes. Nor, until very recently, have mental health staff had much of a say in who gets placed in segregation or how long they should stay under such damaging conditions. Moreover, only security staff can mandate changes in privileges or amenities for individual prisoners in segregation.

Yet most independent psychiatric experts, and even correctional mental health staff, believe that prolonged confinement in conditions of social isolation, idleness, and reduced mental stimulation is psychologically destructive. How destructive depends on each prisoner's prior psychological

---

[510] *Goff v. Harper*, Findings of Fact and Conclusions of Law, No. 4-90-CV-50365 (S.D. Iowa, June 5, 1997), p. 39.

[511] Human Rights Watch visited Graterford, August 12, 2002.

[512] These notes were part of plaintiff's exhibits introduced at trial and cited by the federal court granting plaintiff's request for a preliminary injunction precluding the return of prisoners with serious mental illness to Ohio's supermaximum security Ohio State Penitentiary. See *Austin v. Wilkinson*, Case No. 4:01-CV-71, Order (N.D. Ohio, September 21, 2001) (unpublished opinion), p. 24.

[513] Human Rights Watch interview with Sandra Schank, staff psychiatrist, Mule Creek State Prison, California, July 19, 2002.

strengths and weaknesses, the extent of the social isolation imposed, the absence of activities and stimulation, and the duration of confinement.

The Human Rights Committee, in General Comment 20, said that "prolonged solitary confinement" of prisoners may amount to torture or other cruel, inhuman or degrading treatment or punishment.[514] The European Committee for the Prevention of Torture and Inhuman or Degrading Treatment or Punishment (CPT), which has reviewed a number of prison settings akin to U.S. segregation and supermax facilities, has noted that isolation can militate against reform and rehabilitation and can impair physical and mental health. According to the CPT, "It is generally acknowledged that all forms of solitary confinement without appropriate mental and physical stimulation are likely, in the long-term, to have damaging effects resulting in deterioration of mental faculties and social abilities."[515] It has reminded European governments that:

> The principle of proportionality calls for a balance to be struck between the requirement of the situation and the imposition of a solitary confinement-type regime, which can have very harmful consequences for the person concerned. Solitary confinement can in certain circumstances amount to inhuman and degrading treatment; in any event, all forms of solitary confinement should last for as short a time as possible.[516]

Prisoners have described life in a supermax as akin to living in a tomb. At best, prisoners' days are marked by idleness, tedium, and tension. For many, the absence of normal social interaction, of reasonable mental stimulus, of exposure to the natural world, of almost everything that makes life human and bearable, is emotionally, physically, and psychologically damaging.[517] As Professor Hans Toch has noted, "unmitigated isolation is indisputably stressful, and it reliably overtaxes the resilience of many incarcerated offenders."[518] Psychologist Craig Haney notes:

> Empirical research on solitary and supermax-like confinement has consistently and unequivocally documented the harmful consequences of living in this kind of environment…. Evidence of these negative psychological effects come from person accounts, descriptive studies, and systematic research…conducted over a period of four decades, by researchers from several different continents….[519]

---

[514] Human Rights Committee, General Comment 20, article 7 (Forty-fourth session, 1992), Compilation of General Comments and General Recommendations Adopted by Human Rights Treaty Bodies, U.N. Doc. HRI\GEN\1\Rev.1 at 30 (1994), para. 6.

[515] European Committee for the Prevention of Torture and Inhuman or Degrading Treatment or Punishment, *Report to the Finnish Government on the Visit to Finland,* conducted between 10 and 20 May 1992, Strasbourg, France, 1 April 1993, CPT/Inf (93) 8.

[516] European Committee for the Prevention of Torture and Inhuman or Degrading Treatment or Punishment (CPT), *Report to the Icelandic Government on the Visit to Iceland,* conducted between 6 and 12 July 1993, Strasbourg, France, 28 June 1994, CPT/Inf (94) 8, p. 26. In reviewing the practice of solitary confinement in one of Iceland's prisons, the CPT notes that a report by the country's minister of justice states that "psychiatrists, psychologists and other specialists have stressed that solitary confinement as practiced [at the prison] has a harmful effect on prisoners' mental and physical health, particularly in the case of those detained for long periods."

[517] Human Rights Watch has visited over a dozen supermax facilities across the United States and interviewed inmates confined in them.

[518] Hans Toch, "Future of Supermax Confinement," *The Prison Journal,* vol. 81, no. 3, September 2001, p. 378.

[519] Craig Haney, "Mental Health Issues in Long-Term Solitary and 'Supermax' Confinement," *Crime & Delinquency,* vol. 49, no. 1, January 2003, p. 130.

According to a federal judge, prolonged supermax confinement "may press the outer bounds of what most humans can psychologically tolerate."[520] Even if they have no prior history of mental illness, prisoners subjected to prolonged isolation may experience depression, despair, anxiety, rage, claustrophobia, hallucinations, problems with impulse control, and/or an impaired ability to think, concentrate, or remember.[521]

Prisoners with preexisting psychiatric disorders are at even greater risk of suffering psychological deterioration if kept in segregation for prolonged periods. The stresses, social isolation, and restrictions of life in a supermax can exacerbate their illness or provoke a reoccurrence, immeasurably increasing their pain and suffering. A federal district judge trenchantly observed that placing mentally ill or psychologically vulnerable people in supermax conditions "is the mental equivalent of putting an asthmatic in a place with little air to breathe."[522]

A variety of individuals are especially prone to psychopathologic reactions to the reduced environmental stimulation and social isolation of supermax confinement. Professor Hans Toch's study of prison prisoners led him to conclude, for example, that suicidal prisoners can be pushed over the edge and pathologically fearful prisoners can regress into a psychologically crippling panic reaction.[523] According to Dr. Stuart Grassian, "individuals whose internal emotional life is chaotic and impulse-ridden, and individuals with central nervous system dysfunction," are particularly unable to handle supermax conditions. Yet among the prison population, these are the very individuals prone to committing infractions that result in segregation.[524] Even the expert in prison mental health care retained by the California Department of Corrections for the *Madrid v. Gomez* litigation acknowledged that some people cannot tolerate supermax conditions:

> Typically, those are people who have a pre-existing disorder that is called borderline personality disorder, and there's a fair amount of consistent observation that those folks, when they'[re locked up in segregation] may have a tendency to experience some transient psychoses, which means just a brief psychosis that quickly resolves itself when they're removed from the lockdown [segregation] situation.[525]

Indeed, individuals with psychopathic personality disorders are, by virtue of their condition, particularly unable to tolerate restricted environmental stimulation.[526]

Dr. Stuart Grassian has testified that many mentally ill prisoners suffer from:

---

[520] *Madrid v. Gomez,* 889 F. Supp. 1146 (N.D. California, 1995).

[521] Stuart Grassian and N. Friedman, "Effects of Sensory Deprivation in Psychiatric Seclusion and Solitary Confinement," *International Journal of Law and Psychiatry* (1986), vol. 8, pp. 49-65; Grassian, "Psychopathological Effects of Solitary Confinement," *American Journal of Psychiatry* (1983), vol. 140, pp. 1450-1454; Craig Haney, untitled draft of article on SHUs (2002) (unpublished).

[522] *Madrid v. Gomez,* 889 F. Supp. at 1265 (citations omitted).

[523] Hans Toch, Men in Crisis: Human Breakdown in Prison (1975).

[524] Declaration of Dr. Stuart Grassian, *Eng v. Coughlin,* 80-CV-385S (W.D. New York) (undated).

[525] Testimony of Joel Dvoskin, quoted in *Madrid v. Gomez,* 889 F. Supp. at 1216.

[526] Declaration of Dr. Stuart Grassian, *Eng v. Coughlin,* 80-CV-385S (W.D. New York) (undated), citing H. Quay, "Psychopathic personality as pathological stimulation seeking," *American Journal of Psychiatry* vol. 122 (1965), pp. 80-83.

a combination of psychiatric disorders predisposing them to both psychotic breakdown and to extreme impulsivity.... [S]uch individuals [tend] to be highly impulsive, lacking in internal controls, and [tend] to engage in self-abusive and self-destructive behavior in the prison setting, and especially so when housed in solitary. [T]hey are among the most likely to suffer behavioral deterioration in supermax confinement.[527]

According to psychiatrist Dr. Terry Kupers, the conditions in segregation can cause someone with a vulnerability to psychosis:

to go off the deep end. People who are vulnerable to psychosis have a relatively fragile or brittle ego. When they are made to feel very anxious, or very angry, or very distrustful, their ego tends to disintegrate — in other words, as anger or anxiety mounts, their ego falls apart. They regress, lose control, can't test reality. And this is the beginning of a psychotic decompensation.... If there's nobody to talk to then one is left alone to sort out one's projections, the reality-testing is more difficult — and paranoid notions build up. Activities also bind anxieties and play a role in our testing of reality, so being without activities leaves anxieties to mount — again, there's ego disintegration, and with a disintegrated ego there's even less opportunity or capacity to test the reality of paranoid or unrealistic ideas."[528]

Dr. Kupers also explained the impact of isolated confinement on the mentally ill in his testimony as plaintiff's expert in a lawsuit that challenged, among other issues, the confinement of mentally ill prisoners in Wisconsin's supermax:

[The impact] depends on what the mental illness is. Prisoners who are prone to depression and have had past depressive episodes will become very depressed in isolated confinement. People who are prone to suicide ideation and attempts will become more suicidal in that setting. People who are prone to disorders of mood, either bipolar...or depressive will become that and will have a breakdown in that direction. And people who are psychotic in any way...those people will tend to start losing touch with reality because of the lack of feedback and the lack of social interaction and will have another breakdown, whichever breakdown they're prone to. There are a lot of reasons why these people break down in isolated confinement. First of all, it's almost total isolation and total inactivity. So what happens is that all of us know who we are and maintain our sanity basically by acting, by doing things, by being productive, by mastering things and by relating to other people.... Someone with a mental illness, especially a psychosis, has lots of fantasies. When those fantasies get out of proportion, we call them delusions. The way we check those delusions is to have them in constant social interaction with others so they can say what they're thinking and find out whether they're being crazy or whether that's a realistic perception. When you deprive a person of that kind of feedback on a

---

[527] Declaration of Dr. Stuart Grassian, *Eng v. Coughlin*, 80-CV-385S (W.D. New York) (undated). citing G. Cota & S. Hodgins, "Co-occurring mental disorders among criminal offenders," *Bulletin of the American Academy of Psychiatry and Law*, vol. 18, no. 3, pp. 271-81.
[528] Email communication from Dr. Kupers to Human Rights Watch, April 9, 2003.

constant basis and they have a tendency towards psychosis, they will tend to break down.[529]

In some states, such as California, New York, Arkansas, and Georgia, the stresses of living in a lockdown environment are made worse by the practice of double-bunking prisoners. While companionship is usually a good thing, forced companionship for more than twenty-three hours a day in a cell not much bigger than a closet can lead to violent outbursts, especially amongst mentally ill prisoners.

- In one notorious instance, a seriously mentally inmate at Phillips Correctional Institution, Georgia, warned staff that he was going to snap and attack his cell-mate. Instead of placing him in a single cell, the guards simply gave him a new cell-mate. When he began showing signs of aggression toward this second cell-mate, they removed him and brought in a third. The third was found the next morning stomped to death and with a pencil through his eye.[530]

Lost in Segregation

The longer a seriously mentally disordered individual remains acutely disturbed, the worse the long-term prognosis. Rapid and intensive treatment of acute psychiatric disorders offers the best chance for rapid recovery and serves to minimize long-term symptomatology and disability. The problem of mental breakdown and disability in super-maximum security units is thus two-fold: First, the conditions of confinement tend to exacerbate pre-existing psychiatric disorders to cause decompensation in individuals who are psychologically vulnerable under duress. Second, with continued confinement in these same conditions — particularly in the absence of meaningful psychiatric services — the afflicted prisoner's condition tends to deteriorate even further, and the long-term prognosis worsens.

Unfortunately, the length of time in segregation can be substantial. No longer a matter of spending fifteen days in the "hole," prisoners can end up spending years, even decades, in solitary confinement, sometimes only leaving when they are released from prison at the end of their sentence. Administrative segregation can be indefinite, contingent on "good behavior." Disciplinary segregation can turn endless because of subsequent infractions. Achieving sufficient periods of good behavior to secure release from segregation is particularly difficult for mentally ill prisoners. The same inability to comply with the rules that got them placed in segregation originally then extends the time in isolated confinement. For example, in Texas over nine thousand prisoners are currently incarcerated in administrative segregation cells.[531] Prisoners have to "earn" their way back to general population through abiding by the rules over extended lengths of time. A March 2002 report by forensic psychologist Keith Curry, based on research in eight prisons visited over a fifteen-day period, found that "of the 68 inmates reviewed for whom the length of stay could be roughly estimated from the medical record, the average length of stay in segregation appeared to be 5.2 years with a range of one month to seventeen years."[532] Curry pointed out that:

---

[529] Testimony of Dr. Terry Kupers, *Jones 'El v. Berge*, Civil Case 00-C-0421-C (W.D. Wisconsin, 2001).

[530] Attorneys from the Southern Center for Human Rights told Human Rights Watch of this occurrence. It happened in 2001, while the prisoners were being held in an isolation unit pending disciplinary hearings.

[531] Texas Department of Criminal Justice data indicate that the administrative segregation population peaked in December 2000 at 9,074. Since then it has hovered just over nine thousand.

[532] Keith Curry, Ph.D., letter to the law offices of Donna Brorby, March 19, 2002, p. 4.

> Seriously mentally ill inmates…react more negatively to the relative inactivity and sensory deprivation of 23 hour a day lockdown. As external reality clues recede, their mental functioning often deteriorates with concomitant restriction of their already inadequate coping skills. In the absence of active mental health treatment, seriously mentally ill inmates may become the "bottom dwellers" of the prison system, trapped in segregation units by their illness and unable to adapt to the hard conditions found at the deep end of the correctional system….

As Michael Sullivan, former head of Wisconsin's Department of Corrections, recently testified in court:

> When [the mentally ill] are in segregation, if they're not appropriately engaged they continue exhibiting the behaviors that got them there in the first place. If anything, they heighten that activity, which then puts them back before a disciplinary committee, and they get more time. So instead of getting out, they wind up staying longer and longer and longer, and they deteriorate.[533]

Many prison segregation units have systems of "levels" in which prisoners, through good behavior, can obtain increased privileges. The level system is supposed to offer the segregated prisoner incentives for good behavior, or disincentives for misconduct. Prisoners with mental illness, however, find it hard to leave the most restrictive levels.

> [I]t is plain that seriously mentally ill inmates differentially lack the ability to understand, internalize, and react appropriately to the disincentives of this level system. Seriously ill inmates are overrepresented in the lower levels of administrative segregation and the long periods spent mired there can be attributed to the serious symptoms of their mental illness. In a circular fashion, the extreme social and sensory deprivation of segregation in turn exacerbates those same symptoms that have kept these inmates stuck at the bottom due to repeated disciplinary infractions.[534]

The Lack of Quality Mental Health Services for Segregated Prisoners.

Across the country, the treatment of mentally ill prisoners in segregated facilities is egregiously deficient. However limited the mental health services for general population prisoners, it is significantly worse for those who are segregated. There are typically too few staff to attend to the high proportion of mentally ill prisoners in segregation. Many are untreated or undertreated because staff dismiss their symptoms as manipulation to get out of segregation. The physical design and rules of social isolation and forced idleness preclude treatment measures. Indeed, the very conditions that can exacerbate mental illness also impede treatment and rehabilitation. Few states have sought to develop ways of providing appropriate mental health treatment options within the context of reasonable security precautions for segregated prisoners.

As discussed above in chapter IX, the mentally ill require a range of treatment options besides psychopharmacology — group therapy, private individual therapy or counseling, milieu meetings,

---

[533] Testimony of Michael Sullivan, *Jones 'El v. Berge*, Civil Case 00-C-0421-C (W.D. Wisconsin, September 20, 2001), p. 39
[534] Keith Curry, Ph.D., letter to attorney Donna Brorby, March 19, 2002, p. 7. Curry was describing his findings in Texas, but our research suggests his observations apply equally to supermax prisons generally.

training in the skills of daily living, psychoeducation aimed at teaching patients about their illness and the need to comply with medication regimes, educational programs, vocational training, other forms of psychiatric rehabilitation, supervised recreation, and so forth. In effective mental health programs, some or all of these components can play a crucial part in restoring or improving mental health, or, at the very least, in preventing further deterioration in the patient's psychiatric condition. Many states do not provide such services to prisoners in the general population. But even states that have sought to expand the range of mental health services to prisoners, confront the obstacle of segregation. While medications generally are prescribed to seriously mentally ill prisoners in segregation facilities, therapeutic interventions are conspicuous by their absence.

The cornerstone of segregation is isolation of the prisoner. Out-of-cell time is limited to showers and recreation, and typically requires an escort of correctional officers. Most facilities do not have the security staff — even if they have the office space — to permit prisoners to be escorted for regular private meetings with mental health staff. Mental health staff who want to talk with a prisoner typically must do so standing at the cell front — in full earshot of other prisoners and non-mental health staff. As a result, little cell-front therapy occurs. The rules mandating prisoner in-cell isolation also preclude group therapy, supervised recreational activities, or other forms of group programming. The requirement of isolation flies in the face of the medically accepted fact that most mentally disordered people need to interact with others, even if in incremental steps. They benefit from group therapy and psychiatric rehabilitation activities. They need structured days. If a prisoner is too disturbed or angry to be with others, he needs a treatment plan that will slowly move him in the direction of socialization.

"The mental health team struggles with this," Mule Creek Prison (California) warden Mike Knowles told Human Rights Watch. "There are restrictions within administrative segregation that restrict their ability to do what they need to do — like group therapy. They struggle trying to communicate with inmates from cell doors."[535] Former acting mental health director for Washington State's Department of Corrections, Mike Robbins, is also concerned about limited programming in segregation facilities:

> Not all Intensive Management Units in the state are as attuned to mental health needs as I feel they should be. The offender in an IMU setting has less contact with mental health while they're there. I'd like to see that improved. It's not a good setting for someone with a serious mental illness.[536]

Robbins told Human Rights Watch that mental health staff are supposed to do regular rounds of the IMUs, but that the policy is not formally mandated by Central Office, and accurate data on the numbers, and needs of, seriously mentally ill prisoners within IMUs are not tracked department-wide.

Correctional authorities cite punishment and safety considerations as militating against group activities for prisoners in segregation. But denying mentally ill prisoners therapy, as a form of punishment, is not only counterproductive, it is needlessly cruel. Moreover, to the extent punishment is supposed to function as a deterrence — that objective is misplaced when it is the

---

[535] Human Rights Watch interview with Mike Knowles, warden, Mule Creek State Prison, California, July 19, 2002.
[536] Human Rights Watch interview with Mike Robbins, former acting mental health director, Washington State Department of Corrections, Olympia, Washington, August 19, 2002.

prisoner's mental illness and disorders which prompt acting out or dangerous behavior. Unfortunately, most prison systems function solely on a disciplinary model of punishment for misbehavior; they do not institute, even for the mentally ill, systems of behavioral incentives that might have a greater beneficial impact.[537] As to safety considerations, there is no question that some prisoners are so dangerous and volatile that their interaction with others must be carefully controlled. But even these prisoners, when they decompensate and are transferred to hospital settings, are often able to interact with others without serious incident. Their ability to function in hospital settings raises questions about whether their dangerousness is connected to prison conditions and the treatment they receive there.

If prisoners were on the mental health caseload prior to being transferred to segregation, they are likely to be visited periodically by mental health staff. But because regular segregation units are frequently deeply unpleasant places that are not conducive to therapeutic interactions — noisy, dirty, too hot, or too cold, as well as being crammed full of prisoners who are often intimidating and hostile — mental health staff often spend as little time in them as they can. In prison after prison, our research indicates that visits to prisoners by mental health staff tend to be quick, "how are you doing" cell-front exchanges, what some observers dismissively term "drive-by" visits. Psychiatrists visit even less frequently, and then only to check on medication. Treatment plans other than medication are typically nonexistent; and medication compliance efforts are almost as rare. There is also rarely any monitoring of the mental health of prisoners who were not on the mental health caseload when they begin doing time in the segregation unit — despite the mental health risks of prolonged segregation even for prisoners with no prior mental health histories.

Prisoners who want to talk with mental health staff can wait a long time before anyone shows up at their cellfront. For example, in Nevada a number of prisoners from different prisons, most of them in isolation units, wrote to Human Rights Watch to complain that their requests for medical and mental health appointments routinely were followed by lengthy delays in accessing treatment. One Nevada prisoner in the protective custody unit at the High Desert State Prison in Indian Springs, sent Human Rights Watch copies of multiple request forms he had submitted to see medical doctors and psychiatrists. One request form dated April 20, 2002, responded to ten days later, stated: "you are scheduled for next month or as soon as possible. The medical dept is backed up for months."[538] This sort of delay can prompt acting out and self-mutilation by prisoners desperate to obtain mental health services.

Our research also suggests that mental health staff are unduly quick in concluding that prisoners who request psychiatric assistance are malingering. For example, absent a careful evaluation through diagnostic work-ups, it is impossible to determine whether a self-mutilating individual has genuine psychiatric problems. Staff suspicion of malingering — and the decision to withhold services — is particularly prevalent for segregated prisoners who may have an understandably strong desire to gain even a temporary reprieve from their conditions. Staff also discount the possibility that some prisoners may be exaggerating their psychiatric symptoms because that is frequently the only way to get the help they need. In addition to assuming malingering, mental health staff may be also unduly quick to assign diagnoses of personality disorders rather than Axis I diagnoses.

---

[537] Hans Toch and Kenneth Adams, *Acting Out*, 2002.
[538] The Nevada inmate, J.S., wrote to Human Rights Watch on August 23, 2002, and included copies of his medical treatment request forms.

For example, Dr. Roberta Stellman reported the following about care at Gatesville prison in Texas:

> treatable conditions are not diagnosed and treatment, therefore is not initiated....
> [S]urprisingly, many inmates are not given an Axis I diagnosis. Yet the more difficult
> diagnosis of a personality disorder is readily made, usually antisocial personality
> disorder, without [adequate] documentation...self injury is too often labeled
> "attention-seeking" and again the dynamics of the behavior are disregarded.[539]

Examples of seriously ill prisoners not receiving adequate mental health treatments in supermax units are legion. We note some examples below:

In some of Alabama's prisons, a high proportion of inmates with serious mental illness are confined in segregation, including some inmates who appeared to expert observers to be experiencing even more acute episodes of illness than their counterparts in the prison mental health treatment units. "Despite the fact that the mental condition of inmates segregation [sic] were often worse than those on the mental health units, they had even fewer contacts with mental health treatment staff, were assessed even less frequently by the psychiatrist, and received only psychotropic medication and intensive correctional supervision. When the psychiatrist is available to segregation inmates, interviews are conducted at the open cell front where there is no confidentiality from other inmates or in an open correctional office where there is no privacy from correctional staff." [540]

When Human Rights Watch visited Indiana's Maximum Control Facility in 1997, Dr. Terry Kupers, who joined our research team for the visit, interviewed a prisoner who had been intermittently under psychiatric care since the age of four. He was unable to tolerate solitary confinement and was one of the worst self-mutilators in the history of the facility. Yet he was repeatedly deemed free of psychiatric disorders and received no treatment. He was eventually sent to Indiana's other supermax facility, the Secured Housing Unit, where, despite a regime of psychotropic medication, he was still actively hallucinating, displayed other symptoms diagnostic of schizophrenia, and was very depressed. The psychiatrist at the SHU told us that many of the prisoners receiving psychotropic medications were faking psychotic symptoms "to make an excuse of mental illness." In some cases, the psychiatrist labeled as "manipulative" symptoms that, in the judgment of Human Rights Watch's team of psychiatrists, were clearly signs of serious psychiatric disorders. [541]

In many segregation units, mental health services are so poor that even floridly psychotic prisoners receive scant attention, abandoned in their cells accompanied only by their hallucinations. After reviewing the harrowing testimony of plaintiffs' experts regarding conditions in administrative segregation in Texas, a federal judge concluded:

> inmates in administrative segregation...are deprived of even the most basic
> psychological needs. The scene revealed by the plaintiffs' experts, one largely

---

[539] Dr. Stellman's December 10, 1998 report on mental health services in certain Texas prisons is quoted in Dr. Jeffrey Metzner's letter to attorney Donna Brorby, December 31, 1998, p. 12; on file at Human Rights Watch.

[540] Kathryn Burns, M.D. and Jane Haddad, Psy.D., "Mental Health Care in the Alabama Department of Corrections," *Bradley v. Hightower*, Civ. No. 92-A-70-N (N.D. Ala., June 30, 2000), pp. 85-86.

[541] See Human Rights Watch, *Cold Storage: Super-Maximum Security Confinement in Indiana* (New York: Human Rights Watch, 1997). We were also disturbed by the SHU psychiatrist's stated willingness to give psychoactive medications to prisoners who are not psychotic. He attempted to justify this practice by saying the prisoners had affective disorders, even though it is not standard medical practice to prescribe antipsychotic medications for such disorders.

unrefuted by defendants' emphasis on policies and procedures, is one of a frenzied and frantic state of human despair and desperation. Furthermore, plaintiffs submitted credible evidence of a pattern in TDCJ [Texas Department of Criminal Justice] of housing mentally ill inmates in administrative segregation — inmates who, to be treated, would have to be removed to inpatient care. These inmates, obviously in need of medical help, are instead inappropriately managed merely as miscreants.... Whether because of a lack of resources, a misconception of the reality of psychological pain, the inherent callousness of the bureaucracy or officials' blind faith in their own policies, TDCJ has knowingly turned its back on this most needy segment of its population....

Plaintiffs' experts in *Ruiz* had presented compelling testimony that administrative segregation was "used to warehouse mentally ill patients who need medical and psychiatric attention."[542] Dr. Dennis Jurczak, for example, stated "there was something desperately wrong with a system that would have people this ill sitting in segregation and not being recognized by the mental health staff as needing assistance," including floridly psychotic prisoners. According to the court decision, "Dr. Jurczak found that many of these individuals were not being followed by the mental health staff and many were not identified as mentally ill."[543] Court orders led the department to identify and remove many seriously decompensated prisoners from administrative segregation. However, in 2002, forensic psychologist Keith Curry, retained by the *Ruiz* attorneys, found that prisoners needing sub-acute care remained housed in administrative segregation (indeed congregated in the most restrictive levels) even though the level of care necessary to treat their illness did not exist in administrative segregation. The prisoners instead were only able to receive outpatient care and, according to Curry:

> The quality of outpatient mental health care delivered to inmates surveyed in segregation ranged from adequate to virtually nonexistent.... [The outpatient care suffered from] low and variable caseloads, inadequate and uneven staffing, absent or irrelevant individualized treatment planning, serious and persistent problems with medication administration, and most importantly, the substitution of monitoring for treatment.... Training, supervision, and enforcement of policies and procedures were uniformly weak.[544]

In Louisiana, at Angola Prison's Camp J, a disciplinary housing unit holding 457 prisoners in lock-down conditions, observers who have been allowed into the prison assert that they have encountered a number of overtly psychotic prisoners, several of whom were receiving neither medication nor counseling. According to attorney Keith Nordyke, who has been involved in class action litigation against conditions at Angola, "I was seeing what I considered to be very disturbed, psychotic inmates, who couldn't control their behavior at all. I saw nine or ten. Many were not receiving medication, mental health treatment."[545]

In Florida, until recently, even the pretense of counseling prisoners in segregation was absent. Prisoners in the closed management units (CMUs) lived in cells with external coverings blocking any

---

[542] *Ruiz v. Johnson*, 37 F. Supp. 2d 855, 911 (S.D. Texas, 1999).
[543] Ibid., at 912.
[544] Keith Curry, Ph.D., letter to attorney Donna Brorby, March 19, 2002, p. 10.
[545] Human Rights Watch telephone interview with Nick Nordyke, May 7, 2002. Nordyke has been involved in prison litigation in Louisiana for over a decade.

view out of the windows; they were not permitted radios or allowed to borrow books from the prison library. A 1995 procedural manual on CMUs prepared by the Florida Department of Corrections' Adult Services Programs Office, detailed the prisoner living conditions: "Inmates confined on a 24 hour basis, excluding showers and clinic trips, may exercise in their cells. However, if confinement extends beyond a 30 day period, there shall be an exercise schedule providing a minimum of two hours per week of exercise outside the cell."[546] The1995 manual's one reference to the mental health of prisoners merely stated that a psychologist "shall prepare an assessment if the inmate is assigned to close management for more than 30 continuous days and not assigned to work outside the housing unit. If the confinement extends beyond 90 continuous days a new psychological assessment shall be complete after each subsequent 90 day period."[547] The manual stated that prisoners in Florida's ten close management units must maintain a clean record for six months before being eligible for any form of in-cell programming.[548]

Six years after the manual was written, at the tail end of the *Osterback v. Moore* class action lawsuit filed by mentally ill prisoners against these conditions, in a tacit admission that these units were excessively restrictive, the Florida Department of Corrections sent an internal memo to all its prison wardens.[549] The wardens were ordered to remove external visual shielding on the cell windows; to immediately build exercise stations to be placed in close management yards; to allow closed management prisoners the use of radios; and to allow prisoners to borrow up to three books a week from the prison library (while the 1995 manual had not explicitly documented the denial of library privileges, the 2001 document implicitly acknowledged that this had, in fact, been the case.) In-cell educational opportunities, according to the memo, would now kick in after sixty days, instead of the previously mandated six months.[550] Significantly lacking, however, was any reference to improved mental health counseling on the units.

Three months after the memo went out, without admitting liability, the Florida Department of Corrections offered to settle the *Osterback* case. They proposed consolidating the ten close management units into four sites by October 2003; increasing staff training on mental health issues; performing mental health screening both before and after a prisoner's placement in the units; assessing the behavioral risk of each prisoner so as to better lay the groundwork for mental health planning; and "provid[ing] a full range of outpatient mental health services (e.g., group/individual counseling; case management; psychiatric consultation; psychotropic medications; and timely referral to inpatient care), commensurate with clinical need, as determined by the Defendant's mental health staff."[551] The new plan stated that "all [CMU] inmates shall be allowed out of their cells to receive mental health services specified in the [individualized service plan], unless, within the past 48 hours, the inmate has displayed hostile, threatening, or other behavior that could portend harm or danger

---

[546] *Close Management Procedural Manual,* p. 25 (State of Florida, Department of Corrections' Adult Services Program Office, August 1995).

[547] Ibid., p. 22.

[548] Ibid., p. 25.

[549] *Osterback v. Moore,* Case No. 97-2806-CIV-HUCK (S.D. Florida). The lawsuit alleged that close management conditions were so harsh that they violated the Eighth Amendment to the U.S. Constitution. The case was settled on December 27, 2000, when the court entered a final judgement of injunctive relief in an unpublished order.

[550] Memorandum from Richard Dugger, deputy secretary, Department of Corrections, State of Florida, July 20, 2001.

[551] *Osterback v. Moore,* Case No. 97-2806-CIV-HUCK (S.D. Florida, October 2, 2001), *Defendants' Revised Offer of Judgement,* Phased Consolidation Plan, Part A.5, p. 4.

to others."[552] Plaintiffs accepted the terms of the proposal settlement and it was approved by the court on December 27, 2000.

It remains to be seen whether comprehensive mental health services will indeed be implemented within the time frame laid out in this settlement agreement. Lawyers for the plaintiffs told Human Rights Watch that, as of April 2003, the Florida Department of Corrections was continuing to discipline seriously mentally ill prisoners in the CMUs for such offenses as talking through their doors to neighboring prisoners; and that guards used pepper spray on seriously ill prisoners for creating disturbances, talking, and masturbating. The attorneys also alleged that, while Florida had created a good set of protocols regarding issues of concern such as the monitoring of side-effects of medication and the availability of regular meetings with psych specialists and psychiatrists, the realities do not always match the promise. "In theory they're supposed to monitor side effects," attorney Peter Siegel stated. "The problem is on paper they do everything and on the ground they do very little. People on medications are supposed to be monitored regularly by these psych specialists. And some do it and some don't."[553]

Even within units specifically developed for mentally ill prisoners, such as California's Enhanced Outpatient Units (EOP), disciplinary rules that lead to segregation can frustrate mental health treatment efforts. Mental health clinicians have input into disciplinary hearings for EOP prisoners and can provide information for the disciplinary officers (who are security staff) to consider, but it is the disciplinary officers who have the ultimate say about punishments — including segregated confinement — to be meted out for infractions. When Human Rights Watch visited Mule Creek, fifty-five of the 187 prisoners in administrative segregation were on the mental health roster.[554] Although the duration of such segregation is not prolonged, no more than perhaps two or three months,[555] the prisoners in segregation lack guaranteed, regular access to the mental health programs and services available to them in the EOP. While their EOP status means that the prisoners are supposed to receive ten hours per week of out-of-cell group sessions, in practice, because of staffing shortages and security concerns, most of their interaction with psychologists and mental health staff occurs in cell-front interaction when the staff make their daily rounds in the EOP segregation units. What limited out-of-cell therapy is provided occurs with the prisoners in tiny single holding cells, known to staff and prisoners alike as "cages," in which those perceived as security threats are held while undergoing therapy.[556] It is far from uncommon for EOP administrative segregation prisoners to have to be sent to mental health crisis units for stabilization. According to administrative staff at Mule Creek prison, fully half of all crisis bed admissions at the facility come from the EOP administrative segregation population.[557]

---

[552] Ibid., p. 11.

[553] Human Rights Watch telephone interview with Peter Siegel, attorney, April 21, 2003.

[554] According to the prison, that day twenty-six prisoners were EOP status and twenty-nine were CCCMS status.

[555] Human Rights Watch telephone interview with an attorney who wished to remain anonymous, July, 2003.

[556] When Human Rights Watch visited these units, we saw group therapy rooms set up with a row of three to six cages lined up next to each other. The prisoners are escorted, in shackles, to this room from their cell; they are then locked into the holding cells and are unshackled. The cells are about the size of a priest's confessional; large enough to either sit down in or stand up in, but with no room to take even a single step. This qualifies as group therapy, because the prisoners can all hear the counselor and can all hear each other's comments. They cannot, however, necessarily see each other.

[557] Human Rights Watch telephone interview with an administrative officer, Mule Creek State Prison, August 18, 2003. Mental health staff double-checked the data.

From Segregation Units to Psychiatric Centers and Back

Eleven years ago, the *Journal of Prison & Jail Health* reported that, across the country, prisoners with mental illness move back and forth between segregation and psychiatric centers.

> In segregation, the psychological stressors typically found in corrections are exacerbated and the atmosphere will frequently be counter-therapeutic.... For some [prisoners], this environment causes mental deterioration to the point of necessitating psychiatric hospitalization.[558]

Little has changed in subsequent years. The movement of mentally ill prisoners from segregation units to hospitals and back to segregation remains a prominent feature of their life in prison. When mentally ill prisoners in segregation become unmistakably psychotic, they are transferred in-patient psychiatric facilities. Once the prisoners are stabilized, they are returned to segregation.

- Correctional officers at Valley State Prison for Women, in California, told Human Rights Watch of one prisoner confined in the facility's secured housing unit (SHU) who, "rubs feces all over her body, her hair, her cell. She's been here almost a year. She screams at herself, anybody that walks by there. She floods her cell. She destroys everything that's in it." Periodically, she is removed to a mental unit for crisis intervention. But, the officers reported, after about three days, she is always returned to the SHU.[559]

- In a study of Washington State's Intensive Management Units, four University of Washington researchers found a pattern of:

    > movement between acute care and mental health housing for a time before being admitted to IMU, with IMU admission becoming an increasingly frequent event. In these cases, inmates are described as escalating in violence, unpredictability, or extremely bizarre behavior, and as difficult to manage in other prison settings. They are often recognized as psychotic or seriously mentally ill.[560]

- In New York, numerous seriously mentally ill prisoners are incarcerated in the state's Secured Housing Units (SHU), in a type of isolated cell that prisoners in New York call "the box." Attorneys from the Prisoners' Rights Project who have litigated several mental illness-related cases and are currently engaged in a system-wide mental health lawsuit, allege that a substantial number of seriously mentally ill prisoners spend years, even decades, bouncing back and forth between the SHU and Central New York Psychiatric Center. Prisoners' Rights Project attorney Sarah Kerr stated in a December 2000 presentation to the New York State Democratic Task Force on Criminal Justice Reform:

    > One schizophrenic prisoner whose medical chart we reviewed has been admitted to CNYPC [Central New York Psychiatric Center] on more than 20 occasions since his incarceration in the late 1970s; we know that he has been

---

[558] Article by William J. Rold, "Correctional Health Care," *Journal of Prison and Jail Health*, vol. 11, no. 1, 1992.

[559] Human Rights Watch interviews with correctional officers, Valley State Prison for Women, California, July 17, 2002.

[560] David Lovell, Kristin Cloyes, David Allen, Lorna Rhodes, "Who Lives in Super-Maximum Custody? A Washington State Study," *Federal Probation*, vol. 64, no. 2, Dec. 2000.

> housed continuously in 23 hour confinement for at least the period from early 1991 through May 2000, and that at least six of those ten years in segregation were in SHU.[561]

When the decision has been made that a prisoner should be transferred to a psychiatric unit or facility, the actual move may be delayed by space limitations in those facilities. In Mississippi, for example, it can take several weeks for a prisoner to be removed to an inpatient unit.[562] Such delays are primarily due to lack of staff and lack of space, and sometimes a lethargic bureaucracy plays a part. Also, the hospitals are simply reluctant to accept disruptive prisoners, even if they are acutely ill.

Once removed from segregation and provided a better level of mental health care in specialized psychiatric unit or hospital, many prisoners are stabilized and able to function more normally. But when they are then returned to segregation, they begin again the process of psychiatric deterioration. "Many times, the inmate, upon discharge from a psychiatric hospitalization, is returned to segregation, where the pattern repeats," the authors of the *Journal of Prison & Jail Health* article wrote.[563] In recent years, mental health experts have documented this phenomenon in numerous states whose mental health services were being challenged in litigation. For example, when Dr. Keith Curry toured Texas's prison system in 2002 and reviewed the records of mentally ill prisoners in connection with the *Ruiz* litigation, he discovered that in the six months from September 2001 to March 2002, McConnell prison had sent ninety-one prisoners out of the facility on mental health crisis transfers. Of these, thirty had been removed from administration segregation, forty-four of the ninety-one were repeat referrals, and fourteen of them were for psychotic decompensation while in segregation.[564]

In Oregon, many of the mentally ill prisoners housed in the prisons' Intensive Management Units decompensate and are then sent to the psychiatric intensive care unit. But this is only a short-term solution: two-thirds of those sent to the Mental Health Unit spend only ten to fourteen days there, and the rest at most three or four months. They are then back to the IMU, where many proceed to decompensate again.[565]

Most prison systems recognize that the cycle between segregation units and psychiatric crisis units or hospitals, referred to by some administrators as a "ping pong effect,"[566] is a problem that benefits nobody. The problem is particularly acute for those mentally ill prisoners who are violent and disruptive. They frequently have both serious mental illness (Axis 1) and serious personality disorders (Axis 2) that make their treatment and rehabilitation notoriously difficult yet their mental condition also makes them the greatest management challenge correctional authorities face. These prisoners invariably end up in prolonged segregation or supermaximum security confinement. It

---

[561] Testimony by Sarah Kerr of the Legal Aid Society, Prisoners' Rights Project on Mental Health Care in Special Housing Units in New York State Correctional Facilities, p. 7. Presented before the New York State Democratic Task Force on Criminal Justice Reform, December 4, 2000.

[562] Human Rights Watch telephone interview with John Norton, July 24, 2002.

[563] William J. Rold, "Correctional Health Care," *Journal of Prison and Jail Health*, vol. 11, no. 1, 1992.

[564] Letter from Dr. Keith Curry to the law offices of Donna Brorby, March 19, 2002, p. 16.

[565] Human Rights Watch telephone interview with Gary Fields, administrator, Counseling and Treatment Services, Oregon Department of Corrections, June 24, 2002.

[566] The term "ping pong effect" was first mentioned to Human Rights Watch in an interview with correctional staff, Northern Correctional Institution, Connecticut, June 10, 2002.

may be their Axis 2 disorder that accounts for the behavior that places them in segregation, but because of their Axis I illness, they cannot handle the stressful isolation and they decompensate.

But even in Washington State, Mike Robbins, the acting mental health director for Washington State's Department of Corrections, told Human Rights Watch that many of the most difficult-to-control prisoners in the state end up in Intensive Management Units, the state's supermax facilities. The combination of Axis 2 personality disorders and Axis 1 illnesses renders them too hard to control in the prison system's Special Offender Units (SOU) in which the more intensive mental health programs are concentrated.

> If someone cycles between the Special Offender Unit and the Intensive Management Unit [IMU], if they're troublesome enough the SOU staff will refuse to take them back, because they're not amenable to treatment and they're using up scarce resources. If it's not appropriate to put them in an IMU, where do we put them? We don't want to put them in a mental health program because they're so disruptive they blow up the program. It's a huge problem for corrections in general nationwide. We're struggling with it. The agency has not turned a blind eye to it.[567]

At McNeil Island prison in Washington, the Department of Corrections has developed a different system. The staff emphasize continuity of care, attempting to keep mentally ill prisoners within the same facility and dealing with the same staff for prolonged periods of time, rather than bouncing them between different institutions. They stress the importance of linking mental health treatment to chemical dependency and substance abuse treatment, and they have instituted weekly meetings in which mental health patients have a chance to discuss their illnesses and treatment schedules with case managers. The mental health staff have also worked hard to increase their input into disciplinary processes, and have, in some instances, successfully convinced the prison authorities to reclassify someone out of Maximum Security custody if they believe that prisoner could be better served in a mental health program.[568]

There are no easy answers for how to handle and help dangerous and disruptive prisoners who suffer from Axis 1 or Axis 2 disorders. Mental health experts told us progress is possible, but requires paradigm shifts in which correction officials must relinquish some of the usual rules by which prisons operate. Facilities would have to be run according to treatment protocols as determined by mental health staff. Public officials would have to support a form of incarceration that differed markedly from the traditional prison and be willing to stand up to critics who would argue that such treatment-oriented facilities "coddled" the worst prisoners. Another obstacle, of course, would be funding. No one doubts that a treatment-oriented milieu for mentally ill prisoners who are disruptive must be labor-intensive — and hence expensive. Yet until the expense is undertaken, the vicious cycle of segregation and decompensation and short-term hospitalization will continue until the prisoners are ultimately released, at least as sick as they were upon entry into the criminal justice system, from prison back into the community.

---

[567] Human Rights Watch interview with Mike Robbins, former acting mental health director, Washington Department of Corrections, Olympia, Washington, August 19, 2002.
[568] This information was obtained during a Human Rights Watch meeting with security and mental health staff at McNeil Island, August 22, 2002.

Keeping the Mentally Ill Out of Segregation

Courts have also recognized that conditions that inflict serious pain or injury are constitutionally suspect. "While prison administration may punish, it may not do so in a manner that threatens the physical and mental health of prisoners."[569] As one federal judge cogently noted, if the U.S. Constitution precludes forcibly incarcerating prisoners under conditions that will, or very likely make them seriously physically ill, "these same standards will not tolerate conditions that are likely to make inmates seriously mentally ill."[570]

Several recent court cases indicate the Eighth Amendment prohibition against cruel and unusual punishment may be violated when prisoners with serious mental illness or at increased risk for mental illness are confined in harsh, isolated high security facilities:

- In the landmark *Madrid v. Gomez* case in California, a federal district court in 1995 ruled that it was unconstitutionally cruel and unusual punishment to confine the mentally ill in the secure housing unit (SHU) of Pelican Bay prison. The court ruled:

  > For these inmates, placing them in [a SHU]] is the mental equivalent of putting an asthmatic in a place with little air to breathe. The risk is high enough, and the consequences serious enough, that we have no hesitancy in finding that the risk was plainly unreasonable. Such inmates are not required to endure the horrific suffering of a serious mental disorder or major exacerbation of an existing mental illness before obtaining relief.[571]

  The court also ordered the exclusion from the SHU of:

  > those who the record demonstrates are at a particularly high risk for suffering very serious or severe injury to their mental health, including overt paranoia, psychotic breaks with reality, or massive exacerbations of existing mental illness as a result of the conditions in the SHU. Such inmates consist of the already mentally ill, as well as persons with borderline personality disorders, brain damage or mental retardation, impulse-ridden personalities or a history of prior psychiatric problems of chronic depression.... Such inmates are not required to endure the horrific suffering of a serious mental illness or major exacerbation of an existing mental illness before obtaining relief.... [S]ubjecting individuals to conditions that are `very likely' to render them psychotic or otherwise inflict a serious mental illness or seriously exacerbate an existing mental illness cannot be squared with evolving standards of humanity or decency.... A risk this grave—this shocking and indecent—simply has no place in civilized society.[572]

  After the *Madrid* ruling, new administrators were brought in to Pelican Bay, many of the staff were re-trained, and a new mental health infrastructure was developed for the prison. In January 1998, the prison published plans for the creation of a high security unit specifically

---

[569] *Young v. Quinlan*, 960 F.2d 351, 364 (3d Cir., 1992).
[570] *Madrid v. Gomez*, 889 F. Supp. 1146, 1261 (N.D. Cal., 1995).
[571] *Madrid v. Gomez*, 889 F. Supp. at 1265-66. (citations omitted).
[572] Ibid.

catering to its seriously mentally ill prisoners.[573] Over one hundred seriously mentally ill prisoners were removed from Pelican's Bay's secure housing unit and placed into the new specially designed Psychiatric Services Unit (PSU). In the PSU, prisoners must receive group therapy, regular access to psychiatrists and to counselors, and routine mental health monitoring.[574]

Court monitors appointed under the *Madrid* ruling have generally written favorably on the PSU and on the mental health services the new unit provides. But they have also critiqued the program for failing to live up to certain requirements. In particular, the reports have found that PSU prisoners do not receive enough out-of-cell programming. "During the past three years, defendants have worked to establish various corrective action plans to address shortfalls in their compliance efforts," the Special Master wrote in October 2000.

> Some of these programs, like the development of a data-processing system to measure EOP [Enhanced Outpatient Program] and PSU inmate activity, expansion of the number of rooms that are available for group therapy, implementation of a program for outdoor recreation for PSU inmates, and utilization of a PSU level system have proven successful. Other corrective action plans, including those related to the hiring and retention of staff, and those related to providing EOP and PSU inmates with minimum out of cell structured therapy, have not proved effective.[575]

The report went on to fault the PSU for "chronic staffing shortages, including psychiatrist shortages and a long-term problem with inadequate numbers of psychiatric technicians.... For two and one half years the PSU has failed to meet its structured therapy requirements."

- In October 2001, a federal district judge in Wisconsin issued a preliminary injunction against the confinement of seriously mentally ill prisoners at the state's super-maximum security prison, ruling that plaintiffs had demonstrated a substantial likelihood that such confinement was unconstitutional. The subsequent settlement agreement between the parties approved by the judge establishes a permanent prohibition on the confinement of seriously mentally ill prisoners in the supermax.[576] The state has moved thirty-nine seriously mentally ill prisoners out of the facility (which housed 260 prisoners at the time of the ruling). The settlement permits an exception to the exclusion of seriously mentally ill from the supermax only if the department of corrections establishes the dangerousness of an prisoner and the absence of feasible alternative placements in Wisconsin or outside the state. In such cases, the department must also "identify the additional services that will be provided to the inmate to help him with his serious mental illness and to ameliorate the effect the conditions at Supermax have on that illness."[577]

---

[573] *Psychiatric Services Unit (PSU) Plan*, January 26, 1998.

[574] The settlement to the *Madrid* case resulted in a Special Monitor being appointed to oversee Pelican Bay and the improvements made to its mental health care infrastructure. Human Rights Watch was not able to tour the PSU or interview prisoners held there to ascertain the treatment they are receiving.

[575] *Special Master's Report Re Status Of PSU And EOP Compliance With Health Services Remedial Plan, Madrid v. Terhune*, No. C90-3094-T.E.H. (N.D. California, October 17, 2000).

[576] *Jones 'El v. Berge*, Judgment in a Civil Case, Case No. 00-C-0421-C (W.D. Wisconsin, June 24, 2002) (unpublished).

[577] Ibid.

- A 1998 Ohio Department of Rehabilitation and Correction (DRC) policy specifically stated that:

> Inmates who are seriously mentally ill...will not be placed at Ohio State Penitentiary [the state's supermaximum security prison].... Any inmate who is seriously mentally ill and has been inadvertently transferred to Ohio State Penitentiary shall be transferred to another institution in an expeditious manner.[578]

Nevertheless, in class action litigation against Ohio State Penitentiary (OSP), the presence of seriously mentally ill prisoners at the facility was documented and, under the spotlight, the DRC had to remove them from the prison. A federal district court granted plaintiffs a preliminary injunction preventing the DRC from returning those prisoners to the OSP. It noted there was "little dispute," even from the DRC, that placing seriously ill prisoners in that prison could cause decompensation and deterioration of a prisoner's mental health. The DRC's own psychiatrist acknowledged in his testimony that he had consistently recommended against the return of seriously mentally ill prisoners to OSP because of the likelihood of psychiatric harm.[579] In the settlement concluding part of the class action, the DRC agreed that mentally ill prisoners should not be housed at OSP and that those removed from the prison on grounds of mental illness could never be returned there.[580] Prisoners excluded from supermax confinement in Ohio are those suffering from a serious mental illness or mental retardation, those deemed actively suicidal or suffering from a severe cognitive disorder that results in significant functional impairment, and those with a severe personality disorder that is manifested by frequent episodes of psychosis, depression, or self-injurious behavior.[581]

The Ohio DRC now places seriously mentally ill prisoners who it deems to require high security confinement in the residential treatment unit (RTU) at the Southern Ohio Correctional Facility, a maximum-security prison in Lucasville.[582] However, according DRC policy, when high maximum security classified prisoners are released from the RTU because mental health staff consider them stable and able to cope outside of such a specialized unit, they are placed in the "J-4" administrative control unit. This unit operates with essentially the same rules and restrictions as the supermaximum security prison. There are, nonetheless, substantial differences between the supermax and the J-4 unit. The J-4 cells have open fronts with bars instead of a solid door thus reducing the isolation and enabling prisoners to communicate with each other more easily. There is structural programming, outdoor and indoor recreation, and opportunities for prisoners to interact. The unit also provides more access to mental health treatment than in the OSP. Pointing to these factors,

---

[578] Ohio Department of Corrections Policy 111-07, quoted in Order of Judge James S. Gwin, *Austin v. Wilkinson,* Case No. 4:01-CV-71 (N.D. Ohio, November 21, 2001) (granting plaintiffs preliminary injunction).

[579] Testimony of Gary Beven, M.D., September 24, 2001 hearing, at 216, cited in Order of Judge James S. Gwin, *Austin v. Wilkinson,* Case No. 4:01-CV-71 (N.D. Ohio, November 21, 2001), p. 24.

[580] The settlement was signed on January 8, 2002.

[581] E-mail correspondence from Fred Cohen, to Human Rights Watch, July 9, 2003.

[582] According to Fred Cohen, the Psychiatric Director for the Ohio Department of Rehabilitation and Correction has final say before an inmate is sent to the supermax of Ohio State Penitentiary. At intake, a second full psychiatric evaluation is also conducted. Cohen served as a court-appointed monitor in the Ohio case for five years, and believes the state was very receptive to the proposed changes. Human Rights Watch telephone interview, August 8, 2002.

the federal district court hearing the class action against OSP denied a motion to grant a preliminary injunction preventing the DRC from placing prisoners with serious mental illness in the J-4 unit, concluding they were unlikely to prevail on their claim that such confinement violated the Eighth Amendment.[583]

- In the *Ruiz* lawsuit in Texas, after extensive testimony by plaintiffs' psychiatric experts about the presence of severely ill, including floridly psychotic, prisoners in administrative segregation who were receiving little or no medical care, the federal district court ruled that confining the mentally ill in segregation was unconstitutional. In the *Ruiz* case, a federal court in 1999 noted that in Texas:

> Separately from and independent of, the determination that the conditions of deprivation in administrative segregation violate the constitution, it is found that administrative segregation is being utilized unconstitutionally to house mentally ill inmates — inmates whose illness can only be exacerbated by the depravity of their confinement. As to mentally ill inmates…the severe and psychologically harmful deprivations of [the] administrative segregation units are, by our evolving and maturing society's standards of humanity and decency, found to be cruel and unusual punishment.[584]

The court subsequently ordered the Texas Department of Criminal Justice (TDCJ) to develop plans to make sure:

> seriously mentally ill prisoners for whom the conditions of administrative segregation are injurious or pose a significant risk of serious deterioration in their mental status are not housed in regular administrative segregation, but are rather housed in inpatient mental health hospitals or other facilities appropriate for the level of mental health care that they require.[585]

In conjunction with the University of Texas Medical Branch at Galveston and the Texas Tech University Health Sciences Center in Lubbock, the TDCJ conducted thorough reviews of its prisoner population in high security institutions such as the Estelle Unit, and relocated several dozen of its sickest prisoners into hospital settings. The TDCJ also developed new mental health treatment programs for prisoners who would otherwise be in regular administrative segregation, including one in the Specialized Administrative Segregation Maintenance Program for prisoners who have been stabilized on medication in a hospital setting but have a pattern of discontinuing treatment and decompensating. Another program is the Enhanced In Cell Treatment Program for prisoners with chronic mental illness who do not require a higher level of care but do require treatment and contact to mitigate the effects of the segregation environment.[586] In addition to special reviews of administrative segregation prisoners by mental health staff to identify acutely mentally ill

---

[583] *Austin v. Wilkinson*, Case No. 4:01-CV-71 (N.D. Ohio, September 21, 2001) (unpublished opinion).

[584] *Ruiz v. Johnson*, 37 F. Supp. 855 (S.D. Texas, 1999).

[585] Cited in Intervention Plan for Seriously Mentally Ill Offenders in Administrative Segregation, December 15, 2001.

[586] Plaintiffs' Response to Defendants' Report and Plan Concerning Seriously Mentally Ill Prisoners in Segregation, *Ruiz v. Johnson*, January 14, 2002; on file at Human Rights Watch.

patients, the TDCJ also contracted with a consultant to provide an independent review mechanism to ensure seriously ill offenders are removed from segregation.

- Although Connecticut did not have a lawsuit hanging over its head, it nonetheless changed its rules regarding the incarceration of seriously mentally ill prisoners in its supermax prison. Persistently mentally ill prisoners, registering a four or a five on the five-tiered mental health categorization system used by the Connecticut Department of Correction, are not sent to the supermax Northern Correctional Institution (NCI). "It had to do with the nature of the environment at Northern," Brett Rayford, director of health and mental health services for the department, stated. "Interaction with other people was limited. The facility was designed to contain people even more than other facilities."[587] Nevertheless, mental illness continues to disproportionately plague the supermax prison: of the 450 prisoners at NCI as of mid-2002, 111 were categorized as mental health level three.[588]

---

[587] Human Rights Watch interview with Brett Rayford, director of health and mental health services, Connecticut Department of Correction, June 10, 2002. Human Rights Watch visited Northern Correctional Institution in 2001.
[588] Data provided by Clyde McDonald, field operations director, Correctional Managed Health Care in a Human Rights Watch interview, Connecticut, June 10, 2002; Human Rights Watch interview with Brett Rayford, director of health and mental health services, Connecticut Department of Correction, Connecticut, June 10, 2002.

R.P., NEW YORK

Twenty-four-year-old R.P. has lived in New York State prisons since he was convicted on two counts of attempted assault and attempted criminal sale of a controlled substance in 1998. He is serving a four-to-eight year sentence and is scheduled to be released in September 2004. At one time, he was taking Resperdal, Sinequan, and Cogentin to control his psychosis and to deal with the internal voices that he routinely heard. But R.P. decided to stop taking his medications because they made him feel lazy and sleepy, and, he states somewhat bizarrely, he believed they were killing his sperm.[589]

Before he entered prison, R.P. had had a long history of psychosis. While incarcerated at Rikers Island, New York awaiting trial, he was held incompetent to stand trial and was sent to Mid-Hudson Psychiatric Center to be stabilized. After that, he was tried, found guilty, and sent to prison.

During his five years as a New York State prisoner, R.P., an African-American, has been in several prisons: Attica, Downstate, Clinton, Southport, and Wende. In four of these facilities, he has been placed in Secure Housing Units (SHU) because of his violent outbursts against other prisoners and staff. At the Southport facility, he was housed in D-Block, a unit with solid doors on the cells, resulting in what his attorneys call "significant sensory deprivation."[590] Since May of 1999, he has been in the SHU continuously, brought out only when he decompensates to such an extent that he has to be temporarily removed to one of the satellite mental health units, and involuntarily medicated with shots of Haldol. In fact, he has accumulated so many disciplinary tickets for acts of self-harm, creating disturbances, and unhygienic acts, that he has accrued enough SHU time to keep him there until he has served out his full sentence.

Despite this well-documented history of bizarre behavior, R.P.'s diagnosis by prison authorities continually has changed. Sometimes, he is documented as having anti-social personality disorder; other times he has been diagnosed with attention deficit disorder or adjustment disorder. He has also been diagnosed with "psychosis non-specific." None of these diagnoses have prevented his being housed in the SHU.[591]

In the SHU, lacking daily medications, his mental condition continues to deteriorate. Because he is in the SHU, he has no access to group therapy, no access to the kind of intensive counseling that might convince him to go back on his medications. He says he sees a psychotherapist "once in a blue, but they don't take me seriously." And he says that when they do come around, it is only to provide a couple minutes of formulaic cell-front questions. R.P. says that because he has refused to take his medications, he has not been seen by a psychiatrist in two years. By any definition, R.P. is clearly seriously mentally ill and in need of intensive mental health interventions. He has numerous razor cut scars on both arms, and the center of his stomach likewise has a long, fine scar, the aftermath of R.P.'s attempt to cut himself open.[592]

---

[589] Human Rights Watch interview with R.P., Wende Correctional Facility, Alden, New York, September 13, 2002. Some anti-psychotic medications are known to cause temporary impotence; but sterility is not a known side effect.

[590] Details provided in correspondence with Prisoners Legal Services attorney Betsy Sterling.

[591] Human Rights Watch telephone interview with Betsy Sterling, attorney, Prisoners Legal Services, March 27, 2003.

[592] R.P. showed his scars to Human Rights Watch during an interview at Wende Correctional Facility, Alden, New York, September 13, 2002.

R.P. told Human Rights Watch:

> Living in the SHU is horrible. Voices. A lot of people yelling at you. I'm unable to program. Sometimes I have feelings of killing myself. Nobody to talk to. It's horrible all round. I sit there, look at the walls, talk to myself — about things I want to do, hurting people, hurting correctional officers, hurting other inmates.

"The voices," R.P. stated:

> have got worse. All during the day. At night times it's real worse. There's Bruto, Bad Ass and Funny Man. Bruto is the aggressive one, wanting me to beat people up. Bad Ass talks shit, says things. Funny Man always wants to make jokes on people.

Over the past couple years, R.P. has cut himself with razors, tried to hang himself, and swallowed hoarded painkillers. When he does these actions, he reported, the prison removes him to a suicide-watch observation cell for seven-to-ten days, provide him with no counseling and then returns him to the SHU.

> In the Satellite Unit they just leave you in a strip unit where it's cold. They ask you one time what happened. You ain't got no clothes on. They give you a paper gown. Then they send you back to your cell. It occurs again. Every time, it gets worser. You get tickets, a misbehavior report. If they can't give you no more box time, they give you a restricted diet — bread and cabbage, which is horrible. It's not properly cooked. The cabbage is cold and the bread is hard.

L.J., NEW YORK

In May 2002, Disability Advocates, Inc. filed a lawsuit against the New York State Office of Mental Health (OMH) and the Department of Corrections (DOCS), alleging that:

> prisoners with mental illness subject to DOCS disciplinary sanctions are frequently placed into [SHUs,]…psychological punishing twenty-three hour isolated confinement housing areas…. Prisoners in [SHUs]…have extremely limited opportunities to participate in any form of mental health therapy. Often the only contact with mental health staff occurs during rounds when OMH staff walk through the housing unit and may stop and speak to prisoners from through the bars at the front of their cell or through a slot in the solid door of their cell, all within earshot of neighboring cells and in the presence of a cellmate in the double-celled SHUs.[593]

Not surprisingly, many of the seriously mentally ill in these units routinely bounce back and forth between the Central New York Psychiatric Center and prison SHUs. The story of twenty five-year old L.J., who currently resides in Sing Sing prison, is illustrative.

L.J. has been hearing voices since he was a child. Prisoners Legal Services lawyers told Human Rights Watch he has a history of lead poisoning and had to be schooled in special education classes due to " serious intellectual limitations" and emotional disturbances.[594] Since incarcerated he has been in and out of the Central New York Psychiatric Center. He was arrested in Rochester, when he was nineteen years old, for selling crack cocaine, and received a sentence of three-and-a-half to ten years. He claims to have gone to school for six years, but also thinks he stayed in school until he was twenty-one, two years after he was sent to prison. He claims not to have a mental illness, yet oftentimes forgets to bathe, and in the past has taken Thorazine. Currently, he is refusing to take his medications. Over the past six years, L.J. has been in several prisons and mental health centers: Elmira, the Central New York Psychiatric Center, Cayuga, Elmira again, Great Meadow, and Sing Sing.[595] During his interview with Human Rights Watch, L.J. was clearly confused, his body odor was powerful, suggesting he had not washed in several days, he rocked back and forth continually, and his eyes stared, unblinking and unfocused, throughout the meeting.

L.J. says he was sent to the SHU

> for fighting some dude. They put me in the box. It made me feel upset. I don't think I belong in the box. I started passing out. I hit my head a couple times — on a brick wall. I started talking to myself. Often. Softly. "Wass up?" "What're you doing?" "How you doing?" I didn't want to take any showers. I just ain't go to the shower. The correctional officer asked me why a couple times. I said I don't feel like going to the shower. He walked away.

---

[593] *Disability Advocates Inc., v. New York State Office of Mental Health,* Complaint, No. 02 CV 4002. (S.D.N.Y., May 28, 2002), p. 10.

[594] Information provided Human Rights Watch by Prisoners Legal Services in correspondence dated October 24, 2002.

[595] Human Rights Watch interview with L.J., Sing Sing Prison, Ossining, New York, June 11, 2002.

Nearby prisoners started teasing him about his smell, shouting down the corridor that he stank. "I stopped talking," L.J. reported.

In 1998, L.J. had to be removed to the suicide observation cell and to the Central New York Psychiatric Center, for stabilization. According to Prisoner Legal Services attorneys, he has "repeatedly deteriorated in the SHU only to be cycled out for limited periods to the mental health satellite unit, where he would be stabilized, often on medications, and then returned directly to the SHU cell, for the cycle to start over again."[596] Back in prison, L.J. has stopped taking his medications again, and is tormented by voices. They are, he says, "irritating voices, like somebody coming for me. Whispering voices," that say they are going to kill him. "I want to get rid of the voices. The voices are getting to me," L.J. declared. Then, in the contradictory fashion characteristic of many mentally ill, "I think I need help. I don't need no medications. They say I need it. I don't know — they're lying."

---

[596] Written correspondence from Prisoners Legal Services to Human Rights Watch, October 24, 2002.

III-Equipped

A.O., Illinois, September, 2002

I'm currently diagnosed with Deppression & Anxiety. Upon arriving here I have only been seen by a psychiatrist 2 times in a 6 month period, during which time my condition has gotten worser!!! I've made the psychology staff here aware of my continued deteriorating conditions, but they have ignored my cries for help. The suicide watch cells are deplorable!!! With human feces and urine all over the cell as well as the food tray box where they hand you your food along with depriving you with utensils to eat with. You are treated like a dog and have to eat your food with your hands. The suicide cells are being used as a form of punishment. The windows are kept open on purpose to allow cold fridged air to freeze you while you are without any cloths. You are not even given anything to put around your private parts or anything to sleep on while you are without clothing. There has been 2 actual successful suicide hangings while being on suicide watch since I've been here along with 100s if not 1000s of attempted suicides. The staff here has absolutely no concerns or regards to mental health or human life.... Doctor-patient confidentiality is totally disregarded. The psychiatrist comes to your cell for less than 2 minutes and discusses your confidential mental health problems out loud for everyone on both sides and below your cells can hear exactly what you are discussing with psychiatrist due to cells being open bar cells.

U.L.T., Indiana, June 21, 1999

All afternoon most of the range [the cell bloc] is taking jabs at an ignorant, loud mouthed 'know-it-all,' who is known as a persistent snitch. He has been on the SHU for over 5 years and calls most of the officers by their first names. Not a smart thing to do. This idiot then gives O.Y., a schizoid in the cell next to mine a large paper clip. O.Y. is a known self mutilator. Needless to say, before I can even begin talking to O.Y., he has taken this five inch piece of wire in the paper clip and stuck it all the way up in his penis. Now the idiot that gave it to him is calling for officers to come back here and check on O.Y. O.Y. is bleeding and sore, but there is nothing they can do. They go out to call for a nurse. The shift changes and about an hour later a nurse comes in. The officers take O.Y. out to see the nurse and the nurse gives O.Y. a shot, probably Haldol; but O.Y. isn't sure. The nurse says she'll try to get hold of the doctor. The paper clip is still imbedded in O.Y.'s penis. Now, it is after supper and half of the range is threatening to throw shit on the snitch, and he is threatening to throw it right back. Since every one is locked in these cells, there can be no fights, so they resort to slinging shit.... Our clean laundry is returned at around 8.32pm. Then medications are passed. O.Y. is told that the doctor will check him tomorrow. The paper clip is still where he left it! Everyone is so used to O.Y. doing this stuff it is just like it is part of everyday. O.Y.'s arms are nothing but scars, his neck is just as bad. I have seen him led out of his cell with half of an inkpen sticking out of his neck. I have a pretty strong stomach and I have seen many types of trauma, but this is still extremely gross. Around here, it is 'just O.Y.' There is no regular Psychology staff back here in the SHU. The custody staff has no special training when it comes to mental patients. There is quite a variety of them here in the SHU. But the mental problems are treated the same as the rest of the offenders.

XIII. SUICIDE AND SELF-MUTILATION

Offense: 104. Violation: Dangerous Contraband. Comments: Piece of Glass. Final Result: Guilty. Record of Proceedings: Inmate appeared before the committee to address the charges. Inmate stated: I'm guilty. I was hungry and I was eating my arm that day. I found the piece of glass in my cell after I busted my light out. Disciplinary action: Segregation one year."
—Illinois Department of Corrections, disciplinary hearing, August 22, 1998, Tamms Correctional Center, Illinois:[597]

Human Rights Watch exegesis: a seriously mentally ill inmate in a super-maximum security prison was caught eating his own flesh after having cut open his arm with a shard of glass. He was brought before a disciplinary committee, and was sentenced to a year in the prison's segregation cells.

Self-mutilation, suicide attempts, and suicides are far too common in prison. The prevalence of such self-harm is linked both to the prevalence of mental illness among prisoners and inadequate mental health treatment.

Self-Mutilation

We were not able to find any national or state-wide statistics on the prevalence of self-mutilation in prison. Nevertheless, the extent of the mutilation and the determination exhibited by prisoners to engage in serious acts of self-harm is astonishing. Prisoners have swallowed pins, inserted pencils in their penises and paperclips in their abdomens, bitten chunks of flesh from their arms, slashed and gashed themselves. In many prisons around the country, Human Rights Watch has interviewed prisoners whose bodies are massively scarred from self-mutilation. Both correctional and mental health staff acknowledge that self-mutilation is a major problem.

Elaine Lord, superintendent at the Bedford Hills Correctional Facility in New York, catalogues the remarkable ways women have injured themselves: "cutting their own throat, legs, arms, or wrist; headbanging; inserting foreign objects under the skin or into wounds or surgical sites on the body; overdosing on medication; or swallowing an extraordinary variety of objects including, but not limited to, knitting needles, screws, straight pins, safety pins, pens, pencils, light bulbs, springs, nails, pieces of radiator, screens, uniform name tags, pieces of wall, and chips of paint."[598]

The complaint in a lawsuit against the supermax prison in Tamms, Illinois, drawing on prisoner medical records and psychiatrist interviews, details the self-harm of several mentally ill prisoners.[599] Among the examples cited:

- Twenty three year old D.T.Q. has an extensive psychiatric history that includes a year-long hospitalization at the Illinois State Psychiatric Institute as well as several suicide attempts. After D.T.Q. was incarcerated at Tamms, he

---

[597] *State of Illinois Department of Corrections Adjustment Committee Final Summary Report.* Hearing: August 22, 1998, 8.40 p.m. Hearing was before George C. Welborn, chief administrative officers, Tamms Correctional Center, Illinois.
[598] Lord, "Prison Careers of Mentally Ill Women," p. 376.
[599] *Boyd v. Snyder*, Amended Complaint, No. 99 C 0056 (N.D. Illinois, February 25, 1999).

began hallucinating. He screamed and talked to imaginary people in his cell, once explaining to staff that he was busy having a party. Another time, he saw demons crawling out of his toilet and walls. He began to sit in a tent he had made himself from his blanket, explaining that he was hiding from five drunken correction officers who had threatened him. He began to think his food was being poisoned, that the walls were closing in on him, that the guards were conspiring with one of the inmates to kill him. Eventually, D.T.Q. became violent toward himself and he remains so today. He has repeatedly cut his arms and neck, bitten his shoulders, and bashed his head into a wall.

- T.C. routinely self-mutilates, slicing his arms, neck, and abdomen. He has had to be placed on suicide watch several times, once after he was found with a rope around his neck.

On August 20 [1998], with his arms already swollen from infected self-inflicted wounds, T.C. again cut his arm and began eating small pieces of his own flesh in front of a correctional officer. The officer ignored the medical emergency and also ignored T.C.'s pleas to speak with someone from the mental health unit. Eventually T.C. was removed from the cell and his arm was stitched. Despite the obvious danger T.C. posed to himself, he was returned to the same cell and left unattended (and evidently still in possession of a dangerous instrument); again he cut himself, again requiring stitches to close the wound…. T.C. pulled the stitches out of his arm and lost more than half a pint of blood before he was discovered bleeding in his cell.

In an interview, this prisoner explained to Human Rights Watch that after he had cut his arm with a piece of razor, he had inserted the piece into the gash on his arm. When his arm was stitched up in the infirmary, the razor piece was not removed. Once returned to his cell, he tore out the stitches, removed the razor, and began cutting himself again.[600]

- Another prisoner at Tamms sent Human Rights Watch a letter detailing his experience in Illinois prisons:

I have been in Tamms [for two years]…. I have never had any major mental health issues until I arrived at the Tamms Supermax prison. Also before I came to the Tamms Supermax prison I have never self-mutilated myself. I was placed on (1) crisis in Western Illinois Correctional for saying that I felt suicidal, and I was place on (2) crisis watches while in the Pontiac Correctional Center for making a home made noose and the other for setting my cell on fire. Once I arrived at the Tamms Correctional Center I did not have any problems until about 5 months after my arrival when I was placed on a wing with all inmates who self-mutilated on themselves (at the time I was placed on this wing I had never mutilated myself). After this I soon started to mutilate on myself, this was around October of 2000. When I first started to mutilate on myself it was always labeled as superficial and swept

---

[600] Human Rights Watch interview with T.C., Tamms Correctional Facility, Illinois, November 7, 2001.

under the rug. After a while it started to get worse and worse. But at no time from October of 2000 until January of 2002 was I given any treatment. Around August of 2001 it was getting so bad that I had to be placed in four point restraints when I mutilated myself. Around December of 2001 I had to start getting stitches for my self-mutilation. When I cut they just put me on a crisis watch, they never tried to find out the problem. They never appeared to be concerned about why I mutilated myself. The reason I mutilate myself is because of my anger. When I get angry I cut and it seems that the mutilation calms me down. Then in January of this year when my mother passed it started getting worser and worser. I was placed on enforced medication because of voices telling me to cut then when I cut I started to eat my own flesh. Whenever I cut on myself I have to placed into four point restraints because once I start it is hard to stop. I am housed in a cell that has hard gray plastic caulking all on the wall that makes it very easy for me to cut when I get angry. Prison officials and the mental health staff know that this is what I have used to cut myself but they refuse to remove it from my cell or move me to a more safer cell. I really need some outside help because the mental health staff is working with the prison officials to not properly treat me or diagnose my problem.[601]

Other examples of self-mutilation from around the country include the following:

- Washington prisoner E.X. is imprisoned for manslaughter, robbery, assault, and burglary. E.X. was sexually abused as a child, and as a result has been diagnosed as suffering from Post Traumatic Stress Syndrome and panic attacks. In prison, he has been disciplined several times for fighting with other prisoners. At Walla Walla Prison, in the eastern part of the state, he spent a year in the Intensive Management Unit. There he began seriously hurting himself. He was transferred to Shelton prison, where his acts of self-harm continued. "I really deteriorated in IMU," E.X. aged 30, recalled.

  I was hurting myself, punching myself. One time I took a slipper and was beating myself. I stubbed my finger in my eye socket. I wasn't getting the help I needed. They had a counselor down there, but he was so busy it was very hard to talk to him. One hundred and sixty people with one counselor. I was slipping into depression. I was hearing voices and stopped showering.[602]

  All told, E.X. says he has been in IMUs about seven times during the ten years he has been incarcerated. During some of these occasions he began slamming his head against the wall.

  The lights were on 24 hours a day, cuff ports being slammed all the time, the yelling and screaming, and the absence of human contact magnified my mental illness through the roof, till the only way I could get my mind off it was to hurt myself. The IMU is very detrimental to mental health. It magnifies my illnesses.

---

[601] Letter to Human Rights Watch from prisoner V.Y., dated September 2, 2002.
[602] Human Rights Watch interview with E.X., McNeil Island Prison, Washington, August 22, 2002.

Not until E.X. was removed to the prison at McNeil Island, where the prison is working in conjunction with the University of Washington to up the level of its mental health provisions, did he begin receiving regular mental health treatment.

- In Graterford Prison, Pennsylvania, Human Rights Watch interviewed sixty-year-old mentally ill prisoner X.G., who reported extended episodes of self-mutilation. X.G. is originally from Pittsburgh and says that he has been in an out of mental institutions since he was hit by a bus at the age of fourteen and left with substantial brain injuries. A talkative, opinionated man, X.G. has spent much of his adult life in state mental hospitals, and much of the rest of his adult life in prison for extremely violent crimes. While in prison, he has combined acts of violence against others with ongoing attempts to mutilate and even kill himself, and as a result he has repeatedly cycled in and out of the Restrictive Housing Units (RHUs) in the prison system. When Human Rights Watch interviewed him, X.G. was serving time in disciplinary custody. "Once I set my cell afire and threatened to kill myself. I was setting myself on fire," the prisoner asserted matter-of-factly. His legs are severely scarred from burning; and up and down both arms are literally dozens of scars from where he has cut himself with razors.[603]

- A lawsuit filed against the Georgia Department of Corrections in March 2002, alleges abuse and neglect of seriously mentally ill prisoners at the high security Phillips State Prison, Georgia.[604] Among the allegations, attorneys claim that the prison has systematically ignored the mental health issues of prisoners who engage in acts of self-mutilation, tending to view self-mutilation as a gesture by manipulative prisoners seeking attention, or looking to be removed from the unpleasantly harsh environment of a maximum security prison, rather than as a symptom of bona fide mental health problems.

In addition, the lawsuit alleges that prisoners are routinely disciplined for their acts of self-mutilation. The complaint includes the following examples of self-mutilation:

- o A prisoner with a history of suicide attempts who took a razor back to his cell from the unit control room on September 21, 2001. He "cut his arms several times, and made a four-inch gash on his leg." His action was treated as a disciplinary infraction.

- o Another prisoner "cut himself on his arms, throat, and chest on numerous occasions… even while he was in an administrative segregation unit." Although he was placed in a crisis stabilization unit each time he cut himself at Phillips State Prison, the lawsuit alleges that he was not provided with necessary long-term mental health services. Moreover, his actions were also treated as disciplinary issues and he was punished for hurting himself.

- o In the summer of 2001, a third prisoner "died during a 'cutting party'" — when several prisoners on a cell block begin cutting themselves in tandem — after being

---

[603] Human Rights Watch interviews, Graterford Prison, Pennsylvania, August 12, 2002. Staff let X.G. out of his cell for an interview in the unit's yard.
[604] *Fluellen v. Wetherington,* Civil Case No. 1:02-CV-479(JEC) (N.D., Georgia, March 15, 2002).

placed in a cell with a knife blade left in it. The prisoner "cut himself so severely that he bled to death."

Suicide

Young men, persons with mental illness, alcohol and drug addicts, and people who are in custody, are amongst the most at-risk groups for suicide.[605] Given the prevalence of all of these indicators concurrently among prisoners in the United States, it is not surprising that suicide attempts are a serious problem inside prison. A nationwide survey conducted by prison suicide expert Lindsey Hayes in 1995 found that suicide rates in state prison systems ranged from 18.6 per one hundred thousand all the way up to 53.7 per one hundred thousand.[606] According to The 2001 Corrections Yearbook, the average suicide rate in prison was 0.26 per 1,000 prisoners, or twenty-six per 100,000, two-and-a-half times the rate of suicide in the U.S. population at large, which for 2000 was 10.6 per 100,000.[607]

Mental illness is a high risk factor for suicide; untreated or poorly treated mental illness even more so. NAMI reports research findings that about 90 percent of persons who completed suicides had a diagnosable mental or substance abuse disorder.[608] The organization estimates that between 2 and 15 percent of persons diagnosed with major depression, 3 to 20 percent of persons diagnosed with bipolar disorder, and 6 to 15 percent of persons diagnosed with schizophrenia die by suicide. People with personality disorders are approximately three times as likely to die by suicide than those without.[609]

Human Rights Watch has not been able to find any national or system-wide statistics on the rate of mental illness among prisoners who committed suicide. Nevertheless, correctional and mental health staff and independent experts we interviewed agreed that attempted and completed suicides are more prevalent among prisoners with a diagnosed serious mental illness. A few studies of prison suicides support this view. For example, in Texas prisons, a study of twenty-five suicides committed between June 1996 and June 1997 found that 60 percent of the prisoners had been identified at intake screening with mental disorders, and 76 percent had psychiatric diagnoses at some point during their incarceration.[610] A study in 2002 of New York prison suicide risk factors by New York's Office of Mental Health, which provides mental health services to New York prisoners found that 70 percent of prisoners who committed suicide had a history of mental illness. Forty percent of them had received a mental health service within three days of the suicide; and 40 percent

---

[605] *Preventing Suicide: A Resource for Prison Officers.* Department of Mental Health, World Health Organization (Geneva, 2000) p. 5.

[606] Lindsey Hayes, *Prison Suicide: An Overview and Guide to Prevention* (Mansfield, MA, National Center for Institutions and Alternatives, 1995), p. 4.

[607] Centers for Disease Control and Prevention, National Center for Health Statistics, *Health*, United States, 2000, available at http://www.cdc.gov/nchs/data/hus/tables/2002/02hus047.pdf, accessed on August 26, 2003.

[608] See Jane Pearson, Ph.D., *Suicide in the United States*, NAMI (formerly known as the National Alliance for the Mentally Ill), available online at: http://www.nami.org/update/suicide.html, accessed on August 26, 2003.

[609] Some experts believe the higher range of suicide rates is most accurate. For example, Dr. Jeffrey Metzner told Human Rights Watch that 15 percent of people with schizophrenia commit suicide, and 5 to 15 percent of people with clinical depression. Human Rights Watch telephone interview with Dr. Jeffrey Metzner, July 16, 2003. See also, Douglas Jacobs, ed., *Harvard Medical School's Guide to Suicide Assessment and Intervention* (San Francisco: Jossie Bass, 1999), p. 7.

[610] Xiao-Yan He, A.R. Felthous, C. E. Holzer, P. Nathan, & S. Veasey, "Factors in Prison Suicide: One Year Study in Texas," *Jail Suicide/Mental Health Update*, vol. 10, no. 1 (2001).

had prior stays in psychiatric hospitals.[611] A review by Prison Legal Services of individual reports of New York prison suicides between 1995 and 2001 prepared by New York State's Commission of Correction indicates that many of the prisoners had been on the mental health case load and had discontinued their medication (without receiving adequate medication compliance counseling) or had been seriously mentally ill but had been repeatedly underdiagnosed.[612] In Pennsylvania, prisoners on the mental health/mental retardation roster committed approximately 56 percent of the suicides in 1997 and 64 percent of those in 1998.[613]

Increased Risk of Self-harm and Suicide in Segregation Units

Efforts at self-harm are particularly prevalent in segregated, high security settings. According to Raymond Bonner, suicide prevention expert and chief psychologist at the Federal Correctional Institution at Allenwood, Pennsylvania, "By and large, most self-harm behavior in prison is exhibited by individuals who are confined in conditions of segregation, social isolation, and/or psychosocial deprivation."[614]

The confinement of mentally ill prisoners in segregation also heightens the risk of their suicide, indeed, it heightens the risk of suicide for all prisoners. The World Health Organization has reported that "the majority of suicides in correctional settings occur when a prisoner is isolated from staff and fellow prisoners. Therefore, placement in segregation or isolation cells…can increase the risk of suicide."[615] U.S. statistics reflect the higher prevalence of suicide in segregated settings. One study found that "approximately 68 percent of the inmates who committed suicide were on special housing status (e.g., segregation, administrative detention, or in a psychiatric seclusion unit) and, with only one exception, all victims were in single cells at the time of their deaths."[616]

It is a tragic irony that many of the mentally ill who attempt or commit suicide were originally placed in segregation because of acts of self-harm. Segregation is, however, perhaps the worst possible setting for suicidal prisoners. As Raymond Bonner notes, "Social and environmental isolation is never an appropriate consequence [of acts of self-harm or attempted suicide] as it undoubtedly worsens emotional state, hinders problem-solving and can increase the risk for life-threatening behavior."[617]

The experiences of individual state prison systems bears this out.

---

[611] Correctional Association of New York, "Mental Health in the House of Corrections," forthcoming publication.

[612] Prison Legal Services, Review of New York State Commission of Correction reports on prisoner suicides (undated); on file at Human Rights Watch.

[613] Lance Couturier, Ph.D. and Frederick R. Maue, M.D., "Suicide Prevention Initiatives," 2000, p. 2

[614] Raymond Bonner, "Rethinking Suicide Prevention and Manipulative Behavior in Corrections," *Jail Suicide/Mental Health Update*, vol. 10, no. 4 (Fall 2001), pp. 7-8.

[615] *Preventing Suicide: A Resource for Prison Officers*. Mental and Behavioral Disorders, Department of Mental Health, World Health Organization (Geneva, 2000) p.10.

[616] Lindsay Hayes, *Prison Suicide: An Overview and Guide to Prevention* (the National Center on Institutions and Alternatives, Mansfield, Massachusetts, June 1995), p. 4.

[617] Raymond Bonner, "Rethinking Suicide Prevention and Manipulative Behavior in Corrections," *Jail Suicide/Mental Health Update*, vol. 10, no. 4 (Fall 2001), pp. 7-8.

- Arkansas has had fifteen suicides in the past five years, ten of which were in the state's supermax prison and two of which occurred while the inmates were supposedly under close supervision in mental health units.[618]

According to a study of suicides in New York prisons between 1998 and 2000, 54 percent of the suicides took place in the Special Housing Units.[619] Citing the result of suicide reviews by the New York Commission of Corrections, the complaint filed in 2002 by Disability Advocates Inc. against the New York Office of Mental Health and the New York Department of Correctional Services stated that: "for each year from 1998 through 2001, from 30% to 50% of the suicides for the entire prison population occurred within the 8% of the prison population confined in twenty-three hour isolated confinement housing...[D]eficient mental health treatment and the stresses of isolated twenty three hour confinement have been significant facts leading to suicide."[620]

- In the Mecklenburg Correctional Center, Virginia, twenty-one-year-old Teko Williams committed suicide in a segregation cell in 1997. Williams had a history of serious mental illnesses ranging from major depression to psychosis. He also had a long history of self-harm gestures and suicide attempts. In August 1997, Williams began smearing feces on himself and his cell walls, and also began eating his feces. Because of these acts and the fact that other prisoners on his cell-block were complaining about the smell, Williams was transferred to a segregation unit where he was reportedly kept chained to his cot for much of the last two weeks of his life.[621] The prison psychologist was not consulted about this move. A few days later, Williams used a sheet to hang himself from the bars of the inner-cell door. It took the correctional staff over five hours to realize Williams had killed himself. As a result of this negligence and failure to make the mandatory hourly checks, a correctional officer was fired.[622]

- In June 2000, twenty-year-old Carol Ann Bell, a bipolar female prisoner at the Ohio Reformatory for Women in Ohio, hanged herself in her cell.[623] After an escape attempt, Bell had been placed in administrative segregation. She was kept in solitary confinement for a period of thirteen months, interrupted only by brief periods in the prison's residential treatment unit when she was on suicide watch(which happened at least five times) and after she slit her wrists once.[624] After she was released from solitary confinement, she was moved to maximum security. She allegedly saw her psychiatrist only once every two months, despite guards and prisoners noticing, and reporting, that her mental health was deteriorating. The complaint indicates that the mental health staff simply did not believe her suicidal actions were genuine. Despite a history of suicidal actions and verbal

---

[618] Written communication to Human Rights Watch from Max Mobley, director of mental health, Arkansas Department of Corrections.
[619] "Suicides High in Prison 'Box,'" *Poughkeepsie Journal*, December 16, 2001.
[620] *Disability Advocates Inc., v. New York State Office of Mental Health,* Complaint, No. 02 CV 4002 (S.D.N.Y., May 28, 2002), pp. 14-15.
[621] "Mentally Retarded Man Dies in Mecklenburg Jail the Norfolk Killer, Serving 53 Years, Apparently Hanged Himself in his Cell," *Virginian Pilot and The Ledger-Star,* August 26, 1997.
[622] Information contained in *An Investigation Into the Suicide of A Prison Inmate,* Department for the Rights of Virginians with Disabilities, Case Number 98-0035, June 1999.
[623] Carol Ann Bell was serving a fifteen- to fifty-year sentence for stabbing and robbing a cabdriver when she was sixteen.
[624] *Zertuche v. Timmerman-Cooper,* Complaint (S.D. Ohio, August 22, 2001).

communications with mental health personnel indicating she wanted to take her own life, the complaint asserts that:

> approximately 2 months passed between Carol Ann's last appointment with [the prison psychiatrist] on January 20, 2000 and their next contact on March 15, 2000. At this March meeting, Carol Ann was upset, restless and tearful. Her prescriptions had expired. [The psychiatrist] updated her prescriptions, yet failed to ask Carol Ann about the circumstances leading up to the Crisis Evaluation in February.

In June, shortly before Bell's death, the same psychiatrist failed to read her chart and thus was unaware of the fact that she had been burning herself with cigarettes in recent days. A few days later, Bell ended her own life.[625]

- At the Waupun Correctional Center in Wisconsin, a seriously mentally ill prisoner named Matthew Sanville was placed into a segregation cell after assaulting another prisoner in July 1998. Sanville repeatedly asked guards to arrange for him to see mental health staff and repeatedly threatened to kill himself. Nevertheless, he was never removed from the unit and placed on a suicide watch. On the morning of July 29, Sanville covered all the openings in his cell with paper. He ripped his pillowcase into strips, wet the strips in his sink, tied them together into a noose and hanged himself. Several guards passed his cell during this period, peered in through the paper coverings and then continued on their rounds. Not until 3 o'clock that afternoon did correctional staff enter his cell. By that time Sanville had been dead for several hours. A court subsequently found that the guards had exhibited "deliberate indifference" to Sanville's serious medical needs.[626]

Suicide Protocols

Litigation has established suicide prevention as a required component of mental health services.[627] Nevertheless, in 1995 when custodial suicide prevention expert Lindsey Hayes surveyed prison responses to suicidal prisoners, he found a pattern of neglect and an inadequate invention system. In his Department of Justice-funded report, he urged correctional systems to improve staff training, better identify prisoners at risk of suicide, improve communication between different offices within prisons, provide special housing for suicidal prisoners to be placed within, increase the supervision of these prisoners, and encourage interventions by staff to minimize the chances of a prisoner actually attempting to kill him or herself. Hayes found that only four of the fifty states had all of these elements within their suicide prevention policies. He found that while 79 percent of state departments of correction had suicide prevention policies, only 15 percent of the policies covered

---

[625] Under the terms of the settlement of the lawsuit, approved by a probate court in July 2002, the Ohio Department of Rehabilitation and Correction – in addition to paying damages to Bell's family – agreed to expand mental services at the prison for individuals experiencing mental health crises and to increase mental health training for correctional staff. Bell's suicide also contributed to ongoing discussions within the Ohio Department of Rehabilitation and Correction regarding the confinement of mentally ill offenders in segregation. Human Rights Watch interview with Monique Hoeflinger, attorney, Prison Reform Advocacy Center, which represented Bell's family, September 9, 2003.

[626] Information contained in court opinion in *Martha Sanville v. McCaughtry,* 266 F.3d 724 (7th Cir., September 21, 2001).

[627] Fred Cohen, *The Mentally Disordered Inmate and The Law* (New Jersey: Civic Research Institute, 2000), p. 14-4. Fred Cohen wrote, while "there are constitutional duties to preserve life and to provide medical or mental health care, these duties do not translate into some guarantee of safety, health, the quality of life."

the majority of the elements in the American Correctional Association or National Commission on Correctional Health Care standards.[628]

Eight years later, Hayes believes that, nationally, many of the problems remain: "Inmates reporting that they are taken out of cells and thrown into another cell and stripped naked. That obviously shouldn't happen. Nobody should be stripped naked and left without protective clothing — a paper gown, there are various smocks and safety garments."[629] In fact, prisoners across the country also told Human Rights Watch that all too often suicide attempts resulted in being placed naked for days in cold, barren observation cells. Interaction with mental health staff while in the observation cell is minimal. Some prisoners told Human Rights Watch they do not tell mental health staff of suicidal thoughts because they want to avoid at all costs being put in the observation cells.

- Y.P., a one-time prisoner at the women's prison in Washington, diagnosed with post-traumatic stress disorder, obsessive compulsive disorders, and major depression, told Human Rights Watch:

  > In prison, every time you talked to them about what was bothering you, they'd say "No, you're not feeling that way." They'd shut down my feelings. When I cut myself they put me in one-on-one observation. I was locked in a room, with a mattress on the floor and you're lucky if you get a blanket. You'd have male officers watching you the whole time. I didn't want male officers watching when I went to the bathroom. That's humiliating.

  Y.P. stated that she asked to talk to her counselor once and the nurse refused to send for her. Y.P. responded by swallowing a bunch of pills she had managed to hoard. [630]

- Outside experts found that in Alabama's St. Clair correctional facility, a suicidal prisoner:

  > may be placed in a mental health cell by security staff but is discharged by a psychiatrist. Since a psychiatrist is on-site only one day a week, the inmate may remain nude in the Spartan cell for six days without a psychiatric evaluation. There is no documentation of active treatment of the inmate during the interim…. The delay in the treatment of inmates experiencing a crisis is totally unacceptable by any professional standard of which we are aware for an inmate whose behavior or verbalizations resulted in placement in this restrictive setting. Indeed, if it is a mental health crisis that precipitates…the move…then the inmate suffers needlessly in this cell and there is a strong likelihood of preventable deterioration in the inmate's mental health.[631]

---

[628] Lindsay Hayes, *Prison Suicide: An Overview and Guide to Prevention* (the National Center on Institutions and Alternatives, Mansfield, Massachusetts, June 1995), p. 4; Human Rights Watch telephone interview with Lindsey Hayes, June 18, 2002.

[629] Human Rights Watch telephone interview with Lindsey Hayes, March 26, 2003.

[630] Human Rights Watch interview with Y.P., Seattle, Washington, August 20, 2002.

[631] Kathryn Burns, M.D. and Jane Haddad, Psy.D., "Mental Health Care in the Alabama Department of Corrections," *Bradley v. Hightower*, Civ. No. 92-A-70-N (N.D. Ala., June 30, 2000)), p. 28.

- According to a class action complaint filed on behalf of mentally ill prisoners at Tamms Correctional Center, a supermaximum security prison in Illinois, Robert Boyd, a prisoner with an extensive psychiatric history and a prodigious self-mutilator, has also attempted suicide several times. After these attempts, he has been placed on suicide watch,

> a procedure in which the sole treatment consists of being placed in isolation in a cold stripped cell, without clothes and without conversation, for several days in a row.... At times, while in the isolation of suicide watch, he is placed in four-point restraints for hours at a time and forcibly injected with high doses of a tranquilizer.... Other times he is simply observed, naked, by the guards and nurses. Rarely, is there an attempt at therapeutic conversation; the mental health workers tell him that talking to them is a privilege that he must earn by agreeing not to kill himself.[632]

Independent correctional experts condemn the practice of leaving suicidal prisoners naked, exposed, and without intensive mental health services. According to Lindsey Hayes, such treatment "further enhances the potential of them becoming suicidal or engaging in self-injurious behavior. It's degrading, humiliating."[633] Dr. Terry Kupers told Human Rights Watch that placing suicidal prisoners in barren observation cells:

> is counter-therapeutic in that no therapeutic relationship is formed and the prisoner learns it's better to keep suicidal thoughts and plans to him — or herself. In jails and prisons isolation "safety cells" are used instead of doing what is essential in the treatment of anyone seriously contemplating suicide: talk to them. Thorough evaluation, continuity of contact with mental health clinicians, establishment of a trusting therapeutic relationship — these are the things that prevent suicides and assure the effectiveness of treatment — not fifteen minute checks on a prisoner in an observation/safety cell.[634]

Dr. Janet Schaeffer told Human Rights Watch of a suicidal prisoner she had encountered in a Pennsylvania facility who was repeatedly stripped naked and put into an observation cell despite a history of having been sexually abused as a child that had left him terrified when he did not have his underwear on. "It contributed to his anxiety," Schaeffer reported.

> To have your body that exposed, it's an invasion of your privacy and it causes a great deal of psychological distress. In addition, you're in an environment where you can't get out. You're trapped. You're already feeling pretty horrible. You feel like you want to die and you're at the mercy of people with a lot of power and control. It's a terrible situation, being alone, for someone who's already really suicidal. They already feel very isolated, alienated.[635]

---

[632] *Boyd v. Snyder*, Amended Complaint, No. 99 C 0056 (N.D. Illinois, February 25, 1999). The court denied plaintiff's motion for class certification. *Rasho v. Snyder*, 2003 U.S. Dist. Lexis 2833 (S.D. Illinois, February 28, 2003).
[633] Human Rights Watch telephone interview with Lindsey Hayes, March 26, 2003.
[634] Email correspondence from Dr. Terry Kupers to Human Rights Watch, April 14, 2003.
[635] Human Rights Watch telephone interview with Janet Schaeffer, psychologist, April 28, 2003.

Instead of such isolation, Schaeffer maintains that suicidal prisoners should be talked to by staff, encouraged to interact with their surroundings and with other people; they should, she told Human Rights Watch, be helped to "[re-]establish social relations, not placed in a situation where such interactions are further broken off."

Recognition of their legal obligations, a genuine commitment to avoid suicide (which is one of the most traumatic experiences for correctional staff and surviving prisoners), and the development of national standards for suicide prevention[636] have prompted corrections authorities to begin establishing more effective suicide prevention protocols. Some states have implemented significant measures to limit suicides within their prisons. For example, the Secretary of Corrections of Pennsylvania appointed a Suicide Prevention Task Force to analyze suicide risk factors, department and prison responses to suicide attempts and completed suicides, and to propose recommendations for changes in department policies, procedures and training. Based on the report and findings of the task force in 1999, the department implemented a series of new procedures and policies and expanded the use of others.

Among other things, Pennsylvania prison authorities revised the suicide prevention policy to improve suicide watch procedures, mandate that watches be conducted outside of administrative segregation areas, require that prisoners be provided anti-suicide smocks, and mandate use of a suicide risk indicators checklist. The prison superintendent's prerogative in determining which incidents were suicide attempts and which were merely "gestures" was reduced. The department also undertook to expand the range of mental health treatment services by, for example, increasing the number of psychiatric observation cells, streamlining procedures for committing prisoners in psychiatric crises into inpatient treatment, and increasing the number of Special Needs Units — specialized housing areas where prisoners with handicaps can receive additional services and protection. Recognizing that mentally ill prisoners placed in segregation are at particularly high risk of suicide, the department modified administrative segregation policies to increase the diversion of prisoners with mental illness from these housing areas. Disciplinary proceedings include an assessment of the role of mental illness in the commission of an infraction and the possible impact of segregation on the prisoner's illness. Prison officials are encouraged to reduce disciplinary time for mentally ill prisoners who commit infractions, and to provide enhanced mental health services and tracking for prisoners with mental illness who must be placed in segregation. The department also now uses a suicide risk indicators checklist for prisoners being placed in segregation to ensure that clinical staff visit any at risk prisoners.[637] The aggressive and comprehensive effort is paying off: the number of suicides within the Pennsylvania system declined from fourteen in 1995 to five in 2000, despite an increase of over eight thousand in the size of the state's prison population.[638]

---

[636] In 1981, the American Correctional Association developed widely recognized suicide prevention standards, revised in 1990. The National Commission on Correctional Health Care also first issued suicide standards in 1987, most recently revised in 2003. The ACA and NCCHC standards are adopted voluntarily and are not legally binding.

[637] Lance Couturier, Ph.D. and Frederick R. Maue, M.D., "Suicide Prevention Initiatives in a large Statewide Department of Corrections," *Jail Suicide/Mental Health Update*, vol. 9, no. 4, Summer 2000. We have only touched upon a few of the thirteen new policies and procedures adopted to prevent suicides discussed in the article.

[638] Numbers detailed by Lance Couturier, "Suicide Prevention In a Large State Department of Corrections," *Corrections Today*, August 2001.

In California, the largest prison system in the country, thirty-two prison suicides occurred from October 1998 to December 1999.[639] Underneath these numbers, however, were large discrepancies between prisons. While many California prisons had no suicides, the supermax prisons at Sacramento and Pelican Bay each had three suicides, and Corcoran had five.[640] That is, the three supermax prisons accounted for one-third of the state prison suicides. The authors of a report on California prison suicides wrote that "review of data submitted on individual suicides indicated a delivery of care that was inconsistent with established program guides and/or suicide policies" in twelve California prisons, including the above-mentioned three.[641] While California's prison system, as a whole, had a suicide rate only marginally higher than that found in the American population at large, the suicide rate in prisons such as Corcoran were far higher than the national average. "The five suicides that occurred at Corcoran during the period reviewed reflect the difficulties that facility had in providing adequate mental health treatment to seriously mentally disordered inmates generally, and to inmates at risk for suicide in particular," the report noted.[642] The report authors recommended better training for clinicians and correctional officers alike in recognizing and responding to indicators that a prisoner might be a suicide risk.

California appears to have taken these criticisms to heart and to have expanded its suicide prevention activities. In the year 2000, there were only fifteen suicides throughout the California system. The following year, that number rose again to twenty-seven, suggesting the decline in 2000 might have been a statistical blip.[643] Generally, though, California appears to have dedicated considerable resources to monitoring suicide risks, one of the reform measures it has adopted following a federal court decision that mental health care in California prisons was unconstitutionally deficient.[644]

Punitive Responses to Suicide Attempts
Self-harm is not always a symptom of a serious mental illness. Nevertheless, the desire to harm oneself warrants careful attention by mental health staff. Similarly, all attempts at suicide must be dealt with as a mental health emergency. Yet in prison self-harm or attempted self-harm is frequently dismissed as malingering — without consideration of whether the effort to attract attention is being made by someone with serious psychiatric needs. Dr. Terry Kupers has testified:

> I have in all my tours of prisons checked on the psychological autopsies of suicides…. In reviewing those reports, in 100 percent of cases in about 16 different institutions I have found that successful suicides are preceded by a note in the [medical] chart saying this individual is just malingering or is manipulating or is an antisocial personality; don't pay any attention…. [O]ne can manipulate and be mentally ill or at serious risk or suicide; one can be malingering, and the malingering can be a symptom of the mental illness. Overall my impression is that the mental

---

[639] Information contained in the *Coleman Suicide Report*, written by Raymond Patterson, M.D., and Kerry Hughes, M.D., July 14, 2000. The researchers found that 81.2 percent (twenty-six out of thirty-two) of suicides were by hanging.
[640] Ibid., p. 4.
[641] Ibid., p. 5.
[642] Ibid.
[643] Numbers contained in *Report on Suicides Completed in the California Department of Corrections in Calendar Year 2000*.
[644] *Coleman v. Wilson*, 912 F. Supp. 1282 (E.D. California, 1995). The court accepted a magistrate findings of numerous deficiencies in California's prison mental health services, including the failure to implement its suicide protocols because of severe understaffing.

health staff [at Wisconsin's supermaximum security prison] doesn't take that into consideration.[645]

"Inmates display a variety of self-harm behaviors for different reasons in response to varying problems in living behind bars," Raymond Bonner has written.[646] "Motives may range from actually wanting to die to wanting specific solutions to problems or emotional relief. The term manipulation serves little useful purpose in understanding self-harm behavior and often hinders objective problems-solving and risk assessment…."

Prisoners who injure themselves or attempt suicide are often disciplined, and usually placed in segregation, if they were not there already. The treatment of self-harm as a disciplinary matter is rooted in the corrections paradigm. Self-harm violates the rules, and rule-breaking must be punished. As Fred Cohen explains, corrections officials are also concerned about deterring malingering: "The mind-set in corrections is that there has to be a 'price' for self-mutilation or suicide attempts; otherwise, inmates would begin to believe that they can ensure a transfer to better housing conditions simply by a simple cut or threat of suicide."[647]

The response to self-harm and attempted suicide as a disciplinary rather than mental health matter is also rooted in the way prisons distinguish between what they consider serious mental illness, which they consider to be solely Axis 1, and personality disorders. Self-harm is often a consequence of certain personality disorders. As discussed above in chapter VIII, prison mental health staff tend to discount the importance of personality disorders because they lack the resources to address the high number of prisoners with such disorders, because they get frustrated trying to deal with the notoriously difficult to treat personality disorders, and because they often themselves become "institutionalized," adopting the correctional staff attitude that these prisoners are simply "bad," not "mad." They discount the mental health significance of acting out behavior, including self-harm, by prisoners diagnosed with personality disorders, and see malingering which warrants punishment, rather than illness that needs treatment.

For example, Dr. Thomas Conklin evaluated aspects of mental health care in certain Texas prisons in 1998. Following a review of the charts of thirteen suicide attempts and gestures among prisoners in the Estelle Unit, he found that "all suicide gestures by inmates are seen as manipulating the correctional system with the conscious intent of secondary gain. In not one case was the inmate's behavior seen as reflecting mental pathology that could be treated."[648] Similarly, Dr. Jeffrey Metzner, after reviewing the medical charts and post-mortem psychological evaluation report, made the following assessment about the treatment of a Texas prisoner who committed suicide in 1997:

> This inmate was clearly difficult to treat and had multiple serious self-inflicted wounds. Unfortunately, his problems were ultimately determined to be manipulative in nature and not due to a mental illness but due to malingering and/or an antisocial personality disorder. This ultimately resulted in discontinuation of his medications

---

[645] Testimony of Dr. Terry Kupers, *Jones 'El v. Berge*, Civil Case 00-C-0421-C (W.D. Wisconsin, 2001), pp. 124-25.

[646] Raymond Bonner, "Rethinking Suicide Prevention and Manipulative Behavior in Corrections," *Jail Suicide/Mental Health Update*, vol. 10, no. 4 (Fall 2001), pp. 7-8.

[647] Written communication to Human Rights Watch, June 7, 2003.

[648] Conklin's conclusions are quoted in a letter regarding the Texas Department of Criminal Justice from Dr. Jeffrey L Metzner to attorney Donna Brorby, December 31, 1998, p. 9. Dr. Metzner was retained by Broby to conduct assessments regarding mental health care services provided to TDCJ inmates in connection with the *Ruiz* litigation.

and the later reemergence of a major depressive disorder which was diagnosed one day prior to his suicide. There appeared to be little attempt to understand the dynamics of his behaviors and provide appropriate interventions and/or consultations to the security staff. It is likely his depression was exacerbated by his placement in segregation. This documentation concerning the changes in the diagnosis leading to malingering was poor. This case is another example of systemic problems related to documentation, diagnosis, and treatment which contributed to this inmate's dismal outcome.[649]

The reports of punitive responses to self-harm are legion:

- In his book *Prison Madness*, Terry Kupers reported viewing security files for prisoners in many state prison systems who had killed themselves and been issued "a posthumous citation for violating the prison rule against attempting suicide."[650]

- Todd Winstrom, an attorney with Disability Advocates, told Human Rights Watch of one client at Taycheedah prison in Wisconsin who slit her throat, was patched up by prison doctors and then sentenced to 180 days in segregation for her actions. When she cut her throat a second time, she received another 180 days in solitary.[651]

- According to a New Jersey prisoners' class action complaint:

  A.O. is a prisoner currently confined to Northern State Prison's administrative segregation unit for women in Newark, New Jersey. A.O. has been diagnosed by DOC psychiatrists as suffering from schizophrenia, adjustment disorder, and multiple personality disorder, and she also suffers from seizures as a result of a stroke which she experienced at age fifteen. Her mental illness makes it difficult for her to control her behavior. She has received numerous disciplinary charges, including several for self-mutilation, drug overdoses and assaults on correctional staff.... [She] has attempted suicide or engage in self-mutilation approximately 15 times. Although she attempted to explain the role her mental disorder played in her suicidal behavior at her disciplinary hearings, she received additional time in both disciplinary detention and administrative segregation as a result of her suicidal behavior.[652]

- Dr. Janet Schaeffer, who held senior mental health positions in the Washington Department of Corrections, told Human Rights Watch that:

  Women who attempted to commit suicide were put in [Administrative Segregation] just the same as somebody might be put there because they'd committed some horrible rule infraction. Which is probably one of the

---

[649] Letter from Dr. Jeffrey L. Metzner to attorney Donna Brorby, December 31, 1998, p. 31.
[650] Terry Kupers, *Prison Madness*, 1999, p. 186.
[651] Human Rights Watch telephone interview with Todd Winstrom, June 5, 2002.
[652] *D.M. v. Fauver*, First Amended Class Action Complaint, Civil 96-1840 (D.N.J.). The case ultimately settled. *D.M. v. Terhune*, 67 F. Supp. 2d 401 (D.N.J., 1999).

worst things you could do to a suicidal person. There's a culture that is very powerful and very strong and permeates the entire place. It's very militaristic. They have a chain of command. I'd voice my opinion and argue and it wouldn't go anywhere. After a while it became part of what we knew would happen. That was just the deal. That was what happened. The rules of the prison are driven by issues of power and control.[653]

- As a plaintiffs' expert in the lawsuit against Wisconsin's supermaximum security prison, Dr. Terry Kupers wrote of one prisoner who came to the prison with a clinical chart from the Mendota Mental Health Institute indicating that he had "a pattern of escalation in terms of inappropriate behaviors and deterioration in terms of mental status which are associated with the use of isolation as a management strategy," and noted that the prisoner had a history of suicide attempts.

  [H]e had attempted suicide on more than one occasion in segregation at another institution, and then at SMCI he cut himself badly with broken glass.... He attempted suicide again on 12/10/00, a hanging that resulted in his face turning purple before he could be cut down by staff, and again he was retained at SMCI in isolation. Finally, this prisoner made a serious enough suicide attempt for the mental health staff to transfer him to Wisconsin Resource Center for intensive psychiatric treatment in late August 2001.[654]

- The above-mentioned Disability Advocates, Inc. complaint against the Office of Mental Health (OMH) and the Department of Correctional Services in New York stated that:

  for each year from 1998 through 2001, from 30% to 50% of the suicides for the entire prison population occurred within the 8% of the prison population confined in twenty-three hour isolated confinement housing.... According to State Commission of Correction (SCOC) investigations of suicides, deficient mental health treatment and the stresses of isolated twenty three hour confinement have been significant facts leading to suicide.[655]

---

[653] Human Rights Watch telephone interview with Dr. Janet Schaeffer, May 29, 2002.

[654] Testimony of Dr. Terry Kupers, *Jones 'El v. Berge*, Civil Case 00-C-0421-C (W.D. Wisconsin, 2001).

[655] *Disability Advocates Inc., v. New York State Office of Mental Health*, Complaint, No. 02 CV 4002 (S.D.N.Y., May 28, 2002), pp. 14-15.

FELIX JORGE, NEW YORK

In July 2000, New York State agreed to pay the family of Felix Jorge sizable monetary damages.[656] Six years earlier, on July 28th 1994, the twenty-four-year-old Jorge had stuffed his mouth full of wet toilet paper and suffocated. His suicide occurred in a mental health observation room in Clinton-Dannemora Prison.

Two years before his death, Jorge had been sentenced to three-to-six years in prison for holding up a woman with a toy gun. Despite a history of hospitalizations for mental illness dating back to childhood, despite a long and documented record of schizophrenia, paranoia, and suicide attempts, it took seven months after his admission for prison officials to realize just how seriously mentally ill Jorge was.[657] Only after Jorge had a psychotic attack in September 1993 did the state perform a mental health evaluation on the prisoner. "Mr. Jorge went without correct diagnosis and appropriate treatment for the greater part of his period of incarceration," wrote Dr. Martin Blinder in an opinion letter presented at the civil trial.[658] In the interim, the mental health staff periodically gave him some of the right medications — Haldol, Permitil, Artane — but they did not provide him with any therapy or counseling to ensure he continued taking these medications. In New York State, if patients refuse their medications three times in a row, they can be taken off the medications permanently. And that is what happened to Jorge. Attorney Edward Miller, who represented Jorge's family in their lawsuit against New York, told Human Rights Watch:

> If the inmates who were receiving the service *weren't* mentally ill, they'd work fine.... One of the symptoms of mental illness is refusal to take medication, and the system walks away from them once they refuse medication. They decompensate and they attempt suicide. It's common for them to go out of their minds in silent agony.... You can't forcibly administer medication unless a prisoner presents imminent risk of harm to self or others. But that's a red herring. The major issue is provision of therapy so they'll continue to take medications and not go off them.[659]

In late August 1993, in the midst of a psychotic episode, Jorge began banging his head against a window in the prison van in which he was being transported. He was charged with violating "section 123.10 self-inflicted bodily harm" and "refusing direct order," and received three months in a secure housing unit as punishment. According to prison documents, Jorge was informed that "this disposition is given as punishment for your actions and should serve as a deterrent to future misbehavior of this type by you."[660] In December 1993, Jorge was admitted to the Central New York Psychiatric Center in an acute paranoid, psychotic state. The center did what it is supposed to do: it stabilized Jorge whom the doctors diagnosed with "schizophrenia, paranoid, chronic with

---

[656] In internal prison documents, and court documents, George's name is sometimes spelt "Jorge," sometimes "George."

[657] *Ana Luisa Jorge v. The State of New York*, Claim No. 92210 (Court of Claims, N.Y., August 27, 1999). Page two of claimant Ana Luisa Jorge's Trial Brief states that "after Felix Jorge was incarcerated in May, 1993, New York State did not perform a mental health evaluation of Felix Jorge until September 23, 1993 and then, only after Felix Jorge had a psychotic attack involving auditory hallucinations and paranoia."

[658] "Expert Report of Dr. Martin Blinder," *Ana Luisa Jorge v. The State of New York*, Claim No. 92210 (Court of Claims, N.Y.), exhibit Q.

[659] Human Rights Watch interview with Edward Miller, attorney, New York, New York, June 12, 2002.

[660] In the trial, this document was presented by Attorney Miller as Exhibit A, Bates Stamp #3. See memorandum from Collie Brown to Edward Miller, Esq., December 16, 1999, p. 1; on file at Human Rights Watch.

acute exacerbation." He was then returned to the secure housing unit, to serve six months for "creating a disturbance" and "refusing a direct order" — both the results of the same paranoid state for which he had been sent to the Psychiatric Center.

According to an investigation by the New York State Commission of Correction, in March 1994 a treatment plan was developed for Jorge, recommending mental health staff see him twice a week and that he be re-evaluated for medication by a physician. The report found, however, that "there is no documentation that indicates he was seen twice a week and he was not provided a medication review."[661]

In early April 1994, Jorge swallowed 150 Tylenol (how he obtained this many pills is not documented) and had to have his stomach pumped.[662] Once again, the prison system responded to Jorge's action with punishments rather than treatment. He was given a year in the special housing unit (SHU), was deprived of all commissary, phone calls, and packages for a year, and denied a radio for six months. He was transferred to Clinton-Dannemora prison, to serve his SHU sentence there.[663]

Despite multiple psychiatric diagnoses, somehow Jorge's mental health records did not reach Jorge's new prison. Jorge's family alleged in its suit that:

> Two months after the transfer of inmate Jorge from Auburn to Clinton C.F., the psychologists at Clinton Correctional Facility had not even seen, let alone reviewed the mental health records for Felix Jorge and were totally unfamiliar with his diagnosed condition and consistent history of psychotic breakdown, self injury and suicide attempts.[664]

In May 1994 the Clinton-Dannemora prison psychiatrist examined Jorge before his placement in the SHU and found *no* mental illness problems. Under recommended treatment, the psychiatrist wrote "George declines mental health services at this time."[665] Within a few weeks of this evaluation, Jorge had stopped showering, he was wearing soiled clothing, was incoherent and threatening, was talking to himself about people conspiring against him, was starting fires and cutting himself, and finally became unresponsive and hid under his bed. "His records got lost when he was transferred to Clinton," Miller told Human Rights Watch.

---

[661] *In The Matter of the Death of Felix George, an Inmate of Clinton Correctional Facility,* New York State Commission of Correction report to Glenn Goord, acting commissioner, New York State Department of Correctional Services, April 17, 1996; on file at Human Rights Watch. The information quoted is in Finding 7, p. 3. The report also found that, at Clinton, Jorge was supposedly seen on a daily basis by a psychologist. However, investigators could find no written evidence that these meetings had in fact occurred.

[662] Jorge was treated at Auburn Memorial Hospital.

[663] The forms filled in at the hearing list Jorge being charged with violent conduct, interference with employee, refusing direct order, unauthorized medication, self-inflicted bodily harm. The punishments listed were SHU confinement for 365 days, no commissary for 365 days, no packages for 365 days, no earphones for 180 days, and no phone calls for 365 days. The hearing also recommended the loss of six months good time.

[664] *Ana Luisa Jorge v. The State of New York,* Claim No. 92210 (Court of Claims, N.Y., August 27, 1999), p. 3.

[665] This is documented under Finding 10 of the New York State Commission of Correction's *Final Report into the death of Felix George.* Submitted by Commissioner Thomas Goldrick, April 17, 1996.

When he refused medication [the psychiatrist] simply stopped offering it to him.[666] When he decompensated, which was inevitable, they beat the shit out of him; proceeded to leave him without care in the isolation cell where he was placed, and then the suicide watch was as negligent as the medical care. He was on a fifteen-minute suicide watch. The guards simply took off and left him alone to die.[667]

A month later, one correctional officer was fired for not making rounds of the observation cell on a regular basis, for falsifying logbooks, for failing to video Jorge, and for failing to notify his sergeant when Jorge failed to respond to his pounding on the cell door when he finally did do his rounds. Three weeks later, however, the dismissal was reversed, and the correctional officer was reinstated and only ordered to pay a fine.[668]

In a scathing report the state's Medical Review Board found "the continuity of mental health care in this case deficient. In addition, the Board found the supervision of the observation room in the Mental Health Satellite Unit deficient on the night of George's death."[669]

From January 1995 until March 2002, the New York State Commission of Correction found a total of eighty-three people had committed suicide while prisoners of New York State. At least twenty-five of these were in SHUs at the time of their deaths.[670]

---

[666] At trial, psychiatrist Florence Kaufman confirmed the practice of discontinuing medication for a prisoner who refuses it. *Question*: "If Central Psychiatric issued a blanket order for medication for a psychotic patient, under what if any circumstances could that prescription or order ever be discontinued?" *Answer*: "If the inmate refuses, that's pretty much the reason. Sometimes when they come, they will ask to sign off medication and we'll have them sign a medication refusal form. Sometimes they just never show up for the medication and that's their way of stopping it."

[667] Human Rights Watch interview with Ed Miller, attorney, New York City, June 12, 2002.

[668] The letter of dismissal was sent out on August 15, 1994, under the signature of Thomas Testo, Special Assistant to the Commissioner for Labor Relations. The Disciplinary Settlement Agreement, superceding the initial letter, was sent out September 8, 1994, and was signed and accepted by the correctional officer the next day.

[669] This was documented as Finding 14 in New York State Commission of Correction's *Final Report into the death of Felix George*. Submitted by Commissioner Thomas Goldrick, April 17, 1996.

[670] Information collated by the Legal Aid Society, based on data from the New York State Commission of Correction, and some additional information provided by the New York State Department of Correctional Services.

XIV. FAILURE TO PROVIDE DISCHARGE SERVICES

Some 600 thousand men and women are released from prison in the United States every year.[671] There is growing awareness across the country of the high risk of recidivism for prisoners who are not given support services to enable successful re-entry to society. Virtually every mental health expert that Human Rights Watch interviewed acknowledged the particular importance of providing transitional support upon release to those prisoners who are mentally ill. Nevertheless, many states still do not help mentally ill offenders with the discharge reentry process, despite evidence suggesting discharge planning reduces the likelihood that they will return to prison.[672] Many mentally ill prisoners who were receiving medication in prison are released with as little as a week's supply of medicine. Such a limited supply may well not last until they link up with doctors on the outside and are able to get their prescriptions renewed.

According to a Bureau of Justice Statistics study, 34 percent of the adult correctional facilities in the United States do not help released prisoners obtain community mental health services.[673] For the 66 percent of facilities nationwide that claim to provide some care to released prisoners with mental health problems, the percentage of mentally ill ex-prisoners who actually receive transitional care is unknown as is the quality of that care.[674]

The lack of discharge planning and services by prisons for prisoners with mental illness has been taken to the courts. In *Wakefield v. Thompson*, a federal appeals court considered whether an the Eighth Amendment claim was stated by plaintiff's allegations that correctional staff at a California prison ignored the instructions of his doctor by refusing to provide him upon his release from prison with the prescribed two-week supply of the psychotropic medication that he took because he suffered from Organic Delusional Disorder.[675] The court ruled that state:

> must provide an outgoing prisoner who is receiving and continues to require medication with a supply sufficient to ensure that he has that medication available during the period of time reasonably necessary to permit him to consult a doctor and obtain a new supply. A state's failure to provide medication sufficient to cover this transitional period amounts to an abdication of its responsibility to provide medical care to those, who by reason of incarceration, are unable to provide for their own medical needs.[676]

A class action lawsuit suit was filed in 1999 by mentally ill inmates in New York City's jails who challenged the practice of releasing class members without proper provision for treatment or a way

---

[671] Paige M. Harrison, and Jennifer C. Karberg, *Prison and Jail Inmates at Midyear 2002* (Washington D.C.: Bureau of Justice Statistics, April 2003), table 7.

[672] See Michael Faenza, *Statement on the Criminalization of Mental Illness*, National Mental Health Association News Release, September 21, 2000. Available online at: http://www.nmha.org/newsroom/system/news.vw.cfm?do=vw&rid=228, accessed on July 7, 2003.

[673] See BJS, *Mental Health Treatment in State Prisons, 2000*, 2001.

[674] See Patrick A. Langan, Ph.D. and David J. Levin, Ph.D., *Recidivism of Prisoners Released in 1994* (Washington D.C.: U.S. Department of Justice, Bureau of Justice Statistics, June 2002).

[675] *Wakefield v. Thompson*, 177 F.3d 1160 (9th Cir. 1999).

[676] Ibid., p. 1164.

to continue their medication. Upon release from jail, mentally ill inmates were provided $1.50 in cash and $3.00 in subway fare. They were not provided any mental health services, government benefits assistance, housing referrals, other services, or help in planning their re-entry. A state supreme court granted an injunction requiring mental health discharge planning.[677] It characterized the "irreparable injury" that discharged inmates would face without the injunction as "decompensation for many former inmates, and a return to the cycle of likely harm to themselves and/or others, through substance abuse, mental and physical health deterioration, homelessness, indigence, crime, rearrest, and reincarceration."[678] Under the terms of the settlement, the city agreed to provide mentally ill inmates access to the treatment they need to maintain psychiatric stability after their release, including access to outpatient treatment and medication and the means for pay for those services if the inmate is indigent.[679]

Recidivism

Absent appropriate mental health treatment (as well as supports for housing, employment and income), the mentally ill who commit criminal offenses are likely to repeat them, cycling in and out of correctional facilities for years. According to the Bureau of Justice Statistics, 81.2 percent of the mentally ill in state prisons have prior criminal histories, 26.3 percent have three to five prior sentences to probation or incarceration, 15.6 percent have six to ten, and 10 percent have eleven or more. Jail inmates who have mental illness have similar criminal histories.[680]

For all newly discharged offenders, the highest risk of recidivism is in the first six months after release from prison.[681] Finding housing and employment, gaining access to public assistance, reuniting with friends and family, and other aspects of making the psychological and physical adjustment to a life outside of prison can present challenges to any former prisoner. Mentally ill offenders who do not receive adequate discharge planning or a continuity of treatment upon release are at a particular disadvantage during this crucial readjustment.[682] According to the Council of State Governments:

> individuals with mental illnesses leaving prison without sufficient supplies of medication, connections to mental health and other support services, and housing are almost certain to decompensate, which in turn will likely result in behavior that constitutes a technical violation of release conditions or a new crime.[683]

In a 1985 study in Columbus Ohio, sixty-five patients were followed after their release from state hospitals without discharge planning. Within six months, 32 percent of them had been arrested and jailed, almost all for misdemeanors.[684] In New York, 64 percent of mentally ill offenders tracked

---

[677] *Brad H. v. City of New York*, 712 NYS2d 336 (Supreme Court of New York, 2000).

[678] Ibid., p. 345.

[679] The settlement and complaint in the case (originally titled *Brad H. v. Giuliani*) are available on the website of the Urban Justice Center, whose lawyers brought the case. Available online at: http://www.urbanjustice.org/litigation/index.html, under the project heading "mental health," accessed on September 15, 2003.

[680] Ibid., table 6.

[681] Ibid.

[682] Council of State Governments, *Criminal Justice/Mental Health Consensus Project* (New York: Council of State Governments, June 2002).

[683] Council of State Governments, *Consensus Project* (2002), p. 162.

[684] E. Fuller Torrey, et al., *Criminalizing the Seriously Mentally Ill: The Abuse of Jails as Mental Hospitals* 54 (1992).

after release in a 1991 study were rearrested within eighteen months.[685] In an Ohio study, 63 percent were rearrested in an eighteen-month period.[686] And in Tennessee, the Department of Correction tracked released prisoners with mental health diagnoses for four years after release, and determined that 39 percent were back in the correctional system within twelve months of discharge.[687] In addition to the psychological trauma this cycle of reincarceration causes prisoners with mental illness, reincarceration also results in significant financial costs to the defendants and the community.[688]

Discharge Planning

Mental health professionals widely recognize that "timely and effective discharge planning is essential to continuity of care and an integral part of adequate mental health treatment."[689] Discharge planning for prisoners with mental illness should include making arrangements to ensure — to the extent possible — the ex-prisoner continues to receive an appropriate level of mental health treatment after release from prison.[690] However, among the states that provide some sort of release planning, the extent of arrangements that have been made to connect prisoners with new mental healthcare providers varies widely:

- In Nebraska, mentally ill prisoners typically leave prison with a two-week supply of medication and the names of providers and institutions that may be able to help them. No appointments with providers are made in advance, and no provisions are made for the severely mentally ill who may not be able to explore treatment options independently.[691]

- In Arkansas, discharged prisoners are given a one-week supply of medication and are encouraged to set up appointments with private providers of their own choosing. If the prisoner does not have a private physician that he would like to see upon release, the prison staff will attempt to set him up with an after-care appointment at a Community Mental Health Center (CMHC). Appointments with a CMHC are not guaranteed and are subject to resource availability in a particular area.[692]

---

[685] Lynette Feder, *A Comparison of the Community Adjustment of Mentally Ill Offenders with Those from the General Prison Population (An 18-Month Followup)*, Law and Human Behavior, vol. 15, no. 5, 1991.

[686] Joseph E. Jacoby, Ph.D. and Brenda Kozie-Peak, M.A., *The Benefits of Social Support for Mentally Ill Offenders: Prison-to-Community Transitions*, Behavioral Sciences and the Law, vol. 15, 1997

[687] Unpublished study conducted by the Tennessee Department of Correction, 2003. Human Rights Watch telephone interview with Lenny Lococo, director of mental health services, Tennessee Department of Correction, June 20, 2003.

[688] Amici brief of NAMI and the Bazelon Center for Mental Health Law, et al., in *Brad H. v. City of New York*. Available online at: http://www.bazelon.org/issues/criminalization/bradh.html#4, accessed on September 15, 2003.

[689] American Psychiatric Association, *Psychiatric Services in Jails and Prisons*, 2nd Ed. (Washington D.C., American Psychiatric Association, 2000), p. 18. According to the American Psychiatric Association, discharge planning necessarily includes five essential services: (1) Appointments should be arranged with mental health agencies for all inmates with serious mental illness; (2) Arrangements should be made with local mental health agencies to have prescriptions renewed or evaluated for renewal; (3) Discharge and referral responsibilities should be carried out by specifically designated staff; (4) Inmates should be assessed for the appropriateness of a community referral; and (5) Prison administrative mental health staff should participate in the development of service contracts to ensure access to community-based case managers to provide continuity of service. Ibid., p. 46

[690] Amici Brief in *Brad H. v. City of New York*.

[691] Human Rights Watch telephone interview with Dr. Susan Bohn, director of mental health, Nebraska Department of Correctional Services, June 11, 2003.

[692] Human Rights Watch telephone interview with Dr. Robert Parker, director of mental health, Arkansas Department of Correction, June 10, 2003.

- In Virginia, mentally ill prisoners work with a counselor and a mental health professional on a release plan. Prisoners are given a month's supply of medication upon release, and the prison attempts to set up after-care appointments. However, the community providers do not have the resources to care for every mentally ill prisoner released from prison, and some leave prison without an appointment set up.[693]

- In North Carolina, a prisoner participates in the development of an after-care plan that is tailored to his or her individual mental health needs, and leaves prison with a month's supply of medication, as well as the name, address, and phone number of a provider and an appointment already in place.[694]

Ideally, a range of support and services should be available to discharged prisoners to facilitate reentry. Equally important, the Consensus Project notes, is successful collaboration between "the various agencies and service providers who will be involved in the release, supervision, support, and treatment of the releasee."[695] These agencies should include, at a minimum, corrections, parole (or releasing authority), mental health, housing, employment, health, and welfare, and private providers of treatment and support services.[696] The different agencies should view their individual services as part of an integrated whole, and understand how their mandates overlap, in order to better serve their client populations. This is the goal of Laura Yates, the Social Work Program Director for the North Carolina Department of Correction (DOC). Yates attends meetings of other agencies, making sure that they consider the needs of mentally ill prisoners when they make decisions that affect the service they provide. Attending these meetings also helps her to maintain good relationships with other agencies, and to understand how the DOC fits into the larger picture. "Rather than parceling out the components of an individual," Ms. Yates explains, "we've come to a more unified approach to providing services to an inmate."

Financial Assistance
Continued access to treatment after incarceration is essential for former prisoners who are mentally ill. Yet, mentally ill prisoners typically leave prison without jobs or other sources of income. Without public assistance, many will not be able to pay for and obtain mental health care.

Unfortunately, many offenders leaving prison encounter substantial delays in gaining access to those public benefits to which they are entitled that would enable them to pay for continued mental health care treatment and support services. For example, although federal law does not preclude states from keeping prisoners on the Medicaid rolls while incarcerated, most, if not all, states remove prisoners and require them to reapply upon release.[697] Federal law does require automatic termination of Supplemental Security Income benefits upon incarceration for a period of a year or

---

[693] Human Rights Watch telephone interview with Dr. Robin Hulbert, mental health program director, Virginia Department of Corrections, June 11, 2003.

[694] Human Rights Watch telephone interview with Laura Yates, social work program director, North Carolina Department of Correction, June 13, 2003.

[695] Consensus Project Report, p. 163.

[696] Ibid., p. 164.

[697] Medicaid is a Federal/State entitlement program that pays for medical assistance for certain individuals and families with low incomes and resources. It was established in 1965 as a cooperative venture jointly funded by the Federal and State governments (including the District of Columbia and the Territories) to assist States in furnishing medical assistance to eligible needy persons. States generally have broad discretion in determining which groups their Medicaid programs will cover and the financial criteria for Medicaid eligibility.

more, [698] and it requires that Social Security Disability Insurance (SSDI) benefits be suspended, although not terminated, upon incarceration. [699] Other entitlements are also terminated upon incarceration. [700] Such benefits are not automatically reinstated upon a prisoner's release; it typically takes at least forty-five days and may take as long as eighty-nine days to reactivate these benefits.[701] In the interim period, it is difficult for recently discharged mentally ill offenders to maintain a continuity of care.

Recognizing the importance of enabling ex-prisoners to gain immediate access to public benefits, some states have developed mechanisms to accelerate the restoration process, for example, by securing a prisoners' eligibility for benefits immediately upon release from incarceration. Corrections departments in some states help prisoners fill out benefit applications, although they are prohibited by state law from filing them prior to the date of discharge. Some corrections departments do not help mentally ill prisoners with the process of gaining or regaining public benefits.

States that Confer Eligibility on the Date of Release
Of the states in which prisoners may qualify for medical benefits on the day of discharge, corrections departments cannot guarantee that every prisoner with mental health needs will receive care upon release. As with discharge planning, the success of discharge and transition planning varies significantly from state to state:

- In Maine, the Department of Corrections (DOC) tries to maintain eligibility for prisoners while they are incarcerated. They are not covered while in prison, but do not need to reapply and are automatically eligible upon release. This is a new program; for many years, there was a gap in services during incarceration and prisoners had to reapply upon discharge. A recent change in the law allowed the DOC to do this. The Maine DOC is still "working out the bugs" in this system.[702]

- In Virginia, a counselor and a mental health professional help mentally ill prisoners apply for benefits prior to release. Prisoners can apply for Medicaid so that they become eligible on the date of discharge. Not all eligible prisoners are able to enroll in these services before release.[703]

- In North Carolina, mentally ill and other prisoners begin applications for Medicaid and SSI prior to release. The North Carolina DOC would like to be able to ensure coverage for

---

[698] *Supplemental Security Income* (SSI) is a Federal income supplement program funded by general tax revenues. It is designed to help aged, blind, and disabled people, who have little or no income; and it provides cash to meet basic needs for food, clothing, and shelter.

[699] *Social Security Disability Insurance* (SSDI) is an insurance program for persons who have worked long enough--and recently enough--under Social Security to qualify for disability benefits. Most incarcerated persons do not qualify for SSDI.

[700] The Sentencing Project, *Mentally Ill Offenders in the Criminal Justice System: An Analysis and Prescription* (January 2002), p. 14.

[701] Amici Brief in *Brad H.*

[702] Human Rights Watch telephone interview with Dr. Joe Fitzpatrick, Director of Mental Health Services, Maine Department of Corrections, June 5, 2003.

[703] Human Rights Watch telephone interview with Dr. Robin Hulbert, Virginia Department of Corrections, June 11, 2003.

every prisoner upon release. However, not all benefits offices will enable this early application procedure to go through.[704]

- In Kansas, the Department of Corrections (Kansas DOC) does not assist mentally prisoners with Medicaid coverage. Instead, the goal of the Kansas DOC is to set each mentally ill prisoner up with an SSI disability screening appointment. If the prisoner meets disability requirements and has no alternative health care plan, then the Kansas DOC will help that prisoner apply for SSI coverage that ideally becomes active on the date of discharge. Some prisoners slip through the cracks, either because the Department of Disability Services (DDS) denies coverage, or because there is not enough time for discharge planning prior to prisoner release dates. Although the Kansas DOC would like to see all prisoners that are classified as "persistently mentally ill" covered by SSI disability insurance at the time of release, this is not always a reality. In some cases, the best they can do is send the prisoner to his/her parole officer, who is then mandated to work out a plan, including assistance with benefits applications.[705]

Despite the efforts of departments of corrections, not all mentally ill prisoners who leave prison with medical benefits in place are assured an appointment with a treatment provider. For example, although Kansas helps mentally ill prisoners apply for SSI disability insurance before they leave prison, discharged mentally ill offenders in Kansas experience many of the same difficulties in setting appointments with treatment providers as do their counterparts in Tennessee, where the Department of Corrections does not offer such assistance.[706] The Kansas DOC tries to set up appointments for prisoners prior to their release dates.[707] However, initial after-care appointments can be difficult to obtain. According to Viola Riggins, the Kansas Department of Corrections' Senior Contract Monitor, the Kansas DOC has a difficult time coordinating its services with county mental health departments. As in Tennessee, recently discharged prisoners in some counties may have to wait between six and twelve weeks to see a mental health professional.[708] "The [Kansas] DOC works hard to maintain contracts with county providers," Ms. Riggins explains, "but some counties are just overwhelmed by the number of mentally ill persons in need of services. In a handful of counties, there never seems to be enough resources to handle the need."[709]

States that Help Prisoners Fill Out Applications
Among those states that prohibit incarcerated persons from applying for benefits, some corrections departments help mentally ill prisoners fill out their applications anyway, in preparation for release. A number of state corrections officials are working to change state policy to make prisoners eligible on the date of discharge:

- In Connecticut, although the Department of Correction (DOC) currently has no mechanism to help prisoners apply for Medicaid or SSI while incarcerated, DOC officials are working

---

[704] Human Rights Watch telephone interview with Laura Yates, June 13, 2003.
[705] Human Rights Watch telephone interview with Viola Riggins, contract monitor for Kansas University, Kansas Department of Corrections, June 12, 2003.
[706] Human Rights Watch telephone interview with Viola Riggins, June 12, 2003.
[707] According to Viola Riggins, because some releases happen ahead of schedule, either by court order or another mechanism, it is not always possible to schedule appointments prior to release. In some cases, appointments must be scheduled by parole officers.
[708] Human Rights Watch telephone interview with Viola Riggins, June 12, 2003.
[709] Ibid.

with the Department of Social Services (DSS) to develop a program to help prisoners reapply for coverage while still incarcerated.[710]

- In Massachusetts, the mandate of the Department of Correction (DOC) is to ensure that all mentally ill prisoners have health care coverage upon release. Pursuant to Department of Mental Health (DMH) regulations, prisoners with severe and persistent mental illness are eligible for DMH community-based services. Typically, prisoners who are eligible for DMH are eligible for SSI and Medicaid, either of which can cover the cost of their care. However, the Massachusetts Division of Medical Assistance (DMA) precludes incarcerated persons from applying for MassHealth (Medicaid). In spite of this official policy, the Massachusetts DOC regularly helps prisoners apply for MassHealth and sends in those applications prior to release, hoping that they will be approved. Applications for the neediest candidates frequently are. DOC has been working with DMH to change the policy.[711]

- Up until one year ago, the Tennessee Department of Correction (DOC) had an arrangement with the Department of Mental Health and Developmental Disability (MHDD) that permitted mental health professionals at Tennessee prisons to certify prisoners for mental health disability coverage. This system enabled a majority of Tennessee's mentally ill prisoners to receive Medicaid coverage starting on the day of discharge. This system changed last year; now the only agency permitted to do this assessment is the Department of Human Services (DHS), and DHS will only conduct these assessments for prisoners *after* they have been released. The Tennessee DOC has a verbal commitment from MHDD that prisoners with mental health problems will still be able to secure appointments with treatment providers within two weeks of their release, but in practice, this has not always been the case.[712] "There have been some horror stories," says Lenny Lococo, the Director of Mental Health Services for the Tennessee DOC, "incidents where high risk inmates with serious mental health needs have had to wait as long as two months to get an appointment at a Community Health Center."[713] The Community Health Centers are supposed to help mentally ill offenders apply for TennCare and other benefits; Mr. Lococo thinks that the centers may be less likely to give appointments to uninsured ex-offenders because there is no guarantee that they will be reimbursed for providing this service.

The Tennessee Department of Human Services centralized the eligibility process, Mr. Lococo believes, because it wanted greater control over the admissions process. There was concern that some ineligible persons were receiving benefits, and some eligible persons were being denied. By centralizing the process, Mr. Lococo thinks that DHS was trying to minimize error. In practice, the new policy has potentially dangerous consequences for both mentally ill offenders and the community at large. "A person coming out the criminal justice system already has three strikes against him. This is compounded when that person has a psychiatric disorder. Denying that person an appointment with a mental health professional

---

[710] Human Rights Watch telephone interview with Dan Bannish, health service program director, and Pat Ottolini, director of health and addiction services, Connecticut Department of Correction, June 11, 2003.

[711] Human Rights Watch telephone interview with Gregory Hughes, mental health regional administrator, Massachusetts Department of Corrections, June 12, 2003.

[712] Human Rights Watch telephone interview with Lenny Lococo, director of mental health services, Tennessee Department of Correction, June 20, 2003.

[713] Ibid.

sets him up for failure and puts the community at risk." Mr. Lococo, like many mental health experts, believes that continuity of care is paramount to reducing recidivism.[714]

States that Provide Minimal Help

Many states do next to nothing to help incarcerated persons, including the mentally ill, apply for medical benefits prior to their release from prison. Considering that most state Medicaid and SSI offices will not accept applications from incarcerated persons applying for post-release coverage, some corrections departments simply do not view this type of transitional care as part of their job:

- In Arkansas, prisoners cannot apply for medical benefits while incarcerated. The application process may begin upon release, but the Department of Correction does not assist in this process. When they are discharged, mentally ill prisoners are referred to Community Mental Health Centers that may help them apply for medical benefits and other forms of public assistance.[715]

- In Nebraska, officials at the Department of Correctional Services told Human Rights Watch that they did not know how recently discharged prisoners go about applying for Medicaid and other benefits and that they do not help prisoners apply prior to release.[716]

Ex-offender Programs

Although states have yet to find a seamless way to ensure continuity of mental health coverage and treatment, both are essential to a mentally ill prisoner's successful reentry into society. Open dialogue and stronger partnerships between state agencies, and between those agencies and community providers, may indeed improve the delivery mechanism for mental health care and increase an offender's chances of post-release success. In some communities, special programs operate to provide a range of services, including mental health treatment, to ex-offenders with mental illness.

- In Seattle, Washington, the 6002 Program provides daily mental health services to a fortunate few seriously mentally ill ex-prisoners. 6002 was created after a mentally ill prisoner was released without any access to treatment and stabbed a firefighter to death in the mid-1990s.[717] Following a few years of planning, the program began accepting clients in 1999. It currently has twenty-five clients, all seriously mentally ill and all of whom committed crimes thought to be related to their illness, chosen from within the prison system by a selection committee representing the counties, the prison system, and the mental health system. Because it is funded to accept so few people, the staff picks people they believe have a reasonable chance of benefiting from the services 6002 provides. "We're looking for somebody who has insight into their mental illness and would utilize the services," said coordinator Melanie Maxwell. "We try to avoid giving the spots to people

---

[714] Ibid.

[715] Human Rights Watch telephone interview with Dr. Robert Parker, Arkansas Department of Correction, June 10, 2003.

[716] Human Rights Watch telephone interview with Dr. Susan Bohn, Nebraska Department of Correctional Services, June 11, 2003

[717] Information provided by 6002 staff, including coordinator Melanie Maxwell, and a representative from the King County public mental health system, in a group meeting at the facility, Human Rights Watch interview, Seattle, Washington, August 20, 2002.

who are just using the address for early release." The clients who are chosen are provided with post-prison housing in a 6002-facility, access to counselors and regular group sessions. They are provided with help in managing their money, and are helped in their attempts to find work. "It's been a life-saving thing," Y.P. said.[718]

> I'd not have money to live if it wasn't for them. I'm working part-time on a job. They've supported me, helped me. I have weekly counseling here, and my counselor's really good. I'll be in the program as long as I need it. Till I'm emotionally ready to move on — they don't rush to push you out.

Another client D.E., a drug addict and severe depressive, explained that he:

> need[s] this program. Since I've been here I've been clean for almost forty days. I'm doing really good. I got a membership to the gym. I'm starting to get more active. I go to the library and get books. Everybody's been really great with me. I got my VCR and my Sega System. The hard work of finding who I am and what I want to accomplish when I'm not on drugs is something new to me.[719]

- In Pierce County, Washington, Crisis and Mental Health Coordinator Dave Stewart has begun sending community mental health teams into jails to identify mentally ill people before they even go to trial and to channel community mental health services their way that will stay with them through their involvement in the criminal justice system and into the period following their release.[720]

- In Philadelphia, Pennsylvania, Gaudenzia House, which grew out of meetings between NAMI and the Pennsylvania Department of Corrections, caters to a similar clientele.[721] There, clients are also provided with counseling, with help in finding work and with a supportive post-prison environment. On average, according to a quality review of the program, clients stay at Gaudenzia House slightly over ten months. During that time, staff submit paperwork to the Office of Mental Health in an attempt to find housing for their clients after they leave. In a way, psychiatrist Pogos Vaskanian explained, Gaudenzia serves as a "buffer" between the prison and the community experience. E.O., a forty-five-year-old client at the facility said, "I can talk to the people who work here like a friend; they treat me like family. I see my daughters, my two kids. It's a good place."

- In Maryland, Shelter Plus was founded with a $5.5 million grant from the Department of Housing and Urban Development, and receives matching grants from local communities. The state Mental Hygiene Administration liaises with local mental health authorities and non-profit organizations to find, and lease, housing for this population. Its 2001 annual

---

[718] Human Rights Watch interview with Y.P., Berkeley House, Seattle, Washington, August 20, 2002.

[719] Although the 6002 program lost state funding during the writing of this report, in June of 2003, the program was given a 2-year block grant by the Federal Government. Human Rights Watch telephone interview with Declan Finn, director, 6002 Program, July 2, 2003.

[720] Human Rights Watch telephone interview with David Stewart, crisis and corrections mental health coordinator, Pierce County, Washington, May 15, 2002.

[721] Human Rights Watch interviews with staff, Gaudenzia House, Philadelphia, Pennsylvania, August 13, 2002.

report states that it now operates housing services in twenty-one counties throughout the state.[722] According to Joan Galece, deputy director of the State Mental Hygiene Administration, Maryland, prior to the creation of this program eight in ten seriously mentally ill prisoners were re-arrested within a year of their release from jail.[723] The program claims to have a recidivism rate of only 4 percent amongst the clients it houses. "It's been the best thing we have going for us. It's broken down a lot of barriers that this population had for access to housing. We're unique in that we're a state program working with locals to assist them develop programs for this population."

- In Connecticut, plans are underway to open a series of one hundred-bed Criminal Justice Centers, in which soon-to-be-released prisoners will live in order to help them transition back into life in the community. Although the Department of Correction will pay for these centers, they will be run by treatment organizations. The state is also creating a network of "psychiatric halfway houses," in which seriously mentally ill prisoners can live for up to eighteen months.[724]

- In New York, advocates are lobbying the state to create a Public Safety Demonstration Project to house two hundred homeless seriously mentally ill ex-prisoners. Maryland and Wisconsin are also developing similar programs.

With states under the burden of an enormous fiscal crisis, looking to cut corners wherever they can, programs for the mentally ill are especially vulnerable. This is short sighted, because the cost of the mentally ill returning to prison is greater in the long run than the cost of providing them adequate transition counseling and treatment upon release. Without good discharge planning and post-release programs, seriously mentally ill prisoners are likely to cycle endlessly between prison and the community, their illnesses worsening, and chances increasing that they will end up in the high security units within the prison system. Successful release plans for the mentally ill include partnerships between departments of corrections and other state agencies, the availability of post-release treatment, early enrollment in Medicaid or another form of health care coverage, and pre-release counseling that begins well before a prisoner's release.

The proper funding of discharge planning and post-release programs is a crucial public policy issue. In an era in which the United States incarcerates hundreds of thousands of seriously mentally ill men and women in its prisons, it serves neither the mentally ill nor the broader community to shortchange the transitional programs that could serve to break these linkages between mental illness and imprisonment in 21st century America.

---

[722] *Maryland Mental Hygiene Administration Shelter Plus Care Housing Program Annual Report Summary*, 2001, p. 2.
[723] Human Rights Watch telephone interview with Joan Galece, deputy director, State Department of Mental Health, Maryland, June 7, 2002.
[724] Information provided during meeting with Connecticut Department of Correction mental health staff, June 10, 2002.

R.V., Alabama, June 12, 2002

I am and inmate at W. E. Donaldson prison locked up in seg, and have been for the last 10 years. I have no people left on the outside to help me most all of them have died over the years. I have a very serious problem and need help very bad it's what you could say a matter of life and death. Either during an syst operation or while getting two teeth pulled side by side some type of transmitter and or computer chip was slip into my body without my permission nor me knowing about it till years later. And inmate told me I was being monitored on some kind of super computers, once I found out whoever the monitors are started using it to put me threw living hell, and experimenting on me against my will. I have ask prison staff and medical staff why this was being did to me and they denied it exist. I can not get them to stop what they are doing and it could kill me…. For the last year I have been trying to get help, I have been writing lawyers trying to get them to take my case and file the suits for me but so far I have been unable to get one or get any help. Who ever these people are they have put my mind and insides threw so much hell that at times I have suicidal thoughts, I have also cut my self very bad with a razor blade I stayed in the hospital for 6 hours then sent back to segregation…. In closing I hope and pray that some way you get and investigation into this also get the FBI in Birmingham Alabama to come out here and talk to me befor its to late.

XV.   LEGAL STANDARDS

Under international human rights law, prisoners should not be confined in conditions that constitute torture or that are cruel, inhuman, or degrading. This right includes the right to proper medical care and treatment for mental illness. International human rights law also affirms the separate right to health, which requires appropriate mental health care, to the extent feasible, for all people, regardless of whether they are incarcerated.   International standards include detailed provisions on the treatment of prisoners, including mentally ill prisoners — a resource and set of benchmarks, that, if adhered to, would address many of the deficiencies identified in this report.

The ineffective application of international laws and standards within the United States lies not in their substantive shortcomings, but rather in the failure of U.S. authorities to implement them properly, if at all. International human rights standards are little known and almost never directly applied in the United States. International bodies, including those monitoring compliance with international treaties to which the United States is a party, are typically not heeded in the United States when they issue analyses and recommendations.   By focusing on the federal and state constitutions as the sources of rights, the U.S. government has ignored the development of international legal standards that go beyond constitutionally protected rights.

The U.S. Constitution prohibits cruel and unusual punishment, which the courts have interpreted as requiring prisons to provide mental health treatment to prisoners who have serious mental illness. But the constitution is not violated by malpractice or negligent care. The Eighth Amendment is only violated when prison officials are "deliberately indifferent" to an prisoners need for treatment, not when they provide negligent care or engage in what would otherwise be deemed malpractice. Elected officials — executive and legislative — do not effectively use their respective powers to ensure prison officials provide adequate care, or even meet constitutional requirements. Constitutional standards are primarily enforced through prisoner litigation — litigation which faces enormous procedural as well as substantive obstacles.[725]

While correctional officials acknowledge — as they must — their constitutional obligation to provide mental health care, they have insisted they meet that obligation even when the care was plainly substandard, if not atrocious. To some extent, their position reflects their awareness that conceding constitutional infirmities would either prompt litigation or would lead to verdicts against them in ongoing litigation. Nevertheless our research suggests a disquieting willingness to accept the minimum level of care required by the constitution as the maximum required, and to press for a "minimum" level that is as low as possible. Few express the admirable aspiration of the director of the Ohio Department of Rehabilitation and Correction, Dr. Reginald Wilkinson, who told Human Rights Watch "if you are going to have a mental health system [in prisons], we want the best one possible, even if the constitution does not require it."[726]

---

[725] The role of federal courts in protecting prisoners from mistreatment, and the difficulties inmates face in bringing litigation to vindicate their rights, including the impact of the Prison Litigation Reform Act, are discussed in Human Rights Watch, *No Escape: Male Rape in U.S. Prisons* (New York: Human Rights Watch, 2001).

[726] Human Rights Watch telephone interview with Dr. Reginald Wilkinson, director, Ohio Department of Rehabilitation and Correction, July 3, 2003.

International Protections
International human rights law is a vibrant and evolving body of law that protects all persons, including prisoners with mental illness. Its touchstone is the dignity of each human being. Recognition of that dignity requires respect for numerous other rights articulated in the Universal Declaration of Human Rights and such international treaties as the International Covenant on Civil and Political Rights (ICCPR),[727] the Covenant on Economic, Social and Cultural Rights,[728] and the Convention against Torture and Other Cruel, Inhuman or Degrading Treatment or Punishment (Convention against Torture).[729] Recognition of the unique problems and special abuses faced by persons with mental illness has also led to the development of international instruments providing specific protections for them.

The Rights of Prisoners to be Free of Abuse
The ICCPR is the most comprehensive international human rights treaty the United States has ratified and it includes provisions explicitly intended to protect prisoners from abuse or mistreatment. Under ICCPR article 7, no one "shall be subjected to torture or to cruel, inhuman or degrading treatment or punishment." The prohibition against such abusive treatment applies to prison authorities, governing both actions against individual prisoners as well as the overall conditions of confinement in which prisoners live.[730] The ICCPR does not, however, simply set guidelines for what prison officials and other authorities should not do; it also imposes positive obligations on them. Article 10 states that: "All persons deprived of their liberty shall be treated with humanity and with respect for the inherent dignity of the human person."[731]

Various documents developed within the United Nations flesh out the human rights of persons deprived of liberty and provide guidance as to how governments may comply with their international legal obligations. These documents include the United Nations Standard Minimum Rules for the Treatment of Prisoners[732] (Standard Minimum Rules) adopted by the Economic and Social Council in 1957; the Body of Principles for the Protection of All Persons under Any Form of Detention or Imprisonment,[733] adopted by the General Assembly in 1988; and the Basic Principles

---

[727] International Covenant on Civil and Political Rights, G.A. res. 2200A (XXI), 21 U.N. GAOR Supp. (no. 16) at 52, U.N. Doc. A/6316 (1966), 999 U.N.T.S. 171, entered into force Mar. 23, 1976.

[728] International Covenant on Economic, Social and Cultural Rights, G.A. res. 2200A (XXI), 21 U.N.GAOR Supp. (no. 16) at 49, U.N. Doc. A/6316 (1966), 993 U.N.T.S. 3, entered into force Jan. 3, 1976.

[729] Convention against Torture and Other Cruel, Inhuman or Degrading Treatment or Punishment, G.A. res. 39/46 [annex, 39 U.N. GAOR Supp. (no. 51) at 197, U.N. Doc. A/39/51 (1984)], entered into force June 26, 1987.

[730] The Convention against Torture also prohibits torture and cruel, inhuman, or degrading treatment.

[731] ICCPR, art. 10 (1). Paragraph 3 of article 10 also states the "essential aim" of prison systems is the "reformation and social rehabilitation" of prisoners. The United States, in ratifying the ICCPR, issued an understanding stating that art. 10(3) "does not diminish the goals of punishment, deterrence and incapacitation as additional legitimate purposes for a penitentiary system." While violations of article 7 will also violate article 10, the reverse is not necessarily the case. The criteria by which the Human Rights Committee has concluded certain prisons conditions violated article 10(1) and not article 7 can be difficult to discern. See Nigel Rodley, *The Treatment of Prisoners Under International Law* (Oxford: Clarendon Press, 1999), pp. 286-292.

[732] Standard Minimum Rules for the Treatment of Prisoners, adopted Aug. 30, 1955 by the First United Nations Congress on the Prevention of Crime and the Treatment of Offenders, U.N. Doc. A/CONF/611, annex I, E.S.C. res. 663C, 24 U.N. ESCOR Supp. (no. 1) at 11, U.N. Doc. E/3048 (1957), amended E.S.C. res. 2076, 62 U.N. ESCOR Supp. (no. 1) at 35, U.N. Doc. E/5988 (1977).

[733] Body of Principles for the Protection of All Persons under Any Form of Detention or Imprisonment, G.A. res. 43/173, annex, 43 U.N. GAOR Supp. (no. 49) at 298, U.N. Doc. A/43/49 (1988).

for the Treatment of Prisoners,[734] adopted by the General Assembly in 1990. While these instruments are not treaties, they constitute authoritative guides to the content of binding treaty standards and customary international law.

The Basic Principles for the Treatment of Prisoners establishes prisoners' entitlement to a quality of health care comparable to that available in the outside community.[735] The Body of Principles for the Protection of All Persons under Any Form of Detention or Imprisonment establishes the obligation of authorities to ensure prisoners are given medical screening upon admission and provided appropriate medical care and treatment as necessary and free of charge.[736] The most detailed provisions regarding mental health care for prisoners are contained in the Standard Minimum Rules. According to the guiding principles of the Standard Minimum Rules, the purpose of a sentence of imprisonment is to protect society against crime, a purpose which can only be achieved, "if the period of imprisonment is used to ensure, so far as possible, that upon his return to society the offender is not only willing but able to lead a law-abiding and self-supporting life…."[737] Appropriate medical and mental health services are integral to a properly run prison and to the goal of rehabilitation: "The medical services…shall seek to detect and shall treat any…mental illnesses or defects which may hamper a prisoner's rehabilitation. All necessary…psychiatric services shall be provided to that end."[738]

The Standard Minimum Rules recognize the need to vary the housing, supervision, and care of offenders with mental disorders according to the degree of their illness: those who are psychotic or acutely ill should be placed in mental institutions; those who suffer from "other mental diseases or abnormalities shall be observed and treated in specialized institutions under medical management"; while in a prison, such prisoners "shall be placed under the special supervision of a medical officer." Prison mental health staff should provide for the psychiatric treatment of all other prisoners who need it.[739]

The Standard Minimum Rules recognize that prisons must have sufficient numbers of appropriately qualified competent health care staff to meet their human rights obligations. Medical services should include "a psychiatric service for the diagnosis and, in proper cases, the treatment of states of mental abnormality."[740] To the extent possible, prison staff should also include specialists in

---

[734] Basic Principles for the Treatment of Prisoners, G.A. res. 45/111, annex, 45 U.N. GAOR Supp. (no. 49A) at 200, U.N. Doc. A/45/49 (1990).

[735] Basic Principles for the Treatment of Prisoners, Principle 9 which states: "Prisoners shall have access to the health services available in the country without discrimination on the grounds of their legal situation." See also, European Committee for the Prevention of Torture and Inhuman or Degrading Treatment or Punishment (CPT), *The CPT Standards*, regarding health care services in prisons. "…[P]risoners are entitled to the same level of medical care as persons living in the community at large. This principle is inherent in the fundamental rights of the individual." Ibid., section IV, para. 31.

[736] Basic Principles for the Treatment of Prisoners, Principle 24.

[737] Standard Minimum Rules, paras. 58-59.

[738] Standard Minimum Rules, para. 62.

[739] Standard Minimum Rules, para. 82. The Committee for the Prevention of Torture, a body which monitors prisons of countries party to the European Convention of Human Rights also recognizes that inmates whose illness dictates the need for hospitalization should be transferred from prisons to mental health hospitals. According to the CPT, "a mentally ill prisoner should be kept in a hospital facility which is adequately equipped and possesses appropriately trained staff whether a civil mental hospital or a specially equipped psychiatric facility within the prison system." CPT Standards, para. 43.

[740] Standard Minimum Rules, Rule 22.

addition to psychiatrists, including psychologists, and social workers.[741] Standards of care should not be lowered because those needing medical treatment are prisoners. "Health personnel, particularly physicians, charged with the medical care of prisoners and detainees have a duty to provide them with protection of their physical and mental health and treatment of disease of the same quality and standards as is afforded to those who are not imprisoned or detained."[742] Clinical medical decisions should be governed by medical criteria. International principles of medical ethics require prison medical staff to provide "the best possible health care for those who are incarcerated," with decisions regarding their care and treatment based on the prisoners' health needs, which should take priority over any non-medical matters.[743]

Proper psychiatric treatment in prison as in the community should be based on a treatment plan drawn up for each patient. The plan should consist of more than just medication.

> It should involve a wide range of rehabilitative and therapeutic activities, including access to occupational therapy, group therapy, individual psychotherapy, art, drama, music and sports. Patients should have regular access to suitably-equipped recreation rooms and have the possibility to take outdoor exercise on a daily basis; it is also desirable for them to be offered education and suitable work.[744]

The Right to the Highest Attainable Standard of Health

The International Covenant on Economic, Social and Cultural Rights (ICESCR), in article 12, provides for "the right of everyone to the enjoyment of the highest attainable standard of physical and mental health." The United States, as a signatory but not a party to the ICESCR, is obliged to refrain from acts that would defeat the object and purpose of the treaty.[745] This right has been interpreted as an obligation on governments to take specific steps to protect and promote health — both by instituting measures to maximize health and by protecting people from unhealthy or dangerous conditions.[746] The right to the highest attainable standard of mental health under Article 12 includes a right to services that are available, accessible, acceptable, and of appropriate and good quality, provided by trained medical and professional personnel.[747] Persons who are imprisoned retain this right, and they are entitled to a standard of medical care, including mental health care, equivalent to that available in the wider community.

While under the ICESCR everyone has a claim to some degree of mental health care, prisoners have special claims upon the government for mental health treatment. Incarcerated persons become

---

[741] Standard Minimum Rules, Rule 49.

[742] Principles of Medical Ethics relevant to the Role of Health Personnel, particularly Physicians, in the Protection of Prisoners and Detainees against Torture and Other Cruel, Inhuman or Degrading Treatment or Punishment, G.A. res. 37/194 (1982), Principle 1.

[743] International Council of Prison Medical Services, The Oath of Athens, approved in 1979, quoted in Andrew Coyle, *A Human Rights Approach to Prison Management: Handbook for Prison Staff* (London: University of London. International Centre for Prison Studies, 2002), p. 56.

[744] *CPT Standards*, Section VI, para. 37. This standard for psychiatric treatment applies to forensic as well as non-forensic mental health facilities.

[745] Vienna Convention on Consular Relations, article 18, U.N.T.S. Nos. 8638-8640, vol. 596 (April 24, 1963), pp. 262-512.

[746] Committee on Economic, Social and Cultural Rights, *General Comment 14: The Right to the Highest Attainable Standard of Health*.

[747] Committee on Economic, Social and Cultural Rights, *General Comment 14: The Right to the Highest Attainable Standard of Health*, para. 12.

dependent on the state to provide for their medical services; the state thus has the responsibility to protect their health both in terms of the conditions of confinement and the individual medical treatment they require.[748] Because imprisonment by its nature can damage the mental well being of prisoners, correctional authorities have a responsibility not only to provide appropriate mental health treatment, but to establish conditions consistent with mental health.

In 1991, the United Nations General Assembly adopted the Principles for the Protection of Persons with Mental Illness and the Improvement of Mental Health Care (MI Principles).[749] These principles are "the most complete standards for the protection of the rights of persons with mental disability at the international level."[750] They were developed because of the growing recognition internationally that persons with mental illness often faced unique difficulties in ensuring respect for their basic human rights, both in the community and within mental institutions.[751] Most international and non-governmental organization (NGO) attention to the human rights of the mentally ill has focused on discrimination and the absence of adequate legal protections against improper and abusive treatment. The principles thus address such issues as consent to treatment and medication, loss of legal capacity, discrimination, and rights and conditions in mental health facilities. According to Principle 20, the principles also apply to persons with mental illness serving sentences of imprisonment "with only such limited modifications and exceptions as are necessary in the circumstances." Principle 20 also affirms that all incarcerated persons with mental illness "should receive the best available mental health care."[752]

The United States and International Human Rights Law

The United States has ratified a number of international human rights treaties and instruments but has invested little energy or resources into ensuring they are known and implemented throughout the country. Few prison officials interviewed by Human Rights Watch realize that their work is subject to international human rights standards in addition to constitutional requirements. Few state or even federal officials realize that their responsibilities include ensuring the protection of and respect for human rights under international law, including the rights of prisoners. They are either unaware of [or ignore pronouncements of international treaty bodies and other international entities.

The United States is a party to the International Covenant on Civil and Political Rights and the Convention against Torture. However, it attached limiting reservations, declarations, and

---

[748] See, e.g., Andrew Coyle, *A Human Rights Approach to Prison Management: Handbook for Prison Staff* (London: University of London. International Centre for Prison Studies, 2002). This excellent handbook translates internationally acknowledged human rights and standards relating to imprisonment into guidelines for good prison management.

[749] Principles for the Protection of Persons with Mental Illnesses and the Improvement of Mental Health Care, G.A. res. 46/119, 46 U.N. GAOR Supp. (No. 49) at 189, U.N. Doc. A/46/49 (1991). The MI Principles do not define "mental illness." Principle 4(1) provides that "A determination that a person has a mental illness shall be made in accordance with internationally accepted medical standards."

[750] *The Case of Victor Rosario Congo*, Case No. 11,427, Inter-Am C.H.R. Report 29/99, Ecuador, adopted in Sess. 1424, OEA/Ser/L.V/II., doc. 26, March 9, 1999, para. 54.

[751] The United Nations has appointed three Special Rapporteurs on Human Rights and Disability. See Eric Rosenthal and Clarence J. Sundram, *The Role of International Human Rights in Domestic Mental Health Legislation*, submitted to the World Health Organization on March 31, 2002, and available online at: http://www.bazelon.org/legal/resources/internationallaw.pdf, accessed on July 1, 2003. Rosenthal is executive director of Mental Disability Rights International.

[752] MI Principles, Principle 20.

understandings to its ratification of these treaties that work both substantively, by restricting the scope of the treaties, and procedurally, by restricting their usefulness in court proceedings.[753]

The principal means by which the United States sought to limit the domestic impact of signing the ICCPR and the CAT was by declaring both treaties to be "non-self-executing." That is, without enabling legislation they cannot be relied upon to enforce rights in U.S. courts, and no such legislation has ever been enacted. The United States asserts that existing state and federal laws adequately protect against violations of the treaty. Yet despite many congruencies with the U.S. Constitution, the ICCPR and the Convention against Torture offer additional rights and protections for individuals than has been found under the U.S. Constitution. By declaring the treaties non-self-executing, the United States has left without judicial recourse individuals whose rights under the treaties are being violated.

Under the U.S. Constitution, international treaties are part of the supreme law of the land.[754] Regardless of whether a treaty is self-executing, the president or executive branch remains obligated to ensure they are executed faithfully. At a minimum, the U.S. government should prevent and remedy violations of the internationally recognized human rights of prisoners; should revise existing federal laws to facilitate compliance with treaty obligations; should encourage state correctional authorities to comply with the treaties and should monitor that compliance, and should use all federal powers — including litigation — to make sure prison authorities comply. Although the fifty states are not themselves parties to the treaties, they are obliged to obey federal law, which includes international treaties ratified by the U.S. Senate.

The United States also sought to limit the domestic impact of the ICCPR and Conventional against Torture by limiting the scope of the substantive rights they acknowledged. For example, in its reservation to Article 7 of the ICCPR prohibiting torture or cruel, inhuman or degrading treatment, the United States stated that it "considers itself bound by Article 7 to the extent that 'cruel, inhuman or degrading treatment or punishment' means the cruel and unusual treatment or punishment prohibited by the Fifth, Eighth, and/or Fourteenth Amendments to the Constitution of the United States."[755] The United States has acknowledged that the extent of those constitutional provisions "is

---

[753] The U.S. government attached three reservations, five understandings, and two declarations to its ratification of CAT. Five reservations, five understandings, and four declarations accompanied the ICCPR. The United States has not ratified the First Optional Protocol to the ICCPR and did not declare itself bound by article 22 of CAT. The First Optional Protocol and article 22 allow the committees responsible for monitoring compliance with the treaties to receive complaints from individuals and organizations, in addition to complaints from other governments. The effect of the U.S. positions, combined with inadequate enforcement at the state level of prohibitions on torture and cruel, inhuman, and degrading treatment, is to deny U.S. citizens and others who allege violations of such treaties any forum in which their grievances can be heard or resolved.

[754] The U.S. Constitution's Supremacy Clause, art. VI, cl. 2, establishes that treaties are the law of the land in the United States. As such, treaties have the status of law in the U.S. domestic legal system. The Supremacy Clause declares treaties to be the "supreme Law of the Land" and instructs the courts to give them effect. The Supreme Court has held that customary international law is also the law of the land to be enforced by U.S. courts. See *The Paquete Habana*, 175 U.S. 677 (1900).

[755] Committee Against Torture, "Status of the Convention against Torture and other Cruel, Inhuman or Degrading Treatment or Punishment, and Reservations, Declarations and Objections under the Convention," U.N. Doc. CAT/C/2/Rev5. Available online at: http://www.unhchr.ch/tbs/doc.nsf/0/fa6561b18d8a4767802565c30038c86a?OpenDocument&Highlight=0,CAT%2Fc%2F2%2Frev.5, accessed June 30, 2003.

arguably narrower in some respects" than the scope of article 7.[756] For example, as discussed below, the mistreatment of prisoners through substandard medical care will not be a violation of the Eighth Amendment unless prison officials acted with *deliberate* indifference. Article 7 of the ICCPR does not contain this stringent intent requirement. Prolonged solitary confinement with limited or no human interaction and no opportunity for work, educational, or other activities may violate Article 7 and Article 10.[757] But the Eighth amendment does not give prisoners the right to recreational, vocational, or rehabilitative programs and except with regard to mentally ill prisoners, most U.S. courts have upheld the constitutionality of segregated prison housing in which prisoners are kept, locked up around the clock in small isolated cells, for years at a time.[758]

In 1995, the U.N. Human Rights Committee, which is charged with monitoring the implementation of the ICCPR, found the U.S. reservation to Article 7 of that instrument to be incompatible with the treaty's object and purpose.[759] Human Rights Watch agrees with this analysis, finding that the U.S. attempt to narrow the treaty's coverage is incompatible with its goal of preventing a wide range of human rights abuses. We therefore hold the United States to the full scope of the prohibition on torture and other ill treatment contained in the ICCPR and the Convention against Torture.

Constitutional Protections for Prisoners with Mental Illness

Unlike the ICCPR, the U.S. Constitution does not expressly require federal and state governments to respect the basic dignity of all prisoners nor does it have any provisions that expressly refer to their treatment. The principal constitutional protection for prisoners is the Eighth Amendment's prohibition of "cruel and unusual punishments." It is well acknowledged within U.S. constitutional jurisprudence that the Eighth Amendment requires prison officials to provide prisoners with such basic human needs as adequate food and water, shelter, clothing, sanitation, personal safety, and medical care, including mental health treatment. The courts have acknowledged that when people are incarcerated by the state and as a consequence unable to care for themselves, the U.S. Constitution imposes a duty on the state to assume responsibility for their safety and general well being. "[H]aving stripped [prisoners] of virtually every means of self-protection and foreclosed their access to outside aid," society may not look away and let "the state of nature takes its course."[760]

Yet, despite these constitutional guarantees, endemic problems remain. Prisoners are not a politically powerful constituency; prisoners with mental illness even less so. Governors and state legislatures are reluctant to make the financial commitments needed to ensure prisons are humane and that they provide appropriate mental health services. Correctional authorities may lack the commitment, energy, tenacity, and creativity to change long-established ways of doing business. As

---

[756] U.N. Human Rights Committee, State Party Report (Initial reports of States parties due in 1993), *United States of America* 24/08/94, U.N. Doc. CCPR/C/81/Add.4 (1994), para. 176.

[757] Human Rights Watch, *Cold Storage: Super-Maximum Security Confinement in Indiana* (New York: Human Rights Watch, 1997); Human Rights Watch, "Out of Sight: Super-Maximum Security Confinement in the United States," *A Human Rights Watch Report*, vol. 12, no. 1(G), February 2000; Nigel Rodley, *The Treatment of Prisoners Under International Law* (Oxford: Clarendon Press, 1999).

[758] See discussion of administrative and disciplinary segregation below, chapter XII.

[759] U.N. Human Rights Committee, *Concluding Observations of the Human Rights Committee: United States of America*, U.N. Doc. CCPR/C/79/Add 50 (1995). For further discussion of Human Rights Watch's position on U.S. reservations to these treaties, see Human Rights Watch, *No Escape: Male Rape in U.S. Prisons* (New York: Human Rights Watch, 2001), pp. 58-59; and Human Rights Watch, *All Too Familiar: Sexual Abuse of Women in U.S. State Prisons* (New York: Human Rights Watch, 1996), p. 47.

[760] *Farmer v. Brennan*, 511 U.S. 825, 833 (1994) (internal citations omitted).

a result, it has taken litigation — and the threat of litigation — raising constitutional challenges to generate most of the improvements in U.S. prisons over the past three decades.

The U.S. Department of Justice is authorized by statute to bring criminal charges or civil suits against state authorities for violating prisoners' rights under the U.S. Constitution. It has instituted investigations under the Civil Rights of Institutionalized Persons Act into conditions in a number of jails and prisons that resulted, in findings, among other problems, that mental health services were inadequate, and has secured agreements with the responsible agencies to make improvements.[761] Prisoners, however, have brought most of the suits initiated to reform prison practices and to redress prison abuses. This is also true with regards to cases addressing the treatment of prisoners with serious mental illness. Beginning in the 1970s, and continuing to the present day, prisoners have brought a series of court cases challenging the constitutional adequacy of the care of and mental health services for prisoners with mental illness. Representing mentally ill prisoners, the National Prison Project of the American Civil Liberties Union has, for example, litigated at least sixty-five cases over the past two decades. State and local public legal services organizations have brought many others, in addition to countless suits brought by prisoners representing themselves.

Court rulings or consent decrees have established important benchmarks for the treatment of mentally ill prisoners and mandated major revisions in the ways correctional authorities provided mental health services.[762] Discovery in those cases, as well as court orders, have revealed publicly the appalling conditions under which thousands of mentally ill prisoners have been confined.

Litigation has also enabled prison officials to undertake reforms that politics and lack of resources prevented them from doing. Human Rights Watch interviewed a number of correctional mental health officials who acknowledged that litigation was often the only way they could obtain the financial resources as well as support from elected officials to do what they knew needed to be done. As the mental health director at the Vermont Department of Corrections told us:

> While lawsuits are stressful and time-consuming and, by definition, contentious, they do often expose systems' deficiencies and serve as a spotlight on these areas for a broader audience. This audience would include legislators, high-level managers, the judiciary and executive staff who might be in a position to consider resource allocation needs accordingly.[763]

Similarly, the superintendent of the Washington Correctional Center for Women told us that: "Sometimes lawsuits are useful. It's our aim not to have them. But a part of what got us the

---

[761] The U.S. Department of Justice may criminally prosecute officials for violating a prisoner's constitutional rights under sections 241 and 242 of Title 18 of the United States Code. It may also institute civil suits for violations of the civil rights of prisoners under the Civil Rights of Institutionalized Persons Act, 42 U.S.C. Section 1997 *et seq.* The investigative findings and settlements with Los Angeles County (regarding L.A. County Jail) and with the State of Wyoming (regarding Wyoming state prisons) are available online at: http://www.usdoj.gov/crt/split/index.html, accessed June 9, 2003.

[762] See Fred Cohen, *The Mentally Disordered Inmate and the Law* (New Jersey: Civic Research Institute, 1998); see also the 2000-2001 Supplement to the same volume for a review and analysis of these cases.

[763] Human Rights Watch telephone interview with Tom Powell, director of mental health, Vermont Department of Corrections, April 23, 2003.

resources we have now is *Hallett v. Payne* [class action lawsuit challenging treatment of women prisoners]. We got resources as a result to do it better."[764]

The Right to Mental Health Treatment

In the landmark case of *Estelle v. Gamble,* the U.S. Supreme Court enunciated the legal standard for evaluating medical claims under the Eighth Amendment. Medical care, or the lack there of, is unconstitutional when it involves the "unnecessary and wanton infliction of pain"[765] and because of correctional officials' "deliberate indifference to serious medical needs of prisoners."[766] This standard has been extended to the treatment of mental illness. An prisoner is:

> entitled to psychological or psychiatric treatment if a physician or other health care provider, exercising skill and care at the time of observation, concludes with reasonable medical certainty (1) that the prisoner's symptoms evidence a serious disease or injury; (2) that such disease or injury is curable or may be substantially alleviated; and (3) that the potential for harm to the prisoner by reason of delay or the denial of care would be substantial.[767]

Substandard quality of care, negligence, or even malpractice does not suffice to establish a constitutional violation.[768] To prove an Eighth Amendment violation, prisoners must show both an objective and serious injury, either physical or psychological, and a culpable subjective intent on the part of the prison authorities. The culpable mental state that must be proven is that of "deliberate indifference," meaning that the defendant actually knew of and yet disregarded an excessive risk to prisoner health. Accidental or inadvertent failure to provide adequate care does not suffice. In *Farmer v. Brennan*, the Supreme Court ruled that officials could not be found to be deliberately indifferent based on what they should have known, as opposed to what they actually knew.[769] It stated that:

> prison official[s] may be held liable under the Eighth Amendment for denying humane conditions of confinement only if he knows that inmates face a substantial risk of serious harm and disregards that risk by failing to take reasonable measures to abate it.[770]

That is, the officials must have "consciously disregard[ed] a substantial risk of serious harm" to the prisoners.[771]

---

[764] Human Rights Watch interview with Belinda Stewart, superintendent, Washington Correctional Center for Women, Tacoma, Washington, August 21, 2002.

[765] *Gregg v. Georgia*, 428 U.S. 153, 173 (1976), quoted in *Estelle v. Gamble*, 429 U.S. 97, 104 (1976).

[766] *Estelle*, 429 U.S. at 104.

[767] *Bowring v. Godwin*, 551 F.2d 44, 47 (4th Cir., 1977).

[768] Fred Cohen, *The Mentally Disordered Inmate and the Law* (New Jersey: Civic Research Institute, 1998) provides a comprehensive and periodically updated analysis of legal developments, including how courts have interpreted "deliberate indifference." Another useful source is the bimonthly Correctional Mental Health Report, also published by the Civic Research Institute and edited by Cohen, available online at: http://www.civicresearchinstitute.com/bh2.html, accessed July 1, 2003.

[769] *Farmer v. Brennan*, 511 U.S. 825 (1994).

[770] 511 U.S. at 832.

[771] 511 U.S. at 839.

The requirement of proof of "deliberate indifference" has significantly limited court findings of constitutional violations with regard to mental health services and thus, of course, their ability to order improvements in those services. For example, according to a federal court, plaintiffs' experts in a long-running class action lawsuit against the Texas Department of Criminal Justice (TDCJ) found system-wide deficiencies in the mental health care system, including "not recognizing or minimizing symptoms indicative of major mental illnesses;" underdiagnosis of mental illnesses, inadequate access to psychiatric assessments, and inadequate treatment of those found to be mentally ill; and "wholly inadequate" staffing.[772] However, while the court concluded that the psychiatric care system of TDCJ was "grossly wanting" it was unable to find constitutional violations because of absence of proof that TDCJ officials were "systemically and deliberately indifferent" to prisoners' psychiatric needs.[773] The court stated that it hoped the U.S. Supreme Court would eventually modify its contemporary standards for cruel and unusual punishment regarding medical treatment for prison prisoners. "As the law stands today, the standards permit inhumane treatment of inmates. In this court's opinion, inhumane treatment should be found to be unconstitutional treatment."[774]

There is no clear definition of, or consensus about, what constitutes a sufficiently serious mental health condition to implicate the Eighth Amendment. Reviewing the case law, one of the country's leading experts on legal issues concerning prisoners with mental disorders concluded:

> [T]here is not one clear definition or predictive certainty as to what is or is not a serious mental disorder. [But] schizophrenia, bipolar disorders, and clinically significant depression that causes relative inability to function will all clearly qualify as serious.[775]

In the context of a class action lawsuit in Wisconsin — *Jones 'El v. Berge* — challenging the placement of prisoners with serious mental illnesses in high-security isolated confinement, a federal judge recently approved a definition of "seriously mentally ill inmates" as those who have been:

> Diagnosed with specific conditions such as schizophrenia, delusional disorder, schizophreniform disorder, schizoaffective disorder, brief psychotic disorder, substance-induced psychotic disorder, other psychotic disorders not otherwise specified, major depressive disorders, bipolar disorder I and II.

> Diagnosed with a mental disorder that includes being actively suicidal.

> Diagnosed with an organic brain syndrome that will significantly impair functioning if not treated.

> Diagnosed with a severe personality disorder that results in significant functional impairment.

---

[772] *Ruiz v. Johnson*, 37 F. Supp. 2d 855 (S.D. Texas, 1999), 902-907
[773] *Ruiz*, 37 F. Supp. 2d. at 907.
[774] Ibid.
[775] Fred Cohen, *The Mentally Disordered Inmate and the Law* (New Jersey: Civic Research Institute, 1998), p. 4-33. *The Mentally Disordered Inmate*, which is periodically updated, provides a comprehensive review of legal developments.

Diagnosed with any other serious mental illness that would be worsened by confinement at Supermax.[776]

Constitutionally Required Components of Mental Health Services

The basic components of what is needed for correctional mental health services to pass constitutional muster were outlined in the landmark case of *Ruiz v. Estelle*. Filed in 1972, what became the longest prison-related lawsuit in U.S. history challenged the overcrowding, violence, arbitrary punishments, and grossly inadequate medical care in Texas' sprawling prison system. In his landmark 1980 ruling, Judge William Wayne Justice, chief judge of the U.S. District Court for the Eastern District of Texas, described an unconstitutional mental health services system in which "treatment" consisted almost exclusively of the administration of dangerous medications, prisoners with mental disorders were ignored until their conditions became extremely serious, and acutely ill prisoners were warehoused in an overcrowded special treatment facility with few mental health professionals.[777] He ruled that prison mental health services must include the following:

> First, there must be a systematic program for screening and evaluating inmates in order to identify those who require mental health treatment... Second...treatment must entail more than segregation and close supervision of the inmate patients.... Third, treatment requires the participation of trained mental health professionals, who must be employed in sufficient numbers to identify and treat in an individualized manner those treatable inmates suffering from serious mental disorders.... Fourth, accurate, complete, and confidential records of the mental health treatment process must be maintained. Fifth, prescription and administration of behavior-altering medications in dangerous amounts, by dangerous methods, or without appropriate supervision and periodic evaluations, is an unacceptable method of treatment. Sixth, a basic program for the identification, treatment, and supervision of inmates with suicidal tendencies is a necessary component of any mental health treatment program.[778]

---

[776] The settlement agreement provides that "No seriously mentally ill prisoners will be sent to [the supermax] nor will seriously mentally ill prisoners at the facility be permitted to remain there." The department of corrections sought to have serious mental illness be defined the same as the test for incompetence to stand trial. The court rejected this narrow definition and accepted the definition put forward by Dr. Terry Kupers, a psychiatric expert for the plaintiffs. The court ordered that inmates suffer from a serious mental illness are those who have current symptoms of or are receiving treatment for Axis I disorders; inmates diagnosed with a mental disorder that includes being actively suicidal; with a serious mental illness that is frequently characterized either by breaks with reality or by perceptions of reality that lead the individual to significant functional impairment; with an organic brain syndrome that results in a significant functional impairment if not treated; with a severe personality disorder that is manifested by frequent episodes of psychosis or depression and results in significant functional impairment; or with any other serious mental illness or disorder that is worsened by confinement at Supermax. Included in the settlement agreement between the parties approved by the court were the court's definition of serious mental illness and the court ordered procedures for implementing the definition. As of June 2003, there was only one inmate who the DRC claimed should be held at the facility under this "dangerousness" exception. *Jones 'El v. Berge*, Judgment in a Civil Case, Case No. 00-C-0421-C (W.D. Wisconsin, June 24, 2002) (unpublished). Human Rights Watch telephone interview with David Fathi, attorney with the ACLU's National Prison Project, June 30, 2003.

[777] *Ruiz v. Estelle*, 503 F. Supp. 1265, 1336 (S.D. Tex. 1980), *aff'd in part*, 679 F.2d 115 (5th Cir. 1982), *cert. denied*, 460 U.S. 1042 (1983).

[778] 503 F. Supp. at 1339. In 1999, in response to an effort by Texas to obtain termination of the court's jurisdiction over the Texas prison system, Judge Justice found that Texas continued to violate inmate constitutional rights because of "inadequate and negligen[t] medical and psychiatric treatment."

These six components continue to form the basic outline by which courts assess whether mental health services are adequate. At least two additional components have emerged in the case law. The first is access—the process by which prisoners get to mental health services—and the second is physical resources—whether adequate facilities and equipment are available to meet prisoners' treatment needs.[779]

Americans With Disabilities Act

In recent years, the Americans with Disabilities Act of 1990 has opened up a new avenue for legal challenges to the failure to provide proper treatment for incarcerated persons with mental illness.[780] The act bans discrimination against the disabled, a category that includes persons disabled by mental illness. In 1996, a class action was brought on behalf of prisoners with mental illness in New Jersey alleging that inadequate mental health services in the state's prisons constituted both unconstitutional cruel and unusual punishment and also a violation of the Americans with Disabilities Act. The case was settled in 1999.[781] That same year, attorneys in Illinois filed suit against the Supermax prison at Tamms, also alleging violations of the Americans with Disabilities Act as well as unconstitutionally cruel and unusual punishment.[782] In May 2002, Disability Advocates Inc., filed a class action lawsuit against the New York State Department of Correctional Services and the New York State Office of Mental Health. One of the allegations in the lawsuit, which has not yet been decided, was that the state violated the Americans with Disabilities Act by housing mentally ill prisoners in Secure Housing Units — disciplinary facilities in which the prisoners are kept in their cells twenty four hours a day except for brief periods of exercise a few times a week and in which they have little or no access to meaningful activities and little mental health treatment.[783] Plaintiffs claim the state prison system should "provide alternative punishments as a reasonable accommodation [to the disability of mental illness] so that punishments which exacerbate mental illnesses are not imposed."[784]

Prison Litigation Reform Act

In 1996, federal legislation was enacted that has severely curtailed the ability of prisoners to seek judicial relief for violations of their constitutional rights. Supporters of the Prison Litigation Reform Act (PLRA) insisted it was necessary to curtail frivolous prisoner lawsuits. But its impact — and perhaps its real underlying intent — has been much broader. Prisoners with legitimate and serious complaints are far less likely to be able to have their day in court than they did prior to enactment of the law. A comprehensive set of constraints on prison litigation, the PLRA requires prisoners to exhaust their administrative remedies before they can file a lawsuit. This means they must satisfy all the requirements of prison grievance processes — filing grievances in a correct and timely manner, pursuing their administrative appeals also in a correct and timely manner (the deadlines are typically quite short) — no matter how futile the process may be (prisons rarely recognize the merit of prisoner grievances), no matter how meritorious their claims or how legitimate their reasons for

---

[779] Fred Cohen, *The Mentally Disordered Inmate and the Law* (New Jersey: Civic Research Institute, 1998), p. 7-7. Cohen spells out a larger list of sixteen factors that he concluded are required for a legal and sound system of mental health services.

[780] 42 U.S.C. 12101 et. seq.

[781] *D.M. et al v. Jack Terhune et al.* 67 F. Supp. 2d 401 (D. N.J., 1999).

[782] Plaintiffs were not, however, able to get class certification for the case. *Rasho v. Snyder*, 2003 U.S. Dist. Lexis 2833, Feb. 28, 2003 (Denial of Plaintiffs' Motion for Reconsideration of Order Denying Class Certification).

[783] As noted below in chapter XII, the terminology for punitive, segregated prison units varies among the different prison systems.

[784] *Disability Advocates Inc. v. New York State Office of Mental Health.* No. 02 CV 4002. (S.D.N.Y., May 28, 2002).

failing to follow the administrative process to the letter. The exhaustion requirement applies even if the remedy being sought is not available through the grievance system and even if a prisoner faces an immediate threat to health or safety. The exhaustion requirement is particularly onerous in class action cases, in which all the named plaintiffs must have complied with their prison internal grievance procedures.

The PLRA also: 1) invalidates all settlements that do not include explicit findings that the challenged conditions violate federal law or the constitution, thereby discouraging amicable negotiated settlements, 2) requires that prospective relief in prison conditions suits, such as consent decrees, be "narrowly drawn," 3) arbitrarily terminates court orders against unlawful prison conditions after two years, regardless of the prison authorities' degree of compliance with the orders, and 4) restricts the grant of attorneys' fees for successful prison conditions suits, severely reducing the financial viability of even the most sorely-needed prison reform efforts. Other objectionable provisions of the act limit prisoners' access to the courts by imposing court filing fees on certain indigent prisoners and bar the recovery of damages for pain and suffering not accompanied by physical injury. In short, without explicitly cutting back on prisoners' constitutionally protected rights, the PLRA has created formidable obstacles to judicial protection and enforcement of those rights.